Taxation without Representation
in Contemporary Rural China

The financial burdens imposed on peasants have become a major source of discontent in the Chinese countryside and a worrisome source of political and social instability for the Chinese government. Throughout the 1990s and into the new century, much of rural China has been in a state of crisis as tension has grown between the peasant masses and the state. Farmers who bitterly resented the tax burden began increasingly to protest (sometimes violently) against unpredictable and open-ended financial exactions by predatory local governments. Local rural officials, in turn, are driven by intense pressure to develop and modernize in order to catch up with the more highly developed coastal areas.

Bernstein and Lü show how and why China's developmental programs led to contentious, complicated relationships between peasants and the central and local governments. They discuss the reasons why peasants in grain-growing "agricultural China" have benefited far less during the reform era than those in the industrializing coastal areas. They examine the forms and sources of heavy, informal taxation and shed light on how peasants defend their interests by adopting strategies of collective resistance (both peaceful and violent). The authors also explain why the central government, although often siding with the peasants, has not been able to solve the burden problem by instituting a sound, reliable financial system in the countryside. The regime has, to some extent, sought to empower peasants to defend their interests – informing them about tax rules, expanding the legal system, and instituting village elections – but these attempts have not yet generated enough power from "below" to counter powerful local governments.

The case studies featured here offer rare insight into Chinese political life in the countryside. This is the first in-depth English study of the problem of aggressive taxation by local governments in contemporary China and its social and political implications. Bernstein and Lü help explain how this has played a large role in defining the relationship between the state and peasants in the reform period. Their analysis adds to the larger debate over whether China's growing strength could pose a threat to other countries, or whether China's leaders will be preoccupied with domestic problems such as this one.

Thomas P. Bernstein is Professor of Political Science at Columbia University. A former department Chair and Guggenheim Fellow, he is the author of *Up to the Mountains and Down to the Villages: The Transfer of Youth from Urban to Rural China* (1977) and numerous articles and book chapters.

Xiaobo Lü is Associate Professor of Political Science at Barnard College, Columbia University, and Director of the East Asian Institute at Columbia. He is the author of *Cadres and Corruption* (2000) and coeditor of *Danwei: The Changing Chinese Workplace in Historical and Comparative Perspectives* (1997).

A Study of the East Asian Institute, Columbia University

Through its publication program, inaugurated in 1962, the East Asian Institute has been bringing to public attention the results of significant new research on modern and contemporary East Asia.

Cambridge Modern China Series

Edited by William Kirby, Harvard University

Taxation without Representation in Contemporary Rural China

THOMAS P. BERNSTEIN

Columbia University

XIAOBO LÜ

Barnard College, Columbia University

CAMBRIDGE
UNIVERSITY PRESS

PUBLISHED BY THE PRESS SYNDICATE OF THE UNIVERSITY OF CAMBRIDGE
The Pitt Building, Trumpington Street, Cambridge, United Kingdom

CAMBRIDGE UNIVERSITY PRESS
The Edinburgh Building, Cambridge CB2 2RU, UK
40 West 20th Street, New York, NY 10011-4211, USA
477 Williamstown Road, Port Melbourne, VIC 3207, Australia
Ruiz de Alarcón 13, 28014 Madrid, Spain
Dock House, The Waterfront, Cape Town 8001, South Africa

http://www.cambridge.org

First published 2003

Printed in the United Kingdom at the University Press, Cambridge

Typeface Times New Roman 10/13 pt.   *System* LATEX 2_ε [TB]

A catalog record for this book is available from the British Library.

Library of Congress Cataloging in Publication Data

Bernstein, Thomas P.
Taxation without representation in rural China / Thomas P. Bernstein, Xiaobo Lü.
p.   cm. – (Cambridge modern China series)
Includes bibliographical references and index.
ISBN 0-521-81318-2
1. Taxation – China.   2. Tax incidence – China.   3. China – Politics and government.
I. Lü, Xiaobo, 1959 –   II. Title.   III. Series.
HJ2981 .B47   2003
336.2′00951′091734–dc21   2002025679

ISBN 0 521 81318 2 hardback

Contents

Contents

List of Journals, Newspapers, Translation Services, and Abbreviations

Banyuetan (Fortnightly Chats), Beijing
Beijing Qingnianbao (Beijing Youth Daily)
Beijing Review
Caizheng Yanjiu (Financial Research), Beijing
CAPD, China Association for the Promotion of Democracy
CASS, Chinese Academy of Social Sciences
CC, Central Committee
CCP, Chinese Communist Party
CCTV, Central China Television
CD, China Daily, Beijing
Changjiang Ribao (Yangtze Daily), Wuhan
Cheng Ming (Contention), Hong Kong
China Journal, Canberra (formerly the *Australian Journal of Chinese Affairs*)
Ching Pao (Mirror), Hong Kong
Chiushi Nientai (The Nineties), Hong Kong
Chuncheng Wanbao (Spring City Evening Paper), Kunming, Yunnan
CPPCC, Chinese People's Political Consultative Conference
Dangdai (The Present Age), Nanjing
EBF, Extrabudgetary funds
FA, Farmers' Association
Faxue Pinglun (Legal Review), Beijing
Faxue Yanjiu (Legal Research), Beijing
Fengci yu Youmo (Satire and Humor), Beijing
FBIS, Foreign Broadcast Information Service. Daily Report: China, Springfield, VA
FEER, Far Eastern Economic Review, Hong Kong
FZRB, Fazhi Ribao (Legal Daily), Beijing
Gaige (Reform), Beijing

Gaige yu Lilun (Reform and Theory), Beijing
GLF, Great Leap Forward
GMRB, Guangming Ribao (Guangming Daily), Beijing
Guanli Shijie (World of Management), Beijing
HBRB, Hebei Ribao, (Hebei Daily), Shijiazhuang
Hebei Nongcun Gongzuo (Hebei Rural Work), Shijiazhuang
Hebei Xinfang (Hebei Letters and Visits), Shijiazhuang
Hsin Pao, Hong Kong
Hunan Ribao (Hunan Daily), Changsha
ICHRD, Information Centre for Human Rights and Democracy, Hong Kong
Jiage Lilun yu Shijian (Theory and Practice of Prices), Beijing
Jiangsu Jijian (Jiangsu Party Discipline Inspection), Nanjing
Jingji Cankaobao (Economic Information Daily), Beijing
Jingji Gaige yu Fazhan (Economic Reform and Development), Beijing
Jingji Pinglun (Economic Review), Wuhan
Jingji Tizhi Gaige (Economic Structural Reform), Beijing
Jingji Yanjiu (Economic Research), Beijing
Jingji Yanjiu Cankao (Reference Material for Economic Research), Beijing
JJRB, Jingji Ribao (Economic Daily), Beijing
JPRS, Joint Publications Research Service, Springfield, VA
Kaifang (Opening Up), Hong Kong
Laixin Zhaibian (Extracts from Letters), Beijing
Liaowang (Observer), Beijing
Lien Ho Pao (United Daily), Taipei
Lingdao Canyue (Reference Reading for Leadership), Beijing
MCA, Ministry of Civil Affairs
Minzhu yu Fazhi (Democracy and Law), Shanghai
Ming Pao, Hong Kong
MOA, Ministry of Agriculture
MOF, Ministry of Finance
Nanfang Ribao (Southern Daily), Guangzhou
Nanfang Zhoumo (Southern Weekend), Guangzhou
Neibu Canyue (Internal Reference Readings), Beijing
Neican Xuanbian (Selected Internal Reference), Beijing
NJW, Nongye Jingji Wenti (Problems of the Agricultural Economy), Beijing
NMRB, Nongmin Ribao (Farmers' Daily), Beijing
Nongcun Gongzuo Tongxun (Rural Work Bulletin), Beijing
NPC, National People's Congress
Nongcun Jingji (Rural Economy), Beijing
Nongye Jingji (Agricultural Economy), Shenyang

NYT, New York Times
PAP, People's Armed Police
Ping Kuo Jih Pao (Apple Daily), Hong Kong
PLA, People's Liberation Army
POS, Political Opportunity Structure
Qingnian Yanjiu (Research on Youth), Beijing
RDRI, Rural Development Research Institute
Renmin Gonganbao (People's Public Security Newspaper), Beijing
Renmin Xinfang (Letters and Visits from the People), Beijing
RMRB, Renmin Ribao (People's Daily), Beijing
RMRB-O, Renmin Ribao (People's Daily) *Overseas Edition*, Beijing
SCJP or *SJRB, Shih-chieh Jih-pao* or *Shijie Ribao* (World Journal), New York
Shanxi Nongjing (Shanxi Rural Economy), Taiyuan
Shehui (Society), Shanghai
Shehui Gongzuo Yanjiu (Research on Social Work), Beijing
Shehui Kexue (Social Sciences), Shanghai
Sheke Xinxi Wenhui (Collection of Social Science Information), Beijing
SCMP, South China Morning Post, Hong Kong
Shuiwu Yanjiu (Research on Taxation), Beijing
Sichuan Ribao (Sichuan Daily), Chengdu
Social Sciences in China, Beijing
*SWB-FE, British Broadcasting Company – Survey of World Broadcasts, Third
    Series, Far East*, Caversham Park, Reading, UK
Ta Kung Pao, Hong Kong
Tangtai (Current Age), Hong Kong
Tansuo (Probe), New York
Tong Hsiang (Trends), Hong Kong
TVE, township and village enterprises
VC, Village Committee
Wen Wei Po, Hong Kong
VRA, Village Representative Assembly
XHRB, Xinhua Ribao (New China Daily), Nanjing
Xinhua, New China News Agency, Beijing
Xinhua Neican Xuanbian (New China News Selections for Internal
    Reference), Beijing
Xinhua Wenzhai (New China News Abstracts), Beijing
Xin Shiji (New Century), Haikou
Xinwengao (News Briefs), Beijing
Xingzheng yu Fa (Administration and Law), Changchun
Xuexi yu Tansuo (Study and Probe), Harbin

Yangcheng Wanbao (Guangzhou Evening News), Guangzhou
Zhengzhi yu Falü (Politics and Law), Beijing
Zhongguo Caijingbao (Chinese Financial and Economic News), Beijing
Zhongguo Caizheng (China State Finance), Beijing
Zhongguo Gaigebao (China Reform), Beijing
Zhongguo Guoqing Guoli (China's National Condition and Strength), Beijing
Zhongguo Jiancha (Supervision Work in China), Beijing
Zhongguo Minzheng (Civil Affairs in China), Beijing
Zhongguo Nongcun Guancha (China Rural Survey), Beijing
Zhongguo Qingnian (China Youth), Beijing
Zhongguo Qingnianbao (China Youth Daily), Beijing
Zhongguo Shuiwu (China's Taxation), Beijing
Zhongguo Tongji Xinxi Bao (China Statistical News), Beijing
Zhongguo Wujia (China Prices), Beijing
Zhongguo Xinxibao (China Information), Beijing
ZLTN, Zhongguo Laodong Tongji Nianjian (China Annual Labor Statistics), Beijing
ZNJ, Zhongguo Nongcun Jingji (Chinese Rural Economy), Beijing
ZNTN, Zhongguo Nongcun Tongji Nianjian (China Rural Annual Statistics), Beijing
ZRGYGB, Zhonghua Renmin Gongheguo Guowuyuan Gongbao (State Council Bulletin), Beijing
ZTN, Zhongguo Tongji Nianjian (China Annual Statistics), Beijing
ZTN-Zhaiyao, Zhongguo Tongji Nianjian-Zhaiyao (China Statistical Abstracts Annual), Beijing
ZTS, Zhongguo Tongxunshe (China News Service), Beijing, Hong Kong
ZXB, Zhongguo Xiaofeizhebao (China Consumer News), Beijing
ZXS, Zhongguo Xinwenshe (China News Agency), Beijing, Hong Kong

List of Tables and Figures

TABLES

FIGURES

Preface

In the late 1990s large parts of rural China were in a state of crisis. Households dependent on agriculture for their livelihood were enduring stagnant incomes and there was an increasingly tense relationship between peasants and local officials. Financial exactions to which village households were subject were a major cause. These included formal taxes, a bewildering variety of informally levied fees, and unregulated fund-raising among the households by local officials. Collecting these unpredictable and arbitrary levies often required severe coercion and was a major source of rural discontent. It elicited considerable peasant resistance, increasingly threatening rural stability. Beginning in the mid-1980s, when the problem first emerged into prominence, the leaders of the Chinese Communist Party and government made major efforts to ease "peasant burdens." These efforts failed and the situation became more and more fraught with tension and conflict.

This study sheds light on the nature and extent of the burdens. They were an issue primarily in agricultural areas, rather than in those areas where rural industrialization had made significant progress. It sheds light on the repercussions of the burdens by examining peasant protest and peasant collective action. And it sheds light on the attempts made by the authorities to find effective remedies. In analyzing these issues, the study probes the institutional and behavioral sources of this concrete and practical problem, linking solutions to more deep-going reforms. The burdens were the product not simply of predatory or corrupt local officials. They were the product of a well-entrenched approach to development that set performance targets irrespective of local capacities to meet them (in our case, the local tax base) and that rewarded officials for achievement, not questioning the methods used. The Chinese local state emerges in our study as both predatory and developmental, requiring that it be the former in order to become the latter. The burdens were the product of fiscal practices that had deep roots in imperial and Republican China but they were also grounded in more recent innovations such as fiscal decentralization and administrative deconcentration. Effective solutions required major changes in China's administrative system, thus testing the adaptive capacities of the regime.

Our study reveals a complicated and contentious relationship among peasants, the central government, and local governments. Although the central government sided with the peasants, it lacked the capacity to solve the problem by establishing a sound fiscal system in the countryside, an inadequacy reminiscent of imperial and Republican times. To counter the abusive behavior of local officials, the regime endeavored to empower peasants to defend their interests, introducing freer village elections and broadening access to legal redress. These innovations, although important in their own right, did not generate adequate power from "below" to solve the problem. The burden issue was part and parcel of the underlying challenge of how to make the transition from an authoritarian to a democratic, responsive regime. This book thus brings together major themes in the study of Chinese politics that are often treated separately.

Our research strategy was to construct a generally applicable picture of conditions in "agricultural rural China" rather than to do intensive local research in one or more locales. This approach has advantages and disadvantages. It avoids the inevitable question of just how generalizable case studies are; it also, inevitably, cannot attain an in-depth understanding of how particular factors interacted to produce a specific outcome. In studying protest, for instance, the cases we use are based on press reports, which were sometimes very detailed but did not allow us to say much about possible correlates of collective behavior such as membership in a particular lineage or why a riot took place in village A but not in village B. However, using data from a variety of locales and sources frees the analyst from being tied to case data only.

Our collaboration began in 1997, when we discovered the extent to which our research interests complemented one another or even overlapped. Lü had long been working on the institutional roots of corruption and the changing role of the state, which led him to examine the financial burdens in the context of the administrative system. Bernstein had been working for some years on several issues of rural state-society relations during the reform era, including the transition to household contracting, peasant interest representation, social instability, and the burden problem. We both brought to bear data that we had already collected as well as papers and drafts of chapters.

Both Bernstein and Lü have made numerous research visits to China. In 1985 Bernstein spent three weeks in Zouping county, Shandong, and three weeks in Fengyang county, Anhui, at a time when the burden problem was in its infancy. He later interviewed officials and researchers, in Beijing (1992, 1994, 1998) and in Guangzhou, Tianjin, Shenyang, and Wuhan (1998). Lü interviewed local officials and farmers during his trips to China in Hebei and Henan in 1996, 1998, and 1999. In 1999, Bernstein participated in a collaborative research project involving Zhongshan University, Guangzhou, which entailed short field trips to villages in Guangdong and Hunan. We are very grateful to all those whom we interviewed and to the Chinese scholars who devoted time to extended conversations on our topic. We are particularly indebted to the people who helped us to arrange the interviews and who hosted us in various locales.

Some material in the book has previously appeared in print: Bernstein's "Farmer Discontent and Regime Responses," in *The Paradox of China's Post-Mao Reforms*, edited by Merle Goldman and Roderick MacFarquhar, and "Instability in Rural China," in *Is China Unstable: Assessing the Factors*, edited by David Shambaugh. He is grateful to the publishers for permission to use the material here. Lü published "The Politics of Peasant Burden in Reform China" in *Journal of Peasant Studies*. We are also grateful for permission to use material that appeared in the co-authored article, "Taxation without Representation: Peasants, the Central and Local States in Reform China," which appeared in *The China Quarterly*.

We both owe debts of gratitude to numerous individuals and institutions. To begin with, we want to thank the readers of the manuscript for their comments: Charles Tilly, Edward Friedman, Li Lianjiang, Carl Riskin, Dorothy Solinger, and Vivienne Shue. We also wish to thank the three anonymous reviewers for Cambridge University Press for their comments. Singly or jointly, we have read papers or made presentations on related subjects to various academic audiences, and we would like to express thanks for comments received on these occasions. Bernstein presented papers at the Columbia University Seminar on Modern China in 1994 and 1998; at the conference on "China after Deng," UCLA, 1995; at the conference "China and World Affairs in 2010," Stanford, 1996 (jointly with Dorothy Solinger); at the conference, "Is China Unstable," George Washington University, 1998, and to the China Colloquium of the University of Washington, Seattle, in 2001. Lü presented papers at the Stanford-Berkeley Workshop on Contemporary China, Stanford, 1998, and at the Walter Shorenstein Symposium on "State Legitimation in Contemporary China," Berkeley, 1999. Both authors presented their work at the conference on "Rural China: Emerging Issues in Development," Columbia University, 1995, and to the New England China Seminar, Harvard University, 2001. We are also grateful for permission to quote from unpublished papers by Linda Jakobson, Li Lianjiang, and Murray Scot Tanner.

Thanks must also go to Li Lianjiang, Laura Luehrman, Kevin O'Brien, Stanley Rosen, and Christine P. Wong for providing valuable research material. The Universities Service Centre, Hong Kong, the Hoover Institution, the

Fairbank Center Library at Harvard, the Library of the Center for Chinese Studies at Berkeley, and the C.V. Starr Library at Columbia provided invaluable materials. We would like to thank in particular Nancy Hearst and Annie Chang of Harvard and Berkeley, respectively.

We thank the staff of the East Asian Institute for their support and our colleagues for fostering a congenial intellectual climate.

Over the years, graduate students have provided research assistance and we would like to extend our thanks to them. The most recent were Tao Yifeng and Zhong Hong. Editorial assistance was provided by Ashley Esarey, Bernard Schneider, Edward Wei, and Elizabeth Lacouture.

Research was supported at various times by the Joint Committee on Contemporary China of the ACLS and SSRC, the China Research Committee of the East Asian Institute, and the Luce Foundation in the form of a grant administered by Pacific Lutheran and Zhongshan University. Lü wants to acknowledge the support he received when he was a National Fellow at the Hoover Institution in 1998–9. We are grateful to our editors at Cambridge University Press, Mary Child and Sue Avery. Their guidance and copyediting were crucial to the publication of this book.

And finally, we owe an enormous debt to our spouses, without whose patience, encouragement, support, and advice this book could not have appeared. It is dedicated to them.

T.P.B.
X.L.
New York City

1

Introduction

F OR more than fifteen years China's top leaders called for the "lightening of the peasants' burden," a term that referred to the imposition on villagers of "unreasonable" ad hoc fees, fines, local taxes, assessments on peasant households, or apportionment of governmental expenses among them. Some of these were authorized; many were not; most had at best a dubious basis in law and official regulations. Most were bitterly resented by the peasants for their unpredictability and open-endedness and the coercive manner in which they were collected. Year after year, central leaders and agencies sent edicts, directives, injunctions, exhortations, and pleas down the administrative hierarchy demanding that action be taken to lighten peasant burdens, but to no avail. In 1985 the Central Committee (CC) of the Chinese Communist Party (CCP) and the government's State Council warned that excessive burdens were damaging the authority of the regime and were causing rural unrest and instability. Similar warnings, often in somber tones, have been issued in the years that followed. In the most recent period, rural disturbances arising from burdens and other abuses have become even more worrying to the central leadership. So impressive a record of ineffectuality calls for investigation, analysis, and explanation.

We believe that examination of peasant burdens illuminates two fundamental problems of contemporary Chinese political development. The state faces major challenges in building administrative capacities appropriate to governance in the post-Mao reform era. Just as great a challenge for the state is to develop the means of accommodating the increased assertiveness of society, including demands for accountability, the rule of law, and a voice in policy making.

LOCATING THE CHINESE STATE

A State in Transition. The burden problem has to be seen in the context of China's continuing efforts to reconstruct its state. The Communist Chinese

state was established in 1949 for the purpose of building an industrialized socialist society run according to plan and premised on the absolute primacy of
the collectivist over the individual interest. In the reform period, which began
in 1978, although the goal of industrialization remained, the regime gradually adopted fundamentally new approaches aimed at the establishment of a
"socialist market economy," in which emphasis would be placed much more on
the stimulation of individual incentives. This new orientation required extensive redefinitions of the role of the state away from its primarily transformative,
redistributive, command, and managerial roles during the Maoist era. Redefinitions were required to enable the state to lead, guide, and regulate the transition
to a market economy.

With regard to the economy, the state's dominant role in production and distribution was to be gradually curtailed, and reliance on administrative commands
gradually replaced by fiscal, monetary, and regulatory instruments. A legal system was to be established that would provide security of contracts in horizontal
business transactions, as well as an infrastructure that could sustain ever more
complex market relations. The pursuit of development measured more or less
exclusively in terms of high aggregate growth rates gave way to more complex
goals that would not only promote growth but also pay greater attention to
welfare, education, health, and other aspects of human development.[1]

Numerous decisions had to be made about how far to go in jettisoning Maoist
patterns of governance and administration and about how far the state socialist
system would have to retreat: how much of the planning system should be
retained; how much of a private capitalist sector should be allowed to compete
with state industry; and how much inequality a "socialist" market economy
could tolerate. These fundamental directional questions, which impinged not
just on the economy but on the very nature of the political system and its
relations with society preoccupied the policy makers and, as might be expected,
caused quite a lot of conflict among them.[2]

The reforms signified a conscious retreat from the pursuit of all-embracing
transformative goals imposed by the political system on society and hence a
reduction in the state's autonomy from society. Implementing the goal of radical
transformation of society by means of ideologically based mass mobilization
had entailed the development of extraordinary organizational capacities on
the part of both the Communist Party and the government. These assets
were badly disrupted and damaged during the Cultural Revolution (1966–76).
Reform leaders wanted to continue to make full use of their organizational

---

[1] See the extended and informative analysis of these issues in Riskin et al. (1999).
[2] Fewsmith (1994).

strength to meet the new challenges ahead, but to do so in modified form. Mass mobilization, campaigns, and class struggle were to be replaced by a less disruptive, law-based administrative style, above all one that would allow societal forces greater scope to take initiatives of their own.

As was the case with the economy, the negative goal of repudiating radical Maoism opened up the question of how far political reform should go. The most important answer to this question was given early on, namely that the Chinese Communist Party would retain its monopoly of political power. Within that fundamental constraint, there was considerable flexibility for political reforms that fell short of political liberalization. The latter would have entailed, for instance, the legalization of autonomous interest groups under the one-party umbrella. Chinese society changed very rapidly under the impetus of rapid economic growth and of "reform and opening up to the outside world." New social interests arose, as did demands, grievances, and claims on the state. Yet, political reform lagged consistently behind the societal changes and observers looking at China around the turn of the century widely agreed that there was a deepening disjunction between societal and political development. The state in reform China continued to be shaped to significant degrees by the institutional legacies of the Mao era, a point that will emerge again and again in the chapters that follow.

The process of redefinition and state building was in progress throughout the period that our book covers. Formidable and complex, the tasks were by no means completed during the two decades of reform. This meant that some of the institutions of the old command economy continued to exist, exerting continued powerful influence. For instance, in agriculture the state continued to impose compulsory purchase quotas even after the restoration of family farming. Sowing targets were retained for critical crops. The way the one-child policy program was enforced during the reform era closely resembled the mobilizational approach of the Mao period.[3] Most important for our discussion, rural administrative behavior continued to be strongly conditioned by deeply entrenched old ways. Local officials were free to impose ad hoc charges on peasant households without the authority of law, a legacy from the time of the Maoist campaigns, in which peasant resources were freely appropriated (*yi ping er diao*) in pursuit of developmental or ideological objectives. The structural incompleteness of the transformation of the Chinese countryside was a major factor responsible for the burden problem

Chinese leaders wanted a strong and powerful state, one able to guide, lead, and shape the country's course so that by the middle of the twenty-first century

---

[3] White (1990: 53–77).

China could take its place among the advanced countries of the world. This goal, to which the Chinese were passionately committed, must be understood in historical context. From the mid-nineteenth century on, when China was weak internally and unable to defend itself effectively against imperialist aggression, the Chinese dreamed of their country once again becoming "wealthy and powerful" (*fuqiang*). There was strong consensus that attainment of this goal required a strong state, for without a powerful integrative force, China, in the words of Sun Yat-sen, resembled "a dish of loose sand." Regimes, beginning with the imperial one in its waning days, various local governments, and the Nationalist government in the 1930s sought to restructure the state to enable it to lead the country out of its backwardness and weakness. Communist China also adopted this approach, and for a time, especially the first ten years of the PRC's existence, it seemed as if an effective state had been created that could systematically attain development goals such as industrialization. Much was achieved, but Mao Zedong's successors were deeply chagrined by the disappointing and enormously costly outcome of Mao's utopian efforts to break through to an egalitarian, yet more advanced developmental level. It was this disappointment that prompted them dramatically to change course by gradually turning to the market as a more effective and faster route to wealth and power.

This dramatic turn in strategy did not mean, however, that the state would not play a central role. Markets were important but they could not by any means be left to their own devices. State guidance would go significantly beyond that of interventionist states such as Japan or in Western Europe. The entire state apparatus continued to be oriented to the achievement of rapid development within the new framework of "reform and opening up to the outside world." It continued to exhibit a sense of urgency, impatience, and anxiety about its capacity to catch up with the advanced countries that has always been characteristic of Leninist regimes.[4] In this sense, the reform era represented a path-dependent continuity with the Maoist "Great Leap Forward" mentality. Shorn of its utopian component, the Great Leap slogan of "bigger, better, faster, with more economic results" continued to describe the motivational basis of the Chinese state.

When they changed direction in 1978 China's leaders had in front of them the successes of the East Asian miracle states, the "five tigers" – Japan, South Korea, Taiwan, Hong Kong, and Singapore – whose rapid development in the 1960s and 1970s had left China far behind, mired in revolutionary Maoism. Implicitly at least, they sought to emulate their neighbors in establishing an "East Asian developmental state," in a fully authoritarian variant. The concept

---

[4] See Jowitt (1992: esp. 76 ff) and Jowitt (1970: 233–63).

4

of the developmental state is useful in appraising the nature of the Chinese state. Abstracted from reality, the model of such a state had the following properties: (1) a powerful, highly autonomous state, which defined the goal of achieving rapid development as the major national interest; (2) guidance by a merito-cratically recruited bureaucratic elite imbued with an ethic of public service; (3) authoritative administrative guidance of the economy and close cooperation between public and private sectors, using financial levers and market incentives to implement the state's industrial policies; (4) relative insulation from soci-ety so that the state did not have to accede to demands that would undermine growth, but was able to decide by itself how far living standards could be raised in light of the overriding goal of development. At the same time, to reduce the chances for social unrest, the state sought to avoid the creation of huge dis-parities in incomes; (5) heavy and continued investment in education; and (6) capacity to effectively implement policies.[5]

At the center of the developmental state was the bureaucratic elite, which forged close, usually informal, ties with business but nonetheless retained its autonomy and capacity to play a directing role. These state linkages with outside networks, as Peter Evans suggests in his *Embedded Autonomy*, were "the key to the developmental state's effectiveness . . . combining Weberian bureaucratic insulation with intense connection to the surrounding social structure."[6]

Evans proposes a continuum on which states may be placed with the "preda-tory" state at one end and the developmental state at the other. Zaire under Mobutu approximated the predatory state, one that "preys on its citizenry, ter-rorizing them, despoiling their common patrimony, and providing little in the way of services in return." In one sense, the Zairian state was strong in not being constrained by social forces. It was able to penetrate society for the purpose of appropriating resources. In another sense, it was weak in that it could not achieve any developmental goals. And it was wholly incoherent in that "any slice of public power consists of a veritable exchange instrument, convertible into illicit acquisition of money or other goods."[7] Needless to say, Zaire's GNP steadily declined as Mobutu ran the country into the ground.

In between the predatory and developmental states were intermediate cases such as Brazil and India which contained elements of both. These countries grew, sometimes substantially, but less rapidly and with lower effectiveness than the East Asian newly industrialized countries (NICs). Their state capaci-ties were sapped by dependence on landed classes and, in India, by a general

---

[5] For a succinct statement, see Johnson (1987:136–64) and Amsden (1989).

[6] Evans (1995: 50). This model is applied by Solinger (1991) to the Chinese case.

[7] Evans (1995: 45–6).

orientation of social actors toward securing "particularistic advantage" from the state, especially for favored established industrialists. India's "vast and sprawling state apparatus was even more ambiguously situated in space between predatory and developmental states." It was in part meritocratic and in part deeply corrupt and tied to diverse social interests. There was a lack of the kinds of constructive linkages between the state and business elites that Evans labels "embedded autonomy" which were central to the emergence of a developmental state. India's part-socialist heritage, including the expansion (prior to the 1990s) of state-owned enterprises put "intense strain on state capacity and may well have contributed to the 'erosion of state institutions.'"[8]

In terms of these criteria, China was an intermediate state with both predatory and developmental elements. That this should have been so is suggested simply by size. Evans juxtaposes the two huge states of Brazil and India with the small East Asian development states. He rightly suggests that their size and the consequent greater likelihood of loss of control plus the complexity of very large societies stand in sharp contrast to the compact and cohesive societies of Japan, Korea, or Taiwan. "Given the diseconomies of scale inherent in administrative organizations, it would take a bureaucratic apparatus of truly heroic proportions to produce results comparable to those achieved on an island of twenty million people or a peninsula of forty million."[9] China's population of 1.2 billion people, its sheer size, and the diversity of its economic, social, and ethnic conditions (non-Han minorities inhabit two-thirds of the country's territory) created immense problems for policymakers and administrators, which were aggravated in China because it is a unitary rather than a federal state, and hence the central government shoulders more tasks than would otherwise be the case. The peasant burden problem, mainly found in "agricultural China" in the central and western provinces but far less so in "industrial rural China" in the eastern provinces, was strongly shaped by the state's difficulties in devising and administering suitable policies for both sectors, compounded by the deficiencies of China's vast bureaucracy. The ubiquity of corruption – defined by President Jiang Zemin as a matter of life and death for the Party – together with pervasive clientelism in business-government relations also suggests that China should be located more toward the Zairian end of the continuum.[10]

Yet, in crucial respects, China had the characteristics of a developmental state, if only because under governmental auspices it experienced steady growth

---

[8] Ibid., 69.
[9] Ibid., 68.
[10] Wank (1999) and Lü (2000a: esp. ch. 6).

rates of between 7 to 10 percent per annum for more than 20 years.[11] It is not accurate to say that this immense success was achieved simply by the state relinquishing control and letting market forces take over, although this was an important factor. This achievement suggests that policymakers were able to conceptualize, plan, and pursue a consistent goal-directed set of policies for very long periods of time, despite numerous "twists and turns." And they were able to implement these policies in at least a broad directional sense and in the face of much evasion and obstruction. Evans notes that in Brazil, there were "pockets of efficiency" in the bureaucracy and in the policy-making process that enabled top leaders to play a strong shaping role in development. In his recent study of the new Chinese leadership, Cheng Li points to the "meteoric rise of Chinese technocrats. . . . There was a massive turnover of Chinese leaders at all levels in the 1980s, with a significant number of the promoted elites being technocrats." This change took place at all levels of administration, down to the counties and even to some extent to the townships.[12] Amidst widespread corruption, there were talented and highly motivated technocratic bureaucrats and bureaucrat-politicians – Premier Zhu Rongji comes to mind – who had an increasing impact in the 1980s and 1990s.

THE CENTRAL AND LOCAL STATES

Given the size and complexity of China, one would expect to find sectors where the model of state-led development fits better than in others. One such sector during the reform period was rural industry. "Township and village enterprises" (TVEs), mostly collectively owned by township or village governments, grew at phenomenal rates, came to provide employment for over a 100 million peasants, and enabled the villages in which they developed to achieve modest, sometimes spectacular, levels of prosperity. Their growth was rooted in adapting the East Asian development model to the local level.[13] These industries were able to grow in part because the central government allowed localities to keep and reinvest a larger proportion of their revenue. Jean Oi observes that at the heart of rural industrialization:

> the central state has had to minimize rather than maximize its claim to rev-
> enues generated from the growth process. . . . Localities were allowed to

---

[11] The relationship between corruption and economic growth is complex. As Andrew Wedeman shows, a crucial distinction is whether corrupt money stays in the country and is invested productively or is squirreled away abroad. See Wedeman (1997a: 457–78).

[12] Cheng Li (2001: 35–41).

[13] Oi (1999: 3).

benefit disproportionately from local economic growth. . . . the Chinese reforms succeeded in generating local economic growth because the central state did not get the taxes right.[14]

The fiscal revenue-sharing arrangements that permitted retention of funds locally also required local governments to provide public goods out of local resources. A cadre evaluation system, that rewarded rapid growth and fulfillment of a range of social indicators, motivated local officials to initiate and promote industrialization programs.[15] In these locales, government and Party played critical guiding, entrepreneurial, and managerial roles, for which the term "local developmental state" is appropriate. In this process, resources were generated that could be invested in local infrastructure, used for the provision of a range of services, and for the improvement of living standards. In these areas, local authorities usually did not need to impose burdens directly on the peasants in order to pay for administration or services.[16]

The conditions propitious for the growth of TVEs – market access, availability of skills, proximity to large cities, availability of overseas Chinese investors – were not, however, equally distributed across the Chinese landscape. In the coastal provinces, conditions for the rapid growth of TVEs were favorable, but this was far less the case in the central and western parts of the country where the rate of growth of rural industries was much slower and where their profits and taxes made a far smaller contribution, if any at all, to local development. For our purposes, we distinguish broadly between three parts of the countryside: industrial rural China, mainly concentrated in the eastern provinces, agricultural China, primarily in the central belt of provinces, and subsistence China, located mostly in the western and southwestern provinces.[17]

Our focus is on those parts of the countryside, largely in the central and western provinces, that were far less successful in rural industrialization and that have received less attention in the literature on rural political economy. In these areas, the local authorities often played a predatory role vis-à-vis ordinary peasants in the pursuit of developmental goals. Local authorities in agricultural China, as everywhere, came under intense pressure from their superiors to modernize and develop their localities – to build roads, schools, irrigation installations – but there was never enough money because resource-generating TVEs were few or nonexistent. Hence, local authorities felt compelled to turn to the peasants to

---

[14] Oi (1999: 57). "Not getting taxes right" is a play on Alice Amsden's explanation for Korea's success, namely, that it didn't get the prices right.

[15] Whiting (2001), esp. ch. 3, which analyzes the incentives under which local officials labored.

[16] In addition to Oi and Whiting, see Zweig (1997) and Walder (1998).

[17] The distribution of TVEs in the eastern provinces was also uneven. See Chapter 3.

raise funds for a variety of projects, which provided opportunities for predation. A major theme of this study is that developmental and predatory behaviors were interrelated.

This is not to claim that TVE China was not also subject to predation. TVEs, and indeed all businesses in China, urban and rural, had to pay onerous ad hoc fees and exactions. The fee problem was a national one, besetting state enterprises, TVEs, and other profit-making entities alike, and its sources were a similar combination of "constructive" and predatory motives, in particular undisciplined state entities badly in need of revenue. As the Minister of Finance observed in 1999:

> At present, numerous charges and fees (or funds) are being levied arbitrarily. This puts heavy financial burdens on all sectors of society, arouses great resentment among the people, leads to irrational and chaotic distribution, and causes a drain on revenue and results in failure to prohibit unauthorized departmental coffers.[18]

The burdens placed on TVEs also had developmental and corrupt roots, but what is important from our perspective is that they served to reduce and even eliminate the burdens which otherwise would have been placed on villager households and which became an enormous source of conflict in agricultural China.

A set of institutions – revenue sharing, reliance on localities to supply public goods, an evaluation system to reward successful industrialization – proved dysfunctional when transferred to large parts of China where the prospects for rural industrialization were bleak. When TVEs were few or nonexistent, as in much of agricultural China, peasants directly bore the brunt of the local state's need for resources, which were extracted from villagers in the form of miscellaneous taxes and assorted fees. The process of extraction often turned predatory because of a lack of standardized, legally enforceable procedures limiting the demands of officials for the peasants' money. According to Margaret Levi, "rulers are predatory in the sense that they are revenue maximizers."[19] In these localities maximums were sometimes reached, as illustrated by cases of peasant households that had to borrow money or even sell blood to pay their taxes. In such locales, severe tensions arose between peasants and officials; tensions aggravated by gross abuses of power and widespread corruption. Lack of accountability deepened peasant distrust, since they usually had no way of

---

[18] *Xinhua*, March 6, 1999, in FBIS, no. 305, March 9, 1999. For an article on TVEs and state enterprise fees, see *RMRB*, September 9, 1997, in *SWB-FE*, no. 3056.

[19] Levi (1988: 3).

knowing what proportion of their levies was actually used for a constructive, developmental purpose and what proportion was used to enrich officials.

One answer to this dilemma of inadequate funding could have been for superiors to reduce performance demands on their local subordinates and to provide funds from higher-level governments, especially Beijing. One obstacle was inadequate administrative capacity to calibrate programs to fit different circumstances, despite the stated principle that this should be done (*yin di zhi yi*). Another obstacle was the prevailing developmental ethos of self-reliance, a legacy of Maoism, which rewarded officials for using their ingenuity to achieve results with local resources. Most important, the Center's capacity to redistribute resources to needy provinces was sapped by its own policies of fiscal decentralization adopted in the early 1980s, which, as noted, allowed localities to retain more funds, sharply reducing the flow of revenue to the Center. In 1978, the wealthiest provincial-level entity, Shanghai, turned over a surplus equal to half its GDP to the Center; by 1993, this proportion had shrunk to less than 9 percent.[20] Increasingly wealthy coastal provinces thus benefited from a virtuous developmental circle. Localities acquired "small treasuries" in the form of "extrabudgetary funds" held separately from the regular revenue streams and not subject to appropriation for general government expenditures. This was one source of the chronic revenue shortages that afflicted the central government as well as many local governments. Total regular government budgetary revenues dropped from 31 percent of GDP in 1978 to 12 percent in 1994; the proportion that went to the Center "fell from 60% in the 1970s to 37% in 1993."[21] Furthermore, as Susan Whiting shows, the institutionalization of the revenue-sharing system provided incentives for local officials to evade state taxes levied on collectively owned industry, thereby contributing to the national revenue shortage.[22]

As the redistributive capacities of the central government declined, the financial problems of the poorer provinces worsened. The differentiation in provincial wealth was a product of Deng Xiaoping's dictum that "some can get rich ahead of others" and of a deliberate policy of building on the strong, in this case on the coastal provinces that had the greatest potential to achieve rapid growth. As one part of the country appeared to have fared very well, the other two-thirds lanquished. The disparity in economic growth reflected a policy approach that deferred dealing with the adverse consequences of the coastal development strategy that sought to make the most of immediately available opportunities

---

[20] Wang and Hu (1999: 189–90).
[21] Gang Fan (1998: 210).
[22] Whiting (2001: 94–5, 265–6).

and payoffs. All governments must set priorities and make difficult, often painful decisions. However, we cannot help but conclude that the scale of the problems created by the lopsided coastal development strategy was at least in part the product of a flawed policymaking process, one that was apparently unable to take into account the complexities and diversities of the country and simply overrode the interests concerned.

The central Chinese state demonstrated a strong capacity to stimulate development, but in the process came to face increasingly severe regional inequalities and increasingly severe tensions between local officials and villagers in the agriculture-dependent central and western provinces.[23] The Center leaders did respond energetically to these problems in the 1990s. A tax reform was adopted in 1994 which sought to capture for the Center a larger proportion of revenue. This was quite successful. Center revenues increased from 22 to 48.9 percent of the total. But the proportion of GDP captured by regular budgetary revenue remained remarkably low, 11 percent as of 1997, a rate lower than that of major LDCs, and one that sharply curtailed the capacity of government at all levels.[24] Also, the financial system began to be reformed and efforts were made by the Ministry of Finance to bring extrabudgetary funds under greater control. In the late 1990s, the Center adopted a new program, the western development strategy, to enable these provinces to catch up with the east. As of the year 2001, however, none of these reforms and programs was able to solve the peasant burden problem.[25]

Decentralization made it difficult for the Center to secure the compliance of subnational leaders and bureaucracies. In the past, excessive centralization had stifled local initiative, but decentralization, especially the financial reforms introduced in the early 1980s, created vested local interests, including protectionism, which contributed greatly to the Center's difficulties in monitoring and rectifying deviant behavior of subordinate agents. During much of the reform period, a common saying was "they [the Center authorities] have their policy, but we have our countermeasures" (*zhongyang you zhengce, women you duice*).[26] China, a unitary state, has not arrived at an institutionalized division of power between the Center and the provinces, or between provinces and their subordinate levels of government, one that would subject financial flows between administrative levels to legal regulation and sanction.

---

[23] Wang and Hu (1999). Aside from providing rich data, this book recommends major policy changes to the Chinese leaders.
[24] Riskin et al. (1999). This study focuses strongly on the necessity for financial reform to enable the state to meet its social obligations, for example, to establish a social security system.
[25] Wang and Hu (1999: 190).
[26] *RMRB* (June 12, 1984).

Just how strong local power had become and what kind of threat, if any, it posed to the coherence of the Chinese state, became a topic of vigorous scholarly debate in the 1990s. One analyst concluded that when it came to curbing inflation (often caused by unrestrained local investment in rich provinces, another consequence of the decentralization of fiscal controls) the Center was able to get its way using such levers as its appointment powers. The capacity of the Center to push through the centralizing 1994 tax reform against substantial local opposition reinforces this view. Other scholars took a much more pessimistic view about the extent to which provincial interests prevailed over those of the Center.[27] From the vantage point of this study, both assertions were true: There were incentives for local agents to meet performance targets – the prospect of promotion and bonuses – but their responsiveness didn't extend to compliance with demands for burden reduction, in part because extraction from peasants was required to meet performance goals.

The Chinese state has rightly been characterized as one of "fragmented authoritarianism."[28] In terms of principal-agent theory, there were multiple principals and multiple agents. The twenty-odd generalist leaders of the Party's Politburo who were in charge of making overall policy acted as the bureaucracy's principals. The national-level functional ministries over which they presided were their agents. These agencies themselves functioned as principals with respect to their subordinate counterparts at lower administrative levels. With regard to burdens, numerous ministries – Public Security, Education, Public Health, and so forth – authorized their subordinates to impose a wide variety of fees for delivery of the services for which they were responsible. The Center generalist leadership had great difficulty bringing these practices under control. Principals at lower levels had similar difficulties with their subordinate agents.

Local agents were often not responsive to the demands of the top leaders to curb burdens. In this sense, it is convenient to distinguish between a central state and local states. This point emerges with great clarity on the issue of burdens and stability. The Center leaders were deeply concerned with the maintenance of societal stability, both in the countryside and in the cities, where, from the mid-1990s on, increasing unemployment among state sector workers raised the specter of unrest. In the countryside, the predatory behavior of many local officials was the cause of significant peasant unrest, including riots and violence. The Center was unable to curb their abuses.

---

[27] See Huang (1996). For the pessimistic view, see Wang and Hu (1999).
[28] Lieberthal (1995: 169).

RURAL SOCIETY AND PEASANT COLLECTIVE ACTION

The issue of burden control indicates that the model of a two-player game of state versus society distorts reality. Instead, one can speak of a three-player game between the leaders of the central state, officials of the local states, and various parts of society. On the burden issue, because of their concern with stability, the central authorities sided with the peasants, leading to an implicit alliance between the Center and the peasantry, in which the latter explicitly invoked the authority of Center regulations when protesting against the levies imposed by local officials. Peasants made strong efforts to inform higher-level authorities, up to the Center, of their plight, hoping for favorable intervention. Peasants were "driven by officials to revolt" (*guanbi minfan*), to use the traditional phrase, but they acted in the name of the Center and not against the regime as such. They displayed considerable capacity to act collectively but the scope of their actions was largely limited to the villages and townships.

The core issue was accountability. As the agricultural economist W. Arthur Lewis suggested long ago, locally financed projects can in principle be aligned better to local needs than centrally decreed projects which often fail to take into account local variation and felt needs. But this works only if peasants are involved in the decisionmaking process:

> Farmers resent paying taxes for which they may get no return. However, if the services are provided by local authorities under their control, to whom the taxes are paid, the farmers can see what they are getting for their money, and are more willing to give voluntary labor as well as pay more taxes to meet their own needs.[29]

Or, as a young Shandong farmer put it in 1988:

> Isn't the state building democratic politics? We farmers also want to talk about democracy. We can't bend with the wind anymore. When the higher levels demand this amount of money, they must explain what the reasons are, clearly list the items, and make them known to all. It is both reasonable and lawful to pay grain [taxes]. We farmers are not confused about this. But they just take money from us in some muddled way. We give grain and don't know which 'lord's' (*laoye*) pocket it ends up in.[30]

Taxing Chinese peasants, as the title of our study suggests, was closely linked to demands for accountability, participation, and democracy. The Chinese

---

[29] Quoted in Hunter (1969: 183).
[30] *NMRB*, (January 20, 1988).

leaders recognized this and took a number of steps to enable villagers to defend their rights, a move significantly motivated by their awareness of the link between peasant burdens and social instability. In the 1990s, maintenance of social stability became a paramount priority for China's rulers. To some degree they recognized that without providing some channel for peaceful redress of grievances, peasants were forced to take to the streets, demonstrate, riot, or torch Party-government compounds. Measures taken by the regime included allowing peasants to make use of the "letters and visits" system to lodge complaints and seek redress at administrative levels above the village, by increasing the availability of courts in the countryside, by instituting "open management of village affairs," and, in connection with the latter, by promoting village elections.

The introduction of village elections – a remarkable development in an authoritarian system whose leaders were determined to preserve the Communist Party's monopoly of power – was significantly motivated by the hope that elections would stabilize the rural areas, enlisting peasant cooperation in governance and making village leaders accountable. Thus far, it seems that when village elections have been genuinely open, they have made the management of tax and fee extraction fairer and less arbitrary and abusive. Participation in village-level financial decisions appears to have increased peasant satisfaction and hence contributed to stability. Village democracy also held promise of modest reductions in burdens. The major obstacle to substantial reductions was that direct elections were confined to the villages. Since burdens were imposed not only by village cadres but mainly by higher-level officials, elections would have to be extended upward to the townships before peasants could gain the kind of voice that would make a real difference.

State Capacity and Extraction. These measures of empowerment were not adequate because the burden problem was rooted in larger systemic deficiencies that required solution. Replacement of the ad hoc tax and fee system by a modern system of rural taxation required major reforms of the financial and administrative apparatus. By the end of the 1990s, the country's leaders finally recognized that merely issuing orders to reduce burdens was not enough and that far more substantial measures were needed to change the institutional configuration within which extraction took place. They faced a daunting task. Devising an equitable, fair, and effective tax system for 250 million odd peasant households is a formidable task, as it is in all developing countries. John W. Mellor, an agricultural economist, emphasizes the high transaction costs that inevitably accompany efforts to tax smallholder peasants:

> The problems are compounded in agriculture because of the extreme difficulty of checking accounting procedures. Agriculture, with its wide

variability in productivity, complex depreciation patterns, a system of sales and purchase in small quantities to a multiplicity of buyers and sellers and very substantial home consumption, defies outside checks on accounting procedures. Thus one can expect widespread evasion of agricultural income taxes.[31]

In some countries, notably India, "rural incomes had remained virtually untaxed since independence" in part for political reasons – India's democracy empowered the countryside – but also because of formidable administrative problems.[32] In China, limited administrative capacities were highlighted by one approach to burden control: a rule that levies imposed by the villages and townships must not exceed 5 percent of net per capita earnings of the previous year. Because assessing this by households was too difficult, incomes were averaged on the basis of the townships, a large unit in which incomes often varied greatly, thereby penalizing the poor. A new tax system would have to be predictable and eliminate the elements of arbitrariness and open-endedness that characterized the ad hoc levies. As Margaret Levi puts it, in order to attain "quasi-voluntary compliance" in extracting

> the most from the peasants in the way of tribute, rulers must make a credible commitment not to take more later. Both to ensure stable rule and to keep their costs down, rulers must offer positive benefits to a "minimum winning coalition" of the population in return for allegiance.[33]

As this quote suggests, extraction as a measure of state capacity consists of far more than simply the state's ability to extract funds, as much of the literature on this topic suggests.[34] For extraction to make a genuine contribution to viable state capacity requires an approach that limits extraction and secures societal cooperation. Stalin's Soviet Union displayed extraordinary capacities to extract resources from the countryside but at the cost of thoroughly alienating the peasantry, requiring heavy reliance on coercion and severely distorting the country's long-term development. Not only is the amount that is extracted important – the Chinese regime is in principle sensitive to the capacity of peasants to "endure" (*chengshou*) – but so are fairness and predictability. China has not been able to live up to this standard. Its entire tax system suffered from severe imbalances, including failure to adequately tax

---

[31] Mellor (1966: 91). For a similar view, see Johnston and Kilby (1975: 429).

[32] Varshney (1995: 35, 95, 178).

[33] Levi (1988: 43).

[34] Migdal (1988: 4) summarizes state capacities as consisting of societal penetration, regulation of social relationships, extraction of resources, and appropriation of resources in determined ways.

some sectors of society, widespread tax evasion, either because of administrative difficulties or official connivance, and excessive extraction as in the case under consideration.[35]

As this discussion of extraction shows, the concept of "state capacity" turns out to be quite complex. In the literature it is often presented in the form of a shopping list of attributes, including the following: (1) extractive capacity defined as mobilization of resources to implement Center goals; (2) steering capacity, the ability to guide or steer national development and to define and pursue a national interest; (3) legitimation capacity, the use of symbols to create a consensus or to integrate society around a common set of values so as to enhance the state's ability to achieve popular acceptance, support for and compliance with its policies; (4) coercive capacity, ability to use force to achieve core objectives; (5) capacity to control and administer the nation's territory, including effective monitoring of its subordinate agents, that is, the capacity to implement the state's policies. In some formulations, this includes the capacity to penetrate society and to regulate social relations, and in others, the capacity to respond to societal demands.[36] But only some recognize that "there is not necessarily a positive relationship between different kinds of state capacities. . . . The very unevenness of a state's existing capacities may be the most important structural features to recognize in understanding how it confronts challenges."[37]

The Chinese case demonstrates first that the components of state capacity are not discrete but continuous variables. Each must be broken down into segments. There can be high extractive capacity on one dimension but low capacity on another. China had a high capacity to steer national development in its broad outlines, but low capacity to secure compliance of subordinate agents, at least with regard to burdens. Second, the relations between the various components of capacity must be examined. They should not be measured in isolation from one another. Thus, excessive extraction of resources from Chinese peasants led to loss of support if not loss of legitimacy and therefore required higher levels of coercion to obtain compliance. Inevitably, there is a trade-off, implicitly or explicitly. Therefore, it is not possible to assign one simple ranking to China in terms of the capacities of its state. Inevitably, there are paradoxes, as in the coexistence of development and predation.

---

[35] Gamble (2000: 16–20).

[36] The list is drawn from several authors, including Migdal (1988: 4), Tilly (1978), and Shaoquang Wang (1995: 89–90).

[37] See Evans, Rueschemeyer, and Skocpol (1985: 351–2).

1 Introduction

Chapter 2 provides historical context. It shows that the ad hoc levies were a major issue in state–society relations during the two thousand years of the dynastic era as well as in Republican China. There are striking similarities in the practices used by previous regimes with respect to rural finances and those of contemporary China. Establishing continuities with the past suggests that some of the same structural constraints operated, especially weak administrative capacities at the grass roots, in both contexts. We do not claim that everything stayed the same, especially with respect to state penetration of society. The third part of the chapter covers tax issues during the Communist revolution and the Mao era. The latter fundamentally changed both the institutional and policy contexts, since taxation became embedded in the state's larger quest to extract resources from the countryside for the industrialization program.

Chapter 3 provides basic information: What were the burdens, who imposed them, and what was their impact on peasant incomes? We show that burdens were not simply imposed by localities but also originated from central governmental units and that they were steeply-regressive. This chapter also discusses regional variations and the TVE variable, which separated "agricultural China" mainly in the central and western provinces, from "industrial rural China" in the East. The last part of the chapter sheds light on peasant grievances about burdens, emphasizing the impact of arbitrary, highly coercive, and corrupt methods of collection.

Chapter 4 seeks to shed light on the underlying structural causes of the burden problem. These include the "deconcentration" of power in the Chinese political system, manifested especially in the rise of sequestered extrabudgetary funds and the consequent resort to ad hoc fees; the performance demands made on the rural bureaucracy, which was heavily influenced by the Maoist era; the high costs of unrestrained bureaucratic expansion and the disordered administration of finances, especially at the townships; and finally, the impact of pervasive corruption.

Chapter 5, on peasant resistance, examines mostly illegal peasant strategies to secure redress. We discuss the difficult but not insurmountable data problem. We examine various forms of individual and collective protest and include case studies that vividly illuminate protest activity. To appraise peasant collective protest, we ask to what extent their resistance amounted to an emerging social movement. Our answer is that it did not because major requisites typically associated with social movements were not present, especially urban allies.

Chapter 6 assesses the regime's efforts to bring burdens under control. Center strategies included issuing numerous regulations, launching burden-reduction campaigns, and introducing control mechanisms within the bureaucratic hierarchy. Center leaders also included measures that to some extent empowered the peasants to seek redress on their own. This chapter looks at the complaints peasants were able to lodge, usually to governments above the township level, which took both individual and collective forms. Such activities took place in a context in which the regime allowed the media to report fairly truthfully on the burden abuses, and which in turn encouraged villagers to take action. The chapter also looks at the emerging legal system as an avenue for redress. Two case studies illuminate the difficulties peasants had in securing redress both by complaining to higher levels and by bringing court cases. And finally, the chapter examines institutional reforms, including those of township finance, bureaucratic streamlining, and especially, a drastic attempt to rationalize rural taxes by "turning fees into taxes" (*fei gai shui*). This approach was still localized and experimental, as of the year 2001, but if successful, promised to make a major dent in the problem.

Chapter 7 examines the impact of village elections and of the "open conduct of village affairs" (*cunwu gongkai*) on burden management. Direct election of village chairpersons and village committees was intended to bring about accountability and to orient village cadres toward their constituents and not simply toward their township superiors. Genuine elections thus entailed significant changes in grass roots power relations, especially between the townships and the villages, since the former, under pressure to fulfill the tasks assigned by their superiors, required responsive, obedient village chiefs. This important, indeed ground-breaking reform, was very much a moving target and there are much conflicting data on the impact of the elections on village governance.

The second half of the chapter focuses on the larger issue of peasant interest representation at the Center. Agricultural interests at the Center were woefully underrepresented. The burden problem was, as already emphasized, not simply a local problem requiring local solutions, but also a national one. Communist China was and continues to be a state characterized by "urban bias," a term used by analysts of many developing countries in Africa and Asia which systematically favor the urban sector at the expense of the agricultural one.[38] The Chinese regime was structurally similar to many Third World states, which as Robert Bates notes, were dominated by "a development coalition of industrialists, urban wage earners, bureaucrats, and intellectuals" who viewed agriculture

---

[38] Lipton (1977) and Varshney, ed. (1993, special issue of the *Journal of Development Studies*). Jean C. Oi's article in this issue, "Reform and Urban Bias in China," pp.129–48, focuses on industrial rural China, which was less subject to this "bias."

as the resource for the promotion of industrialization.[39] State agricultural policies, especially the compulsory procurement system, imposed what Chinese
scholars called "hidden burdens" on the peasants whose interests had been systematically subordinated to those of the urban-industrial sector ever since the
First Five-Year Plan was inaugurated in 1953. During the reform era, farmers'
vital interests in state agricultural policies centered on those concerning procurement quotas and pricing of agricultural and industrial products. This part
of Chapter 7 examines demands for a greater voice for China's peasants at the
Center, demands voiced in surprisingly strong form by elite advocates. There
was some responsiveness on the part of the regime, but a fundamental political
realignment resulting from creation of an autonomous national farmers association, did not take place. The lack of adequate rural representation in the
country's policymaking process was another important structural obstacle to
the solution of the burden problem.

Chapter 8, the Conclusion, pulls together our findings and assesses their significance. We review the distinction between "industrializing," "agricultural,"
and "subsistence" rural China; the historical continuities; and the structural
determinants of the problem of tax burdens. Among the latter, we identify as
particularly important central-local relations and their fiscal consequences and
the incentives for officials that grew out of partial decentrialization as well as
from deconcentration of administrative power. We assess the role of the peasants as a third set of players in addition to the roles played by the Center and
local governments, and we evaluate various solutions to the tax burden problem, concluding with an assessment of the potential for further democratizing
pressures arising from "taxation without representation."

---

[39] Bates (1987: 179).

2

Peasants and Taxation in Historical Perspective

HISTORICAL comparison can often yield telling clues about contemporary problems. To a remarkable extent, taxation as an issue in state–peasant relations in the 1990s echoes China's prerevolution past.[1] Then as now, regimes appeared unable to devise, implement, and enforce a fair, equitable, and reasonably honest system of taxation. Then as now, regimes relied heavily on informal, ad hoc ways of funding governmental activities. Then as now, informal levies gave rise to widespread corruption. Then as now, the authorities had difficulty determining just how much households owed in terms of land and other taxes. Then as now, rural taxation was a major source of grievance and social instability.

The aim of this chapter is to illuminate the continuities and differences in the Chinese history of rural taxation by briefly examining the imperial and Republican periods as well as the Communist revolution and the Maoist era.

RURAL TAXATION IN IMPERIAL CHINA

China was an agrarian economy. Land taxes were the major source of revenue for the imperial government. As Table 2.1 indicates, the land tax plus surcharges (*haoxian*) together accounted for more than two-thirds of total revenue.

Because of their dependence on the agricultural population, most Chinese emperors adhered to a low-tax doctrine. They thought of themselves as Confucian benevolent rulers whose task it was to nourish the people. They feared that encroaching on peasant subsistence would threaten dynastic legitimacy and lead to disorder, if not rebellion. The early Qing rulers, for instance, believed that the fall of the preceding dynasty, the Ming, was due to three land tax increases imposed in its last stages of rule.[2] At least in theory, emperors

---

[1] See Bernhardt (1992).
[2] Zelin (1984: 113).

Table 2.1 *Financial Balance Sheet of the Thirty-First Year of the Qianlong Reign (1766)*

Annual Revenues	Amount	Percent	Annual Expenditure	Amount	Percent
Land tax	2,992	62.2	Military	1,704	49.2
Melting			Official		
surcharge	300	6.2	salaries	534	15.4
Salt tax	575	12.0	Royal court	122	3.5
Custom			Local		
revenue	542	11.3	administration	720	20.8
Miscellaneous			Water		
levies	101	2.1	conservation	380	11.0
Regular donations	300	6.2			
TOTALS	4,810	100	TOTALS	3,460	100

Note: 1 unit = 10,000 silver taels.
Source: Caizhengbu (1994: vol. 2: 23).

were not predators seeking to squeeze the peasants to the maximum.[3] During the Ming and the Qing, there was a long-standing commitment never to raise the land tax (*yong bu jia fu*). In 1713, the Kangxi emperor froze the land tax at the 1711 level, regardless of changes in land prices or productivity.[4] Kangxi also called for tax remissions during times of poor harvests and demanded that land-lords pass the benefit on to their tenants. Because the empire depended heavily on the land tax and landowners resisted strongly, this demand was not met. Because formal taxes were kept low, local governments in particular suffered from chronic shortages of revenue. What revenue they were allowed to keep did not cover most basic governmental expenses. Even the most virtuous and frugal of local officials would have found it difficult to operate within the limits set by this system of revenue sharing.[5] Hence, local officials either siphoned off funds going to the Center, squeezed the people by means of informal taxation, or both. Squeezing the people came to constitute a complex system of sur-charges, customary fees, or assessments (*tanpai*). Surcharges were an essential part of local revenues and at times exceeded the land tax. These informal taxes, levies, and impositions were charged and collected by the agents of the county magistrate. The system was easily abused and turned into one of "institutional corruption" at the expense of commoners. Since miscellaneous fees and charges were apportioned among households, the surcharges were regressive.

[3] See Levi (1988).
[4] Yeh-chien Wang (1971: 829–42).
[5] Zelin (1984: 37).

Just as they do today, surcharges posed a formidable challenge to the dynastic rulers, who often vacillated between acquiescence and prohibition. The Kangxi emperor warned twice "against their collection, permitting the people to report officials who persisted in this practice."[6] The governor of Sichuan had signs posted notifying the public of new rates and of their right to report excess collection.[7] The reform regime of the PRC also allowed peasants to petition for relief from abusive taxation. The Ming and Qing emperors sought to rationalize the tax system and tried various means to regularize informal levies to eliminate cheating the ruler and to do away with illicitly burdening peasants. Thus the Yongzheng emperor (1723–36) made vigorous efforts toward reform, permitting the imposition of one major surcharge as a part of the regular tax system (*huohao guigong*) to adequately fund government activities and reduce the need for further informal levies. This effort was remarkably similar to the reform pushed in the late 1990s of converting fees into taxes (*fei gai shui*). Already during the Ming, a famous political commentator wrote that conversion of miscellaneous surcharges and fees into formal taxes could only be effective in the short run.[8] This was indeed the fate of the Yongzheng reforms.

In the sixteenth century during the Ming and again in the Qing, land and poll taxes were merged in to the "single-whip tax system" (*yi tiao bian fa*) but the imperial bureaucracies lacked the capacity to keep track of changing ownership of land, assess the productivity of scattered plots, or monitor changes in the harvest, arduous tasks even for contemporary administrators whether in China or in other developing countries. As was true of the 1990s, officials often relied on estimates. Tax evasion and underassessments of tax – much newly cultivated land escaped the tax rolls – were common problems, benefiting the privileged and powerful. The tax system was supposed to take into account differences in productivity and to equalize burdens, but it failed since powerful gentry were able to evade the rules.[9]

Peasant Tax Resistance in the Imperial Period. Due to onerous taxes, peasants resorted to resistance, which took a variety of forms, ranging from large-scale rebellion to more ordinary, ongoing, and less visible protest. With regard to peasant rebellions, as Charles Tilly observes, increased taxes were the "single most important stimulus to popular rebellion throughout history."[10] The same

---

[6] Zelin (1984: 72).
[7] Zelin (1984: 138).
[8] Gu Yanwu, (1879).
[9] R. Bin Wong (1997: 236).
[10] Tilly (1978: 205–6), quoting from Gabriel Ardant and Eric Wolf.

term of "officials driving the people to rebel" (*guanbi minfan*) by imposing excessive taxes did not lose relevance for the contemporary period. In 1993, during widespread peasant riots against burdens, Wan Li, one of the architects of decollectivization (household contracting), told of peasants who, when asked what they wanted, responded: "We want nothing but Chen Sheng and Wu Guang," the leaders of China's first great peasant rebellion during the Qin Dynasty.[11]

During the dynastic era, revolts, rebellions, and millenarian movements were often triggered at least in part by onerous tax burdens and other state efforts at resource mobilization, such as the corvée. These played a major role in the downfall of the Qin Dynasty. Typically, burdens were heaviest during wars which depleted the imperial treasury, when the dynastic cycle entered its downturn phase, and when state decay, especially corruption, led to widespread abuses. Often a newly risen dynastic regime would begin with lower taxes, learning a lesson from the fall of its predecessors, but then the old ways returned. The early rulers of the Han Dynasty adopted a light corvée and low-tax policy, cutting the land tax. Toward the later years of the Han, however, rulers began to tax heavily and peasant discontent led to several large peasant rebellions. The Sui Dynasty reformed land ownership by implementing equal division of land and a low-tax policy. During the Tang Dynasty, agricultural growth resulted in long-lasting prosperity. Peasants benefited from the low-tax and rent policy as well as a new taxation system. Under the new system, a land-based tax and asset-based tax were collected in the summer and autumn. In the declining years of the Tang, however, levies and corruption triggered peasant rebellions, one of which, the Huang Chao Rebellion, nearly brought the dynasty down. As for the Ming, in the end, natural disasters, heavy exactions, and official corruption made burdens unbearably heavy for peasants. A large peasant rebellion led by Li Zicheng with the appealing slogan, "equal land, no taxes," quickly swept through northern China, forcing the last Ming emperor to commit suicide as the rebellion closed in around the capital.

Small-scale tax resistance was a recurring feature of rural life in imperial China as it has been in the 1990s. In the eighteenth century, tensions between state demands and social expectations of fairness gave rise to efforts to renegotiate the terms of state revenue collection. Protests might erupt when peasants believed that proper procedures or principles had been violated and warranted appeals to fairness and equity, as in cases of unfair apportionment, failure to adjust for poor harvests, or unfair measurements and biased rates of conversion of copper to silver. The belief in equity was shared by officials and commoners alike; hence, inequities such as favoring the rich could become a source of

[11] Li Yusha (1993).

legitimate resistance. In such cases, R. Bin Wong argues, protest was rational, specific, limited, and rested on shared values.[12]

According to Wong, local protest movements usually began with group formation "sometimes numbering less than a hundred" participants, and the emergence of informal leaders. The leaders would present petitions to government officials. Failure of officials to respond set the stage for violent action, including attacks on bureaucrats' homes and offices. This would be followed by the arrest of troublemakers, which in turn mobilized additional people to participate. The outcome might be negotiations or repression or a combination of the two. If the disputes were not resolved, peasant actions might escalate, ultimately threatening the regime. The sequence of events leading up to violent protests and revolts reveals a common pattern of rural protests in traditional, transitional, and contemporary China. The eighteenth century was free of regime-threatening peasant rebellion in part because of official sensitivity to equity and shared expectations of acceptable behavior.[13]

Peasant tax revolts involving violence took place in many provinces during the later years of the Qing. One such episode played itself out in Anfu county, Jiangxi. The magistrate visited some villages in quest of taxes and ordered the collection of tax arrears in a township. When he returned to the county he was met by a group of villagers who surrounded his *yamen* and began beating up the runners who had accompanied him on his tour. The protest leaders charged that the magistrate had employed three ex-bandits to extract the money forcibly. Investigation showed that there had been "undue harassment" of villagers. Nonetheless, the leaders of the riot were punished because they should have pressed their case peacefully by petitioning the magistrate's superiors.[14] Another revolt erupted in 1782, when more than twenty thousand peasants rallied in front of a county government building demanding a reduction of the land tax in Chongyang, Hubei province.[15] Sometimes, when protest against landlords was an important component of a revolt, land contracts were torn up even as tax officials were assaulted. Sometimes, the protestors achieved rate reductions.[16] Acts of nonviolent resistance such as delays in payment, unilateral reductions in the tax, or refusal to pay were reported from Jiangsu, Zhejiang, Anhui, and Jiangxi throughout the nineteenth century.[17] Another form of resistance was the "wildcat" strategy used by migrant farmers who, with government encouragement,

[12] R. Bin Wong (1997: 235–6).
[13] R. Bin Wong (1997: 235–6).
[14] Zelin (1984: 255).
[15] Caizhengbu (1991: 65).
[16] Yan Zhongping (1989: 940–8).
[17] Caizhengbu (1994, v.2: 51).

cultivated virgin land. Migrant farmers would leave these fields after the harvest so governments had no way of knowing who they were or how much they produced and owed in rents and taxes. This happened in Anhui, Jiangsu, Zhejiang, Shaanxi, and Shanxi provinces.[18]

RURAL TAXATION IN THE LATE QING AND REPUBLICAN PERIODS

Three major changes influenced rural taxation toward the end of the dynastic rule and the early era of the Republic. First, the weakening of central power during the decline of the Qing, the period of warlordism, and the era of Nationalist rule permitted a much wider range of intermediate and local authorities, often in competition with one another, to impose taxes and fees; as a result, extraction became less accountable and more corrupt. Second, the collapse of the Confucian ethical basis of government led to increasingly rapacious, predatory, and exploitative practices. And third, the modernization of local governments, entailing expansion since new functions had to be performed, required more revenue. With agricultural involution, namely, the lack of increases in productivity, the process of local state building compounded the peasant tax burdens.[19] In overall perspective, both the central authorities and the peasants lost out, while local officials, often in collusion with local social and economic elites, gained.

As the Qing Dynasty declined in the nineteenth century, the fiscal difficulties of the government became increasingly acute. New sources of revenue, such as customs, became significant. In 1894, customs accounted for 24.6 percent of total national revenues.[20] By the mid-nineteenth century, the growing commercial and manufacturing sector in the Chinese economy led to a proportionate decline in the land tax as a source of national-level revenue, as Table 2.2 indicates.

Yet, this decline and the new revenue sources did not reduce the tax burdens on the peasants. The rise of *lijin*, a transit tax on goods, collected by local governments, is a case in point. *Lijin* was first devised in 1853 when the Qing government was facing fiscal hardship as its army took on the Taiping Rebellion and it needed to empower local officials to impose a new tax. *Lijin*, which literally means "percentage money," first appeared as a local initiative in Yangzhou, Jiangsu province. Most of the other provinces soon followed suit. It played a major role in financing local armies and sustaining the regional warlords in the late eighteenth and early nineteenth centuries. Weak centralized control over the collection process caused the *lijin* to fall prey to various abuses and widespread

---

[18] Zhu Shouming (1958: 3771).
[19] Philip Huang (1990).
[20] Caizhengbu (1994, v.2: 74–80).

Table 2.2 *Land and Other Taxes in the Late Qing*

Taxes	1753		1908		Index
	Amount	Percent	Amount	Percent	1753 = 100
Land tax	54,214	73.5	102,400	35.1	189
Other taxes	19,578	26.5	189,600	64.9	968
Salt tax	8,768	11.9	45,000	15.4	513
Native customs	5,405	7.3	6,700	2.3	124
Maritime customs	–	–	32,900	11.3	–
Lijin	–	–	40,000	13.6	–
Misc. taxes	5,405	7.3	65,000	22.3	1,203
TOTAL	73,792	100	292,000	100	396

Note: 1 unit = 1,000 silver taels.

Source: Yeh-chien Wang (1971: 838).

popular disapproval.[21] To peasants, the *lijin* did nothing but add another tax when they sold their farm products away from home. Viewing it as a detriment to the expansion of commercial and trade growth, the Nationalist government abolished the *lijin* in 1928, but the practice continued well into the 1930s.[22]

In the mid-1930s, the Nationalist government sought to cut taxes. According to a report to a Guomindang (GMD) Central Committee meeting, the Nationalist government abolished 5,200 surtaxes in 1934–5, promised that no new surtaxes would be imposed, that the authorized surtaxes should not exceed the amount of the land taxes, and that more cuts would be made later. Revenues reportedly decreased by 49 million yuan as a result of these measures. However, revocation of surcharges prompted local officials to turn to *tankuan* (apportioned levies) to offset budget deficits not covered by regular revenue, a maneuver familiar to villagers in the 1990s. Provincial authorities were largely powerless to monitor these assessments, since about 85 percent of them were collected by townships (or subcounty districts) and even villages. As Ramon Myers puts it, "The tax [the farmers] dreaded most was the *tankuan*."[23] At the same time, the land tax increased by 8 percent from 1931 to 1934, at a time when the precipitous decline in farm prices during the world depression sharply increased the real cost of the tax.

Fiscal Decentralization. As a part of its fiscal reforms, the Nationalist government decided in 1927 to make the land tax a local tax, breaking a long-standing

---

[21] See Thornton (1999: 1–42).

[22] Caizhengbu (1994, v.2: 74).

[23] See Eastman (1974: 202).

Table 2.3 *Index of Formal Land Tax vs.
Informal Surtaxes (Major
Grain-Producing Provinces, 1931–1933)*

Province	Lowest	Highest
Jiangsu	120	2,603
Zhejiang	134	385
Anhui	48	287
Jiangxi	27	958
Hunan	24	1,280
Hubei	9	8,600
Henan	16	1,019

Note: Formal tax = 100.

Source: Sun Xiaocun (1934: 6).

tradition of classifying it as a central tax.[24] The result was to increase informal surtaxes on the land tax, which became major sources of revenue for provincial and local governments. This was but the legitimization of what had been a long-standing practice in Chinese history.[25] In addition to the land tax and surtaxes, provinces and counties imposed other categories of levies. In Hebei, peasants paid "miscellaneous levies" on sales of peanuts, rice, eggs, sheep intestines, and fur, as well as a hog slaughter tax. In Henan, there was a banquet fee and sales taxes on local products such as whips, sesame oil, and street lamps.[26] A 1934 statistical yearbook lists 127 categories of levies in Guangdong province and 262 categories in Zhejiang province.[27] In Gansu, an impoverished province, people had to pay 44 taxes that took "the fat off their fingers."[28] In Jiangsu, in 1933, surtaxes provided almost eight times the revenue from the land tax. Moreover, there were enormous territorial disparities. According to Ramon Myers, "the land tax varied greatly from county to county and bore little relationship to the value and productivity of the land."[29] In one county in Shandong province the land tax was 2.97 yuan per acre, or 7.5 percent of the harvest; in another, 20 to 25 yuan per acre or 35 to 40 percent of the harvest.[30]

A commentator at the time made a sobering point that resonates with the situation some seventy years later: "After 1927 [fiscal reform], surtaxes grew as the

[24] Ibid., 344.
[25] Caizhengbu (1994, v.2: 74).
[26] Ibid.
[27] *Caizheng Nianjian* (1935).
[28] Clubb (1964: 187).
[29] Eastman (1974: 198).
[30] Ibid., 204.

new reform measures increased. For example, party building, self-governance, road projects, office building, as well as rural revitalization all needed funds. They can only come from the peasants."[31] As the Nationalist government made efforts to decentralize, expansion of local governmental functions was often funded out of surcharges. In 1926, landowners in Chuansha county, Jiangsu, paid a public welfare surcharge, a police levy, a household registration levy, a water conservancy charge, and a levy for education. By 1933, new charges had been added for primary schools, road building, self-government funding, and land surveying. A year later, there were twenty-six different charges. Modernization of local governments burdened villagers in poorer areas much more than in richer ones. In the richer southern counties of Jiangsu, the increases in taxes and surcharges were substantially lower than those in the poorer northern Jiangsu counties. If in the former they doubled, in the latter they rose by three or four times, as in Suining county from 1915 to 1939, or eighteen times in Feng county. The reason was that each county was responsible for the same modernizing programs. Poorer counties with a much smaller tax base had less revenue from the land tax; hence needed revenues had to be sought from large surcharges. "To compensate for a tax base inadequate for their modernizing needs, the governments of Funing and Nantong thus imposed surcharges and levies that were three to four times the amount of the regular tax. In Wuxi and Nanhui, by contrast, the supplementary imposts did not exceed the regular tax."[32] In the 1990s, failure to adjust local tax levels according to local wealth was a major source of burdens on the poorer counties.

The burdens fell disproportionately on ordinary villagers because wealthy landowners refused to cooperate with government tax collectors. As Fei Xiaotong observes, "village elites were not affected by laws [and were] exempt from taxation and conscription."[33] One 1945 estimate suggested that small farmers paid five times more than the official regulations required and that tax burdens took 30 to 50 percent of the harvest. After VJ Day and when civil war was erupting, Chiang Kai-shek bitterly charged that the "rich families in all the provinces usually do not pay the grain levies." Or, as the GMD's *Central Daily* put it, "wealthy landlords, acting in concert with local officials, pass on the burden of the levies to the suffering and inarticulate masses."[34]

Local Power. Another notable aspect of the decentralization reform under the GMD regime was that the power of subcounty officials to tax, especially in

---

[31] He Huiyuan (1934: 6).
[32] Bernhardt (1992: 210–15).
[33] Quoted in Bernhardt (1992: 64).
[34] Bernhardt (1992: 65, 79).

the townships, was greatly enhanced, in part in the name of rationalization. The Nationalist government made substantial efforts to reform and rationalize the structure of local government. Similar to earlier efforts in the late Qing, the Nationalist government's attempts included revamping the fiscal system by decentralizing certain fiscal powers. In 1942, a new system of separate national finance (including provincial finance) and local finance that covered county and subcounty governments was established. The main purpose was to rectify the increasingly irregular subprovincial finance, which had depended heavily on onerous levies and surtaxes. According to the new system, counties would collect and retain certain taxes (including real estate, slaughter, licensing, permit, and deed elimination taxes), while the national government collected other taxes including land, inheritance, sales, and contract taxes. The national government would transfer portions of these national tax revenues to local governments.[35] (In 1994, a similar division of tax revenues into central and local ones was undertaken.) Despite these reforms, for local governments tax revenues were simply not sufficient and they still had to rely on informal levies. For instance, some townships in Sichuan collected levies for administration, protection of schools, teacher salaries, and military family relief funds. In one county alone, there were more than twenty-three local levies imposed by township authorities.[36]

As in the late Qing and early Republican periods, the fiscal reforms under the GMD, especially those aiming at separating national and local finances, had the unanticipated consequence of increasing the burden on the peasants. Fiscal decentralization without accountability – despite the fancy label of "self-governed finance" (*zizhi caizheng*) – spelled trouble for the taxpaying local population. Before the reforms, local levies and surtaxes were illegitimate or quasi-legitimate. The fiscal reforms served to legitimize the authority of local governments to tax. At best they failed to lessen the tax burden on peasants, at worst they exacerbated the problem. These same patterns reappeared in striking form during the reform period of the 1980s and 1990s.

The War of Resistance against Japan generated huge new demands for revenue, especially once the Nationalists were cut off from the rich coastal cities and provinces. In July 1941, the government increased the land tax, which it also began to collect in kind, compelling local governments to search for other sources of revenue. *Tanpai* proliferated. Most were formally illegal but were tacitly tolerated. In Sichuan in 1942, the contributions to the *baojia* (an organization for maintaining local security) and payment of the education charge were the only authorized assessments, but a survey of eighteen counties found a range

---

[35] Caizhengbu (1994, v.2: 425).
[36] *Xinhua Ribao* (Feb. 20, 1945).

of between eleven and sixty-seven additional ones. Peasants had to contribute toward paying for the straw sandals of recruits, supporting families of recruits, road repairs, teachers' stipends, and the training of anti-aircraft crews. The largest exactions accompanying the land tax were the compulsory purchase of grain (*zhenggou*) at half the market price and compulsory borrowing (*zhengjie*) of grain, which was to be repaid in five years. Taxes, contributions, compulsory loans and purchases, the horrendously mismanaged conscription and labor mobilization systems all imposed extraordinary burdens on peasants.[37] Extraction contributed to the Henan famine of 1942–3: "What transformed privation into a terrifyingly severe famine, in which several million persons starved to death, was the government's relentless exaction of taxes and the military grain levy."[38] As was the case during the PRC's Great Leap Forward famine, which to a significant extent was also caused by excessive extraction of grain, the calamity was not a product of conscious intent but one of gross mismanagement.

Tax Resistance. Outbreaks of localized tax resistance were a common feature of the rural landscape in late Qing and Republican China. For the mid-nineteenth century, Elizabeth Perry notes that "the proliferation of militias was associated with a dramatic rise in the frequency and scale of tax resistance in Huai-pei." Surcharges levied to fund the militias caused peasant anger but at the same time "militia detachments offered an organizational base for opposing government policy." In Shandong, "Hundreds of cases have been recorded of militia leading assaults on county offices, burning tax registers, and killing magistrates and other officials."[39] In the twentieth century, as Lucien Bianco concludes, "most peasant riots were directed against tax collectors, local officials, or local bullies, not against the wealthy.... As a rule, rioters and even rebels aimed merely at redressing some wrongs, ending specific local abuses, or getting rid of what they perceived as encroachments on their traditional rights."[40]

During the War of Resistance, as reported by Lloyd Eastman, in early 1942 an estimated sixty thousand people rioted in twenty counties in Gansu with slogans like "Gansu people should rule Gansu! Oppose military conscription and the grain taxes. Kill all the southern barbarians." In 1944, hundreds protesting against levies and corvée labor killed officials and burned tax offices in three townships in northern Hubei. In the same year in southern Hubei, "over ten thousand peasants" rebelled over grain levies and labor services, reportedly

[37] Eastman (1984).
[38] Ibid., 68.
[39] Perry (1980: 86–7).
[40] Bianco (1995: 176).

instigated by Communists allied to the Yellow Spears Society. "Similar uprisings were reported in virtually every province under Nationalist rule – many in the capital province of Szechwan [Sichuan] and some as far away as Fukien [Fujian]."[41]

During the Civil War, according to Lloyd Eastman, peasants in the Nationalist areas did not rise up but nonetheless made a "real, perhaps even decisive . . . indirect" contribution to the Communist victory. This contribution "lay, first and foremost, in depriving the National Government of grain, money, and men." In 1947, "when nominally the Nationalists' territorial control reached its greatest extent during the postwar period, the central government collected only . . . 57 percent of the amount collected in 1942" when the Nationalists controlled far less territory.[42]

TAXES AND THE COMMUNIST REVOLUTION

Exorbitant taxes and levies capriciously and brutally collected were a major, if not the greatest, source of rural grievance. To appeal to the peasantry, Communist revolutionaries necessarily had to differentiate their tax policies from those of their competitors. But as an organized political and military force ruling over large and small parts of the country, the Communists needed revenue as badly as any other governmental authority, especially as they fielded a substantial regular army. At the same time, however, they were not responsible for feeding the cities until 1948 or so. Still, the Communist challenge was to find ways to fund its activities without alienating the people.

When they first arrived in the Shaanxi-Gansu-Ningxia base area in 1935, the Communists abolished all taxes and levies, solely relying on confiscations from rich landlords and local bullies as their revenue base. In 1937, after the Anti-Japanese War started and with the formation of a united front with the Nationalist government, expropriation from landlords could no longer serve as a source of revenue. The Communist border region government received subsidies from the Nationalist government and trade between areas controlled by each brought in some revenue. In 1939 the subsidies ended and in 1941 the Nationalists imposed an economic blockade on the Communist areas. Henceforth, the Communists had to find their own resources, a critical problem in the desperately poor Northwest, one compounded by the rapid growth of the border region government and of its military forces. The Communists addressed the revenue problem in three ways: First, they imposed graduated taxes so that the

---

[41] Eastman (1984: 85).
[42] Ibid., 85.

Table 2.4 *Burdens on Different Social Classes in the*
Shaan-Gan-Ning Base Area, 1942–1943

Social Class	Population (%)	Income (%)	Grain Levy (%)
Landlords	1.9	11.1	29.8
Rich peasants	7.6	16.3	26.2
Middle peasants	28.4	35.5	34.5
Poor peasants	52.6	33.0	8.7
Landless peasants	5.0	1.4	–
Other	4.5	2.7	0.8
TOTAL	100.0	100.0	100.0

Source: Xiang Guang and Zhang Yang (1989).

wealthier paid more than the poorer; second, they used their organizational skills and capacities to administer a procedurally fairer and predictable tax system; and third, they generated new resources from production movements by army and administrative units.

In a 1938 speech, Mao Zedong drew up a blueprint of a new fiscal policy in Communist-controlled areas: "Under the principle of those who make more pay more, all the old taxes and levies should be converted to unified progressive taxes. We should eliminate the tradition of exorbitant levies in order to promote the economy which, in turn, will bring in more tax revenues."[43] Accordingly, the Communist government taxed the local population based on income and social class with an incremental, progressive scheme. As Table 2.4 shows, the tax was a sharply graduated one. Landowners and rich peasants, who constituted only 9.5 percent of the population, paid 56 percent of the tax. Middle-income peasants paid more or less in proportion to their assets whereas poor peasants paid substantially less, while landless ones were exempt. Balancing the interests of the richer and poorer strata was not always easily implemented. As Bianco notes, there were cases in which poorer people had majorities in village organizations and "sometimes made a handful of well-to-do landowners bear most or all of the tax burdens."[44]

A second feature of peasant burdens during this period was the Communists' attempt to transform the grain levy and other taxes into a single agricultural tax based not only on grain production but also on ownership of land and other assets as a way of eliminating the irregular and bitterly resented surcharges, apportionments, and other exactions. A single tax system would reduce both the number of levies and the levels of government that collected

[43] Wei Hongyun (1990: 216).
[44] Bianco (1995: 180).

them. This somewhat complicated scheme of "unified graduated taxation" (*tongyi leijinshui*), which had fifteen scales based on both land and income, was never fully implemented after pilot experiments in 1943 for "lack of well-educated cadres who were able to handle such complex tax schemes."[45] The Shaan-Gan-Ning border region never successfully implemented the new tax system, the most successful case being the Jin-Cha-Ji border region where the tax base was expanded and burdens on individual peasants were reduced overall.[46] According to a report by the government in 1946, in one of the districts in this region, peasants' burdens were reduced from 8 percent in 1941 to 6 percent in 1944 and bounced back to 8 percent of income in 1945 due to major military campaigns against the Japanese.[47] Bianco concludes that "tax distribution in the anti-Japanese bases was less inequitable and tax collection less abuse-ridden than in Nationalist areas. This did not prevent but lessened tax resistance."[48]

In order to reduce their dependence on local populations for tax revenues, the Communists actively pursued a policy of self-reliance and self-production. The production movement was a Communist innovation designed to increase resources while not adding to the peasants' burdens. After the imposition of the Nationalist blockade, the base areas, especially Shaan-Gan-Ning, an impoverished region, faced a serious economic crisis, especially in supplying an army troubled by low morale and some desertions.[49] The rural tax base was simply insufficient. Between 1935 and 1940 the tax grain amounted to only 5 percent of local production, collected on a progressive schedule and paid quite readily by the peasants.[50] But the amount collected was grossly inadequate and higher taxes had to be imposed to lower the government deficits. Thus, in 1941, in some counties, 8 to 12 percent of the harvest was collected under the rubric of the "national salvation public grain," and 35 percent in Yan'an, "at least five times the tax burden imposed on Nationalist Huainan."[51] The Communist leadership found that one sensible way to solve this problem was to practice self-reliance, encouraging the military to engage in productive labor to supplement available tax revenue. New policies of "expanding the economy in order to guarantee supplies" and "unifying management and dispersing [economic] operations" were adopted. Already in January 1939, Mao formally advocated

---

[45] Xiang and Zhang (1988).
[46] Ibid., 76 and Wei (1990: 235).
[47] Wei (1990).
[48] Bianco (1995: 182).
[49] Mao Zedong (1949).
[50] Chen Yung-fa (1995: 267–8).
[51] Ibid., 272.

the idea of "letting the army produce for itself."[52] A production movement (*da shengchan yundong*) was launched in early 1940 by the Central Military Committee, which called on all military units to participate in production of all kinds, including commercial businesses. "Feed and dress ourselves by self-reliance," and "develop the economy in order to guarantee supplies" became the slogans of the hour. Soon, not only army units were engaging in production activities to be self-sufficient, but nonmilitary entities, such as government units, public schools, and hospitals, in Yan'an and the surrounding Shaan-Gan-Ning border region as well. Called "agency production" (*jiguan shengchan*), similar movements were launched in other Communist-controlled base areas in 1942–3. Although set in motion in a mass-campaign style, the "production movement" took on a permanent character. The results were impressive. In 1942 the Communist administrative and army personnel in the base areas had to rely fully on grain taxes; in 1943 and 1944 this ratio dropped to 85 and 60 percent respectively, the difference being made up by self-reliant production.[53]

Although referred to as "production," administrative units did not confine themselves to farming and manufacturing. Commercial retail activities were not only common, but became the dominant type of business conducted outside of agriculture.[54] As of 1941, the Administrative Bureau of the CCP Central Committee alone operated twenty retail stores.[55] In 1944 commercial businesses became the second most lucrative source of revenue. By 1946 there were 348 various kinds of stores, shops, and "mobile production" (*liudong shengchan*, namely, interregional trade) units, plus some 280 consumer co-ops; roughly 2,500 staff worked in these commercial businesses, and revenue from this source increased to 30 percent of revenue.[56] In addition to these commercial operations run directly by units, many large units also invested in two trading companies which monopolized the trade of salt and "special and local products," including opium, and commissioned the trading companies to sell products they produced or possessed, the most lucrative one being opium.[57] According to Chen Yung-fa, profits from opium production and sales by the CCP made a substantial contribution to the economic development of the Shaan-Gan-Ning base area and the financing of its government.[58] In Chen's estimate, in 1942 and 1943 the "special product," the euphemism for opium,

---

[52] Zongzhengzhibu (1989: 77) and Selden (1971: 250–1).
[53] Xiang and Zhang, *Jiefang zhanzheng* (1989: 321).
[54] See Xiaobo Lü (1997a: 269).
[55] Lü (1997a).
[56] Chen Junqi (1987:112–13) and Shangyebu (1984: 18).
[57] See Lü (1997a).
[58] Chen Yung-fa (1995: 264).

Table 2.5 *The Grain Tax in the Shaan-Gan-Ning Base Area, 1938–1945*

Year	Hulled Millet	Grain Tax	Income %
1938	1,270,000	10,000	7.90
1939	1,370,000	50,000	3.63
1940	1,430,000	90,000	6.29
1941	1,470,000	200,000	13.33
1942	1,500,000	160,000	10.69
1943	1,600,000	180,000	11.25
1944	1,750,000	160,000	9.00
1945	1,600,000	125,000	7.80

Note: 1 unit = picul.

Source: Chen Yung-fa (1995: 295) and Selden (1971: 182).

provided 40 percent of the revenue of the base area, and in 1944 and 1945, 26 and 40 percent of total expenditures.[59] Xiaobo Lü's research found, however, that, although opium was a major item of trade, revenue from other local products was also significant.[60] At the same time the grain tax continued at a high level, well above the level of 1940, and only declined significantly in 1945 as Table 2.5 shows.

During the Civil War in the Northeast, the Communists were able to carry out a reasonable policy of extraction that minimized popular discontent. This despite the acute resource demands arising from large-scale military operations and the early occupation of major cities such as Harbin. Steven Levine's careful study of rural policies concludes that:

a factor of major importance in shaping villagers' attitudes toward the revolution was the principle of equity incorporated in the Communist system of taxation and corvée labor (the latter, to be sure, disguised as voluntary contributions). Instead of the arbitrary, capricious methods of the past used to recruit soldiers and civilian support personnel, levy taxes, and secure carts, livestock, food, and fodder, the CCP initiated an equitable and fairly predictable system which spread the burden quite evenly across the rural population and protected villagers from repeated labor service or overly onerous contributions to the military effort.[61]

[59] Ibid., 274.
[60] See Lü (1997a).
[61] Levine (1987: 234–5).

In sum, there were many reasons why the Communists emerged as victors from the civil war; their tax policies and practices were certainly no minor one.

THE MAOIST ERA: THE PRIMACY OF GRAIN PROCUREMENTS

In the quarter century of Maoist rule, fundamental changes took place with respect to rural taxation. The new regime penetrated to the grass roots, gaining unprecedented organizational access to the villages of the whole country. Socialist transformation in its various forms allowed the party–state to gain an unprecedented degree of control over the resources of the peasantry. Peasants became residual claimants to the harvest, after the collectives and the state had taken their share. A portion of the residual was distributed in the form of rations, which all members of the collective unit received, thereby providing basic subsistence. But peasant consumption of grain was strictly limited.[62] At least in principle, disasters were taken into account in calculating peasant needs. Households were also allowed private plots and small private sidelines, although during radical periods these were marginalized or even eliminated. The point of overwhelming importance is that with the onset of planned industrialization in 1953, agriculture became a major source of resources for investment in the urban-industrial sector. This fundamentally changed the situation of China's peasants to their disadvantage. Hitherto they had been subjected to extraction of taxes, levies, and surcharges, as well as to rents paid to landlords, but they could normally sell a part of their output at market prices. Now, the state, through the collective system, controlled the harvest and decided not only the amount of the tax (*gongliang*) but also how much surplus grain (*yuliang*) had to be sold to the state at state-determined prices, often lower than market price.[63] Conversely, high state-set prices governed the sale of industrial goods to the countryside, creating a scissors effect from which the state profited greatly. All this was done through the national unified procurement and marketing system through which the Maoist state massively transferred resources from the countryside to the urban sector. Much of the largest burden placed on the peasantry thus did not come in the form of taxes as such but in the form of the compulsory procurement program.

The contribution that China's peasantry made to the urban-industrial sector, and especially to heavy industry, was stupendous. In 1988 a prominent agricultural economist, Lin Yifu, told the *People's Daily* that in the past 30 years agriculture had contributed "accumulation with a total value of between 600 billion and 800 billion yuan. This means that for the sake of 'industrialization,' China's

---

[62] Oi (1989: 20).
[63] Yang and Li (1980: 206–9).

peasants, whether old or young, have each contributed an average of 1000 yuan," this in an era when annual per capita household incomes peaked at 134 yuan in 1978.[64]

Another economist claimed that from 1952 to 1986 the state each year took nearly 30 billion yuan from agriculture in addition to 3 billion yuan in the form of taxes.[65] Accumulation from the First to Sixth Five-Year Plans (1953 to 1986) totaled 2,243.2 trillion yuan, of which the agricultural sector evidently supplied between a fourth and a third.[66] Moreover, agriculture's share in national investment fluctuated between 8 and 13 percent, systematically retarding that sector's development.[67]

As noted, the regime retained the age-old commitment to subsistence, in sharp contrast to the Stalin regime, from which China adapted its model of industrialization. The government sought to assure subsistence to the peasants but did not by any means always achieve this goal. Before the Great Leap Forward, the "state declared that its claims, both in tax and procurements, should get first priority."[68] During the Great Leap Forward, these claims had catastrophic consequences. China suffered from the greatest famine in all Chinese history, the result of gross mismanagement, including greatly excessive procurements calculated on the basis of grossly exaggerated reports of immense increases in output.[69] After the Great Leap Forward, greater priority was to be given to peasant welfare, but there is "strong evidence that in the decade before 1979, the shares of the collective and the peasants consistently received second and third priority."[70] Grain purchases were reduced, but low rations persisted because of rapid population growth, failure to adjust quotas accordingly, and inept agricultural policies, which did not change until the reform stage, which began with the acknowledgment that around 150 million peasants were living below the subsistence level.

How much sacrifice could be imposed on the peasants was a contentious issue aired occasionally in public as during the Hundred Flowers period in 1957. Five years previously, Mao Zedong had reacted defensively and vehemently to a criticism voiced by Liang Shuming, a Confucian scholar who in the 1930s had led a movement for rural reconstruction based on the revival of traditional values.[71] At a meeting of the Central People's Administrative Committee in

[64] *RMRB* (June 29, 1988, *FBIS*, No. 140, July 21, 1988: 55).
[65] Xu Kongrong (1990: 52).
[66] *ZTN* (1987: 59).
[67] Yang Jianbai and Li Xuezeng (1980: 190).
[68] Oi (1989: 44–5).
[69] See Bernstein (1984: 339–77) and Dali Yang (1996).
[70] Oi (1989: 44–6).
[71] See Alitto (1979: esp. ch. 4–6).

September 1953, Mao "wrenched the microphone away from" Liang Shuming and "burst forth in a stream of technicolor invective against him." "I think you stink," Mao told Liang, an elderly, "frail figure clad in an old-fashioned long gown."[72] What was Liang's crime? He had complained about the burdens the government had imposed on farmers to pay for the Korean War. Even more important, he had "boldly attacked the government for its decision to adopt the Soviet model of economic development because it laid the heaviest burden on the backs of the peasants while making the urban workers a virtual privileged class." Liang reportedly charged that after entering the cities, the Party had abandoned the peasants.[73] Mao rebutted these criticisms. He recalled that in 1941, higher agricultural taxes had to be imposed to counter the blockade by Nationalist forces of the Communist base areas and again to pay for the Korean War and fight U.S. imperialism.

> [W]e will have to collect grain and work among the peasants to persuade them to give something [to the cause]. This alone is a true representation of the interests of the peasants. To squeal and shout is in fact to represent [the interests of] U.S. imperialism. Similarly, the real interest of the peasants and of the country as a whole was to develop heavy industry, which needed funds, hence requiring a limit to the pace of improvement of living standards.[74]

However, from 1956 on, Mao Zedong criticized Stalin's excesses in exploiting the peasants and in lopsidedly emphasizing investment in heavy industry. In his famous article on the "Ten Major Relationships" and later as well he suggested that Stalin's squeezing of the peasants amounted to "draining the pond to catch the fish."[75] During the moderate phase of the Great Leap Forward, when Mao sought to curb the most egregious excesses of the summer and fall of 1958, he spoke out in defense of peasants' vital interests.

> [I]n the communes of Henan, [capital] accumulation, state taxes, administrative costs and the welfare fundal together take up 50 percent of [commune income]. Production costs take up 20 percent, so the peasants actually get 30 percent. But the peasants have to live, and therefore they have to conceal 15 percent [of production], [and they have] several dozen

---

[72] Ibid., 1.

[73] Ibid., 2, 324, fn 17.

[74] Mao Zedong (1986: 390–1). Guy Alitto points out that Premier Zhou Enlai attacked Liang before Mao did. Alitto (1979: 2).

[75] Mao "On the Ten Major Relationships" (1992: 46–8) and "Speech of Feb. 27, 1959" (1976–7: 18).

methods [for doing so]. This is [their] legal right, yet we criticize them for particularism. . . . The peasants are now standing watch and posting sentries to protect [their] ownership of the products and to struggle for the fruits of their labor.[76]

Tragically, Mao forgot these words after the Lushan Plenum in the summer of 1959 when the Great Leap Forward again intensified and millions died of hunger.

State Taxes. These must be understood in the context of the procurement program, which, in the words of a State Council research paper, "represented an integration of exchange and paying taxes."[77] Mao's China relied more on procurements than direct taxation, thus perpetuating the age-old myth that the state benefited peasants by light taxation. As output increased, the share taken by the state tax decreased. In the 1950s, the agricultural tax took between 10 and 14 percent of the harvest. In 1958 it was set at 15 percent of the normal harvest of the time (plus some permissible surcharges); with growth in output, the actual amount of the grain tax had dropped to about 4.5 percent by the late 1970s.[78] Proposals to raise the tax were rejected. Premier Zhou Enlai once responded to such a suggestion: "You take what I say on the record: so long as I am alive, you are not to increase agricultural taxes. Even after I am dead, no one should attempt to burden the peasants."[79] The tax was set for a period of three to five years regardless of increases in productivity but adjustments were generally not made. In contrast to the Yan'an period, because of collectivization and the leveling of incomes the tax was not a graduated one. Reclaimed land was not taxed for a three- to five-year period. The agricultural tax was based on the amount of cultivated land, estimated output, and population. Yields played a small role and there was much local variation. As Jean Oi notes, the small size of the tax masked the burden it imposed in times of poor harvest, since the tax had to be paid "at all costs." The procedures to secure remission were complex and politically ambitious cadres did not want to go on record as having to ask for relief.[80] For the most part, the tax was paid in kind as part of state grain procurement, which meant that grain-short teams had to buy market grain at high prices. Nicholas Lardy suggests the high cost of buying grain to fulfill state procurement quotas in nongrain-growing areas was a major cause of rural poverty.[81]

---

[76] Speech of Feb. 27, 1959 (1976–7: 12–13).
[77] See Oi (1989: 43).
[78] Caizhengbu (1994, v.2); *Zhongguo Caizheng Nianjian* (1997).
[79] Wang Yanbin (1993: 16).
[80] Oi (1989: 21).
[81] Ibid., 24, and Lardy (1983: ch. 4).

Surcharges on state taxes, which throughout history constituted so enormous a problem, persisted to varying degrees, especially in the early 1950s. The government initially approved imposition of local surtaxes of up to 15 percent of the agricultural tax. In 1951 the ceiling was raised to 20 percent. Township and village government spending had risen, again as in the past, due to the expansion of the roles of government and of CCP organization.[82] According to a survey of sixteen provinces in 1951, only a third (34.3 percent) of local government funds for education, administration, social welfare, projects, and other purposes came from the government budget. Local apportionments and donations yielded a third of the funds, 33.4 percent; confiscation from landlords, 19.4 percent; business taxes and revenue from local public businesses, 7.9 percent. Five percent came from other sources.[83] In addition to these surcharges, "voluntary" donations to support the Chinese army in the Korean War and families of "martyrs" or families with men in the military added to the burdens. In many areas, informal exactions added another 24 percent to the state-tax load. In some areas, where local governments still acted in the predatory ways of the pre-Communist regime, miscellaneous charges could equal 560 percent of the formal taxes.[84]

In 1952, the central government ordered the elimination of all surcharges and apportionments. It also decided to provide in the budget for the pay and administrative expenditures of township and village officials and teachers. It left a loophole in that it allowed local authorities to raise funds up to 7 percent in addition to the agricultural taxes, for projects deemed essential.[85] This decree, "Instructions on the 1952 Agricultural Taxes," was the first decree by the PRC central government to address the problem of uncontrolled local extraction under the Communist regime. Just as in the reform years, the limited financial capacity of the central government made it impossible to stick with this decree, which remained in force for only a year.

During the Cultural Revolution (1966–76), there was another surge of miscellaneous charges imposed on peasants. According to one authoritative estimate, the nontax charges during this period raised the tax burden by about 60 to 80 percent. That is to say, despite the continuing decrease in the regular agricultural tax, peasants, as in the olden days, often paid more in unofficial taxes. In some areas, these charges were as low as 1 percent of peasant income but in other areas as high as 18 percent.[86] The Cultural Revolution also substantially weakened control over tax collection and remittances. Large amounts of agricultural

[82] See Caizhengbu (1994, v.2: 100–1).
[83] See Ibid., 102.
[84] Ibid., 109.
[85] Ibid., 102–3.
[86] Ibid., 312.

taxes were misused by local governments and collectives. Violations of financial discipline multiplied while agricultural tax embezzlement also increased.[87]

Major burdens also arose from the heavy corvée labor local governments required from peasants for public projects. Labor service as a form of extraction of resources has been practiced throughout Chinese history. Under the Maoist mobilization regime, and led by an ideological conviction that "humans must triumph over nature," large-scale water/land conservation and reclamation projects quite commonly demanded huge numbers of laborers. Due to the collective structure of rural organization, it is difficult to calculate the exact indirect tax burdens on individual peasants. But clearly, labor service during the collective era, particularly when the Dazhai model was promoted throughout the country in the late 1960s and early 1970s, was a source of indirect burden on the peasants.

Collective Retention. The production brigades and teams claimed a significant share of the harvest and of earnings from sales to the state. Grain stocks were maintained for seeds, fodder, grain reserves, and rations (*kouliang*). If the rations fell below a minimal level of 26 to 30 jin, no tax was imposed and the team became eligible for *fanxiaoliang* – sales to the village. Once the earnings of the team were known, deductions were made for investments (*gongjijin*), which claimed 5 percent of net income, for production and management costs, which were not supposed to exceed 5 percent of total income, and the welfare fund (*gongyijin*). After the cost of the rations was deducted, the rest was distributed in cash to members according to the value of the work points earned.

The distribution ratio among the state, collective (brigades), and individual peasants fluctuated. In 1955, the government collected 9.4 percent of the income, collectives retained 32 percent, and peasants received 58.6 percent. Two years later the proportion going to peasants declined to 55 percent. The Great Leap Forward effort to attain a developmental breakthrough resulted in a dramatic increase in the collective retention, especially for investment. During this period, the practice of "equalization and transfer" (*yiping er diao*) took hold and huge amounts of household and team resources, especially building materials, were appropriated by higher collective and state units. The most dramatic example was the use of cooking utensils to make steel. In the aftermath, communes were reduced in size, confiscated assets were returned, and lofty production goals slashed. Remarkably, it was not until 1965 that the ratio of redistribution came back to a normal level: the state taking 5.7 percent, the

[87] Ibid., 292–4.

collective 39.9 percent, and individuals retaining 54.3 percent.[88] During the mid-1970s, when new efforts to accelerate development were made, the collective retention and government exactions reached other heights, resembling the "equalization and transfer" of the Great Leap Forward.[89]

The first burden reduction campaign of the reform period was aimed at correcting the appropriation of team resources, a practice that stemmed from the GLF's "free transfer of labor, funds, and materials."[90] In the summer of 1978, the *People's Daily* publicized investigations of Xiangxiang county, Hunan, which showed that collectives paid 72 charges imposed by 49 different government departments.[91] The reasons why these charges were imposed foreshadowed the postcollectivization period. First came the growth of administrative staff at the commune and brigade levels. Between 1971 and 1978, some communes in Xiangxiang county added fifty to sixty people to their state cadre force (commune-level officials were paid by the state; production brigade and team cadres were paid out of local resources), 2.3 times more than authorized. Second, local collectives were eager to promote development: education, health, commune and brigade industry, and infrastructure such as transport, but without sufficient state funding. As later chapters show, the informal ways of extracting resources lent themselves to abuse. Some funds, such as state subsidies for local schoolteachers, were diverted to other purposes. County and commune units spent money on office buildings, auditoriums, or hostels, partially paid for by local exactions.[92] It is noteworthy that the localities where peasants' burdens were reported to have been heavy in these early reform years were also the ones where burdens remained substantial in the later reform period, Henan, Anhui, Hunan, and Hubei.[93]

The main difference between these exactions and those of the postcollective reform era is that before the reforms, the exactions were levied mainly on the production teams rather than directly on individual peasants. These practices signified the absence of respect for the property rights of the production teams, later extended to the property rights of the households.

A CCP Central Committee instruction (Circular no. 37) was disseminated nationwide in June 1978, followed by a *People's Daily* editorial, "Implement

---

[88] Ibid., 275–6.

[89] Gao Xiaosheng's short story, "Li Shunda Builds a House," movingly illustrates this form of extraction. It tells of an ex-beggar who time and again patiently accumulated building materials for a house, but each time was pressured into donating them to the collective. Gao Xiaosheng (1979).

[90] *RMRB* editorial (July 5, 1978).

[91] *RMRB* (Nov. 22, 1978).

[92] *RMRB* (July 5, 1978).

[93] For example, Henan, Hunan, Anhui, and Hubei provinces. See *RMRB* (Oct. 5 and Oct. 10, 1978).

Table 2.6 *Peasant Burden over Time in Ningxia Province*

Year	Total Burden (% of Income)	Agricultural Taxes (% of Income)	Collective Retention (% of Income)
1952	10.4	7.9	n/a
1957	11.4	5.9	7.6
1958	27.5	10.4	13.4
1959	41.2	9.5	16.3
1960	47.7	5.8	19.2
1961	20.7	4.3	11.5
1962	22.1	3.5	9.6
1976	36.4	3.6	5.1

Source: Duan Chinglin, (1998: 49–56).

Party Policies and Reduce Peasant Burdens." This early effort in the post-Mao period did have some effect on containing burdens – many counties reportedly reacted to the decree from Beijing by returning money to peasants, possibly because it was connected to the reformers' struggle against the leftist Party Chairman, Hua Guofeng, who was from Hunan.[94] This effort was a forerunner to the burden-reduction efforts made throughout the later reform period. Table 2.6 illustrates burdens during the collective period in a poor province.

The Maoist Legacy. The era of radical Maoism left large parts of rural China deeply impoverished. In late 1978, the historic Third Plenum of the CCP Central Committee disclosed to Party members that 150 million or so peasants did not have adequate rations.[95] In 1978, per capita rations in 463,000 production teams (10.6 percent) were less than 300 jin, substantially below the traditional "no-hunger no-gorging" standard of 400 jin of husked or 480 jin of unhusked grain. In 1978, two-thirds of China's 2,100 counties were less well off than they had been in the early 1950s, and in the remaining one-third, they were less well off than they had been in the 1930s under the GMD.[96] Scholars disagree whether overall per capita rural grain consumption declined between 1957 and 1978, but there is no disagreement that rural living standards stagnated.[97]

---

[94] Caizhengbu (1994, v.2: 360).

[95] See "Decisions" (July 1979: 104–5).

[96] See Chen Yizi (1989: 20) and Yang Jianbai and Li Xuezeng (1980: 182–214).

[97] Nicholas Lardy claims that consumption of commercial grain declined by 5.9 percent from 204.5 kg to 192.5 kg; Kenneth Walker claims that consumption of unhusked grain rose from 245 kg. to 252 kg. See Oi (1989: 33).

The existence of widespread hunger, begging, and chronic poverty thirty years after "liberation" threatened the regime's legitimacy and stability. On January 8, 1979, during the short-lived popular Democracy Wall movement, farmers who had come to petition for redress demonstrated in Beijing. Banners proclaimed: "We don't want hunger!" "We don't want to suffer anymore!" and "We want human rights and democracy!" Led by a woman activist, Fu Yuehua, they asked to present their demands to the then top leader Hua Guofeng as well as to Deng Xiaoping. Toward the end of the month, "an astonishing thirty thousand or so farmers had trekked to Beijing to protest living conditions and seek help." A journalist from *Agence France-Presse* depicted them "as straight out of a Goya painting – sick, on crutches, dressed in rags and tatters, and wretchedly poverty-stricken."[98]

Perhaps influenced by this episode, senior leader Chen Yun told the Politburo in March of 1979 that "there are still beggars in many places." He added that their Party secretaries might lead them to cities to beg for food:

> This is a big question. I said at last year's central work conference that having been liberated for thirty years, if this question is not resolved in ten or twenty years, the branch Party secretaries will lead their teams to go begging in the cities. Not to take this situation into account means that the entire economy will not move forward well. The peasants come first. We cannot but let peasants have a breathing space.[99]

Fear that peasant poverty and suffering might lead to mass migration, unrest, disturbances, and rebellion was not far from the minds of Chinese leaders, who shared the traditional assumption that peasant contentment was the basis of social stability. Chen Yizi, a prominent researcher who had firsthand knowledge of the launching of the rural reforms, reports that the first Party secretary of Anhui province, Wan Li, voiced fears of popular uprisings in 1978, as he would again fifteen years later in 1993. Wan conceded that the Party had yet to prove itself worthy of the right to rule by providing basic subsistence. Chen Yizi quotes peasants in Anhui as saying privately that the Party had "dug a pit of suffering for us." A veteran Party branch secretary in Henan reportedly said that "we hoped and longed for socialism; it was hard to imagine that socialism would bring such sufferings." Even county secretaries and prefectural secretaries in Henan privately told Chen that the CCP had ruined the country. Yao Yilin reportedly heard similar talk in a Beijing suburban

---

[98] See Mab Huang and James D. Seymour (1980: 19). Some of the demonstrators may have been urbanites sent to the countryside from the time of the Anti-rightist Campaign of 1957.

[99] Chen Yun (1982: 74).

county.[100] Evidence on rural disturbances in the late 1970s similar to those in the 1990s has not come to light, but fear of rural unrest and instability played a role in motivating the government to launch the rural reform in the earlier period.

China's leaders took quick and decisive action. They substantially raised state procurement prices and reduced delivery quotas in 1979, thereby increasing the incentive to farmers to sell more above-quota grain which would generate more income. Higher grain prices were a major source of the doubling of peasant incomes that took place in the next four years. Tax relief was also granted to poor communes.[101] According to interviews conducted by Michel Oksenberg, the top leaders made this crucial decision with the backing of a "broad coalition" of officials, who agreed that something had to be done about the deplorable state of agriculture.[102] Most important, the new willingness to experiment and to discard radical Maoist dogma made possible the eventual nationwide introduction of household contracting, a form of family farming in which the land continued to be owned by the collective. When combined with a range of other liberalizing policies in the direction of increasing marketization, the new approach unleashed the peasants' entrepreneurial energies, leading to the rapid transformation of much of the Chinese countryside, especially in the eastern provinces and in the suburbs of major cities as the extraordinary growth of TVEs got underway. At the same time, the less favored central and western provinces experienced a less dramatic transformation and significant areas of poverty remained.

The reform period saw significant continuities with the Maoist period as well as departures from it. The compulsory procurement system remained, after some experimentation with other forms of state purchasing in the mid-1980s. In sharp contrast to the collectivist Mao era, however, households now were required to sell grain directly to the state rather than via collective units. Some could be sold on the free market, and market prices became an important determinant of farm income. As noted, procurement prices were raised substantially in 1979, but from the mid-1980s on, the price the state paid was often below the free market price, and especially during times of inflation could not cover the cost of industrial inputs, thereby creating a "scissors effect" – disadvantageous price differentials between industrial and farm products. Thus, extraction of resources from the countryside via the compulsory sales system continued to be a source of what Chinese scholars came to call the "hidden burdens" on the

---

[100] Chen Yizi (1989: 21–2).
[101] Terry Sicular (1988b: 468).
[102] Oksenberg (1982: 190).

peasants. As Chapter 4 shows, Maoist legacies extended well beyond economic policies. For instance, the "work style" of the Great Leap continued to influence the behavior of officials.

The dissolution of the communes restored formal government at the township level and led to the establishment of village committees at the lowest level of the hierarchy, replacing the production brigades. Production teams were turned into "small groups." Peasants now paid state taxes directly but also continued to make payments to the village collective (committee) for a variety of purposes, as well as to the township. These restorationist policies led to the revival of the pre-Communist practices of informal levies and assessments, which are the focus of this study.

CONCLUSION

Some seventy years ago, an American scholar wrote about the tax burdens in China as compared to other countries. His observations, published in *The New York Times* in 1926, sound eerily familiar to comments on what happened in the 1980s and 1990s:

> While legitimate taxation in China always, in comparison with other countries, has been ridiculously low, other forms of taxation raised the average to the level of normality, which here, as elsewhere, is all the people can be induced or compelled to pay.... In so far as the Chinese masses suffer today from fiscal oppression it is from the kind of taxes which are irregular and unaccounted for.[103]

The examination of historical development in China's rural taxation reveals significant similarities and differences. Some tax problems are age old and still haunt the contemporary regime. The combined burdens of formal and informal taxes fell disproportionately on grain-producing regions both in the past and in the present. The provinces where peasant tax burdens were heavy and resistance strongest were almost the same today as in late Qing. Provinces such as Jiangxi, Hunan, and Hubei, known historically as hotbeds of tax resistance, saw their share of similar collective action in the post-Mao period. There are also continuities in central–local relations. Similar reforms aiming at political and fiscal decentralization took place during the Republican and the post-Mao periods. In both cases, efforts to redesign central–local relations by means of fiscal decentralization often resulted in more local taxes and levies.

---

[103] *NYT* (April 4, 1926).

This is not to claim that the current drama of excessive levies is playing itself out in the same way as it did in the past. There are important breaks with the past. A fundamental break took place early during the Maoist period, when the rural social and economic elite was overthrown. In the past, there had always been four players, not three, in the game of rural taxation. In addition to the central authorities, local officials, and peasants, there had been the rural social and economic elites playing major roles. Their tax exemptions, whether legal or not, shifted the tax burden to ordinary farming peasants. At times, officials found themselves in conflict with landlords over such issues as passing tax remissions on to their tenants. More often they colluded with the nonofficial elite. At times, conflict between landlords and peasants over rents took precedence over tax conflict, but on the whole, the major line of cleavage was between peasants and officials over taxes and fees.[104] In reform China, too, the conflict between officials and peasants over taxes was far more important than conflict between farming peasants and the emerging new elite of entrepreneurs and managers of TVEs and private businesses; conflict over taxes was concentrated in areas where nonagricultural enterprise did not as yet play a major role. Where diversification did give rise to such an elite, excessive tax burdens were not so great a problem for farming peasants, since resources from nonagricultural enterprise could be used to pay for governmental services.

[104] See Bernhardt (1992).

3

Extracting Funds from the Peasants

It is the obligation of peasants to pay taxes to the state, to fulfill the state's procurement quotas for agricultural products, and to be responsible for the various fees and services stipulated in these regulations. Any other demands on peasants to give financial, material, and labor contributions gratis are illegal and peasants have the right reject them.[1]

DESPITE this and similar regulations repeatedly issued by central agencies, peasant burdens continued to exceed their legal obligations. This chapter describes and analyzes just what the burden problem was. We make five major points: (1) Exactions were open-ended and often arbitrary; (2) excessive tax and fee burdens were a problem throughout most of the reform period and by all accounts rose over time; (3) taxes and fees were highly regressive both locally within townships and across the country; (4) the severity of burdens varied with the presence or absence of TVEs whose resources could be tapped to pay for services and development projects; and (5) tax burdens – their size, variability, and the often brutal collection methods – were a major source of peasant grievances.

Burdens have to be assessed against peasant incomes, hence, we begin with a brief discussion of this topic. Analysis is complicated by enormous intrarural disparities. In 1999, the per capita income of peasants nationwide was 2,210 yuan; it was 5,409 in rural Shanghai and 1,357 in Gansu. In most of the agricultural provinces of central China, incomes were either below or at the average, because many of the villages did not have much income from nonagricultural sources, that is, from township and village enterprises (TVEs). Nationally, incomes rose dramatically in the 1980s, but in

[1] *ZRGYGB* (1992: 1432).

Table 3.1 *National Rural Incomes Compared with Those in Agricultural Provinces (per capita)*

Year	1985	1990	1995	1996	1997	1998	1999
National	398	686	1,577	1,926	2,090	2,162	2,210
Shanxi	359	604	1,208	1,557	1,738	1,859	1,773
Anhui	369	539	1,303	1,607	1,809	1,863	1,900
Jiangxi	377	670	1,538	1,870	2,107	2,048	2,129
Henan	329	563	1,232	1,579	1,734	1,864	1,948
Hubei	421	671	1,511	1,854	2,102	2,172	2,217
Sichuan	314	558	1,158	1,453	1,681	1,789	1,843
Shaanxi	295	531	963	1,165	1,273	1,406	1,456
Gansu	255	431	880	1,101	1,273	1,393	1,357

Note: In yuan. Until 1997, Sichuan included what is now Chongqing municipality.

Sources: ZTN (1998: 346); *ZTN* (2000: 332). Numbers are rounded off.

the 1990s the rate of growth slowed down, especially from 1997. Table 3.1 compares average national incomes with several predominantly agricultural ones:

The income differences between primarily agricultural areas and those in industrializing rural China would be even starker than the table shows, because most provinces had some areas, especially around large cities, where income from nonagricultural sources played a major role. The table shows that income declined in Shanxi in 1999 by 4.6 percent and in Gansu by nearly 3 percent, a disturbing development that also occurred in the three northeastern provinces. In early 2001, the annual Rural Work Conference found that "farmers' incomes in some grain production regions are declining" and called for urgent measures to increase incomes.[2] These data do not control for inflation, which at various times significantly eroded gains in income. In the years 1989–91, incomes actually rose by only 0.7 percent per annum. In 1992, real income was only 432 yuan and in 1995, it rose by only 5 percent, again much lower than the nominal amount in the table.[3] In 1998, according to the Ministry of Agriculture's annual survey of twenty thousand households, real incomes decreased by 2.36 percent.[4] By all accounts, the situation of farm families that relied on agriculture for a living became bleaker in the late 1990s.

---

[2] *Xinhua*, January, 5, 2001. Incomes in 2000 increased by only a minuscule 46 yuan.

[3] CD (Jan. 12, 1996), quoting Chen Jiyuan and Han Jun, scholars at the Chinese Academy of Sciences (CASS).

[4] Lu Mai (Sept. 20, 1999).

Table 3.2 *Peasant Burdens*

Types of Charges	Items and Explanations
State taxes	Agricultural tax and surcharge; special products tax; slaughter tax; farmland utilization tax; contract tax; animal husbandry tax; education surcharge
Township and village levies (*jiti tiliu and tongchou fei, village retention and township comprehensive fee*)	Village: Three purposes – collective investments; welfare, cadre compensation. Township: Five purposes – schools, family planning, support for veterans, militia, and road construction and maintenance
Corvée labor services, often monetized	5–10 days of labor on flood prevention, afforestation, roads or school construction; 10–20 days on "accumulation labor" on state water conservancy or afforestation projects
Fees, apportionments, and fundraising	For road or school construction and other local improvement projects; newspaper subscriptions, purchase of insurance, marriage certificates, etc.
Fines	Collected by numerous government agencies for infractions such as birth control violations
Burdens connected with peasant sales to state ("hidden burdens")	Compulsory grain sales to state at below market prices; scissors differential between industrial and agricultural prices; local abuses such as payment in IOUs not cash

BURDENS: AN OVERVIEW

"Peasant burdens" (*nongmin de fudan*) refer to an array of formal and informal exactions both legitimate and illegitimate. See Table 3.2 for a survey of peasant burdens.

State Taxes. In 1999 the six state taxes listed in the table brought in a total of 42.4 billion yuan, reflecting astonishing growth. In 1980 revenue from the agricultural sector amounted to 2.7 billion; in 1990, to 8.8 billion; and in 1995 to 28 billion.[5] In per capita terms, these increases were reported as 7.65 yuan per capita in 1985, 13.21 yuan in 1990, 28.10 yuan in 1995, and 38.92 yuan

---

[5] *ZTN* (2000: 258). This excludes the animal husbandry tax as well as a banquet tax, which presumably was levied on both urban and rural sectors. See *ZTN* (2000: 274).

in 1998. The doubling of state taxes as of 1995 was a consequence of the 1994 tax reform, which required localities to rely more heavily on the various agricultural taxes since the central authorities now took a larger share of other taxes.[6] Still, state taxes constituted only a small percentage of incomes. In 1998, when net incomes averaged 2,161.98 yuan, it was 1.8 percent. However, in March 2001, Premier Zhu Rongji told a press conference that state agricultural taxes amounted to about 30 billion yuan, which he said was 5 percent of peasant incomes.[7]

The agricultural tax was based on regulations issued in 1958 and set at 15 percent of normal grain yields averaged over three years. Because it was not adjusted as yields rose over time, the actual tax rate gradually dropped, by the 1980s to about 3 percent of output.[8] As had been traditionally the case in China, the regular grain tax was deliberately kept low as a measure of the state's concern for the peasants. But local governments could impose a surcharge of up to 15 percent or more depending on circumstances. This tax was traditionally paid in kind, but from 1985 it could be paid in cash at current prices. The fact that the agricultural tax contributed a declining share of total revenue was a major factor motivating various local governmental authorities to compensate by imposing additional burdens.

The special product tax was levied on nongrain farm products, such as animal husbandry, tobacco, sericulture, horticulture, lumber, and so forth. It and the slaughter tax lent itself to abuses such as equal assessment of all households whether or not they actually produced a special product or had slaughtered a pig. This is one instance of a general pattern that characterized the tax problem and that arose from the administrative difficulties of imposing taxes on households. From the collectors' point of view, it was much simpler to impose a flat rate on everyone than to ascertain each family's circumstances. In 1996, a central document demanded that localities and departments should not "levy special agricultural tax or the animal slaughter tax according to population" or to acreage farmed, but instead on households.[9]

Township and Village Levies (T and V). Table 3.2 shows the purposes of the two sets of levies, often called *santi wutong* – the three "retentions" and five "unifieds" – which were set by the township and collected by the village committee but administered by the townships. According to national regulations later enshrined in the Law on Agriculture passed in 1993, the combined payment

[6] *ZTN-Zhaiyao* (1998: 84) and Sun Meijun (1998).
[7] *RMRB-O* (March 16, 2001).
[8] See Oi (1999: 17–26). Oi emphasizes the regional variability of the tax.
[9] *Xinhua* (Dec. 9, 1996, *SWB-FE*2797, S1/4).

was not to exceed 5 percent of the average net per capita income of township inhabitants for the preceding year.[10] However, "in the absolute majority of localities," the levy in fact significantly exceeded this level in the later 1980s and early 1990s. Nationally, it rose from 6.71 percent of incomes in 1985 to 7.94 percent in 1991 but this concealed enormous variation.[11] Just how much peasants paid after 1991 is not at all clear. In the wake of a major burden reduction campaign in 1993 the T and V levy fell below 5 percent of incomes but then "rebounded," only to drop again to a minuscule 1.12 percent of per capita incomes in 1998. But the latter percentage was eclipsed by Premier Zhu Rongji in March 2001, who stated that the T and V levies amounted to 60 billion yuan or 10 percent of incomes. The lower percentages probably were supplied by rural officials who responded to the pressures to limit the levies to 5 percent either by concealing the real amounts exacted or by shifting exactions to other sources, especially fees. The higher figure may well have come from sample surveys conducted by the Ministry of Agriculture and other units.[12] Widely reported abuses included collection ahead of schedule, addition of new charges after the county or city administrations had approved the exactions, and especially exaggeration of income to increase the size of the 5 percent.

Labor Services. Each able-bodied laborer was required to contribute five to ten days of work per year (*yiwu gong*) on local flood prevention, afforestation, roads, and school construction. A second requirement, called accumulation labor (*jilei gong*), demanded ten to twenty days of work per year on state water conservation projects and afforestation.[13] With the decline of collectivism during the reform era, the corvée requirement was not always enforced, but greater efforts to do so were made in the 1990s. In 1991 contributed labor days rose by 22 percent compared to the previous year.[14] Officials often pressured peasants to pay cash in lieu of labor services, a practice that was forbidden in 1993 but nonetheless continued. Reportedly, when family members worked in the cities, their families had to pay the labor equivalent for their absentee members as well.[15] Paying taxes in cash, including the T and V taxes, added significantly to

---

[10] In discussions both within and without China, the 5 percent limit is often erroneously applied to the entire tax burden of peasants. See *NMRB*, editors (1998: 15).

[11] Li Qin (1992) and Chen Youfu (1994).

[12] *Liaowang* (no. 43, Oct. 26, 1998: 16–18) and see the "Notice" of the CC and State Council General Offices which called for strict checking on collections that exceeded 5 percent, in *Xinhua* (July 27, 1998).

[13] *ZRGYGB* (1992).

[14] Li Qin (1992).

[15] Interviews, Wuhan (Sept. 1998). However, *FZRB* (May 21, 1996) asserts that this was not the case.

Table 3.3 *Peasant Cash Payments, 1994–1997*

Year	Cash income (% of total income)	Cash payments (% of burdens)	Burdens (% of income)[a]	Cash payments (% of cash income)
1994	64.9	87.3	5.5	7.5
1995	62.6	86.8	5.6	7.8
1996	63.3	88.0	5.6	7.8
1997	67.2	90.5	5.2	7.0

[a] Burdens include agricultural taxes and the T and V levies but not fees.
Source: Sun Meijun (1998: 7–12).

the peasants' burdens, because a substantial proportion of their income was in kind. Table 3.3 shows cash income and cash payments by peasants.

Fees, Fundraising, Apportionments. The "three irregulars (*sanluan*)," indiscriminate collection of fees, fundraising, and apportionment of expenses (*luan shoufei, luan jizi, luan tanpai*), were the most indeterminate and open-ended of the burdens. (Often the triad "*sanluan*" included fines; see below.) Fees or service charges were imposed when a villager needed a building permit, a license, or to register a marriage. All households were sometimes required to pay fees for services that some of them did not need, such as veterinary services. Donating funds for projects was supposedly voluntary, but contributions were often compulsory. Cadres embarked on fundraising drives for various development projects, such as school building, or for the cost of receiving visiting officials, frequently going from house to house in quest of contributions.[16] Household assessments were often uniformly distributed regardless of ability to pay, thereby contributing to the regressiveness of the burdens. The scope for abuse, especially for corruption, of the "three irregulars" was large. They elicited the greatest anger and proved most difficult to bring under control. See Figure 3.1.

Peasant funds, unless embezzled or otherwise misused (for instance, for "wining and dining"), became part of the township extrabudgetary and self-raised funds, which were outside the regular budget. Townships relied heavily on such funds because of the inadequacy of regular budgetary allocations, creating strong incentives for officials to extract money from the peasants informally (see Chapter 4).[17] Because fees benefited the local authorities, they could rise to grotesque heights. Marriage registration was supposed to cost nine yuan and

[16] *Xinhua* (June 19, 1985, *FBIS*, no. 121:K 14–15) and *RMRB* (Nov. 17, 1985).
[17] See Christine Wong (1997: 167–212).

等肉下锅

韦启美 画

Figure 3.1 The words on the goat read "irregular fees" and a group of cadres is eagerly
awaiting having the goat cooked in a hot pot as part of their banquet. *Source: Fengci yu
Youmo*, No. 2, January 2000.

was reduced to two yuan in 1993. The *Legal Daily* reported in 1996 that in
some Shandong villages, marriage fees cost eight hundred and even twelve
hundred yuan. The fee for registering a first birth was eight hundred yuan,
for a second birth, fifteen hundred, plus three hundred yuan for each child's
household registration.[18] See Figure 3.2.

The townships were not by any means solely responsible for the *sanluan*.
Many of them originated from Center agencies. In 1991, the Ministry of
Agriculture found 148 documents issued by 48 ministries and commissions that
authorized the collection of fees or fundraising. Two years later, the General
Offices of the Party Central Committee and the State Council published a list
of 99 fees and fundraising schemes imposed by 24 Center-level units.[19] The

---

[18] *FZRB* (May 21, 1996) and *RMRB* (Oct. 19, 1993, in *FBIS*, no. 204: 53). A circular on nine fees
was issued in October 1993 by the State Planning Commission, the Ministries of Finance [MOF]
and Agriculture [MOA] which, inter alia, stipulated the fee for marriage registration. See *RMRB*
(Oct. 19, 1993, *FBIS*, no. 204: 53–4).
[19] *ZRGYGB* (1993: 850–57).

Figure 3.2 The sign on the truck reads "agricultural tax" and the sign on the trailer reads "assessments," which are much larger than the regular tax. *Source: Fengci yu Youmo*, August 20, 1999.

State Education Commission raised money for educational development; the Ministry of Public Health for subsidies to rural doctors; and the Ministry of Water Resources for building power plants. The Ministry of Agriculture, which was in charge of implementing burden reduction, also charged fees, for the management of farm machinery, for instance. The Ministry of Communications charged a fee for highway maintenance and a fee for the management of highway transport. The Public Security Ministry charged fees for the control of public offenses, for handling major traffic accidents, for ID cards and household registration. The Ministry of Water Resources imposed fees for the control of soil erosion. The Ministry of Public Health collected funds for a truly worthwhile purpose: improving toilets in rural areas. These Center-level fees cascaded down the hierarchy. Lower-level units might add to the higher-level fees or add fees of their own. In 1985, in Songhuajiang prefecture, Heilongjiang, farmers paid 95 different fees: 58 to provincial units, 10 to prefectural units, and 27 to county and township departments.[20] In Hebei in the mid-1990s, 18 provincial-level units issued 56 documents authorizing 83 types of fees. The 19 counties of Shijiazhuang city issued 125 such documents on the basis of which 852 fees or fines could be charged, assessments imposed, or fund drives launched.[21]

Projects launched by Center-level agencies often entailed the setting of targets (*dabiao*) handed down to the local authorities and for the meeting of which they competed, and for which officials demanded cash, goods, or labor from the peasants. This might include targets for law enforcement and security, purchase of

[20] *RMRB* (Nov. 17, 1985).
[21] Zhu Shouyin (1998).

insurance policies, sports competitions, sanitation, primary health care services, and the building of schools, agriculture and science centers, old-age homes, or police stations. Attainment of such targets affected the salaries and promotions of officials' and hence prompted them to squeeze the peasants. We discuss this in Chapter 4. Moreover, the political reputations of counties, townships, and villages hinged on designation as "advanced," which prompted fierce competition among them. In 1993, the Center identified forty-three target-setting programs and ordered the abolition of every one. Despite the cancellation of programs, fees, assessments, fundraising drives, and target setting by the Center authorities, these practices persisted.

Fees for Education. How localities were to pay for basic education was an enormous problem. The Chinese state grossly neglected paying for elementary education. Only some of the costs of rural education were funded by the state in the expectation that other sources of funds would be found. In 1984 the central government imposed a surtax for education amounting to 1 or 2 percent of net per capita incomes.[22] Much of the township levy, as well as corvée labor, was devoted to education and school construction. But these resources were often inadequate to fund school construction, maintenance, and acquisition of equipment, or to pay not only local teachers (*minban jiaoshi*) but often also those supposed to be paid from the regular state education budget. Moreover, local officials came under great pressure to provide nine years of education in their districts to fulfill a national plan to raise educational levels. Because this was implemented without provision of adequate funds, localities without their own resources had to put increased pressure on peasants to pay even more for education.

Fundraising for education because the major source of burdens.[23] National statistics indicate that the per capita peasant expenditures for education, entertainment, and culture – official statistics lump these categories together – rose from 31.38 yuan in 1990 to 168.33 yuan in 1999, absorbing 3.9 percent of per capita incomes in 1990 and 8 percent in 1998, far more than state taxes.[24] Peasants no doubt spent some money on entertainment and culture, but most of the money went to education, judging by the grievances that arose from this issue.

In addition to burdening all households, the education levies imposed extraordinarily high expenses on those with school-age children. The Education

---

[22] West (1997: 213–82).

[23] Interview, Beijng (Aug. 25, 1998). In his March 2001 press conference, Premier Zhu observed that fees "actually found their way to support education." See *RMRB-O* (March 16, 2001).

[24] *ZTN* (2000: 334).

Figure 3.3 In an unnamed county, teacher salaries represented by the pot are eaten up by various exactions. From right to left, they are assessments, fundraising, local savings, donations, a construction fee, and a fee for fighting floods. *Source: Zhongguo Jiaoyu Bao*, July 19, 1997.

Law forbade charging tuition but allowed "miscellaneous fees." According to Loraine West, "In the 1993 academic year, an average of 21.55 yuan ... was collected from rural primary school students and 44.03 yuan from rural junior high school students in miscellaneous fees." In sharp contrast, in the early 1980s, "students paid less than 10 yuan to attend primary school."[25] In 1995, Wang Yanbin reported that "the average primary school student paid 90 to 250 yuan per academic year and middle school students 110 to 500. In Meitan county, Guizhou, peasants reported that preschool (*xueqian ban*) cost 154 yuan plus 20 catties of rice; primary school, 40 yuan plus miscellaneous fees."[26] Officials were extremely inventive in finding something for which an education fee could be imposed: construction equipment, recreation, tree planting, broomsticks, desk use. In Heilongjiang, there were over a dozen such fees, including a bicycle parking fee.[27] It is not surprising that children of poor peasants often dropped out of school.

[25] West (1997: 238–9).
[26] Wang Yanbin (1995).
[27] Zhao Xin (1992) and West (1997).

Figure 3.4 This cartoon satirizes a slogan used in the schools: "each day progress upwards." But the student's progress consists of climbing on boxes, each of which has the name of a different fee. The first set on the left consists of fees for transferring to another school, for class handouts, for attending school temporarily, for dossiers, and maintenance. The second set lists fees for examination papers, insurance, and hygiene. The last three are for substitutes, after-school lessons, tuition, and miscellaneous expenses. *Source: Zhongguo Jiaoyu Bao* (November 18, 1993).

Fines. Levying fines on a wide range of pretexts and for minor infractions was a very common practice, as indicated not only by reports from localities but by the language used in Center documents. One document, promulgated in 1997, called for "resolute prohibition of illegal fines and cancellation of those lists of fines that lacked legal authorization."[28] Rural officials used fines to secure compliance, as the 1997 decree put it, "we should resolutely correct such erroneous practices as imposing fines on peasants who fail to complete planting tasks," and also as a means of raising money to pay administrative expenses. In 1992, the inadequate budgets of many units, according to the *Sichuan Ribao*, prompted reliance on fines.[29] In 1998, "some localities" instructed the public security organs to impose fines in order to cover their costs.[30] Violations of the rules on family planning yielded a lucrative income in fines. If, for instance, a second child were born within five years of the first, cadres would fine the couple two to five thousand yuan or take their property.[31] Households in arrears

---

[28] *RMRB* (April 1, 1997).
[29] *SCRB* (June 11, 1992).
[30] *ZXS* (Oct. 17,1998, *SWB-FE*, no. 3366, G/6).
[31] Interviews, Wuhan agricultural economists (Sept. 1998).

in the payment of taxes and other levies were fined and charged high interest rates. These fines served corrupt ends since cadres didn't keep accounts of fines.

The burdens resulting from fees, fines, and apportionments were the most difficult to account for. An official in the Ministry of Agriculture, Li Qin, wrote that as of 1991 they had "doubled and redoubled" (*chengbei zengzhang*). According to "incomplete" statistics compiled by this ministry, they amounted to 12 billion yuan, 13.8 yuan per capita or 2.3 percent of net per capita income. The author disaggregated the 12 billion as follows: Farmers "unwillingly" paid 1.7 billion yuan in administrative fees; 4.1 billion yuan in apportionments, 3.81 billion yuan in other "social loads" (*shehui fudan*), plus 2.31 billion yuan in fines, or 11.92 billion yuan.[32] In 1996, according to an official in the State Statistical Bureau, the amount collected from the *sanluan*, the "three irregulars", nationwide was only somewhat higher than in 1991, 13.12 billion yuan, or 14.7 yuan per capita. But a 100-county statistical survey by the Ministry of Agriculture indicated that these burdens exacted 46.1 yuan, that is, three times as much.[33] In the latter half of the 1990s, fees, fines, and assessments became an even more serious problem. The *sanluan* became a substitute for the regularization of township and village taxes, a point noted by Center-level analysts.[34] Thus the Ministry of Finance found that in 1996 the aggregate peasant burden load in a Hebei county totaled 27.7 million RMB, of which an extraordinary 71.5 percent came from various fees and only 28.5 percent from regular taxes. A nationwide survey done in 1997 confirmed this ratio: Only 24 percent of the 195 yuan burden came from formal taxes.[35] At his March 2001 press conference, Premier Zhu stated that a total of 120 billion yuan "or even more" was being extracted from the peasantry, which, in view of the earlier figures of 30 billion in state taxes and 60 billion for T and V levies, implies a figure of 30 billion yuan "or even more" for "unauthorized fees" (*luan fei*). "Everywhere the peasants complain: state taxes are light; township and village taxes are heavy, and third and fourth category taxes (that is, fees) are bottomless" (*toushui qing, ershui zhong, sanshui sishui wu didong*).[36]

Impact on the Poor. Based on their analysis of income distribution in 1988 and 1995, Azizur Rahman Khan and Carl Riskin conclude that "the burden of net rural taxes is largely borne by households who are poor in the rural context and extremely poor in the context of China as a whole. Therefore, a reduction in net

[32] Li Qin (1992).
[33] Sun Meijun (1998: 9).
[34] Lu Mai (*RMRB*, Sept. 20, 1999).
[35] Guojia Shuiwu Zongju Nongshuiju Ketizu (2000).
[36] Gu Kang, et al. (1999: 2–7) and *RMRB-O* (March 16, 2001).

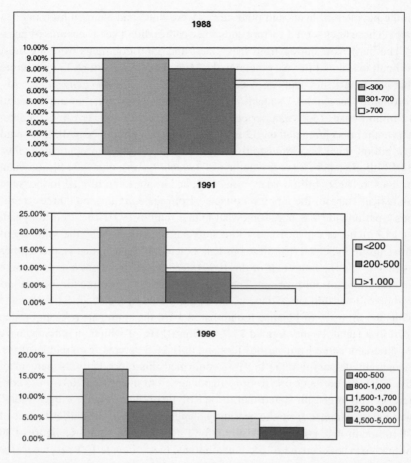

Figure 3.5 Burdens as Proportions of Incomes (in yuan). *Sources:* Zonghe Jihuasi
(1990: 58); Tang Ping (1992), Sun Meijun, (1998: 7–12).

taxes on rural households would have a strongly equalizing effect."[37] Moreover,
they show that the regressiveness of rural taxes had become far worse in 1995
compared to 1988: "the poorest decile's share of net taxes was 12 times its share
of income while the richest decile had a high negative rate of net taxes (net of
positive transfer from state and collective)."[38] National-level data demonstrate
the severity of the regressiveness of the burdens for three different periods. See
Figure 3.5.

[37] Khan and Riskin (1998: 249).
[38] Ibid, 240.

These data probably exclude fees, fines, and apportionments. "The fees are in most cases uniformly assessed regardless of whether a household is rich or poor."[39]

Application of the rule that T and V levies must not exceed 5 percent of average incomes of townships for the preceding year often resulted in grossly regressive tax burdens because of variations in household incomes. When business families were taxed together with farm households – they also had to pay the levies but separately from farm households and their payments were not restricted by the 5 percent limit – the extent of the regressiveness increased further.[40] One extreme example was a township in Guannan county, Jiangsu, where the average per capita income in 1993 was 700 yuan which yielded a T and V tax of 35 yuan. The per capita income of prosperous households, however, averaged 6,500 yuan and that of impoverished ones, 200 yuan. The former paid 0.5 percent of their income and the latter, 17.5 percent. In 1997, a Center directive called for lowering the unit of assessment from the township to the village. Cadres were told to check actual incomes carefully and not to submit false reports. According to scholars and officials interviewed in 1998, these policies were generally not implemented.[41] Ascertaining the actual incomes of households was an administratively formidable task. Cadres therefore often confined themselves to aggregate estimates. This source of inequity can be removed only when taxes are based on the actual income of each household, a step suggested by Chinese scholars but one difficult to implement.

Center directives called for full or partial exemptions from taxes for the very poor and for those stricken by disasters. But these were often not granted, one reason being that richer peasants resented having to shoulder the extra burden. The impact of taxes on the rural poor is strikingly illustrated by the case of Miaogang village in Jinzhai county, Anhui, a poor area close to the Hubei border. The per capita income was 606 yuan in 1996, less than a third of the national average. In this village, 30 to 40 percent of households found it difficult to grow enough food for subsistence. When bad weather damaged crops, as in 1995, more than half the households had to borrow money to buy grain. The next year, things improved a bit, but one-third or so of the households were still in dire straits because taxes had substantially increased:

> The ruthless pressure of taxes and fees on the impoverished households emerges with striking clarity. They either have to sell ration grain or

---

[39] Wang Yushao (1997: 30).

[40] Regulations called for taxing private business separately. See *ZRGYGB* (1992: 37) and *RMRB* (April 1, 1997).

[41] *RMRB* (April 1, 1997).

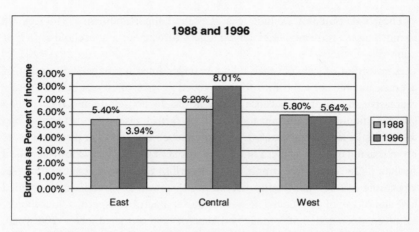

Figure 3.6 Peasant Burdens in Three Regions. *Sources:* ZTN (1989: 746), Zonghe Jihua Si (1990: 58), Wang Yaoxin and Lu Xianzhen (1997: 7–12). Another report from the State Statistics Bureau shows that in 1995, peasant burdens constituted 4.1 percent of incomes in the eastern region, 5.5 percent in the western region, and 8 percent in the central region. See Ketizu (1998a: 21–30).

borrow money [to pay taxes]; but in the final analysis, either method has one result: They are thrown into the abyss of high-interest indebtedness.[42]

The researchers reported that Miaogang received thirty thousand yuan in government antipoverty funds each year but paid seventy thousand yuan in taxes. They observed that alleviation of the tax burden was the simplest way to help the rural poor, a point also emphasized by Khan and Riskin.[43]

Regional Regressiveness of Burdens. If China's provinces are divided into three categories according to their level of economic development, a clear pattern emerges: those in the mid-level development areas defined in terms of income bore the heaviest burden. Rural incomes were high in the coastal belt of provinces, medium in the central provinces, lowest in the western ones because poverty was so severe, whereas the relative tax load was lowest in the richer East and highest in the central region where most grain-producing provinces are located. See Figure 3.6.

Hidden Burdens. Chapter 2 discusses the massive extraction of resources from the countryside during the Mao era via the state procurement system and state

---

[42] Shanghai Lingdian Shichang Diaocha Youxian Gongsi (1998). We are indebted to Professor Stanley Rosen for this article.

[43] Khan and Riskin (1998: 253).

control over input prices, the latter of which allowed the regime to secure a profit from the price differential between input and peasant sales prices, thereby imposing a "hidden burden." During the reform era, the compulsory state procurement system was continued, particularly for grain and cotton, even as a free market for agricultural inputs and commodities developed and as market prices became an important determinant of the sale of agricultural commodities. Although the regime abandoned the extremely extractive and exploitative policies of old, procurement burdens continued to be a problem, especially from the mid-1980s on. Hidden burdens arose from official price policies, local violations of Center directives, from the vagaries of the market, and from broader economic forces such as inflation.

State procurement policies fluctuated over time as did the severity of the hidden burdens. During some periods, notably between 1979 and 1984, the state bought all grain and cotton surpluses, greatly benefiting farmers because prices of quota and above-quota grain and cotton were raised substantially in 1978 as a way of radically boosting peasant incentives. This favorable situation for farmers ended with a reform in 1985 that sought to reduce the huge expense incurred by the state for grain purchases, which, for political reasons, could not be passed on to the urban consumer in the form of higher food prices. In the years that followed, grain marketing became a severe source of conflict between the state and the peasants. Sympathetic Chinese scholars agree that the procurement prices during the reform period continued to disadvantage the agricultural sector, especially grain farming, in favor of the urban-industrial sector. In 1991, the editors of the journal *Nongye Jingji Wenti* (*Problems of the Agricultural Economy*) wrote of the "severe erosion" of the interests of grain growers, which had reached "a stage where we have no choice but to solve this problem." In their view, Chinese industry "has long passed its primitive accumulation stage" and was no longer in need of resource transfers from agriculture. "No longer can we continue to allow a fragile agricultural sector to be the source of industrial accumulation. In contrast, industry needs a robust agricultural sector to give it momentum for continued development."[44] In 1996, CASS scholars Chen Jiyuan and Han Jun attributed China's enormous urban-rural income disparity "to the government's policy of taking funds from the agricultural sector for industrial development through price mechanisms," causing heavy losses for farmers.[45]

Hidden burdens for farmers arose from the differentials between the state procurement prices (both the lower quota grain and the higher negotiated price

---

[44] Editorial Department, *NJW* (1992: 43).
[45] *CD* (Jan. 12, 1996).

offered after farmers had met their base quota) and the free market price. Market prices were often higher than the state prices at which peasants had to meet their quotas.[46] A 1997 World Bank report compared state quota and negotiated prices with the market price in 1995 and found that the lower state prices "imposed a total implicit tax of 40.7 billion yuan on grain producers.... Since incomes of grain farmers are typically below those of aquatic, livestock, fruit, and vegetable producers, the tax is discriminatory as well."[47] In Weixian county, Hebei, in 1995, the state wheat quota was 30.1 million jin and the corn quota 4.1 million jin. The differential between the quota and the market price cost peasants 2.0 million yuan, almost three times the state agricultural tax of 7.1 million yuan.[48] Moreover, in designated state "grain production bases," the grain sales quotas were especially high. In these "grain bases" farmers reportedly were not allowed to transfer labor to more remunerative purposes, disadvantaging farmers.[49] Hence the common complaint that there was no profit in grain farming.

During inflationary times, hidden burdens arose from widening the "price scissors" between what farmers paid for essential industrial inputs such as diesel oil, chemical fertilizer, plastic sheeting, and pesticides and what they received in agricultural purchase prices, whether from the state or in the free market. When the scissors opened wide, that is, when input prices rose without a corresponding rise in farm prices, farmers suffered losses. As do farmers worldwide, those in China naturally had a crucial stake in these price relationships and often protested when they turned against them.

According to a 1996 report, the relation was generally adverse: Between 1979 and 1992, rising grain procurement prices increased farmers' income by 184 billion yuan, but rising prices for producers and consumer goods cost farmers 193 billion yuan, "wiping away all their profits."[50] According to official data, the price scissors widened by an average of 14.5 percent per year between 1985 and 1991. In 1991, when the price ratio had fallen to only 5.1 percent, the per capita cost of the price differential was 217.1 yuan. In that year, state taxes, the village and township tax, labor, and fees added up to 108.22 yuan,

---

[46] Zhu Shouyin (1998).

[47] *At China's Table* (1997: 23). In the later 1980s, the following price differentials between grain and other produce were reported from a Hubei prefecture: One mu planted to wheat earned 10 yuan; one planted to paddy rice, 108 yuan; one to sesame, 980 yuan, and melons, 440 yuan. Quoted in Shu Hua (1987). See also Sicular (1988a: 671–705).

[48] Zhu Shouyin (1998).

[49] Interviews, Wuhan (Sept. 1998).

[50] *CD* (Jan. 12, 1996) quoting Chen Jiyuan and Han Jun of CASS.

or only half the hidden burdens. "How can farmers bear so heavy a load?" the author of the study asked.[51] Price scissors widened again in the mid-1990s.[52] The state responded by substantially raising procurement prices, and these increases contributed to the increases in peasant incomes between 1994 and 1996 shown in Table 3.1.

Bumper harvests in the later 1990s dropped the market price below the state price and also made it difficult for peasants to sell their crops either to the state or on the market. State purchasing units, now responsible for their own profits and losses, would often refuse to buy grain directly from farmers, preferring to do so more cheaply on the market. The PRC introduced a "protective price" (*baohu jia*) to provide a floor below which grain prices were not supposed to fall, thereby protecting peasant interests. A 1999 directive ordered state purchasers to buy grain "as much as possible at the protected price," even while undercutting this order by demanding that they also resell at a profit in order to reduce state subsidies.[53] In the year 2000, Premier Zhu Rongji emphasized that purchasing departments should buy grain at protected prices "without limitation," but he also made clear that such prices applied only to certain varieties, the intent being to motivate peasants to grow higher-quality grain.[54] He acknowledged that in "some localities," purchasing units were restricting purchases, lowering quality grades, and reducing prices. Protective prices evidently were not of much help.

Data from an unpublished paper by the noted economist Hu Angang reveal that per capita incomes from the sale of all types of agricultural commodities dropped from a peak of 1,092.3 yuan in 1997 to 600.6 yuan in 2000, a staggering decline of 45 percent. In 2000 alone, according to the Ministry of Agriculture, the aggregate loss from grain farming amounted to 110 billion yuan or 125 yuan per capita. One-third of this decline was due to reduced production and two-thirds to the drop in the grain prices.[55]

As the surpluses piled up, peasants were beset by the "one high, one low, and one heavy" (*yigao, yidi, yizhong*), that is, high input prices, low purchase prices, and heavy tax burdens.[56] Many farmers bitterly complained that they could not make ends meet by farming because market prices had dropped and because of heavy tax and fee burdens.[57] A poignant plea sent to the State

---

[51] Li Qin (1992).

[52] *RMRB* (June 1, 1998).

[53] *RMRB* (Oct. 26, 1999; *SWB-FE*/3682, G/15–16).

[54] See, e.g., his May 2000 speech, *Xinhua* (May 28, 2000, *SWB-FE* 3856, G7–9).

[55] Hu Angang (2002).

[56] Sun Meijun (1998).

[57] These were major reasons behind riots in several townships in Fengcheng city, Jiangxi, in August 2000. See *NYT* (Sept. 17, 2000).

Council in February 2000 by a township Party secretary, Li Changping, in a major grain-growing county in Hubei, strikingly illustrates the combined effect of procurement and taxes on peasants and the local economy. His township had a population of forty thousand of whom eighteen thousand were able-bodied workers. A total of twenty-five thousand people had left to seek work in the cities, among them fifteen thousand of the able-bodied. Migrants had formerly had a definite goal; now they just ran off. "If we have to die we might as well die in the city; the next generation won't be peasants." Formerly, only surplus laborers and girls left; now, everyone was leaving. Extraordinary efforts had to be made to transfer abandoned land to others, but still, an estimated twenty thousand out of thirty-five thousand mu was left fallow in the year 2000.[58] Burdens assessed on land and on a per capita basis added up to 350 yuan. But procurement prices only covered the costs of production other than labor and 80 percent of peasants lost money, but they still had to meet their tax and other obligations. Because people couldn't pay, the villages in the townships were deep in debt. In 1985, 85 percent of villages made collective investments in infrastructure or money-making enterprises; now 85 percent were unable to do so. "The peasants' burdens are getting worse year by year." The Center's propeasant policies were "very hard to implement." Grain purchases were not made according to the protective price; in addition, the state purchasing agencies required that peasants pay for storage. If they retained the grain for themselves they were fined or it was confiscated.[59]

Assessment. How much did the average peasant household have to pay at any one time? It is difficult, if not impossible, to come up with a simple number. Most national statistics do not include all the burdens and income data from primarily agricultural villages are averaged in with villages enjoying TVE incomes where household burdens were much lower. An accurate calculation would have to be based on a sample of agricultural villages only.[60] In addition, official reports sent up the hierarchy from villages to townships to counties probably understated the amounts actually collected from peasants. A careful investigation of actual household incomes in a Hubei village by Li Xiande found an official level of burdens of 202 yuan per capita in 1996 or 12.8 percent of per capita income. Actual payments made by peasants averaged 292 yuan or 18.6 percent.

---

[58] *Nanfang Zhoumo* (Aug. 24, 2000).

[59] *Nanfang Zhoumo* (Aug. 25, 2000). Compare Chapter 6, for the State Council's response to this plea. For a book-length account of this situation and its ramifications, see Li Changping (2002).

[60] However, see Guojia Shuiwu Nongshuiju Ketizu (2000: 24), where it is implied that a major survey done in 1997 did focus on areas where burdens were a particular problem, thereby lending greater credence to its data.

Table 3.4 *Rates of Increasing Incomes and Burdens*

	1995[a]	1996[a]	1997[a]
Rate of increase of cash incomes	37%	21%	6.50%
Rate of increase of state taxes, T&V levy, contract fee	32.40%	16.4%	19.6%

[a] January through July.

Source: Wang Yaoxin and Lu Xianzhen (1997: 7–12).

The T and V levy accounted for only 3 percent of income, enabling officials to boast of having complied with the 5 percent limit. The entire village was officially assessed a quota of 434,560 yuan and actually paid 630,000 yuan. The official quota was the product of a complex process of negotiation between the county, the township, and the village, which included assessment of incomes but essentially aimed at meeting the expenditure responsibilities of each level. Once each village's total had been handed down, it was disaggregated to the households on the basis of land farmed. The administrative difficulties of determining actual household incomes prompted the widespread use of this surrogate, which further distorted the relation between levies and incomes. But as the higher unofficial total shows, even once the official quota had been handed down, substantial additional sums were extracted.[61]

Unquestionably, burdens rose over time. In the late 1980s in "many places," according to a State Council report of 1990, burdens rose faster than farmer incomes.[62] Between 1985 and 1991, peasant incomes rose at the rate of 10 percent per year; state taxes at 16.9 percent, and township and village levies at 15 percent.[63] During the first six months of the years 1996 and 1997, the rates of increase of incomes and of the three burdens – agricultural taxes, T and V levies, and contract fees – varied as shown in Table 3.4.

One survey of five thousand households in twelve provinces, sixty counties, and one hundred and twenty towns or townships found that burdens rose from 73.7 yuan per capita in 1990 to 195 in 1997, whereas another source based on statistics from government departments put the amount at 180 yuan.[64] These sums took about 10 percent of the preceding year's net income or 16 percent of

---

[61] Li Xiande (2000).

[62] *RMRB* (Feb. 14, 1990).

[63] Li Qin (1992).

[64] Guojia Shuiwu Nongshuiju Ketizu (2000: 22–32).

their cash income.[65] Another study published in 1997 concluded that "in recent years the farmers have had to pay agricultural taxes and other charges to the tune of up to 20 percent more of their incomes."[66] In 2001 Zhu Rongji suggested that 20 percent of incomes "or more" was being extracted.[67] This excludes the "hidden burden," the losses suffered by peasants from the procurement system and adverse market trends. The cumulative impact of taxes, fees, and "hidden burdens" allows us to understand why many peasant families relied on remittances from migrants working in the cities to survive, why some peasants resorted to selling their blood, and why still others took to rioting.[68]

THE TVE FACTOR

As emphasized in the Introduction, the availability to localities of resources for development was a major variable determining the severity of the burdens. The most important determinant of income levels and the severity of burdens on farmers was the extent of development of township and village enterprises, whether collective or private, commercial or industrial. (Other factors, such as specialization in technical crops, also played a role.) The income differentials in Figure 3.6 correlate well with the distribution of TVEs. Township and village enterprises were concentrated in the eastern belt of provinces, especially in the coastal regions of Guangdong, Fujian, Zhejiang, Jiangsu, and Shandong, less so in the central and especially the western provinces. The coastal provinces were advantaged by easier access to markets, proximity to large cities, better transportation, preferential policies that were the product of the coastal development strategy of the 1980s, and, especially in Guangdong and Fujian, availability of overseas Chinese investment. TVEs became the pillars of the local economy and the source of revenue for local development. Local governments were able to count on TVEs to generate profits and taxes. A high level of nonagricultural enterprise held out the prospect that revenues from TVEs could relieve farm households from some or all of their burdens. Highly industrialized villages in southern Jiangsu, parts of Shandong, or the Tianjin suburbs were able to build infrastructure and provide free schooling – sometimes including college expenses – health care, social welfare, and other benefits, sometimes on a remarkable scale.[69] In Qufu

---

[65] *Liaowang* (No. 43, Oct. 26, 1998: 16–18).

[66] Gao Changquan and Chi Fulin, eds. (1997: 94).

[67] Zhu Rongji in *RMRB* (March 16, 2001).

[68] See Solinger (1999: 162–76) for an analysis of migration patterns. On sales of blood, see *NYT* (Oct. 28, 2000).

[69] See Oi (1999: 79–80) and Cheng Li (1997: chs. 5–6) for vivid descriptions and analysis of the impact of rural industrialization on southern Jiangsu.

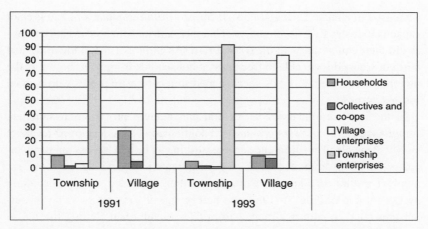

Figure 3.7 Percentage Shares of Township and Village Levies Paid by Different Producers in Shaoxing County, Zhejiang Province. *Source:* Zhang Jun and Jiang Wei, (1998: 36–44).

prefecture, Shandong, enterprise profits enabled "the government to finance some 400,000 yuan in public expenditure aside from reinvesting in TVEs." In contrast, villages in Guizhou "spend nothing for education and health; their public expenditures are confined to paying nominal salaries ('a subsidy') to village officials."[70] *Farmers' Daily* wrote in 1988 that "in some economically developed areas where village-run enterprises have developed rapidly, there are fewer kinds of fees and taxes levied by village authorities on peasants, resulting in better relations between cadres and the masses."[71] Figure 3.7 strikingly illustrates the decline in family tax burdens as TVEs developed in an eastern county.

As noted earlier, there was much variation within the provinces with respect to TVEs. The Pearl River Delta was more developed than northern Guangdong and coastal Fujian was far richer than the remote, mountainous western villages of the province. Comparison of southern and northern Jiangsu (Jiangnan versus Subei) shows that in 1997, net profits of TVEs in Jiangyang county, Wuxi city, amounted to 173.85 million yuan but in Weining county, Xuzhou city, to 13.74 million yuan, and in Haian county, Nantong city, to only 940,000 yuan.[72] In central and western China, suburban villages with good market access and other favorable conditions – Zhengzhou city and Jiquan prefecture in Henan,

---

[70] Christine Wong (1997: 199).

[71] *NMRB* (Sept. 26, 1988, *FBIS*, no.195: 12–14) and see Oi (1990: 18, 30).

[72] Jiangsu Sheng Tongji Ju (1997: 243–4).

Changsha in Hunan, Chengdu in Sichuan, and Xi'an in Shaanxi – had greater capacity to foster TVE development. Their peasantries benefited in similar ways as did their counterparts in the coastal East. As early as 1984, a township just north of Chengdu was able to free peasant households from contributing to the investment and welfare funds because township enterprise profits were tapped for this purpose.[73]

In the vast hinterlands of the central and western provinces, in contrast, "empty shell" villages (*kongke cun*) predominated. TVEs developed far more slowly if at all. The differences were striking: The net profits of rural industry in 1988 amounted to four billion yuan in Shandong but only six hundred million in Sichuan, whose population exceeded that of Shandong by twenty-five million. In 1989, the percentage of rural gross value of output generated by industry ranged from 57.5 in suburban Beijing to 13.4 in Guangxi.[74] "During 1989 and 1991 investment in fixed assets in rural enterprises totaled 29.6 billion yuan in the East, compared with 662 million in central China and 292 million in west China."[75] In 1998, gross value of industrial output of TVEs per rural laborer yielded stark variations. See Table 3.5.

Thus, only a subset of all townships and villages in rural China were able to "take off."[76] According to an MOA survey of 717,000 villages nationwide in 1997, 63.7 percent of the villages (457,000) had incomes from collective economic activities, whereas 36.3 percent (260,000) had no income from such sources. However, among those that had collective business incomes, nearly two-thirds earned less than fifty thousand yuan from such sources.[77] Only a relatively small portion of villages in China built up a genuinely solid economic base in the form of collectively or privately owned enterprises. In the least developed regions, mainly in western and southwestern China, where poverty still remained a daily threat, there was no significant surplus that could be extracted. These regions relied heavily on government funds and relief. Many of them were inhabited by minorities, for whom the central government implemented favorable policies, including financial assistance. But in the central belt of provinces, where grain and cotton were the main sources of rural incomes, such state assistance was low, outside investors were scarce, and self-reliance was the norm. In these regions, resources to meet development

---

[73] *RMRB* (June 16, 1984).

[74] *ZTN* (1989: 242) and *ZTN* (1990: 334).

[75] *CD* (Jan. 11, 1996), quoting Wang Weinong of the Economic Institute of the State Planning Commission.

[76] See Oi (1999).

[77] Zhougquo Shehui Kexueyuan (1999: 42–3).

Table 3.5 *Annual Gross Value of Industrial Output per Rural Laborer, 1998*

	GVIO[a] (billions of yuan)	Size of Rural Labor Force (millions)	GVIO[a] Per Rural Worker (yuan)
Eastern Provinces			
Jiangsu	590.6	27.4	21,585.2
Zhejiang	391.8	20.1	18,687.0
Guangdong	428.7	26.3	17,389.1
Shandong	457.4	35	12,732.6
Central Provinces			
Hubei	226.9	17.7	12,814.0
Shanxi	63.9	9.7	6,516.1
Henan	117.7	40.8	4,320.1
Anhui	88.8	27.2	3,267.2
Hunan	100.0	27.9	3,589.4
Jiangxi	38.0	15.4	2,464.6
Western Provinces			
Sichuan (excl. Zhongqing)	66.3	38.3	1,730.3
Shanxi	14.3	13.6	1,051.0
Guizhou	11.0	16.8	653.1
Gansu	37.0	9.1	408.5

[a] Gross Value of Industrial Output.

Source: ZNTN (1999: 42 and 295). Numbers are rounded off.

programs imposed by higher levels (compare Chapter 4) had to be squeezed from the peasants. This may have contributed to the curvilinear pattern noted in Figure 3.6 which shows that relative burdens were highest in the central belt, where producing provinces such as Hubei, Hunan, and Anhui extracted more than 15 percent of peasant incomes. Other provinces where peasant burdens were heavy included Jiangxi, Hebei, and Sichuan.[78] Not surprisingly, a large majority of peasant petitions for relief from burdens came from the central region and protests and violence were concentrated here.[79]

The role played by TVEs in eliminating or mitigating burdens requires additional qualification. The profitability of TVEs fluctuated and then declined in the later 1990s, affecting the size of the surplus that could be tapped by the local authorities. According to the rural statistical annual of 1998, total employment

[78] Zhai Liensheng (1997).
[79] Personal communication from an editor of a Beijing newspaper.

in TVEs fell in 1997 from 130.5 million to 91.6 million, but this is contradicted by the annual of 2000, which indicates stagnation rather than wholesale decline.[80] By 1999, the agricultural economist Lu Mai reported that because rural industries had been running at a loss, "local governments increased taxes on rural areas in order to maintain their scale of expenditure."[81] One of the authors found during a research visit to rural Changsha in 1999 that most of the TVEs were working at half capacity or less due to flagging demand.[82]

TVEs too were subjected to a wide variety of fees and assessments. By no means did the TVE funds taken by local governments serve only local developmental purposes and hence reduce burdens on households. These fees also elicited numerous vehement complaints and remedial directives. In 1992, teams from several State Council agencies investigated burdens in Zhangjiagang city, and in Jiangdu and Huaiyin counties, Jiangsu. The teams found that out "of every 100 yuan of net output value created by township enterprises, 30 yuan will be taken away in the name of various apportionments, fund-raising, and fees. . . . In effect, the excessive burdens borne by the peasants have been shifted onto the township enterprises." Formal taxes in these places were still kept within the 5 percent limit, but peasants were still burdened by fees, fundraising, and apportionments, which "were out of control" and "could be seen everywhere."[83] A 1997 study found that "the problem of all quarters of society apportioning expenses among township and town enterprises, imposing fines on them, and collecting fees from them arbitrarily is still a serious one. Some localities have even transferred on to the township and town enterprises the burden so unreasonably imposed on the peasants in the past," weakening their capacity to absorb more peasant workers.[84] These qualifications notwithstanding, TVE-generated profits and taxes greatly reduced the burden load on ordinary households. It is not surprising that policymakers and researchers alike saw the ultimate solution to the burden problem – and that of rural poverty, generally – in the industrialization of the countryside.

---

[80] *ZNTN* (1998: 295) and *ZNTN* (2000: 29). *ZNTN* (1999: 18) claims a reduction of 4.6 million in 1997.
[81] Lu Mai (1999: Sept. 20).
[82] For an excellent anthropological study of successful TVE development in a village in Sichuan but one that experienced a severe downturn from the second half of the 1990s on, see Ruf (1998: esp. chs. 1, 5).
[83] *XHRB* (Oct. 30, 1992, *JPRS*, no. 95, Dec. 22, 1992: 32). The team came from the Ministry of Agriculture, the Bureau of Legislation of the State Council, and the Ministry of Supervision.
[84] RDRI (1997).

GRIEVANCES: LACK OF ACCOUNTABILITY AND BRUTALITY
OF ENFORCEMENT

Burdens and the way they were collected caused peasants to harbor deep grievances. There is, however, an issue of perception. It can be argued that to some extent grievances arose because hidden burdens became overt with decollectivization. During the commune period, members of production teams only received residual work points after various deductions had been made about which peasants often knew little. Now, villagers had to hand over tax and fee money directly or see it deducted from procurement payments. In the reform period, even when burdens shrank, peasants might complain. Aggregate burdens in Benxi county, Liaoning, had actually dropped from 9 million yuan before 1978 to 4.35 million in 1984, but villagers complained because they now had to pay them directly.[85] This is one reason why fees and apportionments that cadres collected directly from households elicited the greatest discontent. "The arbitrary collection of fees has been the problem most complained about by the masses in recent years."[86] Misperceptions, however, can by no means account for peasant protests, nor for the seriousness of the Chinese regime's response to "unreasonably" heavy burdens.

Grievances were rooted in beliefs about the equity, fairness, and justice of state demands that had their origin in premodern times as discussed in Chapter 2. These beliefs included both procedural and substantive aspects of taxation: lack of fair apportionment of the tax burden among richer and poorer households, failure to take poor harvests into account when assessing taxes, downgrading the quality of grain, and forcing peasants to accept unfavorable ratios between payment in copper versus silver. Tax resistance often resulted from the anger generated by these abuses.[87] Contemporary rural complaints were not dissimilar.

The expectation that the state should deal fairly with peasants was reflected in state justifications for burden imposition. The state explicitly depicted burdens as based on analysis of what was tolerable and what was fair. A lengthy explication of the 5 percent T and V levy in the 1993 Law on Agriculture claimed that "this ratio was arrived at after comprehensive statistical and survey investigations. It is based on the actual income level of the peasants and on their economic capacities (*chengshou nengli*)."[88]

---

[85] *RMRB* (May 24, 1985, *FBIS*, no.105: K 11–12) and Li Qin (1992) who reports that about 3 percent of incomes were withheld by the collectives.

[86] *RMRB* (July 8, 1994, *FBIS*, no.130: 30).

[87] R. Bin Wong (1997: 236–7).

[88] Luo Fasheng and Sun Zuohai, eds. (1993: 56).

Villagers had strong ideas about the legitimacy of particular exactions. In Taoyuan county, Hunan, where farmers were beset by heavy burdens, they reportedly distinguished between "reasonable" and "unreasonable" burdens. They felt an obligation to pay the agricultural tax, to support military dependents, and the poor "five-guarantee" households, who depended on village welfare. But they objected strenuously to paying for cadres, for the training of Party members, for the high cost of the collective investments, and for a charge imposed to pay for construction of a power station, the completion of which had been long delayed, and which, once in operation, would still charge them for electric power. Farmers also thought the state ought to pay for teachers and for one-child family awards.[89]

Chinese peasants accepted both the inevitability and the legitimacy of taxes, of handing over "the imperial grain" (*huangliang*). Burdens enraged them because of their arbitrary, unpredictable, and open-ended nature, and the coexistence of what was legal and what was illegal.[90] A major peasant demand was that the open-endedness of burdens be stopped and replaced by a system in which burdens would be set at the beginning of the agricultural year, allowing peasants to plan ahead.[91]

Hapless villagers were at the receiving end of the demands of a vast bureaucratic apparatus whose various levels and innumerable departments thought nothing of adding a charge for one or another function or service, and who rationalized each charge as too small to harm increasingly prosperous farmers. Exactions were unpredictable in scope, form, and source. They could rise without rhyme or reason. Officials who extracted funds were not accountable to farmers and often not to their superiors either. Rules that detailed approval processes were often disregarded. Villagers were often not adequately informed about the purposes of the project in question, nor about the benefits that would accrue to them, nor was there accountability about whether the funds were in fact used for the stated purpose.[92] The number, variety, and size of the exactions boggle the mind.[93] "The peasants said that now either seven or eight hands all have stretched out toward us."[94] As one observer noted, every locality or department saw peasants as fair game, as the "Tang monk's meat" (*Tang seng rou*), referring to the monk Xuanzang's encounters with man-eating

---

[89] Chen Yimin (1983: 19–20).

[90] Zonghe Jihuasi (1990).

[91] *Lingdao Canyue* (no. 16, June 5, 1999).

[92] Zonghe Jihuasi (1990).

[93] For some telling examples from Shandong, see *FZRB* (May 21, 1996).

[94] *XHRB* (Oct. 30, 1992, *JPRS*, no. 95, Dec. 22, 1992: 32), reported by the State Council Inspection Team in Jiangsu cited earlier.

Figure 3.8 A peasant woman is shivering from cold since her house has numerous holes, labeled irregular fees, assessments, and apportionments. *Source: Fengci yu Youmo*, No. 7, April 20, 1997.

monsters during his journey to the West in quest of Buddhist scriptures.[95] In one year, officials might solicit money to build a revolutionary martyrs' monument; in another to add a transportation charge to fertilizer sales; in still another to charge farmers the higher market price rather than the state price for an industrial input, or to add new charges to existing ones. Officials skillfully concocted various pretexts to rationalize their practices. Extraction of fees for education, for instance, was said to demonstrate that "the people were now running things."[96]

Specific grievances that arose from lack of accountability include the following:

1. Failure to deliver services. A 1988 study by the Ministry of Agriculture quoted a farmers' ditty on this point: "You hand over the security fee but you don't have a feeling of security; every year there is supposed to be militia training but you never see them march; every year you pay the broadcasting fee but you don't hear any broadcasts; every year you pay for cooperative health care but they charge you the market price for medicine."[97]

2. Turning user fees into de facto taxes. Resentment focused particularly on fees imposed on all households regardless of whether the individual benefited from the purpose for which the fee was charged. Those who didn't raise hogs

[95] Chen Youfu (1994).
[96] Wang Yaoxin and Lu Yanzhen (1997: 7–12).
[97] Zonghe Jihuasi (1990).

had to pay the slaughter tax; those who had no special products to sell were charged the special products tax. Those who were illiterate had to pay for magazine subscriptions. All households were forced to buy insurance regardless of individual preferences.[98]

3. Imposing multiple charges for the same service. Local traffic departments required tractor owners to purchase a license plate, but so did local departments of agricultural machinery.[99] The same farmer whose labor had been requisitioned to build or repair a road was also charged a road user's fee when he drove his tractor to take produce to market. In a Sichuan county, "150 tons of Chinese-made chemical fertilizer reached the peasants after undergoing 26 procedures, during which 15 units collected various charges, resulting in a rise in the price of fertilizer from 446.4 yuan to 756 yuan a ton."[100] Formerly, when a villager built a house, only one department had to approve construction; now, there were three and each charged its own fee.[101]

4. Diversion of funds. "How funds were used was largely at the discretion of local officials, which left plenty of room for misusing funds, whether for private gain or the benefit of their administrative units."[102] A wide range of bitterly resented practices was quite common. These included using the peasants' money to add unnecessary staff to village and township bureaucracies, to buy expensive automobiles, televisions, cell phones, and other items, to construct impressive and costly buildings, to give feasts, and engage in corruption pure and simple by embezzling funds (see Chapter 4).

5. Exaggeration of peasant incomes. During the Great Leap Forward, millions of peasants starved because local officials grossly inflated the size of the harvests in their reports to higher authorities, leading to correspondingly inflated procurement quotas. In the reform period, the press carried quite a few stories showing that local officials again inflated local output and incomes as a way of increasing levies. In 1996, *Banyuetan* published letters from Fujian farmers from Anxi county complaining that when filling out a questionnaire on attainment of the national target of "modest prosperity," nine out of ten peasants were required to state that they had attained it.[103] A group of peasants from a poor

---

[98] See especially Sha Qiu and Jiang Nan (1993).

[99] *RMRB-O* (May 26, 1984), reported by NPC deputies from Heilongjiang.

[100] *JJRB* (Feb. 22, 1989, *FBIS*, no. 42: 49).

[101] They were the State Land Administration, the Forestry Department, and the Department of Rural Construction. *SCRB* (June 11, 1993).

[102] Tang Ping (1992).

[103] *Banyuetan* (no. 4, Feb. 25, 1996). An editorial note reminds readers of the destructive consequences of the "wind of exaggeration" during the Great Leap Forward. See also Yongshun Cai (2000: 783–805).

county in Jiangsu wrote to complain that the township government "brazenly" demanded that they tell a higher-level inspection team that their burden load was 100 yuan when in fact it was 340 yuan.

6. Abuses connected with grain procurement. First, cadres often deducted taxes and fees from the procurement payments due peasants. In principle, only the state agricultural tax (*gongliang*) was supposed to be deducted as part of grain sales to the state. However, as of 1991, in one-third of the nation's townships and villages, the T and V levies were deducted from sales to the state.[104] This was administratively convenient from the point of view of cadres because it reduced the task of direct collection. Deductions were also often made to pay for assessments, fundraising, and even fines. And earnings were further reduced when purchasing agents downgraded the quality of the grain.

Tragic and pathetic cases of victimization occurred. There were families that worked hard all year and at the end found themselves with virtually no cash income or even in debt, much as used to be true of peons in Latin American latifundia. According to a 1985 *People's Daily* article, half the procurement payments in six Henan townships were misappropriated.[105] In one of them, 85 percent of the procurement payments due were deducted. One family of seven, having sold 1,260 catties of wheat to the state, ended up owing 24 yuan. Sometimes farmers had to sell property to cover their debts. Farmers were "extremely disgusted" and their anger was shared by the paper's authoritative "Commentator."[106] Center directives forbade deductions from procurement payments but these injunctions were often ignored.

Purchasing officials could reduce peasant incomes by downgrading the quality and hence the price of the produce offered or by refusing to buy altogether when the state price was higher than the market price. In the late 1990s, state-owned grain enterprises became responsible for their own profits and losses, prompting them to use market criteria to the disadvantage of grain farmers. Another abuse widely practiced in the late 1980s and early 1990s was to issue "white slips" or IOUs (*baitiao*) rather than cash for sales to the state. Often this was the result of local officials' diversion of state procurement funds to more profitable undertakings, for example, investment in the 1992–3 speculative real estate boom, or, more generally, to pay for other expenses. It goes without saying that this greatly angered farmers who needed cash if only to buy inputs for

---

[104] Li Qin (1992).

[105] *RMRB* (July 22, 1985) and article by Commentator. See also *Banyuetan* (No. 18, Sept. 25, 1985, *JPRS*, no. 15, May 22, 1986: 10–12) Similar instances of deducting money due were reported from Jiangsu and Shandong. See Commentary, *Xinhua* (Aug. 3, 1985, *FBIS*, no. 150: K–18) and *Radio Jinan* (Aug. 2, 1985, *FBIS*, no. 156: O–l).

[106] *RMRB* and *RMRB* Commentator (July 22, 1985).

the next farming season.[107] During the widespread rural rioting in 1992–3, in which IOUs were a big target, the central regime sought vigorously to eliminate IOUs, but scattered reports of payment in IOUs continued to appear.[108] In addition, local post offices also sought to profit by issuing so-called "green slips" – promissory notes – for remittances from migrants working in cities to their families in their home villages and by deducting a fee for handling the transaction, reportedly a "fairly common practice."[109]

Brutal Enforcement. Given the combination of villager suspicion and resentment and the pressures on local officials to meet targets, it stands to reason that for cadres the collection process was difficult, time-consuming, and frustrating. As Xu Yong, a researcher on rural selfgovernance put it, "when burdens increased and exceeded peasants' capacity to meet them, complaints would result and peasants would petition for exemptions or hope for reductions, giving rise to severe conflicts."[110] At the very least, the task could only be accomplished by *"pian, hong, and he* (deception, roaring, and intimidation)."[111] Accounts in the Chinese media depict insensitive, officious, brutal, callous, and cruel officials.[112] "Crude and simple" work methods, bullying, beatings, and other lawless methods were common.[113] In some Hunan villages, there were the "six arbitraries" in cadre style: "Fining, detaining, tying up, beating, torturing, and interrogation." Some townships practiced "police rule," dispatching "public security forces" and "local police to deal with the masses . . . with absolutely no regard for any party mass line and painstaking ideological work."[114]

A circular on rural Party rectification distinguished between those who raised funds "to the serious detriment of the personal safety and property of the masses" and those who only acted out of "impetuosity and rashness in performing heavy tasks under higher level pressure."[115] Fines and property confiscation were the "favorite means [used by] some local cadres against disobedient farmers."[116]

---

[107] For an excellent account of the IOU issue, see Wedeman (1997b: 805–31).

[108] In 1995, the Center authorities again forbade the issuing of IOUs. See *SJRB* (December 18, 1995). Interviews at the Liaoning Academy of Social Sciences, August 1998, confirmed that the practice continued in various places.

[109] Interviews, Liaoning Academy of Social Sciences, August 1998, and with Wuhan economists, September 1998.

[110] Xu Yong (1997: 278).

[111] Shanghai Lingdian Shichang Diaocha Youxian Gongsi (1998).

[112] A good example is Sha Qiu and Jiang Nan (1993).

[113] Tang Yinsu (1991) and also *NMRB* (Sept. 20, 1988).

[114] Wang Xijia (1991, Nov. 21, 1991).

[115] *HBRB,* article and editorial (Nov. 19, 1985, *JPRS*-1986-015, April 22, 1986: 37–9) and *Xinhua* (Nov. 24, 1985, *FBIS*, no. 228: K 34).

[116] *Beijing Review* (Jan. 13–19, 1992: 37–8).

In 1996, an internal journal reported that when cadres came to a Hubei village to collect, peasants would shout "*guizi jin cun le*" ("the devils have come"), a term from the Anti-Japanese War.[117]

Center directives fully confirm the widespread use of force. One issued in December 1996 stipulated that: "We should strictly forbid the mobilization of armed policemen to arrest people illegally; the dispatch of 'small detachments' or 'work teams' to extract money or gifts from peasants; and the entry into peasants' homes to confiscate property forcibly."[118] A Center "Decision" on burdens made public in April 1997, stipulated that "The use of instruments and methods of dictatorship to collect money or goods from peasants is strictly forbidden."[119] Like orders issued in previous years, officials were told not to use "shock teams," not to seize grain, livestock, or furniture in lieu of taxes, not to force peasants to borrow money to meet their obligations, and not to force peasants to give money in lieu of labor services.[120]

"Shock" or work teams were typically organized by townships. On arriving in a village, the team would mobilize village cadres, split into smaller groups and go from house to house in search of money. Local police, hired thugs, and assorted enforcers might accompany these invaders.[121] In August 1998, the *Nanfang Zhoumo*, a muckraking weekly, reported on a search mission that had taken place in Mengzi county, Yunnan, the month before. The head of the township, accompanied by forty thugs, invaded the house of peasant Liang Faling, shouting, "whoever moves will be beaten to death" (*shui dong jiu da si shui*). After beating Liang and his young son while Liang's wife pleaded for them on her knees, the team took various goods, including their television and bicycle. Liang owed a tax of 75 yuan levied on pomegranates, which had not ripened and hence had not yet been sold. He was told that if he didn't pay within three days, he would be fined five times the amount owed and he would have to buy back his property.[122]

Chinese media reported a number of cases in which individual peasants were either beaten to death or driven to suicide. (Suicides were also committed as acts of resistance and defiance; see Chapter 5.) "In connection with requisitioning of money and grain, vicious killings have occurred in Jilin,

---

[117] *Xinhua Neican Xuanbian* (no. 4, 1996: 4–5).

[118] *Xinhua* (Dec. 8, 1996, *SWB-FE*, 2797: S1/3–4).

[119] *RMRB* (April 1, 1997).

[120] *RMRB* (April 1, 1997). For an earlier directive, see *ZRGYGB* (no.18, Sept. 2, 1993: 856).

[121] For detailed descriptions of several such cases, see Chen Daolong (1994: 2–22). Chen was an investigative reporter for *Xinhua Ribao.*. We are indebted to Professor Li Lianjiang for this important source.

[122] *Nanfang Zhoumo* (Sept. 11, 1998).

Hubei, Hunan, Sichuan, Anhui, Jiangsu, Hebei, Henan, and elsewhere."[123] In Muyang county, Jiangsu province, a death connected with burdens occurred in each of three unspecified years.[124] Some of these cases elicited nation-wide attention, for example, that of a Hunan farm woman who drowned her-self after relentless harassment by township cadres to pay 320 yuan in as-sessments and after they had taken away her television set and bicycle. The cadres responsible were not punished but rather promoted.[125] A case that "shocked the nation" occurred in 1994 in a village in Zhengzhou city. A peasant, Chen Zhongshen, had appealed repeatedly to higher levels against township and village fees. In response, several village cadres beat him to death.[126]

That these were not isolated cases is indicated by a joint Central Commit-tee/State Council ruling, published in April 1997, which called for subjecting the responsible leaders of townships or villages to criminal investigation, "when higher tax burdens lead to grave incidents including deaths or serious injuries." Leaders of provinces in which "a series of grave incidents that lead to vicious cases of deaths or serious injury occur" must submit written investigation re-ports to the Center.[127] Several years earlier, the Ministry of Supervision issued an internal circular that ordered all cases of bodily injury caused by peasant bur-dens to be accurately reported to the Ministry and in some cases to be exposed in the media.[128]

Impact on Peasant–Cadre Relations. Burdens, it can be safely stated, were the major single cause for the widespread deterioration in the relations between officials and the peasants, a development which greatly alarmed Chinese of-ficials and others from the late 1980s on. Burdens were not the only cause. Village and township cadres were charged with implementing five unpopu-lar "hard policies": tax collection, grain procurement, allocation of land for house building, cremation of the dead, and birth control, all of which caused friction between cadres and the masses. One report, by Party Secretary Wang Chongru of Zhongxiang county, Hubei, was entitled: "The danger of a rift:

---

[123] Chen Daolong (1994: 5).
[124] Wang Yanbin (1995).
[125] *Xinwengao* (1992: No. 8,315, Nov. 19, 1992: 23). Other cases of peasants driven to suicide by zealous tax collecting cadres were reported by *JJRB* (Feb. 23, 1993, *JPRS*, no. 27, April 29, 1993: 41–2) from Xiangxiang county, Hunan; for a case from Pizhou county, Jiangsu, see *FZRB* (June 7, 1996) and for one from Anhua county, Hunan, see *SJRB* (Nov. 11, 1996).
[126] Wang Yanbin (1995).
[127] *RMRB* (April 1, 1997).
[128] Jianchabu (1995).

The tearing apart of the ties between the rural Party and the masses."[129] The author compared the "fish-in-water" relations of the revolutionary period with the current "oil and water" relations, which were worse than they had been even during the leftist era of the Cultural Revolution, when farmers' "capitalist tails" were cut off. In Zhongxiang county, the prestige of a proportion of Party members in the eyes of the masses dropped. They didn't get mass support (the masses were dissatisfied with them) and couldn't get much done. There was open strife and veiled struggle. Secretary Wang added: "The masses see that Center policy cannot deal fairly with farmers. Basic level cadres are powerless. They seek out farmers to press them for grain, for funds, for labor, for life (*cuiming*, referring to abortions). They are skillful, even resorting to armed force. Farmers vent their grievances on the basic level cadres."

According to the Ministry of Civil Affairs, relations lacked harmony or were tense in more than two-thirds of twelve counties in Guizhou. In Tangyin county, Henan, half the villages were in the same situation. In some places, farmer-cadre relations were explosively dangerous (*yichu jifa*).[130] A researcher who investigated some one hundred villages in twenty townships in Yiyang region, Hunan, found relations "quite strained" in at least half of them.[131] In 1992, *Farmers' Daily* published a letter from a Shandong township official entitled "Why do peasants distrust the township government?"[132] A 1991 investigation in Xinfeng county, Shanxi, showed that 43 percent of farmers lacked confidence in township and village cadres, believing they were merely after the farmers' money and not in serving their peasant clients.[133] Burdens created "a confrontational relationship between cadres and the people, which damages the party's image among the peasant masses" and had a big impact on the way cadres performed their jobs generally.[134] Or, as a Shanxi agricultural official put it:

Peasants think that the fees from their various burdens, no matter whether they are reasonable or unreasonable, no matter what level or department imposes them, all go to the state, that they are "exorbitant taxes and levies" collected by the state. Therefore, the opinions and complaints of the peasants

[129] Wang Chongru (1990). We are indebted to Joseph Bosco for this article. See also *NMRB* (Sept. 26, 1988), Tian Zelin and Zou Haisen (1989), and Wang Xijia (1991).
[130] Li Jingtian (1991).
[131] Wang Xijia (1991).
[132] *NMRB* (Aug. 24, 1992).
[133] Wang Dagao (1991). The author was Party Secretary of Xinfeng county.
[134] Li Qin (1992).

Figure 3.9 The caption reads "cultural relic." The stone reads "Serve the People" and the man is consulting an encyclopedia. *Source: Fengci yu Youmo,* No. 8, April 20, 2001.

are very often directed against the Party organizations and the governments of various levels.[135]

One observer concluded in 1999 that "cadres take the masses as the objectives of the dictatorship and the masses see the cadres as the enemies."[136] See Figure 3.9.

In sum, the extraction of taxes and fees from villagers in agricultural China created a crisis which worsened over the years and caused increasing anxiety among the Central leaders.

In appraising the extent of the crisis, one can ask whether the open and hidden burdens created a crisis of subsistence. Judging by peasant collective actions the answer is no, since no evidence has come to light of assaults on granaries or of protest marches against hunger. Nonetheless, when the abuses documented in this chapter included the seizure of household grain, subsistence crises were indeed created in such cases. At the same time, however, peasants did not lose their land because of tax delinquencies. Under the household responsibility

[135] Chen Youfu (1994).
[136] Yang Hao (1999: 68).

system land was owned collectively and each household was entitled to a share of the arable land. Peasants under China's partially socialist system were thus protected from complete destitution and from losing their membership in the village. The main impact of the the burdens was to greatly aggravate the shortage of cash with which to buy basic necessities such as health care. In this sense the contemporary tax and fee problem can be differentiated from its counterpart in Republican and imperial China.

4

Institutional Sources of Informal Tax Burdens

WHY were many of China's farmers subjected to financial burdens to the
point at which some were driven to suicide and others to violent protest?
In this chapter, we look for the underlying causes in the institutions and structures of China's political–administrative system. We identify five structural
sources of peasant financial burdens: the vertical and horizontal deconcentration of power; performance pressures on local cadres and officials; state sprawl –
the costly expansion of the bureaucracies down to the townships;[1] muddled
finances at the township level; and deeply embedded opportunities to engage in
corruption. Some of these were strongly influenced by Maoist legacies. Others
were based more specifically in the financial system. This chapter demonstrates
the extent to which inadequate state capacity rooted in changing and deterio-
rating institutions was at the heart of the burden problem.

DECONCENTRATION OF STATE POWER

The norms of the PRC's political–administrative system prized unity of purpose and action in accordance with the top leaders' policies and instructions.
Functional ministries at the central level were responsible to the Party Central Committee and the State Council and to their coordinating groups. Below
Beijing, there was a dual vertical chain of command of Party and government
from province down to township. Government agencies reported to their respective superior agencies as well as horizontally to their corresponding Party and
government leaders, and, most important, to the territorial Party committees.
These vertical and horizontal (*tiaotiao* and *kuaikuai*) lines of control sought to
minimize the deviations of "departmentalism" and of "localism," that is, the
inevitable tendencies of bureaucratic agents to pursue their own "minor public

---

[1] See Vivienne Shue (1995: 90–112).

interests" (*xiaogong*) at the expense of the public interest.[2] During the reform era, these tendencies became a serious problem and a major source of peasant burdens.

In the reform period a process of "deconcentration" of governmental power took place, a term that encompasses not just vertical decentralization but also the horizontal expansion of the power of agencies that had gained more regulatory power.[3] Vertically, deconcentration took the form of deliberate decentralization as the central leaders delegated power to their lower-level subordinates to stimulate them to take developmental initiatives. Because funds were scarce, these agencies, as well as numerous public units such as state-owned enterprises (SOEs), were given the authority to mobilize their own resources outside of the regular, unified state budget and thus enable them to carry out their missions even under conditions of severe budgetary constraints. This gave rise to "extrabudgetary," and "self-raised" funds, which, in rural areas without industrial resources (that is, TVEs) were largely raised from the peasant population and were a major source of burdens. Horizontally, deconcentration allowed ministries and commissions as well as their subordinate agencies to accumulate off-budget resources, in part by imposition of a large variety of fees. These authorizations took on a life of their own. They were an open invitation to various governmental units to accumulate their own "small treasuries" (*xiaojinku*). These funds were not subject to control by the regular budgetary authority, the Ministry of Finance, and therefore they enhanced the units' operational autonomy. An unusually clear statement of these consequences was made in 1999 by a researcher in the Ministry of Finance: "driven by their own interests, various government departments always sought to gain maximum benefit by expanding their extra-budgetary or nonbudgetary incomes."[4] See Figure 4.1.

Authorized and unauthorized fees proliferated. A 1992 report from the State Tax Bureau indicates that, of the thirty or so levies commonly imposed in China, only a few were grounded in tax laws and regulations. Most were levied according to various local and agency "ordinances," "regulations," or "pilot procedures."[5] These agency-levied fees led to an enormous drain on regular tax revenue, and a vicious circle developed: the portion of regular (in-budget) tax revenues shrank in the overall fiscal revenue structure. These in-budget revenues were less able to meet the funding needs of the agencies at the local level, hence

---

[2] For a detailed discussion on the historical roots of public units pursuing economic interests, see Xiaobo Lü (1997a: 21–41).

[3] For this concept, see Xiaobo Lü (1997b: 113–38).

[4] *ZXS* (June 21, 1999, in *FBIS*, June 21, 1999).

[5] Hua Sheng (1993).

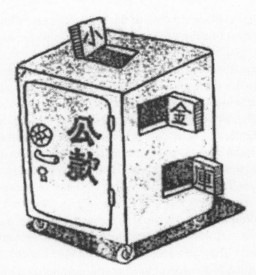

Figure 4.1 The cartoon shows a safe containing public funds. The openings are labeled "small treasuries," referring to public funds squirreled away by various units. *Source: Fengci yu Youmo*, April 20, 1995.

exacerbating the proclivity of government agencies to raise money in ad hoc and informal fashion. Fiscal dispersion led to the loss of in-budget revenue by the central government and hence to the sharp decline in the proportion of GDP that accrued to the central treasury in the form of tax revenue, from 31 percent in 1978 to 12 percent in 1994. In contrast, other developing countries usually collected 15 to 25 percent of GDP. The regular unified state budget was in deficit for several years in the 1980s and then chronically so in the 1990s. Despite strenuous efforts to curtail fees and other exactions, an internal report by researchers in the Ministry of Finance revealed, in 1993 for every yuan collected in fees, 2.25 yuan flowed into tax revenue. In 1996, after the fiscal reform, this ratio decreased to 1:1.46. The report also revealed an astonishing datum: As of 1997, in-budget tax revenues amounted to 11.6 percent of GDP, but if all the off-budget revenue (mainly fees) were included in the regular budget, the government's share of GDP would actually be 25 to 30 percent.[6] Only a fraction of this was accounted for by fees extracted from peasants since fees were a nationwide, urban, and rural problem. These data indicate that the burden problem was an indicator of a deep-seated, structural fiscal crisis.

Extrabudgetary revenues or funds (EBF) actually originated in the early 1950s as a central government strategy for encouraging local initiatives in

[6] Jia, Bai, and Ma (1999: 2–7).

86

economic development. The term *yusuanwai zijin* was first officially used at a national meeting on finance in 1953.[7] In the late 1950s, when planning was decentralized to accelerate growth by encouraging local initiative, extrabudgetary funds grew rapidly. With the policy of "walking on two legs" (efforts by both the central and local governments to promote economic recovery and growth), the central government allowed local governments to retain a certain amount of revenues outside the budget to encourage their active promotion of economic development.[8] By 1960, EBFs reached a peak of 20.6 percent of regular fiscal revenues. In the wake of the disastrous Great Leap Forward, the central government recentralized control and implemented an economic retrenchment policy. EBF funds decreased to 15.1 percent in 1963. A second rise in EBFs occurred in 1976 when extrabudgetary funds amounted to 35.5 percent of the total state revenues.

During the reform period, EBFs became even more significant in the overall fiscal structure. Decentralizing fiscal reforms initiated in the early and mid-1980s, called "eating from separate kitchens," allowed well-off provinces to keep more of their revenue to enable them to develop at maximum speed. This put a new strain on the unified regular budget and on the state's redistributive capacities. Inability to fund the growing needs of an expanding state from regular revenues further encouraged officials to raise off-budget funds, thereby further reducing remittances to the Center by well-off provinces. This in turn generated pressure to allow local governments and government agencies to seek additional revenue by raising off-budget funds.[9] In 1983, when the first of a series of government regulations on EBFs was issued, these funds already amounted to 77.5 percent of regular revenue. Five years later, EBFs were almost as large as regular fiscal revenues and 5.5 times as large as they had been in 1978. From 1994, however, major efforts were made to incorporate more of the EBFs into the regular revenue stream and by 1996, the proportion of EBFs to regular budgetary revenue had shrunk to a still sizeable 53 percent.[10]

This fiscal structure not only generated conflicts of economic interests between the central and local governments, but also, and perhaps more important, a trend of *individual agencies* or units utilizing government authority or monopoly control over critical resources to serve the particularistic interests of their units. Administrative and nonprofit public agencies became economic agents. Success in securing off-budget, off-regulation revenues was one of the most

---

[7] Wang Qixiang (1997).
[8] Zheng Xuwei (1997).
[9] Zhongguo Shehui Kexueyuan Nongcun Fazhan Yanjiusuo (1999: 42).
[10] *ZTN* (1998:169, 282).

important tests of how an agency leader was judged by his or her subordinates, so much so that "organizational rent-seeking" – by agencies all the way down to the townships, often in violation of fiscal regulations – was uninhibited and widespread.[11] State capacity was thus increasingly eroded by ineffective control of the Party/state over its own agencies and agents. The consequence of institutional changes in fiscal and political structures was further to "cellularize" power in China.[12] The Chinese fiscal system, in its entirety, faced, in the words of a Chinese economist, an "extreme anomaly" in which inadequate (in-budget) tax revenue coexisted with a surfeit of (off-budget) funds.[13] The institution of EBFs not only weakened the steering and redistributive capacity of the central government, but also contributed greatly to misallocation of resources, irregularities, and corruption.

THE LOCAL STATE: DEVELOPMENTAL PRESSURES AND INCENTIVES

The main point of this section is that "unfunded mandates" – an American label for demands placed on the states by the federal government – provided organizational incentives for local agencies to maximize their quest for financial resources, as evaluation of performance of local officials created personal incentives to raise revenues. The hallmark of the reform era was pursuit of economic growth and rapid attainment of modernization. This goal required immense investments by governments, collectives, and individuals. It was not only a matter of funding rural industrialization and modernizing agriculture but of building a vast infrastructure, as anyone who in the past has traveled on rural roads readily understands, and of enlarging small towns that could serve as the nuclei for local development. Local governments in China were responsible for the provision of public goods which could not be secured through the market mechanism. More schools and roads were to be built, more electricity supplied, and more services provided, causing a sharp rise in the funds needed for such public goods.

Public Goods and Taxpayer Choice. Despite decollectivization, the basic principle of local provision of public goods did not change. During the collective era, public goods were provided not through taxation but by means of collective burden sharing. Resources were allocated and incomes distributed in accordance with government decrees. Peasants were not clearly informed about the size of the financial burdens that arose from the provision of public goods. Under

---

[11] For a detailed discussion, see Xiaobo Lü (2000b).

[12] For further discussion, see Xiaobo Lü (1999).

[13] See *ZNJ* (no. 4, 1997: 21–4).

the old system, the collectives paid taxes, retained the necessary revenues for public goods (in the form of public accumulation funds and public welfare funds) and funds for production, depreciation, and management. The residual was distributed to commune members. In 1978, revenues were allocated as follows: for agricultural taxes, 3.4 percent; for management, production, and equipment depreciation, 34.4 percent; for public accumulation and welfare funds, 9.1 percent; and for commune members, 53.1 percent.[14]

Governments everywhere are responsible for the provision of public goods and services not readily available through market mechanisms. These goods may be provided without the consent of the consumers and taxpayers. In China's nondemocratic system, the provision of rural public goods and services was usually not a result of negotiation between government and society but of unilateral imposition by government. Each ministry, claiming to serve the interests of the public, imposed its public goods without consideration of their impact on peasant incomes or in the belief that the sums needed were too small to hurt. Peasants, as consumers of public goods, had to pay for these goods with or without their consent. The imposed nature of public goods provision in rural China was to a significant extent responsible for the complaints about the tax and fee burdens. Some studies suggest that the contemporary Chinese countryside faced an "oversupply of public goods" – too many costly public goods supplied regardless of the local resources required to pay for them.[15]

There were three characteristics of the imposed provision of public goods and services. First, local governments often charged large fees for services such as issuance of marriage or birth certificates, frequently far in excess of the official rules and far more than an average farmer could afford. Second, governments provided goods for which there was little demand or need relative to economic conditions. Some poor areas, for instance, built high-cost cultural facilities which rural residents did not regularly utilize. Third, some goods could have been allocated through the market but continued to be provided by government agencies. A good example was newspaper and magazine subscription. In China's countryside, one of the most frequent complaints was that peasants were forced to subscribe to newspapers or magazines by the government agencies that published these journals.

Provision of public goods and services became a handy excuse for local leaders to exact revenues. They rationalized their practices on the grounds that "we collect from those who will benefit" or that "people's roads are built by

---

[14] Ye Xingqing (1997: 57–62).

[15] Ibid. During and after decollectivization, when many collective assets were distributed, there was an acute shortage of public goods.

the people," or "community-run schools (*minban*) are run by the people." In interviews some officials and scholars contended that without local governments pushing for more public projects, peasants would remain perennially short-sighted and selfish about long-term development needs. "They complain now, but they will know how much benefit they can enjoy with the money they put in," said one scholar who studied peasant burdens in Henan province.[16] Many township officials considered peasant payments as reasonable and rational because the money collected was used in the collective interest. Everyone benefited from these funds. They vehemently rejected an across-the-board condemnation of burdens.[17]

As explained in Chapter 3, in industrializing rural China local resources were generated from TVE profits, largely obviating the need to raise funds from the peasants. In contrast, in "agricultural China," the peasants had to be squeezed for at least a portion of the necessary funds. Except for areas designated as "poor" and those which received government assistance – mostly located in the western provinces and in areas inhabited by minority nationalities – neither the central government nor the provinces provided adequate resources to meet developmental objectives. Unlike urban public projects, rural public projects could rarely count on the state to allocate funding. Here, the urban-rural divide and discrimination against the rural sector could not be more salient, especially with regard to school and road construction.[18]

Ironically the pressure to achieve unrealistic developmental goals that so burdened the peasants came from the very authorities who called for burden reduction.[19] As Loraine West suggests, "unfunded mandates abound in the delivery of public services in the rural areas. Central and provincial governments often announce targets, such as a specific reduction in the infant mortality rate or schools equipped to meet certain standards, but do not themselves provide the funds needed to achieve their targets."[20] Thus governments demanded the attainment of nine years of schooling in rural areas, but without supplying adequate funds. As a senior researcher who specializes in rural issues pointed out, "the social and economic tasks assigned to rural areas by the central and provincial governments . . . require villages to build schools, hospitals, and sanitation departments, but they receive no financial allocations to do this."[21]

[16] Interview, November 1997.
[17] Interviews, July 1998.
[18] *Liaowang* (No. 4, 1997: 37–8).
[19] *HBRB* (March 10, 1997).
[20] Loraine West (1997: 281).
[21] Chen Xiwen (May 28, 1998, in *SWB-FE*/3263, S 1/7).

Performance and Individual Incentives. "Compounding the problem of unfunded mandates is the fact that local officials were judged and evaluated based on their fulfillment of these mandates. This placed pressure on local officials to levy additional fees on an already overburdened community to fund the mandates."[22] Salaries and especially bonuses and promotions were tied to performance measured by the extent to which they fulfilled targets, such as that of universalizing nine years of education. In the reform era, to reduce the incidence of unmotivated time serving in the bureaucracy, concrete and specific achievements came to be regarded as the way to measure "scientifically" the performance of administrative agents. The criteria for good performance varied with the position of the individual and the priorities of higher-level governments.[23] Local officials signed "position responsibility contracts" (*gangwei zeren zhuang*) – sometimes as many as twenty – with higher authorities that specified targets to be attained. This practice began in 1987 when county governments in several provinces signed "rural work reward and penalty contracts" with township heads. Later, similar contracts were drawn up between township agencies and their staffs and this became standard practice.[24] In Jitong county, Hunan (where heavy burdens caused peasant riots), some township officials had to sign a dozen such "contracts" and some even had to pay deposits, which they lost if they failed to achieve the contracted goals. In addition, their chance of being promoted could be adversely affected.[25] In some cases, local officials' salaries were tied to the amount of money they could raise. In Henan province, for example, one township began in 1993 a so-called "performance salary system," in which salaries of township officials came not from township budgets but from fines and surcharges imposed during the enforcement of family planning and state grain purchases. According to this system, a township official would receive two fen (cents) for every half kilo of grain he or she purchased from farmers, 25 yuan for every vasectomy, 50 yuan for every abortion, and 100 yuan for a late-term abortion.[26] Some villages in Hubei province set up awards for revenue collection as a way of motivating officials.[27] In 1996 burden reduction was actually made a part of the performance criteria for local officials but without much effect since the other criteria

---

[22] West (1997: 281).

[23] For an excellent discussion, see Susan Whiting (2001: esp. ch. 3). Whiting's book focuses on industrializing coastal villages, where the main criterion for cadre performance was growth of TVEs.

[24] See *Xinhua Wenzhai* (No. 12, 1997: 12–24).

[25] *Neican Xuanbian* (No. 9, 1997).

[26] *Neican Xuanbian* (No. 1, 1997).

[27] *Neican Xuanbian* (No. 6, 1997).

remained, requiring officials to make choices about the ones in which they aimed to excel.[28]

Legacies of the Past. The eagerness among local cadres to meet targets was not only a matter of tangible incentives. It also reflected a deeply embedded mentality and organizational ethos rooted in the prereform era. Four such legacies came into play.

First, the Maoist mobilization regime was characterized by campaigns that aimed at fulfilling "core tasks" (*zhongxin gongzuo*, assignments that took priority over others and on the fulfillment of which leadership resources were concentrated). Core tasks were a defining feature of Leninist mobilization regimes, as Ken Jowitt has shown.[29] Although other characteristics of Maoist mobilization regimes such as class struggle disappeared, and even as the Chinese Party-state increasingly turned to tasks of regulation and provision of services, core tasks remained a significant part of the modus operandi of the Chinese bureaucracy.[30] An investigation in the late 1980s of township governments in Pinggu county of Beijing found that half the staff's workload was devoted to core tasks. The newly implemented annual merit assessment of cadres was composed of three criteria: functional work, 100 points; core tasks, also 100 points; and assessment by the Party committee (*dangwei zhangwo*), 30 points.[31] Accomplishing core tasks usually required additional resources, including recruiting staff and setting up ad hoc offices, which could well add to burdens.

Second, the "bigger and faster" mentality of the Great Leap Forward and the competitive pressure that this generated between territorial units continued. This orientation contrasted with the pragmatic and realistic line of the reform era ("truth through facts"). Government policies that stimulated and rewarded success regardless of the cost re-enforced the Maoist mind-set. This included completing plans ahead of time in the hope that the administrative unit (county or township) would be designated as "advanced." For instance, a local road might originally be planned to be built with local revenues in five years. The township government, however, would be eager to finish the work in three years, resulting in heavier levies on the peasants.[32]

A practice that contributed significantly to the peasants' growing financial burdens was the *dabiao* – reaching certain standards or planned targets – or *shengji*, upgrading. The idea of *dabiao* was lofty: Who would not want to

[28] Whiting (2001: 286).
[29] Ken Jowitt (1992: 56).
[30] Liu Guoguang (1998: 243).
[31] Li Kang (1990).
[32] See *Neican Xuanbian* (No. 9, 1997).

modernize and improve local schools and roads? Yet each *dabiao* required funding. As noted in Chapter 3, there were at least forty-three different kinds of *dabiao* activities in the countryside that required peasants to pay for them in one way or another. Examples included targets for the construction of militia training camps, schools, and homes for the aged, targets for the elimination of rodents, for subscriptions to newspapers and magazines, and for the purchase of insurance policies.[33] Actually, there were far more than these. In 1991 alone, there were 619 various kinds of *dabiao*, competitions, and inspections in Shandong province.[34]

One indication of how these "reaching higher standards" projects fueled the rise of burdens was an "Emergency Notice on Seriously Reducing the Burden of Peasants" (March 19, 1993), issued by the CCP Central Committee and the State Council. This decree ordered suspension, pending examination, of all *dabiao* activities for which peasant funds, goods, or labor had to be requisitioned.[35] Later that year another decree ordered cancellation of forty-three such *dabiao* programs. Again, in December 1996, the Central Committee and the State Council issued another warning on the still prevalent *dabiao* activities: "Some localities blindly pursue growth rates that surpass their financial capacity. So they extend their hands to the peasants for money by using all sorts of excuses. Some departments are overeager in carrying out projects in rural areas. They unrealistically practice raising and upgrading targets (*dabiao*), formalism, and increasing peasant burdens."[36]

Cases of heavy tax burdens caused by local *dabiao* activities abound. In one instance, in order to be ranked first in the national *dabiao* of rural old-age insurance coverage, Suizhou city government in Hubei province in 1985 compelled villagers to take out such insurance and pay the premium. It was in this locality that a well publicized case of farmer suicide as a result of heavy burdens took place. When confronted by reporters investigating the case, local officials showed a number of contracts (*zeren zhuang*) signed by the mayor of the city, the heads of the townships, and the directors of local agencies, such as the education bureau and civil affairs bureau, who were simply implementing the policy of their superiors.[37]

Among all the *dabiao*, the one that involved population control quotas probably caused the most popular resentment. Township governments faced a particularly difficult task in this policy area. As intermediaries between the central

[33] *ZRGYGB* (No. 18, Sept. 2, 1993: 854–5).
[34] *Banyuetan* (No. 1, 1993).
[35] *ZRGYGB* (No. 7, May 27, 1993: 286–8).
[36] *RMRB* (April 1, 1997).
[37] *Liaowang* (No. 12, 1996).

state and the peasants, they were obliged to implement the quotas set by higher authorities while faced with frequent resistance from peasants. Enforcing birth control quotas required a great deal of coercion, but also provided opportunities for corruption, such as sale of quotas, bribery, inflated fines levied on violators, or encouraging families to have excess children in order to levy fines. In addition, the pressure to meet birth targets invited falsification of statistics.

Then there was the difference between decision makers and implementers. Local officials who had to fulfill demands from higher levels commonly complained about being caught between pressures from above to develop faster and pressures from below, from the peasants. If they did not comply with demands from higher authorities, they faced reprimands and even cuts in salary and if they did, they faced the prospect of collective protests. Village cadres complained about the insensitivity of their superiors, who cared only about fulfillment of specific assignments and not about relations with the peasants:

> The higher authorities assign tasks uniformly and as absolute requirements. They don't explain about methods, resulting in rigid relations between peasants and the cadres. When higher-level departments evaluate basic-level cadres, they often only look at the rate of progress in fulfilling specific tasks, but don't care how they are carried out. They don't evaluate basic-level cadres according to whether they have done farmers some good. . . . As a result the basic-level cadres . . . do whatever has to be done to get the job done.[38] Caught as they were between the state and the peasants, the cadres felt that they should not be blamed for the resulting troubles.[39]

The campaign mentality of the past was significantly modified in the post-Mao period but in a destructive way. During the Mao era, officials were supposed to practice frugality and to avoid ostentatious display. During the reform era, however, officials widely believed that displays of visible progress, such as construction of impressive and expensive Party and government compounds, guesthouses, and monuments, or purchase of expensive automobiles added to their status and prestige, intensifying the tendency to spend. Extravagant spending, overcommitment of resources, and overinvestment were typical of the rural political economy and became systemic sources of peasant burdens.

Third, as during the Mao era, competitive pressures to achieve results distorted the upward information flow, a problem typical of command economies and more generally of principal–agent relations. During the reform period,

---

[38] *NMRB* (Sept. 26, 1988).
[39] See Chen Daolong (1994).

complaints of statistical padding were common, strikingly reminiscent of the "wind of exaggeration" (*fukua feng*) of the Great Leap Forward. Several township officials we interviewed admitted that they had to inflate results to meet the targets and satisfy their superiors. The demand to keep peasant T and V levies under the official ceiling of 5 percent of incomes prompted officials to inflate their reports of peasant incomes. One study found that peasant income figures submitted by officials in Liu'an city, Anhui province, were exaggerated by 100 percent.[40] Other investigations showed that in some places peasant incomes were reported as having been 25 to 30 percent higher than actual incomes, thereby enabling officials to extract more while pretending to comply with the legal limit.[41] In recent years, the competition for the label of "modestly well-off village" – a goal of national agricultural policy – led to income overreporting so officials could lay claim to this achievement and in the process tax more. A recent Central Organization Department report suggests that this type of cheating was a major source of peasant burden.[42]

Higher authorities always demanded loyalty from their subordinates. If the county statistical bureau wanted favorable statistics or reports, the townships had to provide them. Or, if the county planning bureau wanted numbers that would allow the setting of high targets, townships also had to comply. One township official quoted three lines of verse pasted, in traditional fashion, on a house door, that illustrated the predicament of officials. The top verse read: "Officials generate numbers, and numbers produce officials." The left verse read: "Supervisors press their subordinates; every level demands more of its subordinates." The right verse read: "Subordinates cheat their supervisors by watering numbers, and as water passes, the channels are dredged open." The analogy to the Great Leap Forward was not lost on farmers: "Things were done in a big way in the past, which caused us disasters. Today, with this type of fundraising, we are made to suffer again."[43]

Finally, the Maoist legacy also manifested itself with regard to the concept of self-reliance, the expectation that achievements would be judged by relying on local resources. As Christine Wong puts it, "rural finance in the PRC today shows strong continuity with the pre-reform past. The dualistic development strategy of 'walking on two legs' spawned policies in the 1960s and 1970s that called for a self-reliant rural sector. The countryside had to take care of itself

---

[40] Fang Xiancang (1998: 41).
[41] *NJW* (No. 7, 1994: 55).
[42] Zhonggong Zhongyang Zuzhibu Ketizu (2001: 84).
[43] Authors' interview, August 1998.

and not impose financial burdens on the modern sector of government. . . . This concept of local self-reliance still guides rural finance today."[44]

STATE SPRAWL: CHINA'S EXPANDING BUREAUCRACY

One of the remarkable aspects of the reform era was the expansion of the Chinese state from the Center down to the townships, remarkable because as marketization gained ground and the government increasingly relinquished the task of directly micromanaging the economy, the number of bureaucrats should have declined. In modernizing, however, the state acquired numerous new regulatory and service functions and these help account for the growth of the bureaucracy. But there can be little doubt that a significant proportion of the expansion was parasitical and indicative of a deep erosion of an ethic of public service. The added personnel often made little or no contribution to the achievement of the goals of their administrative units. The Chinese bureaucracy suffered grossly from overstaffing, buck-passing, and inefficiency.[45] Excessive hiring of administrative staff was another sign of the loosening of state control and of lowered state capacity. More significantly, the increasing costs of administration were in varying degrees passed down the hierarchy to the peasants, often in the form of fees and other charges for regulatory or other services. Several campaigns were launched in the 1980s and early 1990s to cut staff. As with burden reduction, the central government issued many decrees demanding strict control over the number of both offices and staff, but to no avail, due in no small part to resistance and distortion at the local level.[46] A new major policy initiative to reorganize and downsize government by cutting the bureaucracy in half was adopted in 1998. It began at the central level and was expected to be implemented in due course down to the townships. According to preliminary official statistics, government personnel in the central ministries were cut by nearly half from 32,000 to 16,000. By mid-2000, provincial government personnel had also been reduced by 47 percent.[47] Still, the progress of downsizing local governments, which was to remove some three million public officials at the county and township levels, has proven to be quite difficult. According to a March 2002 report, the pace of county and township government restructuring has slowed markedly, lagging the original plan to implement such restructuring by the end of 2001.[48]

---

[44] Christine Wong (1997:167–8).
[45] *ZNJ* (No. 10, Oct. 1992: 3–7).
[46] Liu Jinghuai (1992: 18–19).
[47] *RMRB* (Oct. 4, 2000).
[48] *Liaowang* (No. 10, Mar. 4, 2002: 11).

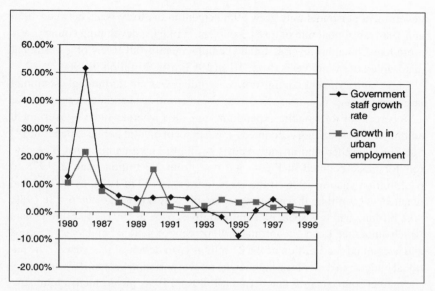

Figure 4.2 Government Staff Increase Rate, 1980–1999. *Sources: ZTN* and *ZLTN*, various years. Staff size rose from 4.6 million to 10.93 million in 1996.

In the two decades of reform, the number of government personnel – defined as staff of government and Party agencies as well as official social organizations such as trade unions – more than doubled and increased more rapidly than the growth of urban employment, an annual average of 4.7 percent versus 3.4 percent. The statistics in Figure 4.2 actually include only a fraction of those who "ate the imperial grain," those on the government payroll. A much larger figure was reported for 1991 by an investigative journalist: "The number of those who depended on budgetary appropriations for their wages grew from 15 million in 1979 to 34 million in 1991 and actually to 40 million if substitute staff (*yi gong dai gan*) are included."[49] In 1951, the ratio of cadres (officials) and other employees in public units was 1:600; by 1991, this ratio had decreased to 1:36.[50] As of 1998, according to a NPC report, there were about 41.2 million state functionaries, each one of whom required the support of about thirty people.[51] Compared to mature market economies, the expansion of administrative staff in China was staggering. In Japan, for example, where the government plays a large role judging by the standards of free market doctrine,

[49] Liu Jinghuai (1992: 18–19).
[50] Zhao Yining and Ye Shudong (1997: 12–13).
[51] In early 1998, thirty people sustained one "state functionary," which means there were about 41.2 million of them. *Xinhua* (March 17, 1998, *FBIS*, March 22, 1998).

government personnel only grew 59.8 percent in the forty years between 1950 and 1986, an annual rate of just 1.3 percent.[52] India, a developing country, was more like China, however. Estimated employment by all levels of government quadrupled in twenty years, from 4.1 in 1953 to 16.2 million in 1983.[53]

China's government administrative spending was one of the highest among large developing countries. In 1995, administrative spending accounted for 12.8 percent of total public expenditure in China whereas India's government administrative spending accounted for 6.6 percent of total public expenditure.[54] Salaries and other administrative costs swallowed up gigantic sums. The payroll for those counted in Figure 4.2 rose from 2.7 billion yuan in 1978 to 67.2. billion yuan in 1996. If the wage index was 100 in 1978, by 1996 it had reached 967.9, although real wages reportedly only doubled to 206.6.[55] In 1980, 40.4 billion yuan was spent on administrative costs; in 1991, 140 billion yuan, which amounted to an extraordinary 40 percent of national budgetary revenue and accounted for 3 billion of the 21 billion yuan deficit of that year.[56] The national budget ran deficits throughout the reform period, except in 1978 and 1985.

Another source claims that between 1980 and 1996, government administrative spending increased 15.6 times while total public expenditure increased only 5.5 times. In 1980, administrative spending accounted for 5.43 percent of the total public expenditure; 6.51 percent in 1986; 9.83 percent in 1990; 12.79 percent in 1995; and 13.1 percent in 1996.[57] One significant factor in the growing government administrative expenditure was the long-standing practice of "*bianzhiwai*" – hiring outside the formal table of organization – extra staff who were not part of the regular government payroll. According to one source, from the province to the townships, staff rose from 2.8 million to at least 5.4 million in 1991, or 6 million if officials sent to lower levels to set up counterpart offices are included.[58] Ten percent of the 6 million were *bianzhiwai* personnel, with one hundred thousand at the provincial level and the rest at the prefectural level down to the townships. Most, if not all, of the *bianzhiwai* staff were paid out of extrabudgetary funds. In the early 1990s, the number of administrative personnel of most provinces exceeded the budgeted payroll, sometimes by 50 percent.

Staggering proportions of local revenue were spent on administrative costs, especially in poor provinces. For example, in Gansu province where peasant

[52] Hu Jiayong (1998).
[53] David C. Potter (1986: 159).
[54] Yu Tianxing and Wang Shisheng (1999: 14–18).
[55] *ZLTN* (1997: 39, 45).
[56] Liu Jinghuai (1992: 18–19).
[57] *Neibu Canyue* (No. 15, April 21, 1999).
[58] Liu Jinghuai (1992: 18–19).

incomes were among China's lowest, administrative personnel increased from two hundred thousand in 1980 to six hundred sixty thousand in 1990. In the latter year, 79 percent (2.6 out of 3.3 billion yuan) of this province's revenues were "eaten up" by administrative costs.[59] The salaries of administrative personnel alone took up 42 percent of total provincial spending in 1993.[60] In 1989, Henan spent nearly 70 percent of its budget on administrative costs. In many provinces, the proportion was around 65 percent.[61]

In most counties nationwide, administrative costs took up 80 to 90 percent of county revenue, a situation that some scholars viewed as a genuine fiscal crisis.[62] In more than 70 percent of counties, including Anhui, which ranked twenty-seventh out of thirty provinces in peasant income, all budgetary income went to administration. In 1992, 1,091 of China's 2,181 counties or county-level cities ran deficits and suffered from "overstaffing, bloated bureaucracy, buck-passing, and inefficiency."[63] In Xinjiang Autonomous Region, 88 percent of all counties were "deficit counties" in 1994. In 1997 an MOA study of ten provinces showed that 60 percent of counties ran deficits.[64] In some poor provinces, counties not only used up their own revenue, but also subsidies allocated from higher levels. One poor county (unidentified) with a population of three hundred thousand had 1,600 government administrative personnel or 187 per capita versus a national average of 36 per capita. Neither the county revenue nor outside subsidies could cover administrative costs. Hence, the county diverted a portion of the antipoverty funds allocated by the state. As the author of the study plaintively commented, "If there is no investment, how can poverty ever be ended?"[65] See Figure 4.3.

Naturally, the population paid. Data on public security organs gathered by Murray Scot Tanner and associates provide striking evidence of how shortages of budgetary funds drove agencies to rely on informal modes of collecting money. In 1996, real public security expenditures in Hubei amounted to 790 million yuan, a portion of which was generated by personnel outside the regular payroll, but only 450 million yuan was paid by the finance departments. Some poor regions only paid 20 percent of total expenditures. In one county, a county public security bureau which was allocated only 40 percent of its budget request was told by the finance official: "You are the police. You have special powers.

---

[59] Ibid.
[60] *Neican Xuanbian* (No. 35, 1993).
[61] Liu Jinghuai (1992: 18–19).
[62] Ketizu (1998b).
[63] Du Ying (1992) and Huang Yanxin (1994).
[64] WenTiejun in *Nanfang Zhoumo* (Aug. 24, 2000).
[65] Liu Jinghuai (1992: 18–19).

我为什么走不快　　仗其作

Figure 4.3 The caption reads, "Why can't I walk faster?" The characters on the fat man's jacket say "government agencies." In his hand he carries "funds." *Source: Liaowang*, No. 36, September 7, 1992.

You can fine people."[66] Elsewhere, as well, "some localities have been unable to ensure that the costs of the public security organs are covered and in some cases have instructed the public security organs to impose fines."[67] In sum, chronic shortages of funds that to a significant degree arose from escalating administrative costs were a major reason why government agencies from the central ministries down to the townships charged fees for services and imposed fines.

Township Bureaucracy. Towns and townships, the lowest level of the state bureaucracy, were not exempt from costly bureaucratic sprawl. According to Wen Tiejun, a prominent MOA researcher, in the early 1980s an average township supported eight cadres. In the late 1980s, the number had risen to thirty; as of 2000, the number had grown to a stupendous average of three hundred, and in advanced towns, to eight hundred to a thousand.[68] During the commune era (1958–83) in Shulu county (now Xinji city), Hebei, an average of

[66] Murray Scot Tanner et al. (2000: 15, 26).
[67] *ZXS* (Oct. 17, 1998, *SWB-FE*/3566, G/5–6).
[68] Wen Tiejun in *Nanfang Zhoumo* (Aug. 24, 2000).

7.5 administrators served at the top tier of the communes (the equivalent of to-day's townships). By 1989, the average had grown to 11.4; by then new offices had already been established, which in one township brought the number up to thirty-one, not including the five people responsible for Party work, the ninety-nine on the state payroll in state-managed nonprofit professional institutions (*shiye danwei*), and sixty-four staff in numerous branch offices of higher-level public units.[69] According to a Ministry of Civil Affairs report, in Kaiyuan county, Liaoning province, during the commune era about twenty cadres ran each commune, but by 1991, the cadre force of the township governments, excluding functional agencies, had increased to seventy or so.[70] In Sichuan, a township in Jiaoge county had a staff of 1,056 persons; its authorized strength was 220.[71] One township in Henan had 87 cadres on the state payroll in 1996, 70 cadres on the nonstate payroll, 350 public school teachers, 120 retired teach-ers, and 30 temporary teachers. All told, this township had to cover the salaries of 657 people at a cost of 1.7 million yuan annually. The total revenue of this township, including allocations by the higher levels, was only 1.9 million yuan.[72] For our purposes, the last point is the crucial one: Only a fraction of the township personnel were paid out of the regular state budget. Most of the staff was *bianzhiwai*, paid with extrabudgetary or locally-raised funds. See Table 4.1.

Increases in the local cadre force came in several forms. First, the number of permanent government offices grew. During the period of 1984–91, some fifty thousand new "section-level" (*ke*) offices were created or upgraded with nine thousand additions every year, staffed by over four million officials.[73] Blecher and Shue found that in Shulu county since the mid-1980s, a series of new government offices were set up in the townships, including offices or stations for economic management, legal services, family planning, finance, land man-agement, and urban construction. Ultimately a township's table of organization came to include twenty-odd offices.[74] In this way, the so-called "seven bureaus and eight stations" (*qisuo bazhan*) emerged as township government became more and more complex and differentiated. According to a recent survey of township governments in Henan province, a typical township had more than

---

[69] Vivienne Shue (1995: 110–11).

[70] *Zhengzhi yu Falü* (No. 4, 1991: 53–6).

[71] *RMRB* (June 11, 1992).

[72] Bi Jingquan, Xiong Zhongcai, and Wang Caiming (1996).

[73] Zhao Yining and Ye Shudong (1997: 12–13).

[74] Marc Blecher and Vivienne Shue (1996). Additional ones included national tax collection, local tax collection, industry and commerce, police, and environmental protection. There were also post offices, stations for grain and cotton purchases, power management, road management, farm machinery, veterinarian services, water management, supply and marketing cooperatives, credit coops, and courts.

Table 4.1 *Administrative and Service Personnel in the Towns and Townships*

	1979	1989	1992
State organs, Party organs, Mass organizations[a]	370	1,370	1,520
Land administration, housing, utilities, services for residents, consulting	130	1,510	1,660
Health, sports, social welfare	1,170	1,320	1,440
S&T services	80 (1980)	180	210
Education, culture, broadcasting, and TV	3,620	3,060	3,080
Finance and insurance	110	210	253
Totals:	**5,430**	**7,650**	**8,160**

Note: In thousands.

[a] The rural section of the statistical yearbook for 1992 reports that there were 1.519 million township economic organization management cadres. See *ZTN* (1993:331).

Sources: ZTN (1990: 128), (1993: 115), and Christine Wong (1997: 191). Later statistical volumes did not carry such breakdowns.

thirty functional agencies in addition to the Party committee, people's congress, and township government. Some agencies performed overlapping functions. A clinic for family planning and one for regular medical care were administered out of separate offices.[75]

A proportion of township agencies were new branch agencies set up and directly supervised by their superior units in the county government. This was a form of "vertical expansion" of government. Such units were created to correspond to similar departments, bureaus, or offices at higher levels. Since they were responsible to their county-level superiors, the horizontal leadership of township Party committees and governments often had little control over their operations, including charging of fees.

Second, administrative expansion was found in the constant appearance of new ad hoc offices. As explained earlier, one of the legacies of the Mao era was the continued identification of designated core tasks, which often entailed creating new ad hoc offices. As one observer put it, when there was an "urgent task" and an office wasn't set up to handle it, local officials feared that their superiors would not regard them as giving enough attention to the task. These ad hoc offices often took on a life of their own, becoming more or less permanent, some lasting for a decade. Even when a temporary office closed, its personnel had to be absorbed into the bureaucracy. In one county there were 176 such offices in

[75] Bi, Xiong, and Wang (1996).

1989; two years later 98 were still in existence.[76] In the suburban counties of Tianjin there were 117 such ad hoc offices with 15 of them maintaining regular office functions and staff.[77] In townships in Pinggu county, Beijing, where, it will be recalled, half the staff's workload was devoted to core tasks, investigators found that eight different such ad hoc offices had been set up in one township in just one year between 1989 and 1990. These included the "leadership group for raising educational funds," the "leadership group for village committee elections," the "command post for guarding against riots and improving public security," and, amazingly, the "office for supplies to the Asian Games."[78] All needed funds were explicitly devoted to the task of raising money from the population.

Only a portion of the township administrators – usually half to two-thirds – were state cadres (*guojia ganbu*), paid for out of the state budget. Those who staffed the branch offices of county-level units were paid from a lump sum sent by the appropriate county departments. Often the lump sum was not adequate to cover the actual personnel costs, meaning that townships had to supplement the salaries with funds from their own, off-budget sources. The categories of cadres who were paid out of local resources reflected the complexities of these different statuses: contract cadres (*hetongzhi ganbu*), workers-as-cadres (*yi gong dai gan*), farmers-as-cadres (*yi nong dai gan*). The off-budget funds also had to cover the salaries of staff of not-for-profit public units, such as community-run (*minban*) schools and medical clinics. Some were paid out of the portion of the township levy which violated the rules. Others were paid out of a share of township-owned business profits, assuming there were any. Public units at the county and township levels that practice the "two-nos and three-reliances" (no administrative budget and no state payroll; reliance on fees, fines, and self-raised funds) have mushroomed in the last decade or so and account for much of the increase in personnel.[79] Last but not least, the very task of collecting a myriad of taxes and fees itself required large and costly allocations of personnel. In a township in Huoyang county, Anhui province, nineteen people were sent to the villages just to collect the special products tax. They spent two months at this complex task, which required finding out about sales of the relevant products from each household. They collected forty thousand yuan in taxes but their expenses just about equaled that amount.[80] In another Anhui county, townships each "had to collect six to seven taxes and fees. . . . They had to go to each peasant household two or three times before

---

[76] See Liu Jinghuai (1992: 18–19).
[77] Liu Guoguang, et al. (1998: 243).
[78] Ibid.
[79] Li Xueju, Wang Zhenyao, and Tang Jinsu (1994: 26).
[80] Zhu Shouyin (1998).

they were able to collect even one levy item." The number of such visits was astronomical.[81]

New functions acquired by the local state as the result of reform – development, public goods provision, and regulation – explain some of the expansion. Desires among local officials for status and better-paid jobs were other important factors. Government employment conferred visible status and authority on cadres as a representative of state authority. More important, obtaining a cadre job in a township enabled one to "eat imperial grain" – get on the government payroll, be it regularly or locally funded. It provided an iron rice bowl, as well as bonuses and opportunities for promotion for those who performed well. Even those paid out of local resources had more economic security than many ordinary farmers, especially in poor areas. More generally, stagnant farm incomes in the later 1990s sharply increased the desirability of jobs in the bureaucracy. One benefit that many local cadres enjoyed that contributed directly to the fund-raising by agencies was official uniforms, for which government employees received allowances. Why rural officials coveted the wearing of uniforms may sound puzzling, but to rural officials whose incomes were relatively low compared to their urban counterparts, the extra allowance for uniforms was no small bonus. Uniforms were worn by cadres in numerous agencies, including those administering commerce, taxation, police, courts, financial affairs, the militia, road management, administration, power management, forestry, public health, city planning, land management, and fisheries. In some localities, uniforms even extended to holders of CCP offices, including those in charge of combating corruption and waste. Some members of the Communist Party committee who were not regular state agents wore the uniforms of the agencies they supervised.[82]

The quest for a state job helps explain why the poorer the place, the larger the township staff. In Jilin province, the ratio of state cadres to the general population was eight percent higher in the province's twenty-four poor counties than in the better-off ones. In Qinghai province, the ratio of administrative staff to general population was 1:30, but in some poor counties it was as low as 1:13.[83] In addition to offering job security, government employment in poor areas was attractive because there were few TVEs or other opportunities open to returning PLA veterans or to college graduates, some of whom were assigned to work in the poor areas. The trick was to get hired. Incumbent

---

[81] CCTV (Aug. 5, 2000, *SWB-FE*/3914, G/3–4).

[82] Li, Wang, and Tang (1994: 62, 120).

[83] Ketizu (1998b).

office holders often came under pressure to go through the "back door" by hiring family members or friends. However, even if there had been no parasitic padding of payrolls, an incoherent township bureaucracy with its multitude of offices responsible to different superiors greatly inflated administrative costs.

As for village administration, the average number of cadres whose pay came from the village portion of the T and V levies increased only slightly from 4 in 1985 to 4.3 in 1992. But there was enormous variability. In 1992, according to the Ministry of Civil Affairs, in Tieling city, Liaoning, villages had an average of 5.5 members per village committee, with committee memberships ranging from 5 to 12.1. In Jiangsu, in the late 1990s, villages quite often had as many as a dozen cadres, and in extreme cases, 20 to 30.[84] In poverty-stricken Gansu, there was an average of 3.8 cadres per village committee in 1996 plus about one cadre for each village small group (the former production team).[85] Villagers became particularly angry when village cadres demanded wages for administrative work that exceeded local per capita incomes, all the more so because cadres also derived income from farm work and because administrative compensation had to be paid in cash.[86] In Liaoning, a 1989 survey of 72 percent of the villages showed that a fifth of cadres were getting four to six times the allowance permissible.[87]

MUDDLED FINANCES AND THE RURAL FUNDING CRISIS

Uncontrolled bureaucratic expansion burgeoned in the context of uncontrolled township finance. Township funds came from three major sources: in-budget funds and two off-budget funds, that is extrabudgetary funds (EBF) and, before 1996, self-raised funds. Their exaction and disposal were governed by different rules and regulations. Table 4.2 shows the relationship between the three, and strikingly, the growth of self-raised funds. Since the in-budget funds were always inadequate, township governments had to resort to more and more off-budget financing.

Townships acquired their own budgets beginning in 1983 after the dismantling of the communes. Until then, all tax revenues were collected by the counties and disbursed by them. (This change in itself entailed the doubling of the number of bureaucrats involved in fiscal work, as shown in Table 4.1.) Township

---

[84] *Xinhua* (Oct. 30, 1998, *SWB-FE*/3372, G/7).
[85] Gansu Sheng Tongji Ju and Gansu Sheng Nongyeweiyuanhui (1997: 175).
[86] Zonghe Jihuasi (1990: 57–60).
[87] *NMRB* (Jan. 20, 1988).

Table 4.2 *Township Finance, 1986–1993*

	1986	1987	1988	1989	1990	1991	1992	1993
Total Revenue	100.0	100.0	100.0	100.0	100.0	100.0	100.0	100.0
Budgetary revenue	83.3	82.7	80.0	75.9	74.6	72.0	71.5	73.8
Extrabudgetary revenue	5.0	4.7	5.6	6.0	6.4	6.9	7.1	6.5
Self-raised funds	11.7	12.6	14.4	18.1	19.0	21.1	21.5	19.8
Total Expenditure	100.0	100.0	100.0	100.0	100.0	100.0	100.0	100.0
Budgetary expenditure	77.5	76.6	74.3	69.4	69.0	66.3	65.9	67.6
Extrabudgetary expenditure	6.4	6.1	7.0	7.2	7.4	7.7	7.6	7.0
Self-raised funds	16.2	17.3	18.7	23.4	23.6	25.6	26.5	25.4

Note: Percent.
Source: Christine Wong (1997: 200), citing data from Ministry of Finance.

governments collected a variety of state taxes (see Table 3.2) but shared them with the counties, and received some subsidies. Complex rules governed revenue sharing, remittances of revenue to the counties, and disbursement of subsidies downward.[88] According to data gathered by Christine Wong, the central government earmarked grants for the support of agriculture, welfare and disaster relief, and administration. In 1993, for instance, the twenty towns and townships of Penglai county, Shandong, received 7.45 million yuan in earmarked subsidies, which financed 23 percent of their total expenditures, the rest being funded from local sources.[89] Wong notes wide variation in the size of these subsidies and she also points to a nationwide trend of reducing subsidies in the name of encouraging self-reliance. In a poor county, such as Puding in Guizhou, revenues increased by 10.2 percent per year between 1988 and 1993, but expenditures grew by only 2.9 percent because subsidies were cut. This situation was of concern because per capita fiscal expenditure in Puding remained very low. At 69 yuan it was only 37 percent of the national average in 1993, and very low compared with some other counties, some of which spent as much as 194 yuan. Pushing an already underfunded county toward self-financing meant prolonging the government's inability to meet its responsibility of providing basic services.[90] Profits from TVEs enabled rich counties to offset the reductions in subsidies; middle-income counties squeezed the peasants, and poor ones such as Puding, which could not extract more from the villagers, were compelled to reduce whatever public services they

[88] Christine Wong (1997: 178–90).
[89] Ibid., 195.
[90] Ibid., 188.

had managed to provide, unless the national poverty program provided some offsetting funds.

The 1994 tax reform – intended to consolidate and rationalize the entire tax system and especially to insure an increasing flow of revenue to the Center – exacerbated the difficulties of subprovincial administrative levels, especially the townships, as major taxes were redirected to the Center.[91] This effect was apparently an unanticipated consequence. Three-fourths of the very significant new value-added tax (including that on TVEs) went to the central government; the rest remained with local governments. Other taxes were also transferred to the national coffers, inflicting real harm on localities. Examples were the tobacco and liquor taxes, which had been major sources of revenue for Guizhou and Yunnan. After the reform, agricultural taxes along with a new land-use tax and a sales tax became the main revenue sources of local governments, increasing their incentives to impose surcharges on the land tax.[92]

The adverse consequences of the 1994 tax reform increased the incentive for local governments to squeeze money from the peasants outside the regular tax system if they were to pay salaries, maintain their services, and implement central government policies. There was enormous variation in the proportion of revenue that came from off-budget sources. A 1996 study of four agricultural provinces – Anhui, Hubei, Hunan, and Jiangxi – in which burdens were heavy, showed that some townships had a 2:1 ratio of off-budget to in-budget financing.[93]

Extrabudgetary and Self-Raised Revenues. In the rural fiscal system, the term "extrabudgetary funds" had a specific, narrow meaning, referring to funds that were raised, managed, and disposed of by government or public units outside of the regular annual budget. Until 1996, "extrabudgetary funds" derived from four categories of revenues in rural areas: (1) centrally approved local surcharges, such as the agricultural surtax, the public utility surtax, the salt tax surtax, the educational development surtax, and the urbanization surtax; (2) revenues from enterprises under the supervision of some central or local government agencies; (3) revenues from administrative sources such as fees, fines, confiscation; and (4) revenues remitted by enterprises such as TVEs that were not under regular budgetary control. Most important from our perspective was the third item, revenues from such administrative sources as road

---

[91] See the 1996 investigation reported in *Zhongguo Caijingbao* (Jan. 21, 1997).
[92] The reform stipulated that the Center would kick back significant proportions of its newly increased revenue, but evidently this hasn't made a difference at the grassroots.
[93] Ketizu (1997: 40–5). In industrializing rural China, high extrabudgetary revenue from TVEs played a major role in local funding. See Fan Gang (1998: 212) and Susan Whiting (2001).

maintenance and transport management fees, school fees, market management fees, and so forth.

"Self-raised funds" as a separate category of off-budget revenues were formally merged into the EBFs in 1996, but as Table 4.2 suggests, they had played a major role in rural public finance before. The line between extrabudgetary and self-raised funds was murky since there was no clear consensus as to what each should include.[94] The origin of "self-raised funds" can be traced back to the early 1950s when the new government allowed townships to raise funds in order to meet needs for roads, school buildings, or water conservation projects, which could not be met by county financing. From 1983 on, townships were allowed to raise still more such funds. In the "Administrative Regulations on Fees and Labor Services borne by Peasants" issued in late 1991, self-raised funds were defined as a supplement to the budget *and* to extrabudgetary revenues.[95] According to the regulation, extrabudgetary revenues in the rural areas included various revenues from TVEs and from fees.[96]

Off-budget Funds and Peasant Burdens. The collection and disposal of off-budget revenues were in the hands of local governments. The funds were theoretically subject to fiscal regulations and laws. They were not supposed to be transferable and were to be used only for the specific purposes for which the money had been collected. In reality, however, it was very difficult to enforce the regulations despite annual "general inspections of fiscal and financial discipline." There were few real constraints on the collection, management, and expenditure of off-budget funds. In Hunan, the township part of the T and V levies was supposed to be managed by the agricultural department of the townships and allocated by the township government. But getting a piece of this pie became the subject of contention among various government agencies. First, the county superiors of the five township agencies that were supposed to receive the funds (education, family planning, civil affairs, communications, and armed forces) forced their township counterparts to turn the money over to them, ostensibly for administration. Second, there was a tug of war to decide which units got what proportion of the pie (despite rules on this). Since the T and V levies constituted 5 percent of peasant incomes, the education departments demanded 1.5 to 2 percent; family planning agencies demanded 0.5 percent; civil affairs demanded that deserving veterans receive the equal of the annual year's average income of households in the township, whereas those in charge

---

[94] For example, according to Chen Dajie and Wu Junpei (1994), income from administrative fees was part of extrabudgetary funds. Qu Liangsheng (1997) lists them as self-raised funds.

[95] See Qu Liangsheng (1997). See also *ZRGYGB* (No. 41, Jan. 7, 1992).

[96] See Chen Dajie and Wu Zunpei (1994).

of assisting poor families wanted to provide each impoverished villager with 70 percent of average peasant income. Faced with these multiple pressures, all the townships could do was to increase burdens.[97]

Conflicting decrees and rules issued by different ministries were in part responsible for these jurisdictional disputes. With regard to the T and V levies, the MOA required that township levies be controlled by the agricultural economy station, but the MOF required that the township finance departments take charge. As of 1996, finance departments in two-thirds of townships controlled these funds; one-third were handled by the agricultural stations.[98]

Townships were not simply troubled by lack of coordination and unified funding. The underlying problem was the acute shortage of funds, which, inter alia, was the result of the extremely costly bloating of staff and of the target and performance evaluation systems. The fundamental reality was that by the later 1990s a huge number of townships and villages ran chronic and rapidly escalating deficits. Even after squeezing peasant households to the maximum possible, townships and villages still found it impossible to meet all their expenses. Indebtedness increased dramatically both at the township and village levels. An MOA study of ten provinces in 1997 showed that the average township had debts of 4 million yuan and the average village, 200,000 yuan.[99] Li Changping, the Hubei township Party secretary quoted in Chapter 3, who wrote to the State Council about burdens, reported that as of the year 2000, township indebtedness was increasing at an annual rate of 1.5 million yuan. Village debts were increasing at an annual rate of 100 to 150,000 yuan. Townships had to pay 15 percent interest on their loans and villages 20 percent.[100] Table 4.3 provides a striking example from Anhui.

EMBEDDED CORRUPTION

Corruption contributed greatly to the burden problem. The political and financial arrangements at the grassroots level created opportunities and incentives to engage in numerous types of corrupt practices, ranging from misuse or diversion of public funds from their stated purpose to outright graft, bribery, or extortion. While peasants felt the pain of being levied and charged, local government agencies and officials often squandered considerable proportions of the money thus raised. Without accountability to their constituents, officials had plenty of opportunities to "use their power for private gain" (*yi quan mou si*).

[97] *Neican Xuanbian* (No. 9, 1997: 8).
[98] Su Ming (1998: 58–62).
[99] *Nanfang Zhoumo* (Aug. 25, 2000).
[100] Wen Tiejun in *Nanfang Zhoumo* (Aug. 24, 2000).

Table 4.3 *Township and Village Indebtedness in Anhui*

	Debt	1997	1998
Township	Total township debt (billion yuan)	3.60	5.90
	Average township debt (million yuan)	1.60	3.04
Village	Total village debt (billion yuan)	4.64	5.16
	Average village debt (thousand yuan)	150.00	169.00

Source: Sun Zifeng (2001:33–5).

As one article put it, "the decision as to how these funds are used is usually a subjective one that depends on the whim of the local authorities."[101] Corruption in the rural areas was evidence of lack of effective control from above and of other institutional shortcomings, especially ill-defined property rights which did not delimit the private from the public sphere. Arbitrary extraction of funds was also a legacy from the collective era when local authorities had the right to requisition peasant property and funds.[102] The salaries of cadres and officials were low and therefore the temptation to garner extra income by means of corrupt practices was high. In the richer areas, newly wealthy private entrepreneurs greatly exacerbated the pressure on cadres to engage in conspicuous consumption. Cadres were pressed by their families, potential marriage partners, and peers to emulate the lifestyle of the wealthy by supplementing their incomes through corruption.[103] The incentives to yield to the temptation were strengthened by the strong likelihood that one would not be caught and by a pervasive "climate of corruption," characterized by the assumption and expectation that everyone was on the take.[104]

An important systemic source of corruption was the ubiquitous requirement imposed by Chinese bureaucratic agencies for permits, licenses, authorizations, and certificates for anyone wanting to start even a small business or to go to the cities to work. The process could become extremely cumbersome. Reportedly, one province had as many as fifteen hundred permits for the vast variety of activities that citizens or foreign investors wished to undertake. The complex approval process was another source of inflation of staff needed to investigate

[101] Tang Ping (1992: 32–4).
[102] Wang Yuexin (1995).
[103] Interview, Hebei, 1997.
[104] On the concept of a culture of corruption, see Melanie Manion (1996).

applications. Most important, it was a major source of corruption, since bribery was a common part of the transaction.[105]

Exposure of corruption at higher levels would always cause an outcry, yet abuse and corruption at the grassroots level in the rural areas often went unnoticed. This is not to say that the central leadership did not seek to root out corruption at the grassroots. Detailed laws and regulations aimed at corruption and establishing good governance were issued from the late 1970s on. In 1997 alone, six new national anticorruption laws and disciplinary regulations were promulgated.[106] Numerous local anticorruption rules were also issued. Moreover, there was an overall improvement in the technical training of legal and disciplinary enforcement agencies, but the hairsplitting details of the regulations made them difficult to enforce at the township level. Most important, corruption showed up in new forms and patterns, especially in informal behavior that was not easy to regulate. Defining illegal actions was not always easy. The boundary between public and private was blurred and provided incentives for officials to impose fines and fees arbitrarily and at will. Some of these funds served to supplement budgetary shortfalls for operating expenses, which could be seen as legitimate, unless the unit's payroll had been padded.

A major opportunity to misuse funds came from the existence of the off-budget funds raised and controlled by the local government agencies. Undoubtedly, some of these funds were spent on developmental projects and served to improve the quality of life of local residents. But a substantial proportion was misused for such unauthorized or illegal activities as wining and dining, giving of gifts, bribes, and embezzlement.[107] According to an investigation of twenty-two township government agencies that collected fees from peasants, 80 percent of all revenues from this source was retained by the agencies, but only a minuscule 4 percent was actually spent on local public projects.[108] Off-budget funds were commonly used to provide staff members with extra bonuses and other income in cash or in kind (such as groceries, local products, and so forth). Some agencies spent the money to buy various consumer goods that were distributed among the staff for free.[109] Sometimes, money from fees or fines was pocketed by individuals in the agency in question rather than becoming part of the off-budget fund, but the more common practice was for the unit in question

---

[105] Interview with a senior editor of *RMRB*, October 2000.

[106] These include, the "Disciplinary Action Rules of the CCP," the "Implementation Measures on Intra-Party Supervision," the "Ethical Code of CCP Cadres," the "Rules Against Luxury Spending," and the "Administrative Supervision Law." See *Liaowang* (No. 18, 1997: 30–1).

[107] Xu Hongbing (1992: 32–3).

[108] Li Wenxue (1997).

[109] Xinwengao (Feb. 1, 1990).

to profit as a unit, as through the purchase of cars, construction of impressive buildings, a major sign of status and prestige, and by holding lavish banquets.

The scope of these abuses was often remarkable. Between 1994 and 1996, a township urban development office, which had several staff members, raised 180,000 yuan from a "town construction supplementary fee," despite clear regulations forbidding such a fee, and spent 150,000 yuan on wining and dining in the same period.[110] The dramatic increase in the number of uniforms worn by law enforcement and regulatory agencies in the last few years is another indicator of how money was spent. In Jiangsu province, 30 percent of the uniformed state agency employees, or 114,972 people, wore uniforms without approval but funded by the agencies nonetheless.[111] In some places, there were as many as forty-two kinds of uniforms; most of those who wore them had some power to extract funds. Hence the popular saying, "forty-two caps (uniformed agents) eat one broken straw hat (peasants)."[112] A familiar situation in the countryside was that, despite the poverty of many ordinary farmers, ostentatious office buildings housing local government agencies were built in the towns, and local officials rode government cars carrying mobile phones in their hands.[113] During a field trip to a rural township in Hebei province in 1994, one of the authors found that whereas the local education bureau had several passenger cars, occupied a good-sized building, and ran a for-profit restaurant, the bureau chief complained about lack of sufficient funding for local schools and their poor equipment.[114] In Hubei province, where peasant burdens were heavy, one county had over four thousand mobile phones, over half of which were used by local officials at a cost of 2,400 yuan, even as the average per capita income was 2,000 yuan.[115]

In 1987 an audit of 3.02 billion yuan in state poverty-relief funds – half of the total allocated in 1985 and 1986 – found that in 995 counties at least 6 percent and probably more was misspent. One hundred thirty three million yuan were diverted for cars, for the building of offices, apartments, guesthouses, movie theaters, and for unnecessary administrative expenses. Financial departments in Shaanxi prefectures and counties levied a 0.5 percent "user charge" and a "management fee" when they allocated economic development funds to poor areas; the money went to buy cameras, tape recorders, and motorcycles. He Yu, the "eating and drinking Party secretary" of Zi'an county, Shaanxi, reportedly

---

[110] *Liaowang* (No. 17, April 1997).

[111] *Jiangsu Jijian* (No. 8, 1993).

[112] See *Sheke Xinxi Wenhui* (No. 13, 1993: 29).

[113] *Neican Xuanbian* (No. 13, 1998).

[114] Author's interview, Hebei, 1994.

[115] *Changjiang Ribao* (March 27, 1997).

Figure 4.4 The person in rags on the left is an official from a well-off county who pleads for unnecessary emergency relief. The one on the right, who wears a suit jacket, is from a poor county and reports fake good news to his superiors for promotion. *Source: Fengci yu Youmo*, No. 12, June 20, 1994.

misappropriated 250,000 yuan of poverty funds, which he used to lead twenty cadres on a thirty-seven-day tour of China's major cities, ostensibly to conduct a survey.[116]

Abuses sometimes took on truly grotesque forms. According to a *Legal Daily* article, in Tongxin county, Ningxia, one of the poorest in the Northwest, various county officials, including county Party secretaries, judges, and procurators, appointed their own schoolchildren who were still in primary school to government posts. One girl reportedly had accumulated years of work from the age of four.[117] Between 1991 and 1998, 340 persons were improperly appointed to state cadre posts. The county's population was 330,000; its table of organization was 2,800, but 11,000 people were actually on the government payroll. This was paid for in part by diverting poverty-relief funds that should have gone to farmers.[118] All these practices pointed to the severe erosion of a sense of public service and financial discipline, and to a lack of accountability. Figure 4.4 lampoons two other kinds of official malfeasance.

[116] *ZTS* (July 3, 1989; *FBIS*, No. 131: 30).
[117] *FZRB* Website (May 28, 2000, *SWB-FE*/3868, G/6–7).
[118] Ibid.

At the village level, financial matters were usually handled without much accountability to the villagers. Bookkeeping was often chaotic.[119] After the annual audit of village finance in 1996, Liaoning province discovered 119.2 million yuan worth of funds spent in violation of financial regulations. Of this amount, 1.3 million yuan was involved in 199 corruption cases.[120] According to an audit of rural public finance in thirteen villages located in seven townships, nearly half the village cadres had embezzled public funds.[121]

Corruption alone cannot account for the burdens, but the public naturally suspected the worst. To peasants, the most obvious and most resented practice involving abuse of village funds was wining and dining (*gongkuan qingke*), especially when involving visitors from higher levels. Villages often spent several thousands, and sometimes tens of thousands, on receiving or entertaining visiting officials from higher authorities.[122] One pretext to justify extraction of money was for the visits of cadres at the county level from whom locals allegedly acquired information of use to the villagers.[123] Perhaps villagers failed to see that in Chinese society any significant transaction required a banquet, but the sums expended were often disproportionate to the benefits gained. In 1988, a Hebei village of 403 households spent 35,000 yuan on eleven feasts. Every individual had to pay 29 yuan for the privilege of watching the cadres eat.[124] In 1989, a Sichuan township investigation showed that sixteen village and township cadres spent 3,754 yuan on banquets over a three-year period. (Reportedly they had to return the money.)[125] According to a seven-hundred household survey, peasant contributions for cadre feasts and gifts increased by 10.7 percent in 1989 alone.[126] Numerous directives forbade these practices but they continued nonetheless. According to some estimates, village cadres nationwide spent some six billion yuan on wining and dining every year in China.[127]

CONCLUSION

This chapter analyzed the institutional foundations which generated both organizational and individual incentives to exact taxes from peasants. These

---

[119] For an exposé of the chaotic state of village funds, see *FZRB* (June 9, 1996).
[120] Sun Jun and Li Yuchen (1998: 38).
[121] See *FZRB* (June 9, 1996).
[122] Li Wenxue (1997).
[123] Interviews, Liaoning Academy of Social Sciences, September 1998.
[124] *RMRB* (June 28, 1989), *ZTS* (July 3, 1989, *FBIS*, No. 131:30).
[125] *NMRB* (Sept. 12, 1989).
[126] *JJRB* (Sept. 25, 1990, *FBIS*, No. 198: 35) and interviews, Liaoning Academy of Social Sciences, August 1998.
[127] Li Wenxue (1997).

institutions, both formal (such as bloated bureaucracy and off-budget public financing) and informal (such as developmental pressures and corruption), contributed in different ways to the peasant burden. We do not wish to suggest that they all weigh equally. Some of them, such as deconcentration of state power, existed in all regions regardless of their developmental and socioeconomic profiles. In regions where this factor was most salient in affecting peasant tax burdens, namely "agricultural China," the weakening of both vertical and horizontal integration of state power gave rise to local government agencies whose financial and political power depended to a great extent on the exaction of off-budget revenues. Other causes such as developmental pressures and incentives had a more direct impact in the grain-producing provinces where peasants had to pay for local economic development and public goods and service provision. In "industrializing rural China" TVE profits provided a substitute, whereas in "subsistence rural China" less could be extracted to begin with, prompting officials to divert state poverty funds. But everywhere, especially in the townships, there was a cancerous growth of local bureaucracies which ate up most available resources and were a major source of burdens. Despite several major efforts to reduce the size of the government, as of 2001 the government bureaucracy at the township level had not been significantly reduced. Given the gross inadequacy of state budgets, funds to pay staff had to be found locally, giving rise to the unique institution of off-budget finance that has helped to offset the budgetary shortage but at the same time has made possible irregular practices to raise unauthorized levies and fees. Finally, corruption among township and village officials added to the burden of the peasants since unaccountable power provided the necessary opportunities. It should be emphasized, however, that the primary source of excessive burdens was systemic, in that even honest officials sympathetic to the plight of the peasants found themselves in situations in which they felt compelled to impose oppressive taxes and fees.

5

Burdens and Resistance: Peasant Collective Action

E XCESSIVE taxes and fees combined with brutal collection methods have led to protest and violence. Forms of resistance fall into two categories, more or less legal efforts to seek redress of grievances, which are examined in Chapter 6, and those clearly illegal, the topic of this chapter. Legal and illegal protest overlapped if only because the rules were ambiguous. Illegal resistance occurred at both the individual and the more serious collective levels. Peasant strategies ranged from evasion of taxes or fees and attempts to delay and postpone payment, to demonstrations, sit-ins, and blockades of roads and railroads, to sacking Party-government compounds, and beating and killing cadres.

Acts of illegal protest and violence, both at the individual and collective levels, have occurred on numerous occasions. By all accounts, they rose in frequency as the 1990s progressed and into the twenty-first century. An authoritative analysis of both urban and rural protest published in 2001 by the Central Committee's Organization Department stated that "frequently hundreds and thousands and even up to ten thousand" have participated, adding:

> What is especially worthy of attention is that at present the frequency of collective incidents (*quntixing shijian*) is rising more and more, their scope is broadening more and more, the feelings expressed are becoming fiercer and fiercer, and the harm they do is becoming greater and greater.[1]

Some of the protests have involved spontaneous eruptions of anger, rage, and despair, but others were strategic in having a clear purpose, to call the attention of higher-level officials, especially the Center, to the peasants' plight in the expectation that officials would act to resolve their grievances. This is one reason why illegal protests often grew out of what had begun as "collective petitioning"

---

[1] Zhonggong Zhongyang Zuzhibu Ketizu (2001: 67, 285).

(*jitishangfang*), group visits to higher authorities – which were more or less legal but frowned on – especially to levels of Party and government above the township. In terms of a principal–agent model, peasants, as clients, appealed to the principals over the heads of local officials, the agents, on the grounds that these agents were violating the policies and directives of the principals.

This chapter first discusses individual-level and collective resistance in the form of brief case studies and one longer one, that of the 1993 riots in Renshou county, Sichuan. It also provides some aggregate statistics. It then discusses organization, leadership, and the goals and demands put forth by the protestors and the incentives and disincentives for engaging in illegal acts. The report of the CC Organization Department just quoted also had this to say about trends in collective actions:

> The organizational level is visibly becoming higher. Formerly, incidents were mostly spontaneous and fairly loose (*songsan*). Now, many have leaders, are organized, and behind the participants there are core elements who exert influence and control. Some even hire lawyers and seek media support.[2]

Trends toward greater coherence of collective actions raise the question of whether rural collective actions were turning into social movements as defined in the literature. If so, the political significance of tax-and-fee protests would clearly be much greater. Although we find that there are constituent elements of social movements in some collective actions, such as the presence of leaders and organizers, they fall far short of qualifying as the term "social movement." This is particularly true when it comes to coordination across space, finding allies and the broader ideological framing of grievances. One of the striking features of protest in China is that there has not been a linkage between urban protesters – the large number of recently unemployed state workers – and their rural counterparts. The last part of the chapter asks why it is that peasant protestors seem to have few allies. Tax-and-fee collective actions were defensive or reactive – reducing burdens satisfied most protestors – and hence did not threaten the regime.[3] A threat could arise if collective protests mushroomed, together with disorders arising from other issues (see below), so as to overwhelm the repressive capacities of the system.

Given the secrecy with which Chinese rulers have treated outbreaks of disorders and disturbances, some remarks about sources are in order. Neither PRC press coverage nor official statements have left doubt about the seriousness of

---

[2] Ibid., 385–6.
[3] Bianco (2001: 86).

rural discontent. Since the mid-1980s the Chinese press has written regularly on this topic and the threat the protests pose to rural stability. In 1987, the journal *Liaowang* wrote of a "rebellious mentality" (*zaofan xinli*) among peasants. The same term was used in a Ministry of Agriculture report on burdens published in 1990.[4] Discontent with burdens was clearly widespread and chronic. Villagers grumbled, groused, complained, and worried about new exactions and how they could cope. Anger often rose to high levels. The existence of overt anger was so well known that it is not necessary to resort to analytical devices such as James C. Scott's "hidden transcripts," that is, the critical and hostile attitudes of ordinary people toward powerful and oppressive elites that they keep hidden but that may suddenly and dramatically burst forth.[5]

The government has not disclosed statistics on type, frequency, and trends on the violent protests that have been occurring in all of China. Even sources that deal quite frankly with the topic only provide some percentages. Thus, in Sichuan province, urban and rural incidents with fifty or more participants rose by 142 percent in 1999 compared to the previous year, while the number of participants rose by 157 percent.[6] Statistics, albeit incomplete, appear in Hong Kong publications, such as *Cheng Ming*, *Kaifang*, or *Ming Pao* which claim access to confidential Chinese sources. Mainland publications, such as *Minzhu yu Fazhi* and *Nanfang Zhoumo* occasionally carry detailed accounts of individual and collective protests. In 1993, the Sichuan Information Office published an account of the Renshou county riots of 1993.[7] The presence of Hong Kong journalists probably prompted this lapse into frankness. In recent years, western journalists have managed to visit places where riots occurred, as in the case of the Ningxiang riot outside Changsha in early 1999.[8] Some journalists telephoned officials in the counties or even townships to obtain some details or at least confirmation of the event. The Information Centre for Human Rights and Democracy in Hong Kong (ICHRD) has also collected data on incidents. Detailed and sometimes graphic accounts of individual-level peasant violence appear sporadically in the Chinese media. Interviewing Chinese researchers and officials has on occasion yielded additional information. On the whole, however, the official media have confined themselves to euphemisms such as "vicious incidents" (*exing shijian*) of villagers being "fiercely dissatisfied" (*qianglie buman*) or "fiercely reacting" (*qianglie fanying*), terms suggestive of violence.

---

[4] *Liaowang* (No.8, Feb. 23, 1987) and Zonghe Jihuasi (1990).
[5] Scott (1990).
[6] Zhonggong Zhongyang Zuzhibu Ketizu (2001: 285).
[7] *ZXS*, Chengdu (June 12, 1993, *FBIS*, No. 112: 28–9).
[8] *NYT* (Feb. 1, 1999).

The regime perceived peasant reactions to excessive burdens as an ongoing threat to social stability. A Center document issued as early as 1985 complained that the Central Committee and State Council had "time and again" called for reducing peasant burdens, only to see them increase.[9] It warned that burdens greatly exceeded peasants' capacity to pay and damaged peasant incentives, that is, their interest in farming. Burdens damaged Party-mass relations and the worker-peasant alliance, lowered the prestige of Party and government, caused severe discontent, and threatened rural stability and public order. Burdens constituted "a major political problem." If burdens were not checked, even greater harm would be done to Party-peasant relations.[10] Similar alarming diagnoses were frequently made in the 1990s.

In March 1993, at the time of the annual meeting of the National People's Congress (NPC), Center leaders were panicked by rural rioting over burdens and IOUs, which reached a peak in that year. The specter that China's history of "officials driving the peasants to revolt" (*guanbi minfan*) might repeat itself reportedly "shocked Zhongnanhai."[11] Wan Li, the outgoing chair of the NPC Standing Committee and one of the pioneers of decollectivization in the late 1970s, reportedly spoke of local "landlords," "despots," and "tyrants," who had undone the work of the land reform of the early 1950s and decollectivization in the 1970s. Wan Li had heard that when some peasants were asked what they needed, the response was, "We need nothing but Chen Sheng and Wu Guang," the leaders of China's first great peasant rebellion in the Qin.[12] In Wan's view, the countryside was in a desperate state. If the state failed to solve the problem, peasants would end up turning against the state and chaos would ensue.[13] Vice Premier Tian Jiyun reportedly told Tianjin city NPC deputies that "If there are problems in the villages, no one in the present regime can hold on to power.... Farmers have been most tolerant. They will not rebel if it has not gone too far. But if they did, the consequences are unimaginable."[14] Also in 1993, State Council investigators reported "with a heavy heart," that "the rural villages have become like a stack of dry firewood and the peasants are stretched to the limit." A provincial-level leader in charge of rural work warned

---

[9] *ZRGYGB* (1985: 1043–6).

[10] See also *Xinhua* (Nov. 1, 1985, *FBIS*, No. 213: K 16–17); *Banyuetan* (No.18, Sept. 25, 1985, *JPRS*-86-015, May 22, 1986: l0–12); *Xinhua* (June 25, 1985, *FBIS*, No. 135: K16). On damage done by burdens to incentives and willingness to invest, see also *RMRB* Commentator (Sept. 7, 1983); *NMRB* (Aug. 8, 1988); *RMRB* (Feb. 14, 1990); and *Xinhua* (Oct. 15, 1990, *FBIS*, No. 202: 31–5).

[11] Sheng Jung (1993: 10–15).

[12] Lu, Yu-sha (1993: 13–14).

[13] *ZXS*, Beijing (July 3, 1993, *FBIS*, No. 128: 34–5).

[14] SCMP (March 22, 1998, *FBIS*, No. 54-1993: 46).

that "when the blowup finally does occur, it may be impossible to set [things] right again."[15]

In retrospect, apocalyptic pronouncements of impending doom were exaggerated. But in the years since, Center edicts have continued to contain somber warnings. In 1996, burdens were causing "extreme anger"; in 1997, they were "a problem that still arouses the most vehement peasant reaction." In that year, Premier Zhu warned officials that "underestimating the strength of the peasants would be to make a historic mistake."[16] In 1998, conditions were "extremely unfavorable to the maintenance of overall social stability."[17] Similar statements were made later as well, as indicated by the report of the Central Committee Organization Department cited above.

INDIVIDUAL AND COLLECTIVE PROTEST AND VIOLENCE

This section presents data in the form of brief case studies of peasant resistance that illustrate the situations in which violent protest occurred and that convey the flavor of these incidents.

Individual-Level Violence. From the late 1980s on, peasant violence against cadres has included beatings, destruction of property, arson, killing farm animals, and cutting down fruit trees. The culprits were hard to detect. Hidden revenge "terrified cadres," some of whom resigned. In Hebei, one Party secretary's property was torched repeatedly for five years. He finally took the hint and quit.[18] Some of this behavior fits one of James C. Scott's concepts of how the oppressed react, that is, with "everyday forms of resistance." Rather than engaging in dangerous public protest or public defiance, peasants adopted the "safer course of anonymous attacks on property, poaching, character assassination, and shunning."[19] But what is striking about this resistance is that much of it was boldly overt in the 1990s. Thus, instances of peasants openly killing cadres occurred, clearly reflecting their intense despair and rage. See Case 5.1.

Case 5.1. In June 1993, the heads of the township and the agricultural cooperative in Fanjing xiang, Santai county, Sichuan, led a group to Wenming village to press for payments. Two cadres entered the house of thirty-year-old Zi Junnai demanding payment. Zi refused because the amount was too

---

[15] Xu Baojian (1993).
[16] Yue Shan (1997: 21–3).
[17] *RMRB-O* (May 7, 1996); *RMRB-O* (April 1, 1997); and *Xinhua* (July 27, 1998).
[18] Wang Chongru (1990) and Huang Jizeng (1990).
[19] Scott (1990: 17).

large. Both cadres ruled against Zi, who then demanded that they leave. They didn't, whereupon Zi picked up a carrying pole, beat the coop chief to death and inflicted severe head injuries on the township chief, whereupon Zi fled. An investigation revealed that the township's peasants had had to pay 86 yuan each in addition to the state tax, their total burden claiming 31 percent of their average incomes.[20]

Chen Daolong, an investigative journalist from the Nanjing paper *Xinhua Ribao*, commented that cases of killing cadres engaged in tax collection were very rare. But he added that some young peasants were prone to brawl and cadres sometimes got killed in the process.[21] Two similar cases that occurred in Shaanxi and Shandong in 1997 and 1998 reportedly elicited the sympathy of villagers who hailed the killers as heroes resisting official oppression. In the Shaanxi incident, the culprit, who killed an entire cadre family, was arrested but reportedly not tried, as he had the support of the villagers.[22]

In some cases, peasants sought to combine suicide with killing. See Cases 5.2 and 5.3.

Case 5.2   Liu Shu, a peasant from a town in Yantai prefecture, Shandong, had refused to pay taxes since 1980 and now owed 470 yuan. During the tax collection campaign in 1993, Liu "publicly announced that he would refuse to pay, while instigating other villagers to do the same." The deputy town head, accompanied by county and township public security officials, came to the village office to pressure him by doing "ideological face-to-face work with Liu Shu," arousing Liu to fury. Ordered to pay on pain of legal sanctions, Liu got hold of seven kilograms of explosives, "wrapped them around his body with a fuse," and blew himself up, killing the deputy town head in the process.[23]

Case 5.3   Wang Yongsheng, a 26-year-old head of a poverty stricken household of three in Linquan county, Anhui, was experiencing unusually severe difficulties because he owed 1,000 yuan in medical costs due to the difficult birth of his son. The area had also suffered from natural disasters. In 1992, the village was exempted from the state tax but not from the T and V levy of 30 yuan. In 1993, new disasters left the family short of grain to eat. Despite this, the village cadres decided to collect the village portion of the township and village levy and to do so in the form of wheat. But they

[20] Chen Daolong (1994: 7).
[21] Ibid.
[22] *SJRB* (Jan. 28, 1998).
[23] *Beijing Qingnianbao* (Jan. 19,1994, *FBIS*, No. 20: 30–1).

did not convene the village assembly to approve this, nor did they notify the households. The town deputy head and seven cadres came to assist in collecting the grain. They threatened that those who failed to hand over the grain that same day would have to give a third more. Wang Yongsheng managed to hand over 120 jin but still owed 48 jin. He wanted to pay this in cash and his wife went to her native village to borrow the money.

The cadres now raised the penalty for laggards from a third to half of the grain specified in the quota. They started to search houses. In one house they found no grain but only an 83-year-old woman, so they took a sheepskin and the family bed. When they came to Wang's house, he pleaded with them not to condemn his family to starvation as the money was on its way. When the cadres started to search, Wang tried in vain to stop them, whereupon he blew himself up in the presence of the cadres. He died but the four cadres present suffered only superficial injuries.[24]

According to the investigative journalist, Chen Daolong, "Not a few peasants resort to suicide to protest the excessive loads and the simple and crude (*cubao*) methods of the collecting cadres."[25] Suicide as a form of protest and resistance occurred in pre-Communist China. As Bianco writes, "one of the most popular ways to take revenge upon a pitiless creditor is to commit suicide before his door," leading to loss of face for the creditor.[26] In contemporary China, instances have occurred of peasants depositing a corpse in front of or in a cadre's house as a way of shaming the culprit. See Cases 5.4 and 5.5.

Case 5.4 In August 1993, fourteen township cadres arrived in a village in Huaiyang county, Anhui, at the request of the village Party secretary and the chairman of the village committee to assist with tax collection. A small team went to the home of two brothers in their fifties, Sun Dachang and Sun Dapeng, who lived hardscrabble lives, and demanded 209 yuan which the brothers didn't have. The team then searched for but did not find grain. Instead, they took a pregnant sow whose piglets the brothers had hoped to sell. The group head, also named Sun, intervened and was told by the Party secretary that the brothers could redeem the sow for 20 yuan, which the group head then lent them.

Before this transaction could be completed, however, the township and village cadres sold the sow and divided the proceeds among themselves. Sun Dachang fruitlessly sought compensation from the village cadres. He

---

[24] Chen Daolong (1994: 7–9).
[25] Ibid., 7.
[26] Bianco (1978: 280, 301). Also Lee and Kleinman (2000: 221–40).

cursed the chairman for his lack of humanity. The chairman responded by saying "If you curse me I'll beat you." Dachang, in despair, prepared to commit suicide. His brother sought to dissuade him, saying that begging was preferable to death. Dachang confronted the Party secretary, threatening to kill himself if they were not compensated. The secretary rebuffed him.

Dachang drank pesticide and became severely ill. His brother sought help but the cadres responded with callous indifference. Finally, the group chief and others carried him to the village dispensary but were told to take him to the township hospital, where he died. His brother claimed the body and deposited it in the Party secretary's house. The frightened and superstitious occupants fled and the body stayed there for four days, when county and township cadres came to settle the matter.

The township eventually paid for the medical and funeral costs of the Sun family and also awarded the surviving brother 1,300 yuan in compensation. However, the Party secretary's family received 8,000 yuan for the emotional pain of having Dachang's corpse in their house. The Huaiyang Party Committee and government investigated the case. The village Party secretary was dismissed and the other cadres were put on a year's Party probation.[27]

Case 5.5 The following story was carried on the front-page of the *Legal Daily* (*Fazhi Ribao*) in 1996. Qiankaiyuan village in Shulan city, Jilin, had signed a contract with its township in March 1995 that called for per capita payments of 49 yuan or 5 percent of average incomes in the township. At the end of the year, however, the township imposed new assessments for eight programs, which increased the taxes to an average of 13.7 percent of township incomes. In low-income Qiankaiyuan village, however, the increase amounted to a total 230 yuan, or 28.5 percent of incomes.

The peasants were extremely angry. In January 1996, twenty people appealed to the Shulan Party Committee's Visits and Letters Office and to the Provincial Discipline Inspection Committee. These authorities instructed the township to take immediate steps to reduce such heavy burdens. The township secretary refused.

---

[27] Chen Daolong (1994: 9–10). Liu Binyan (1989: 148–9), also an investigative journalist, reports a case from 1989, a time when peasants resisted both tax and grain collection, in which a farmer who refused to turn over tax and quota grain, fearing that his family would die of starvation, was arrested and beaten to death while in custody. His family sought to shame the officials by leaving the body to decay outside the township government compound. Despite mediation by the county officials, the body stayed for 260 days.

On January 26, the township deputy head and a group of cadres went to Qiankaiyuan village to cajole the village cadres to start collecting. The village chairman said that if the villagers don't pay, they'll just take goods. An 82-year-old farmer unsuccessfully protested and resisted removal of his tractor. In despair, he drank pesticide and died in the township hospital.

The case prompted a large-scale investigation of the taxation system from the province on down. Township and village Party secretaries as well as government officials were dismissed. The village chairman was expelled from the Party. Administrative penalties were imposed on Shulan city officials, who were also subjected to severe criticism. A judiciary committee was called upon to investigate the case.[28]

Statistics on Cases of Collective Action. From late 1992 to mid-1993, according to Hong Kong press reports quoting internal sources, "more than 170 antigovernment disturbances" occurred in rural areas in up to twelve provinces.[29] According to a 1994 Central Committee document on rural instability, cited by *Cheng Ming*, 6,230 cases of turmoil (*dongluan*), defined as violent collective actions, occurred in the countryside in 1993. In 830 of these cases, five hundred or more people took part and more than one township was involved. In seventy-eight cases, over one thousand people participated. In twenty-one, more than five thousand people participated and in these cases the disorders spread to several townships and even to other counties. "Serious cases" consisted of the burning of county and township Party, government, public security, and bank offices. Eighty-two hundred injuries or deaths of officials and peasants resulted, as well as 200 million yuan in damage. In 340 cases, local police, mobile People's Armed Police, or even PLA units were required to pacify the populace. These forces reportedly suffered 2,400 casualties, including 385 deaths.[30] These incidents were caused by a variety of grievances, but unbearable taxation was a major one. Given the alarmist comments made by central leaders in the spring of 1993, these numbers do not seem implausible.

For subsequent years, similar thumbnail sketches were published.

1. In the first four months of 1994, 2,300 instances of turmoil broke out, of which 370 involved more than 500 participants and more than one township. In 22 cases, more than 1,000 people took part, and in nine cases, over 5,000 people were involved. In these nine latter cases, approximately 5,000 county and township officials as well as peasants suffered injuries.[31]

---

[28] *FZRB* (April 10, 1996).

[29] *FEER* (July 15, 1993: 68–70); *SCMP* (June 27, 1993, *FBIS*, No. 122: 21).

[30] Lu Nong (1994). Lu writes of a total of 1.67 million "cases," but gives no definition.

[31] Ibid.

2. In the fall of 1995, confrontations occurred in 80 townships or villages in 22 counties in Shanxi, Henan, and Hunan, involving an aggregate of 100,000 peasants. Violent clashes reportedly took 100 lives, including 30 officials and 70 peasants. Peasants hurled rocks and Molotov cocktails.[32]

3. In the fall, winter, and early spring of 1996–7, confrontations in the form of parades and demonstrations as well as petitioning erupted in 36 counties in nine provinces, with 380,000 participants. Two hundred thirty were labeled cases of "turmoil, riot, or rebellion."[33]

Between mid-May and mid-June 1997 and again in late July and early August, another major wave of unrest occurred in four provinces involving a reported half a million participants. See Table 5.1.

For 1999, the Information Centre for Human Rights and Democracy in Hong Kong quoted a security official as saying that in all of China, about 100,000 cases of unrest had occurred, while another journal reported 53,000 rural incidents with around 5,352,000 participants. But it did not give details on types of protests. In 2000, major disturbances took place in Jiangxi and again in April 2001.[34]

Cases of Collective Actions. Five types of collective actions appear in the data: collective boycotts or refusal to pay, spontaneous eruptions, actions characterized by a high level of prior organization, collective actions in response to new demands for funds, and violence in connection with collective petitioning. With regard to the first, an instance of collective boycotts occurred in a Hubei village where villagers who refused to pay the T and V levies rose from 5 percent in 1983 to 90 percent in 1989.[35]

An instance of a spontaneous eruption of collective protest took place in May 1987 in Cangshan county, Shandong, as detailed in Case 5.6.

Case 5.6   County leaders had recklessly encouraged farmers to grow as much garlic – a specialty of the area – as they could, based on a forecast of unlimited market demand, which turned out to be a gross miscalculation. Beginning on May 22, farmers brought a record harvest of garlic to the state

[32] Guan Jie (1995).

[33] Li Zijing (1997). For a report on one major outbreak in September 1996 in Qidong county, Hunan, see *SCJP*, November 11, 1996. The Chinese terms for demonstrations, parades, and petitioning are *youxing, shiwei,* and *qingyuan*; turmoil, riot, and rebellion are *dongluan, saoluan, baodong.*

[34] Yue Shan (2000); Agence France Press (August 29 and 30, 2000); *Baltimore Sun* (Feb. 12, 2001), quoting the Information Centre for Human Rights and Democracy, Hong Kong; *Baltimore Sun* (April 18, 2001); *NYT* (April 20, 2001).

[35] *ZXS* (July 12, 1989, *FBIS*, No. 135: 31–2). There were also cases of villagers leaving their homes and hiding when officials arrived to collect taxes or grain.

Table 5.1 *Major Peasant Protests in 1997*

Place	Dates	People Involved	Collective Actions
Anhui	May 20 to June 17, 1997	70,000	Peasants living in 40 townships in five counties in three prefectures staged some 60 incidents. Aside from attacks on official buildings, in two counties, peasants seized guns and ammunition. In Xiaoxian, 500 blocked a cargo train and seized goods, resulting in armed confrontation with the Public Security branch of the railroads. The cost was 40 injuries and 11 deaths, five of whom were police.
Henan	May 17–22, 1997	200,000	In Yiyang and Changde prefectures, peasants in 80 townships in five counties staged 80 incidents of assembly (*jihui*), demonstrations and submission of petitions. In several instances, peasants burned vehicles and attacked county governments. Three deaths and 54 injuries resulted.
Hubei	May 14–19, 1997	120,000	Peasants in 60 townships in four counties in Jingzhou prefecture staged 70-odd demonstrations in opposition to peasant exploitation and official appropriation of peasant fruits of labor. In Tianmen county, 3,000 villagers attacked county Party-government buildings; 90 injuries resulted.
Hubei	July 30–August 2, 1997	200,000	Peasants demonstrated, petitioned, and protested. This involved 12 counties and 75 townships. In 8 of the latter, the protests were labeled *saoluan* and *baodong* (riots and rebellions). The main cause was payment in IOUs, overpriced inputs, and 21 taxes and levies that violated national policy. In one prefecture, peasants looted a local armory and participated in a bloody fight in which more than 40 of them were wounded or killed.

Place	Dates	People Involved	Collective Actions
Jiangxi	Mid-May to mid-June, 1997	100,000	Peasants in three prefectures – Jiujiang, Yichun, and Jian – in 70 townships in five counties staged a hundred protests. Peasants occupied county Party and government buildings, attacked supply and marketing cooperatives, plundering fertilizer and cement. In Yifeng county, 800 people attacked the Public Security Bureau. In some cases, leading cadres from the province and the prefecture were surrounded and had to be rescued by the military.
Jiangxi	July 28 to August 5, 1997	200,000	Peasants in 15 counties and 78 townships staged protests against IOUs, low grain prices, the high cost of inputs, and increased taxes and levies. In four counties, bloody clashes occurred when thousands attacked county Party-government buildings. 200 peasants were hurt, as were 50 Public Security and PAP personnel. In two counties, peasants torched township Party-government compounds. In one of them, Yongfeng, the county Public Security opened fire, allegedly because peasants had explosives, causing 70 peasant casualties.

Sources: Li Zijing (1997: 19–21) and Yue Shan (1997: 21–3).

purchasing stations. The glut prompted the stations to cut the promised purchase price of 0.80 yuan per kg by increments down to 0.04 yuan per Kg. On May 27, an estimated forty thousand peasants crowded into town bringing in cartloads of their product but purchasing stations were ordered to stop buying altogether. The loss of promised income was greatly aggravated by the prior collection of an "avalanche" of fees connected to the growing and marketing of garlic, which included handling fees, transaction fees, quality control fees, and so forth.

Large groups of farmers searched for the county leaders who were afraid to show up. Enraged peasants now went on a rampage. Some shouted: "We are the offspring of Liangshan. It is time for us to rebel." (Liangshan was the lair of the legendary bandits in the novel *Water Margin*.) They smashed window panes, wrecked offices, and looted stores. "All documents, personnel files, and data were torn to pieces or looted and 750 articles of public property were smashed, with a direct loss of some 60,000 yuan."

The superior prefectural Party committee apparently advised letting the riot run its course, which it did for five hours until police reinforcements and a deputy Party secretary arrived. Investigators blamed the riot on the "bureaucratism" of county leaders. The county deputy Party secretary was removed and his boss suspended pending investigation. A handful of "criminal elements" among the protesters was sentenced to terms ranging from one to five years.[36]

The next case, Case 5.7, organized and sustained protest, provides a counterpoint to the preceding case.

Case 5.7 Daolin town in Ningxiang county, outside Changsha, Hunan, had a history of abusive tax collection and resistance. Sometime in 1996–7 farmers from several villages formed an organization, innocuously named "Volunteer Propagandists for the Policy of Reducing Burdens." Each village had at least one member. Members met regularly and studied documents. They used tape recorders to reach households and rented a loudspeaker truck to propagate the official policy of reducing burdens.[37] Similar groups were formed in at least four of the twelve other townships in Ningxiang county. The leaders of these groups were known as "peasant heroes" or "burden reduction heroes."[38] In June 1998, a large and peaceful demonstration was staged in Daolin, which reportedly led to a reduction in school fees, a success that no doubt inspired villagers to engage in further protest.[39]

Organizers planned another rally on January 8, 1999. They put up posters asking peasants to attend. One poster invoked the support of the central leaders for the lightening of burdens: "Resolutely unite around the Center of the Communist Party headed by President Jiang Zemin and Prime Minister Zhu Rongji." Another account claimed that the police planned to arrest the ringleaders and disband the group. On the 8th, approximately four thousand villagers gathered at the town government compound to demand lower taxes and an end to corruption, but before the protest leaders were able to speak, the crowd surged toward the compound.

---

[36] Zheng Ying (1988). Based on a Shandong Party document. A slightly different account appeared in *Zhongguo Fazhibao*, as reported by AFP (July 17, 1987, *FBIS*, No. 197: 01).

[37] *Banyuetan* (*neibuban*) (No. 4, 1999: 10). A western account gives different names, such as "Volunteers for publicizing policies and regulations" and "Association for reducing taxes and saving the nation." See *NYT* (Jan. 16 and Feb. 1, 1999).

[38] *Banyuetan* (*neibuban*) (No. 2, 2000: 8–30). An article reporting on Daolin appears on pp. 8–10. For more on the issue of leadership, see below.

[39] *NYT* (Feb. 1, 1999).

The authorities mobilized an overwhelming force of one thousand police officers and five hundred soldiers. Police ordered the crowd to disperse and used clubs and tear gas. A tear-gas canister killed one peasant; many were injured and hundreds were arrested.[40] A different report claimed that the peasants' efforts to prevent police from arresting the organizers was the source of the clash.[41]

Apparently, protesters reassembled on the following day but were dispersed. A week later, two hundred village representatives petitioned the Changsha government, demanding to know the identity of the officer who had caused the death. Three demonstrations against official violence were held against the Changsha government, which responded by paying the family of the victim 60,000 yuan in compensation. Three of the protest leaders went surreptitiously to Beijing to petition national government offices and to contact the popular investigative TV program *Jiaodian Fantan* (Focal Point), hoping to have their case publicized. They wanted a central work team to be sent to Ningxiang. At the 1999 NPC meeting, Premier Zhu expressed deep concern about rural stability in Hunan and anger at violent repression.[42]

Two leaders hid in the village until summer, when they were arrested. In August, nine organizers were sentenced to terms of from two to six years for attacking government agencies and holding illegal rallies.[43]

Case 5.8 illustrates collective violence in response to cadre violence.

Case 5.8   In 1998, in Liangping county, Sichuan, the chief of Xinsheng town and several cadres from the Land Bureau argued with a farmer, Luo Changrong, who refused to pay land taxes. The cadres beat him and he died two days later. Several hundred villagers carried the body to the town government building. Police sought to remove the corpse. A clash ensued; one villager was killed and others were wounded. The county investigated.[44]

Case 5.9 shows how violence was sparked by new burden demands.

Case 5.9   In Zhouhan township, Hua county, Henan, peasant incomes dropped in 1994, but forcible collection of funds continued. In December 1994, the government started collective fund-raising for road and canal

---

[40] Ibid.
[41] *NYT* (Jan. 16, 1999), *SCJP* (Jan. 15, 1999).
[42] *NYT* (Feb. 1, 1999), *SCJP* (Feb. 1, 1999 and April 3, 1999), and *NMRB* (March 8,1999).
[43] *NYT* (June 16, 1999), Reuters (Aug. 13, 1999), in Current@aol.com.
[44] *SCMP* (Nov. 3, 1998).

construction and also imposed new education fees. Each peasant was required to pay within three days between 120 and 145 yuan. Failure to comply would result in the closing of schools and the dispatch of heads of households to a study class.

On December 26, nearly one thousand peasants attacked the town government. The Ministries of Supervision and Agriculture learned of this and sent a team which imposed Party and governmental disciplinary measures. The article noted that similar incidents (*exing shijian*) had occurred in Hunan and Guizhou.[45]

And finally, violence erupted in connection with collective petitioning. When groups of villagers visited higher-level authorities to seek relief, officials might refuse to meet with their leaders, fob them off with empty, placating promises of investigations, or simply pass the buck by sending them to other offices. In such cases, anger might be publicly voiced, and more villagers might arrive to reinforce their vanguard. Public Security officials might then order the group to disperse and violence would ensue.[46]

The Renshou Riots. These were the most thoroughly reported examples of collective protest in the wave of rural protests in 1992–3. They illustrate the extent of pent-up farmer fury, the ease with which it could be ignited, the rise to prominence of informal leaders, the role of the media in mobilizing farmers, and the interplay between central and provincial directives, local officials, and villagers. As in Case 5.7, Renshou peasants also protested in the name of the Center.

The riots erupted during a period of increasing pressure from both Center and provincial authorities on local officials to undertake genuine burden reduction programs. In June 1992, *Sichuan Ribao* complained about the failure to enforce provincial regulations promulgated in October 1991. Some localities not only failed to reduce burdens but even increased them. The paper also carried a "Notice" from the Provincial Party Committee and Government, dated May 28, annulling any documents that violated Sichuan regulations "without exception."[47] As for central responses, in December 1992, Jiang Zemin and Li Peng both ordered urgent burden reduction measures. On March 19, 1993, a central "Urgent Circular" charged many localities and departments with foot dragging and resistance to cuts. "Peasants were outraged and the stability of the entire society was threatened." The circular ordered a freeze on all exactions

---

[45] Wang Yanbin (1995).
[46] For a complex case of this nature, see Chen Daolong (1994: 11–12).
[47] *SCRB* (June 11, 1992).

"without exception" pending review, excluding only the agricultural tax and the T and V levies, which were to stay within the 5 percent limit. On May 26, the Ministry of Agriculture ordered cancellation of forty-three target-setting and fee-charging programs.[48] The riots took place in the context of these Center actions which favored the peasants.

Renshou is a poor and primarily agricultural county located sixty miles southeast of Chengdu. In 1993 the great majority of its 1.5 million people depended on agriculture. Forty percent of the county's able-bodied labor force was working in the cities. Renshou's annual per capita rural income in 1993 was 680 yuan, far below the national average of 922 yuan. Five percent of the population lacked basic subsistence.

Burdens were high. Each villager had to pay "close to 100 yuan" in exactions, or about 15 percent of 1992 per capita net incomes.[49] Households were paid in IOUs rather than cash for agricultural sales to the state. Post offices also handed out IOUs in the form of "green slips" to villagers who received remittances from migrant relatives. Quite a few villagers had to borrow money from credit cooperatives to pay their fees. Some who did not get loans and couldn't pay on time were fined.[50]

In Sichuan, road building was considered the key to development. In November 1992, the county authorities launched a project to complete paving a segment of Route 213 through Renshou to Chengdu. The road would significantly increase market access and hence was potentially of great benefit to the Renshou populace. It also had the potential of attracting investors to build enterprises in the county.[51] The project cost 145 million yuan, of which 5 million yuan was to be met by grants and 50 million yuan would come in the form of loans from the provincial and city governments. Villagers were expected to contribute 45 million yuan in labor for the two-year project. Each laborer had to pay 30 yuan in cash.

In three districts – the county's 107 townships were divided into 13 districts – some peasant households reportedly preferred to pay in cash because their able-bodied members were away working in cities but remitted part of their earnings. This led the district authorities to believe that peasants had adequate cash reserves. Hence, they asked for cash, intending to contract the road work out to construction crews, thereby eliminating the onerous task of mobilizing peasants to work on the road. The difficulties of collecting money directly from

---

[48] *ZRGYGB* (No.7, May 27, 1993: 286–8), *Xinhua* (May 26, 1993, *FBIS*, No. 33: 33–4).
[49] Chou Wen-tao (1993).
[50] *ZXB* (May 10, 1993).
[51] Pan Wei (1996: ch. 4, 92–4). Professor Pan interviewed in Renshou county in 1994. We are indebted to Professor Pan for shedding much light on the disturbances.

villagers led the authorities to require payment all at once. In addition, the officials raised the road building fee to 55 yuan.[52] Cadres explained that the increment was for investment in TVEs. Peasants believed the add-on was for purchase of official cars. In any event, as the official account put it, "Peasants found it hard to bear such a burden."[53]

Collecting the road construction levy turned into a campaign. One township broadcast to the peasants that they should contribute one hundred catties of rice, even if this meant eating only two rather than three meals a day: "In ordinary times, you don't eat meat twice a day, so pay the road fee and live the way it used to be in the 1950s and 1960s."[54] In their quest for money, township cadres took away TVs, hogs, and grain redeemable when the household in question found the money. Cadres beat peasants with police batons. When a child obstructed the taking of grain by the village Party secretary, he knocked the child to the ground while another cadre tied up the mother. In another township, when a peasant complained that the burden was too heavy, he was handcuffed to a tree for several hours.[55]

Around the turn of the year, a peasant leader emerged: Zhang De'an of Xinmin village, Xie'an township in Fujia district, an educated fifty-two-year-old PLA veteran who "knew state policies and law," and who had often argued with township and village cadres over burdens. Zhang traveled around Fujia, making speeches and posting the rules. He organized classes to educate peasants about their obligations and advised them to resist paying the extra 25 yuan which cadres demanded for TVE development. "As Zhang had the nerve to confront officials and speak the minds of the broad mass of peasants, he was universally supported."[56] In January 1993, Zhang was elected to the people's congress of Xie'an township without having been nominated by the township government. The county prosecutor thereupon tried to have him arrested on a charge of tax evasion.

Zhang publicly tore up the arrest warrant as seven to eight hundred peasants carrying farm tools and shoulder poles gathered in Xie'an township. They drove the arresting officers out and burned a police vehicle. Violence erupted in Xie'an township in January and February. Stores closed and the government was paralyzed. "Hundreds of peasants were said to have been involved in a 'guerrilla war' of throwing stones."[57] Farmers marched to the

---

[52] Ibid., 95.
[53] *ZXS*, Beijing (June 12, 1993, *FBIS*, No. 112: 28–9), by Sichuan Government Information Office.
[54] Pan Wei (1996: 97) and *ZXB* (May 10, 1993).
[55] *ZXB* (May 10, 1993).
[56] Chou Wen-tao (1993) and Pan Wei (1996).
[57] Pan Wei (1996).

county seat and jostled into the government compound, loudly demanding justice.[58]

This popular mobilization aroused the Sichuan Party and government leaders to send a work team to Renshou in February. Given the national offensive on excessive burdens, the provincial and Renshou county officials "affirmed that Zhang De'an was reasonable in giving publicity to the policy about lessening peasants' burdens and calling on people to refuse to pay the excess cash levy." Zhang De'an, enjoying provincial support, became a recognized leader who spent days "negotiating with different levels of important officials on behalf of his peasants."[59]

Under provincial guidance, the Renshou leaders decided to stop collecting the highway levy and turned funds already collected into an investment pool paying 7.2 percent interest, repayable after completion of the highway project. They also decreed that the peasants should pay for the road with labor only whose value would be included in the official 5 percent T and V levy. The county government sent twenty-one work teams to the villages to implement the burden reduction policy. It sent 2,100 copies of "Explanations on Applying the Laws on Managing Peasants' Burdens in Sichuan Province" to the townships and villages. The county ordered a freeze on all fee collections exceeding 5 percent of average per capita township income in accordance with national rules. The plan for burdens for 1993 was set at 4.8 percent. "Serious measures" were also taken to correct cadre work style. "District and township cadres were required to visit peasant households [and] build close ties" with them. According to the official account, tranquillity was restored in March and April. As the work teams left, peasants celebrated their victory, setting off firecrackers.[60]

Rumblings of discontent continued, however, over the application of the 5 percent rule. As Pan Wei observes, "There was no way for rural cadres accurately to calculate the 1992 per capita net income of every peasant household."[61] Many arguments erupted. Fees beyond the 5 percent limit continued to be collected, if only because some of them had been set by higher levels, including Center ministries (see Chapter 4). "Many" local cadres believed these fees were legitimate and continued to collect them.[62]

The Center's March 19 "Urgent Circular" clarified this point in that it proscribed the collection of any fee beyond the 5 percent level, pending review. Some townships, however reportedly sought to prevent the peasants from learning

---

[58] Chou Wen-tao (1993).

[59] Ibid.

[60] *ZXS*, Chengdu (June 12, 1993, *FBIS*, No. 112, 1993: 28–9) and *SCMP* (June 13, 1993).

[61] Pan Wei (1996: 100).

[62] Sheng Jung (1993).

about the circular. The plausibility of this is buttressed by a *Sichuan Ribao* article of January 3, 1993, which complained that some localities in the province were treating burden regulations as an internal document to which peasants did not have access. One report claimed that some townships cut off electricity during news broadcasts to block access.

New peasant spokespersons emerged. One, Xiang Wenqing, posted the "Urgent Circular" and provincial documents in "nearly every village of Fujia district," prompting police to arrest him on March 28. During the arrest, he shouted, "Long live the CCP," whereupon his captors put a handkerchief over his mouth. Onlookers angrily demanded his release. Peasants posted a slogan: "Jiao Yulu, Li Xiangnan, where are you?" Jiao was a national model from the 1960s who cared for the peasants and Li a popular TV actor who portrayed such models. On April 3, more than ten thousand peasants gathered in Fujia town to celebrate "the Center's voice," shouting "Long live the Communist Party."[63]

Apparently because of this agitation, Sichuan's deputy governor, Liu Changjie, came to Renshou, walked five kilometers with a crowd of Fujia peasants, visited poor families, and ate a meal in Zhang De'an's home. As he departed, several thousand peasants spontaneously gathered and lit firecrackers to encourage him to help them. No doubt this event contributed to their belief that the higher authorities were on their side. Xiang Wenqing was released.[64]

Serious rioting resumed in late May and reached a peak in early June. According to the Sichuan Information Office, the turmoil was precipitated by two false articles published on May 10 in *China Consumer News* by two TV journalists. The articles charged Renshou county officials with concealment of Center directives from farmers and with continued defiance of the "Urgent Circular" by imposing irregular levies on peasants. The paper proclaimed: "No one is allowed to defy the Center's 'Urgent Circular,'" attacking local officials. As Pan Wei put it, "The article thus painted Renshou leaders as a gang of bullies resisting the central and provincial governments' orders."[65]

Zhang De'an apparently having dropped out of the picture, Xiang Wenqing, together with seven others, made more than a thousand copies of the *Consumer News* article, sold them to farmers for 40 *fen* each and posted them on walls and trees in Fujia district. The impact of the inflammatory *China Consumer News* accusation was exacerbated by publication of new central documents on May 26, which detailed lists of fees for forty-six target-setting programs that had to be canceled. Previous Center documents had not provided such specific

[63] *ZXB* (May 10, 1993).

[64] Pan Wei (1996: 100–1).

[65] See *ZXB* (May 10, 1993) and Pan Wei (1996: 102).

detail. The charge made by *China Consumer News* that Renshou county officials were deceiving farmers seemed borne out, undermining the morale of Renshou cadres: "The central authorities have betrayed us."[66]

Just as the new Center documents ordered large-scale cutbacks in fees, *Sichuan Ribao* published an article on May 27 that reassuringly praised Renshou's burden reduction efforts and claimed that cadre-peasant relations had improved. The article noted that whereas in January the county had received thirty-nine letters and nine visits by complainants, only three letters and two visits were registered in April and none in the first half of May. The article was apparently written in rebuttal to the *China Consumer News* charges. (On June 3, *China Consumer News* published the *Sichuan Ribao* article, presumably on higher-level orders.)

Xiang Wenqing allegedly manipulated the article to fan farmer demands and anger. He and others insisted that even the "reasonable" 4.8 percent levy be rescinded and that refunds be given for levies paid since the institution of household contracting. Farmers said: "According to the regulations announced by the central authorities, we have already paid taxes and levies up to the year 2000." The county budget was running a 20 million yuan deficit at the time and could not possibly have met these demands. Xiang exhorted the masses: "The central newspaper is now supporting us. If we do not take action now, when should we? We must give them hell (*zheng si*), and we must destroy the county Party committee and county government. We must organize and send ten thousand people to Beijing to lodge our complaints."[67]

Large-scale riots erupted in Fujia district in late May and early June. Farmers beat cadres, attacked police, held some hostage, and smashed or burned all cars in sight. "Serious incidents" of "beating, smashing, and looting" occurred. Ten to fifteen thousand farmers surrounded the Fujia government offices. Some broke into the compound and excoriated and beat forty to sixty cadres. The streets of Fujia town were packed with villagers. Peasants carried "pitchforks, rods, and placards."[68] In Huafang township, angry peasants took a deputy Party secretary hostage. There was looting, arson, and stone throwing.[69]

Leshan city and Renshou cadres went to Fujia seeking to mediate but instead were beaten. One plainclothes policeman was held in a minivan for more than ten hours. Unidentified "peasant leaders" dissuaded the crowd from setting the vehicle on fire. Finally, county police found "a few known ruffians" – also

[66] Sheng Jung (1993). Jung Sheng reported on the riot from Renshou.
[67] Sheng Jung (1993) and Pan Wei (1996).
[68] Sheng Jung (1993).
[69] Pan Wei (1996: 104).

unidentified, but possibly indicative of ties between police and village thugs –
who freed the captive at knife point.[70]

Reportedly, the Central authorities set up a hotline to Renshou. The provincial
Party committee formulated two plans, the first of which was to take a soft
line, mediate, and calm the peasants, and only arrest the ringleaders. A second
plan would become operative if the first one failed and if Renshou county fell
"into peasant hands." If this were to happen, the Renshou case would have
to be handled as a "contradiction with the enemy," invoking Chairman Mao's
distinction between conflicts "among the people," which could be handled by
persuasion and those with enemies, which would necessitate the use of force, the
mobilization of armed forces to suppress the rising "at all costs."[71] Access to the
county was closed because people from other places were coming, perhaps to
support the Fujia rioters.[72]

On June 6, an attempt was made to arrest Xiang Wenqing and seven other
ringleaders. Nine detachments of PAP and ordinary police succeeded in arresting four, including Xiang, in surprise raids on their homes, but the rest could
not be detained because hundreds of peasants protected them. One detachment
radioed for reinforcements, and tear gas was fired, whereupon farmers threw
rocks and bricks, forcing the detachment to retreat.

The riot subsided without the authorities taking the drastic steps envisaged
in the second plan. The official account claims that the authorities acted with
great restraint in the belief that farmers had a genuine grievance and that on the
whole, the riot was a "contradiction among the people," not with the "enemy."
Reportedly, no farmers were injured, but numerous cadres and police were.[73]
Arrests were aimed at those who had committed acts of "beating, smashing, and
looting," but most farmers were exonerated. Xiang Wenqing and Zhang De'an –
who apparently had also been arrested – were released in 1994. The Fujia and
Huafang Party and government leaders were dismissed. The province allocated
a fifty million yuan emergency fund to highway 213, thereby obviating a peasant
contribution.[74] In 1994, a new county Party secretary was appointed, transferred
from neighboring Pengshan county where there had been no rioting. Some
Renshou villagers reportedly had asked their Pengshan compatriots to join in
the protests, but they refused on the grounds that their burdens had been imposed
legally and with their participation. An elected village committee had involved

---

[70] Sheng Jung (1993).

[71] Ibid.

[72] O'Brien and Li (1995: 763), quoting a rural researcher.

[73] *ZXS* (June 12, 1993) and Sheng Jung (1993).

[74] Pan Wei (1996: 104).

villagers in the discussion and management of their burdens, thereby reducing anger.[75]

How close did rural collective actions come to qualifying as "social movements," as analyzed in literature such as Sidney Tarrow's *Power in Movement*?[76] We do not claim that collective peasant protest and resistance in China actually were social movements, but the concept provides a yardstick, crude to be sure, against which to appraise peasant protest. Social movements are contentious "collective challenges by people with common purposes and solidarity in sustained inter- action with elites, opponents and authorities," who find it difficult or impossible to press their claims within normal channels, if only because their demands are not acceptable to established authority and hence are perceived as posing a chal- lenge.[77] In western democracies, such causes as civil rights, the environment, and women's liberation gave rise to social movements. In communist Poland, the trade union, Solidarity, became a full-scale movement. The East German peace groups that functioned with the support of Protestant churches were incipient social movements, which in 1988 and 1989 took on a greater but short-lived role in the transition from communism.[78] Peasant social movements in Third World countries such as Guatemala have played important roles in struggles for land, human rights, and social justice.[79]

Major propositions about such movements include the following: (1) Social movements arise when the "political opportunity structure" (POS) of those hitherto excluded from the political process changes, lowering the risks and costs of engaging in collective action. (2) Typically, social movements are loosely organized, often lacking strong formal structures. Leaders – "polit- ical entrepreneurs" – tap into social networks and face-to-face groups, and mobilize solidarities based on recognition of common interests. It is social sol- idarity that differentiates social movements from James C. Scott's everyday forms of resistance, for example, "footdragging, petty sabotage, backbiting and tricks" by individuals, although such acts, as Tarrow notes, may develop into collective actions. (3) Social movements engage in disruptive and destabilizing actions which can turn into violence depending on the state's propensity and

[75] Epstein (1996: 416).
[76] Tarrow (1994).
[77] Ibid., 2–3.
[78] Kamenitsa (1998: 313–33).
[79] See, for instance, Brockett (1991: 253–74).

capacity for repression.[80] (4) Social movements shape specific grievances into broader claims, for example, from integration at lunch counters to demands for civil rights as a whole, a process which requires the building of coalitions with various allies and potential supporters and allows the movements to gain momentum without which they could easily lapse into quiescence. In premodern times in Europe, movement formation was limited because claims were specific, localized, segmented, and therefore short-lived. As Tarrow notes, in writing of premodern France, "The major constraint on turning these grievances and the collective actions that they triggered – food riots, land occupations – into social movements was the limitation of the forms and goals of collective action to people's immediate claims . . . and direct targets."

Modern movements, in contrast, have overcome the episodic and localized nature of premodern protest by using new means of communication and new repertoires of collective action, although memories of past modes of protest still exert some influence.[81] In Central America, for instance, allies and support groups played a critical role in enabling peasants to assert themselves collectively. These came from church activists, trade unions, parties, people engaged in local development projects, as well as guerrillas, whose mobilizational efforts fostered a change in the peasants' fatalistic outlook and hence facilitated establishment of peasant organizations.[82]

The following sections apply some of these concepts to the Chinese case, including the concept of political opportunity, the demands and goals of tax-and-fee protesters, the intensity of repression, leadership, organization, and the question of allies. We make three major points. The support by central leaders for burden reduction was a key component of peasants' POS, legitimating protest, but at the same time serving to confine peasant demands to remedial measures rather than for broader political change. Second, protests against financial burdens largely lacked sustained leadership, organization, and capacities to coordinate protests, but there are some signs of change in this regard. Third, in successful social movements diverse grievances are aggregated into a broader program, which serves as the basis for the forging of broader protest coalitions. Tax-and-fee protesters did not link up with those peasants who harbored different grievances against the authorities. Nor was there any linkage between rural and urban protestors, which could have greatly enhanced the prospects for the emergence of a major social movement. Nor did most tax-and-fee protest take on a distinct ideological coloring.

[80] Tarrow (1994: 19, 101).
[81] Ibid. 20, 39.
[82] Brockett (1991: 258).

Political Opportunity Structures. Movement theorists argue that grievances and deprivation are far more widespread than instances of collective action. Hence, favorable political opportunities are needed which potential organizers can use to mobilize people.[83] In rural China, new opportunities for villagers to engage in unauthorized activities arose from China's rural reforms themselves and the modernizing changes that they brought. The reforms altered the political environment, providing new opportunities to engage in collective action. Peasants' social and political space widened with decollectivization. They acquired greater control over resources and became less dependent on the collectives. No longer bound to the land, they enjoyed increasing mobility. Villagers had greater access to outside sources of information such as newspapers and television which increasingly penetrated even into the remote countryside. This reduced their dependence on local officials who had an interest in preventing ordinary people from learning about national policies and rules. Peasants also acquired a greater capacity to reproduce and disseminate information, as seen, for instance, in the case of the Renshou riots. Political reforms such as village democratization and the opening of legal avenues further expanded the space in which villagers could maneuver.

The most important resource that emboldened villagers to engage in strategic, rational collective action was the belief that the central authorities themselves opposed excessive burdens and therefore sided with them against their own agents. When peasants learned about Center policies and laws, they were emboldened to assert themselves, perhaps peacefully at first, but if appeals failed, resorting to violence. Central leaders' assurances that they did care about the plight of the peasants added to peasants' incentives to engage in what Li Lianjiang and Kevin O'Brien call "rightful" resistance.[84] The Center authorities naturally did not deliberately encourage illegal collective actions, which were an unanticipated consequence of the shortage or ineffectiveness of legal modes of securing redress. Nevertheless Center signals held out promise that when peasants protested on a large enough scale, a response from them would ensue. For instance, during the July and August 1997 riots in Jiangxi and Hubei, NPC Chairman Li Peng sent a powerful work team to investigate. It ordered payment of all IOUs and abolished twenty-one taxes and fees. It also ruled that most peasants who took part were not to be held responsible. Premier Zhu accused the provincial leaders of the two provinces of dereliction of duty and ordered swift punishment of "local tyrants" in authority. "In the majority

---

[83] Tarrow (1994: 81, 18).
[84] Lianjiang Li and O'Brien (1996: 28–61), O'Brien and Li (1995: 756–83), and O'Brien (1996: 31–55).

of cases," Zhu acknowledged, peasants engaged in violent protest because of the acts of local government leaders who violated central policies and were corrupt.[85] The hope for such higher-level intervention encouraged villagers to assert themselves.

The Renshou county riots were by no means the only example in which Center documents played an important mobilizing role. Three years later a similar large-scale drama played itself out in Qidong, Hunan. This time a traveling villager brought back a copy of provincial "Document 9" which demanded that local authorities reduce burdens. Copies of the seven-page document sold for as much as 10 yuan. It was read aloud to peasants before movie showings. When towns and townships persisted in assessing excess levies and continued to use brutal methods, demonstrations erupted under the slogan "implement the provincial Party committee's Document Number Nine, relieve the peasants' burdens." Protests escalated, prompting violent suppression, but eventually the peasants were propitiated and pacified.[86] In the Ningxiang county disturbances in early 1999 (see Case 5.7) central leaders and policies were also invoked. The riots in August 2000 in Jiangxi were reportedly inspired by a booklet of central documents of which a sympathetic editor of a Jiangxi journal published twelve thousand copies, which were eagerly bought up by villagers (see Chapter 6).[87]

Peasants' positive orientation toward the authorities turned more and more negative as they moved down the hierarchy, as this verse suggests:

> At the Center the sky is blue,
> in the provinces clouds are gathering,
> in the counties there is flooding,
> in the townships people are drowning
> and are running for their lives.[88]

This helps to explain cases of violence that occurred in the course of peasant searches for help from higher levels using such channels as collective petitioning. Peasants needed to be able to inform the higher levels of the hierarchy of their plight. But since the township cadres, against whom the peasants were complaining, had an interest in preventing information from reaching the higher-level authorities, violent efforts at communicating grievances sometimes resulted. Illegal forms of protest such as sit-ins or blocking automobile

---

[85] Yue Shan (1997).

[86] *Ming Pao* (Nov. 8, 1996, in *SWB-FE*, 2765G/4–5), based in part on the Qidong county Office for Relieving Peasant Burdens.

[87] See *Nanfang Zhoumo* (Oct. 12, 2000) for a report on the publication of the handbook.

[88] Yang Hao (1999: 90). See also Li and O'Brien (1996: 43). A 2001 survey by Li Lianjiang confirms this. See Li Lianjiang (2001).

or railroad lines were often the only way to get attention from higher-level authorities.[89]

Demands and Goals. The peasants' positive orientation toward the Center legitimated but also limited protests. Most evidence suggests that their demands were specific and narrow. Peasants wanted relief, concrete tangible reductions in burdens, and perhaps punishment of abusive officials. If these were granted, they were satisfied and protest subsided. Their actions, in other words, were defensive in nature. In Renshou, when burden reduction was implemented and steps were taken to curb cadre abuses, protests ceased. Because many villagers had faith that the Center was on their side, they did not challenge the regime as such. Invoking central rules limited peasant demands to remedial ones in line with those rules. Peasants wanted to restore a proper balance between the claims of the state and their own. They had always "obediently" paid their taxes, but the burdens and price scissors "have forced the broad masses of peasants not only to negate the tradition but to go against it."[90] This mind-set built on a long tradition of tax resistance against illegitimate extractions.[91]

Limited demands were probably also conditioned by fear that protestors might be accused of counterrevolution or trying to overthrow state power. They no doubt remembered the fierce class struggle against enemies under Mao and may well have known of current harsh punishments for subversive crimes. Villagers' tactics of clothing protest in the authority of the Central Committee and State Council undoubtedly made it more difficult for local officials to assign negative political labels to such acts. But this limitation also meant that tax-and-fee collective actions did not turn into social movements, which would have required that demands be broadened and generalized to attract larger and diverse support.

This is not to say that peasants did not want political reforms. The Shandong peasant quoted in the Introduction prefaced his complaint about the lack of accountability in taxation and fund-raising with the statement "we also want democracy."[92] As noted in Chapter 7, demands for village and township democratization were related to peasant demands for accountable officials. Many peasants looked to the law for protection from abuse (see Chapter 6).

In contrast, Hong Kong sources claiming access to internal documents report that more radical political demands were voiced in many places. In the disorders

---

[89] Interview, September 10, 1998.
[90] *NMRB* (Sept. 23, 1988, *FBIS*, No. 193: 25–7).
[91] See R. Bin Wong (1997: ch. 10) on tax resistance.
[92] *NMRB* (January 20, 1988).

in Shanxi, Henan, and Hunan in the fall of 1995, rural underground organizations reportedly adopted political slogans that aimed at peasant autonomy and emancipation from the control of outsiders: "All wealth of the land should go to the peasants"; "end the exploitation and oppression of the peasant class"; and "long live the peasant communist party and the unity of the peasants."[93] In August 1993, about two thousand villagers from seven villages in Qingyang and Ningguo counties in southern Anhui reportedly held prolonged meetings to protest the issuance of IOUs and other abuses. Some township cadres took part, displaying banners similar to the ones already mentioned. Others read "down with the new landlords of the 1990s," and "[oppose] the 10,000 taxes" of the CCP.[94] In the May–June 1997 disturbances in Jiangxi, some county and village cadres reportedly put up these slogans: "Down with the urban bureaucratic exploiting class," "divide the wealth of the new rural despots," and "establish peasant political power."[95] In the July and August disturbances, slogans were said to have included "down with the county bosses" or "down with the county tyrants." In Lianhua county, peasants called for a "third revolution," the first having been land reform and the second decollectivization.[96] These slogans were political, transcending the tax-and-fee issue, and some were directed against the existing political order. In the absence of confirming indicators from the mainland, these reports must be treated with caution. What is interesting about them is that the demands were directed against the cities rather than toward alliances with them, indicative of deep rural resentment of the urban sector.

Repression. Collective protest probably was also encouraged by the regime's ambivalent approach to the repression of outbreaks. As Charles Tilly notes, a high risk of repression and severe punishment is a strong deterrent to participation in collective action, especially violent action. Conversely, awareness of governmental reluctance or incapacity to use force stimulates participation.[97] In the Chinese countryside, the swiftness, certainty, and harshness of repression and punishment appear to have attenuated in the later 1980s and into the 1990s, certainly in comparison, not only with the ferocity with which suspected "counterrevolutionary" acts were handled during the Maoist period, but also

---

[93] Guan Jie (1995: 18–19). The Chinese for these slogans is, in order, *"tiandi caifu yiqie gui nongmin," "jieshu dui nongmin jieji de boxue he yapo,"* and *"nongmin gongchan dang wansui; nongmin jieji tuanjie wansui!"*

[94] "Anhui nongmin kangshui shijian" (1993). The Chinese terms are *"dadao jiushi niandai de xin dizhu,"* and *"gongchan dang wan shui."*

[95] Li Zijing (1997), citing *Neican* of Xinhua News Agency. The terms used were *"dadao chengshi guanliao boxue jieji," "fen xiangcun xin diba de caifu,"* and *"jianli nongmin zhengquan."*

[96] Yue Shan (1997).

[97] Tilly (1978: 158).

in comparison to the early reform period. Elizabeth Perry, writing about the early 1980s, points to the Party-state's "impressive coercive capacity" in the countryside, enabling it swiftly to suppress rural unrest.[98]

For several reasons both the capacity and the propensity swiftly to crush collective resistance declined. First, within the villages, the political control system became significantly less intrusive than it had been in Maoist times. Mass campaigns, punitive class labeling, and class struggle ended. The major mission of village organizations became economic development and the pursuit of prosperity. Intravillage social control institutions such as the security defense committees first set up in 1954 often became inactive. Security officials complained about the slackness of networks of supervision and the difficulty in mobilizing villagers to guard against unauthorized behavior.[99] The widespread practice of township mobilization of "shock detachments" that invaded villages to enforce tax collection was testimony to the lack of enforcement structures in the villages able to protect individual tax collectors.

Second, public security organs also were lax in rural law enforcement. The overall decline in the effectiveness of the Chinese state in the reform era weakened the ability of rural public security to control protests, crime, and social disorder. An official from the Ministry of Civil Affairs interviewed in 1992 observed that public security officials at the township and county levels tended to be reluctant to intervene in armed feuds and quarrels within the villages.[100] Lax public security not only opened space for villagers to protest but also gave rise to increasingly vociferous complaints about the inability of the authorities to protect them from gangs, the kidnapping of women and children, and robberies, the incidence of which rose greatly in the later 1980s and the 1990s. At the 1993 NPC session, 160 (or one-third) of all motions submitted by deputies dealt with social order. Deputies voiced villager complaints about lack of police protection, the poor quality of law enforcement, and the frequency with which criminals could bribe their way to freedom.[101] But when public security and judicial organs did enforce the law, appalling instances of cruelty and corrupt abuse of power often occurred, as we have seen.

In major cases of collective protest, such as the "garlic riots" in 1987 (Case 5.6) and the Renshou riots in 1993, the response of the police was slow, hesitant, incompetent, and ineffectual. In Renshou, mobs were able to surround, beat, and hold police hostage without eliciting a massive show of force.

---

[98] Perry (1985: 192).
[99] See *Renmin Gonganbao* (May 25, 1995, *FBIS*, No. 183: 24–5); *Xinhua* (Dec. 21, 1995, *FBIS*, No. 247: 26–7), and *NMRB* (June 22, 1993, in *JPRS*-071, Sept. 23, 1993: 42–4).
[100] Interview, Beijing, June 1992.
[101] *NMRB* (June 23, 1993, *JPRS*-071, Sept. 23, 1993: 42–4).

Elsewhere, when farmers attacked cadres, police protection was not necessarily available: "The masses beat cadres, who complained in vain, further encouraging the masses."[102]

As social instability became a growing regime concern in the 1990s, major efforts were made to strengthen the security apparatus, the police, the People's Armed Police, township-based militias, and also local PLA garrisons. One goal was to develop the capacity for rapid deployment of overwhelming force; another, to train in riot control techniques that would obviate the use of massive, lethal force as at Tiananmen.[103] The thumbnail descriptions given in Table 5.1 indicate a high degree of police mobilization. In early 1999, the Ningxiang disturbances (see Case 5.7) elicited the deployment of a reported one thousand police and five hundred troops. They used clubs and tear gas, resulting in one death.

In another case, in late November 1998, seven hundred police were sent to Shaocun village in Weixian county, Hebei, a poverty-stricken area, to arrest four "criminals" accused of having obstructed officials in the performance of their public duties. The Weixian county Party committee decided on the crackdown because it felt that problems in Shaocun village were undermining the stability of the whole county. This village had a long history of cadre-peasant tensions going back to 1989, when cadres had contracted an orchard out to themselves, yet required all villagers to pay the special products tax. Because one of the four "criminals" had lodged complaints with higher levels, his house was searched and his property confiscated. Villagers complained that the conflict with cadres was due to the lack of democracy. Elections for the village committee and within the Party branch had not been held in twenty years. When the police came, they carried a lot of rope and handcuffs, indicating intent to arrest numerous people, not just the four suspects. A clash with villagers ensued in which police fired fifty-three shots, killing one of the suspects and wounding five others. They also inflicted beatings. Provincial-level agencies investigated the incident.[104] And in a Jiangxi riot in April 2001, two peasants were killed by police and seventeen injured.[105]

Chinese officials were divided over the issue of how far to go in cracking down. In November 1997, a Sichuan Party secretary spoke about an incident in which peasants in Zhongjiang county had vandalized the township government compound and the police station. "Because of this, some comrades advocated

---

[102] *NMRB* (May 9, 1989) case from Anhua county, Hunan.
[103] Shu Szu (1993: 34–5, in *FBIS*, No. 63: 28–30).
[104] Lian Jimin (1999).
[105] *NYT* (April 20, 2001).

sending troops, but I resolutely disagreed. I believe that the peasants were not rebellious, but simply angry about some of our work." He blamed the township leaders for angering the peasants. They had delayed paying peasants for their grain while insisting on early tax payments.[106]

In April 1998, the State Council promulgated regulations on how to deal with rallies, parades, demonstrations, and petitions. These forms of protest were rapidly increasing, and in some cases local authorities were unable to handle them. Each outbreak was to be analyzed by differentiating between those that constituted "contradictions among the people" and those that involved "contradictions with the enemy," using Mao Zedong's distinctions. An immediate report was to be made to the central and provincial authorities. Most cases, according to the document, fell into the within-the-people category in that they were apolitical, unorganized, and not premeditated. Such cases were often characterized by misunderstanding or dissatisfaction with government work and policies. They might have been caused by encroachments on the masses' legitimate rights and interests or failure to find a legal and reasonable solution to their grievances, but they could also be the result of unreasonable peasant demands that could not at present be met. In such cases persuasion was to be used, lawful grievances were to be resolved, and bureaucratic styles of work corrected. The goal was to pacify the masses and avoid exacerbating and escalating the outbreak.

Cases which had a hostile component included those in which protestors resorted to violence, engaged in "beating, smashing, and looting" (a phrase from the Cultural Revolution), attacked organs of Party and government, and blocked railroads, roads, or bridges. Hostile cases were also those characterized by political organization and goals, linking up (*chuanlian*) with people in different jurisdictions and departments, or by connections with "hostile forces" within China (that is, dissidents) and from the outside world. The 1998 document focused special attention on those who organized and planned collective actions and on their political backgrounds, and called for arresting the ringleaders. But it did not specify whether all cases of peasant organization should be treated as "hostile."[107] Three years later, an assessment by the Central Committee's Organization Department claimed that as "contradictions among the people have become visible rather than hidden, enhanced contradictions of an antagonistic character (*duikangxing*) have become a prominent feature" of incidents.[108] As collective protests increased in numbers, size, and organization,

[106] Chen Weihua (1998: 28–31).
[107] Li Zijing (1998: 17–18).
[108] Zhonggong Zhongyang Zuzhibu Ketizu (2001: 67–8).

suspicions arose that conspirators and plotters must be at work, suspicions well-rooted in Communist political culture. In any event, the guidelines left much of the interpretation to the discretion of local officials. Judging by the Ningxiang county example, some local authorities were quick to assign an enemy label and therefore to resort to force. An additional factor favoring harshness was the "strike hard" campaign against crime then in progress.

Premier Zhu Rongji's 1999 Work Report to NPC suggested that in the handling of within-the-people cases, excessive force had been used. Zhu said that legal, economic, and administrative means should be used, combined with "in depth" ideological and political work. "Under no circumstances should we take an oversimplified or blunt approach to exacerbate a problem. Still less should we use dictatorial means against the masses of people." This apparently was a reference to the Ningxiang incident, with the handling of which Zhu was reportedly dissatisfied.[109]

The regime thus continued to send out mixed signals on the management of disorders, calling for the use of soft and hard methods. Since the regime attached overriding importance to the maintenance of social stability, local officials' promotion chances were adversely affected if their bailiwicks became known for a high frequency of collective protest. This gave them an incentive to use overwhelming force to crush large-scale collective protests. Yet, since officials were also criticized for excessive harshness, villagers could not be sure just how they would respond and this may explain why collective protests continued to erupt. Inefficiency is another explanation for the continuity of protests. Despite their intention to act quickly, the reaction of the authorities to large protests continued to be slow, judging by a major eruption in Yuandu township, Fengcheng city, Jiangxi, in August 2000. On August 16 and 17, hundreds of farmers protesting against taxes and fees ransacked the township government offices. Thousands more villagers – some estimates claim twenty thousand – participated in the protest. But the police, including the People's Armed Police, took a full week to respond.[110]

LEADERS, ORGANIZATION, AND COORDINATION

Who were the leaders of collective actions against excessive taxes and fees? Many of the protests were spontaneous flare-ups that apparently lacked leadership and organization, often the product of a string of abuses, the latest of which was the straw that broke the camel's back. These were sometimes large-scale

---

[109] CCTV (March 5, 1999, in *SWB-FE*/3478.S /11) and *SCMP* (April 3, 1999).
[110] AFP (Aug. 17 and 30, 2000), *SCMP* (Sept. 9, 2000), and *NYT* (Sept. 17, 2000).

eruptions, such as the "garlic riots" (Case 5.6), when large numbers of aggrieved and angry villagers on market day were suddenly galvanized by someone loudly voicing anger, leading to instant formation of a mob. Such protests fit Theodore Shanin's analysis of peasant riots as characterized by "short outbursts of accumulated frustration and rebellious feelings" followed by quiescence.[111] Tarrow explains the link between riots and social movements:

> Is a riot or a mob a social movement? Usually not, because their participants typically lack more than temporary solidarity. But sometimes, even riots reveal a common purpose or solidarity. The ghetto riots [in the United States] were not movements in themselves, but the fact that they were triggered by police abuse indicates that they arose out of a widespread sense of injustice. . . . Mobs, riots, and spontaneous assemblies are more an indication that a movement is in the process of formation than of movements themselves.[112]

A subset of the collective protests did have leaders. They came from among three groups: "troublemakers" (*diaomin*), members of village elites not in office, and elected village officeholders. Troublemakers, "policy-based resisters" in the classification of villager activism offered by Li and O'Brien, were "shrewd, unyielding, and assertive individuals who made things difficult for cadres, disputing their demands by invoking laws, regulations, and policies." They differed from obedient and passive villagers, *shunmin*, who at most engaged in grumbling and furtive evasion. They also differed from *dingzi hu,* literally "nail households," recalcitrant villagers who "boldly defy orders as well as policies and laws and frequently challenge village leaders who confront them. . . . Recalcitrants are more than willing to resort to force to defend their harvest and to employ violence when cadres crowd them." Their influence on other villagers was limited, however, in part because they defied all higher-level demands, including both legal and illegal levies, and all implementation, whether abusive or not.[113] Nail households probably lashed out as individuals, whereas leaders emerged among the assertive and disputatious troublemakers if only because they clothed their resistance in issues of general concern.

Not all villagers had policy-based troublemakers. In a poor village in mountainous Sichuan, according to the field researches by Xu Yong, three groups emerged on the issue of taxes and fees. One small group, mainly cadres and people close to them, paid on time. The majority took a wait-and-see attitude,

---

[111] Shanin (1971: 258).

[112] Tarrow (1994: 5).

[113] Li and O'Brien (1996: 28–61).

sought delays, and paid only when the cadres threatened them. A smaller group delayed for long periods. Most of these were in fact unable to pay, but a subset of "nail households" were defiant, refusing to pay altogether and hence subject to harsh coercion. The influence of the nail households was contradictory: On the one hand, their refusal had the potential of encouraging the wait-and-see middle group to join them, but on the other hand, those who hesitated were worried that if the hard-line resisters succeeded in their refusal, cadres would shift their debt to them. Most villagers didn't see any point in complaining or taking action. Apart from acts of individual defiance, the chance of the emergence of collective action in this village was low.[114]

Respected villagers who did not hold any office were potential leaders of protests. In early 2000, the internal edition of a popular journal, *Banyuetan,* gave this introduction to a twenty-two-page report on and analysis of informal leaders, called "peasant heroes," in Hunan:

> In recent years, in some villages where cadre-mass relations were tense, "peasant leaders" have appeared. Under their leadership, organization, and slogans, peasants engage in collective petitioning, accuse cadres, even surround and attack basic-level Party and government organs. What are they, heroes or troublemakers? Where does their "magic power" come from?[115]

Many or perhaps even most of the peasant leaders came from the relatively well educated village-level elite such as PLA veterans who had acquired organizational and communications skills in the army. This was so in the case of Zhang De'an in Renshou county. In a Shanxi tax outbreak, several hundred peasants confronted local authorities led by a PLA veteran.[116] Many veterans, like Zhang De'an, did not have positions commensurate with their background and experience. Zhang, for one, may have aspired to replace current office holders.[117] In Ningxiang, Hunan (Case 5.7), one of the "peasant heroes," Yang Yaojin, was a veteran who became a teacher in a locally run school.[118] There was a vast reservoir of PLA veterans in the countryside, estimated at twenty million, many of whom reportedly were disgruntled at having had to return to their home villages upon demobilization.[119] At the same time, however,

---

[114] Xu Yong (1997: 279–80).
[115] *Banyuetan* (*neibuban*) (No. 2, 2000).
[116] *SCMP* (June 26, 1993, *FBIS*, No. 122: 19).
[117] See O'Brien and Li (1995: 758).
[118] *Banyuetan* (*neibuban*) (No. 2, 2000: 8).
[119] Yang Po (1992: 26–7).

evidence that militias provided a support base for protest similar to that of the nineteenth century has not come to light.[120]

Leaders also came from among rural teachers. Some built networks based on their relationship with parents. One, just mentioned, Yang Yaojin of Ningxiang, Hunan (Case 5.7), held meetings of parents to check school accounts, which apparently helped him to build groups of supporters in the villages of Daolin town. In Hubei, a schoolteacher who had been dismissed for some time led resistance to taxation, including beating tax officials and organizing demonstrations. And another case, from Sichuan, also involved a teacher.[121] In another, Huang Guoqing of Lianyuan city, Hunan, had run afoul of the authorities by opening a school and hiring teachers without permission. To "assist" higher administrative agencies in reducing burdens, he set up a "board of directors" which formulated demands on government. Huang had failed his college entrance examinations by one point (reminiscent of Hong Xiuquan who led the massive nineteenth century Taiping Rebellion).[122]

These leaders had information and organizational skills and enjoyed prestige and authority among the masses, often for their past activities of leading protests, petitioning, and engaging in conflicts with township cadres. Huang Guoqing led or manipulated a large attack on his township headquarters in 1996. He was arrested but released shortly thereafter because of "pressure" from various unnamed quarters, much to the anger of basic-level cadres. When interviewed by a reporter in 1999, Huang was surrounded by a large entourage of villagers who said "whatever Huang says is what we all want." Peasants from neighboring counties came to him to obtain instructions, literally the scriptures (*qu jing*) – an allusion to the popular novel, *Journey to the West*.

These "burden-reduction heroes" posed a dilemma for the authorities. Three approaches presented themselves. One was the straightforward authoritarian response of arresting them in the name of preservation of order. Basic-level officials naturally preferred this course, but doing so could backfire because of the popularity of the informal leaders and the militancy of infuriated peasants. In Yizhang county, Hunan, an arrest elicited widespread peasant mobilization amidst the beating of drums, the assembly of about two thousand, the surrounding of one hundred Public Security officers, and the smashing of the town government compound, including the living quarters of the cadres. A second, more effective approach was for officials to take concerted action to reduce burdens and meet peasant grievances, thereby demobilizing both leaders and activists.

---

[120] See Perry (1980: 86–7).

[121] *Ming Pao* (Feb. 14, 2001, *FBIS*, No. 214, 2001) and *Washington Post* (May 8, 2001).

[122] *Banyuetan* (*neibuban*) (No. 2, 2000).

The third approach was to co-opt informal leaders into formal positions, taking advantage of their popularity and organizational abilities. This happened in a village in Hongshi town, Hengyang county, Hunan. In 1996 one of its villages was invaded by a team of two hundred township and village cadres on a mission to collect levies. When they began taking hogs and grain, they were blockaded by several hundred peasants organized by "peasant hero" Yi Shunlao, who had earlier led collective petitioning. A work team investigated and learned that township and village cadres wanted to make Yi the target of attack. Instead, the team interviewed Yi and mobilized him to run for election to the village committee. He won hands down. Together with the accountant, also a veteran at organizing petitions, he instituted an open finance system, informing villagers of how their money was spent. There was no further collective petitioning and the village was designated a model. The price to township and some village cadres was that they saw their authority undercut.

To what extent did clan or lineage organizations provide an existing or potential organizational base for protest? During the reform period, lineages resurfaced, after having been long suppressed. The state considered them a threat because they undermined the regime's political power in the villages, especially when lineage leaders were elected to village committees, when Party members followed clan rules rather than those of the Party, or when the local police protected clan activities, as in the following case.

> In remote counties, cadres and even police officials have become active clan members. During a recent celebration in Qidong county, Hunan [it will be recalled that Qidong was the site of a major tax-and-fee protest in 1996] police vehicles were on hand to maintain order and the event was broadcast on local television for more than two hours. More than 90 percent of the leaders of clans in Dingcheng and Hanshou districts in the same province are Party members.[123]

Little seems to be known, however, about the connection between lineages and organized protest.

Village Elections. The introduction of liberalized democratic village elections added an important new element to the interest calculus of village leaders. When village elections (discussed in more detail in Chapter 7) allowed peasants to make a genuine choice rather than one explicitly or implicitly dictated by the townships and the village Party branches, the chairpersons and members of the

---

[123] Quoted in *SCMP* (April 28, 1995, *FBIS*, No. 82:14–15). For a particularly striking case of clan dominance of local politics in the suburbs of Yueyang city, Hunan, see *RMRB* (April 16, 1989).

village committees (henceforth VC) were more likely to promote the demands of their constituents rather than respond to orders from above, sometimes to the point of leading protests.[124] In October 1999, two elected village cadres in Henan reportedly led an antitax demonstration at their township compound.[125] Li Lianjiang found other cases of chairpersons of village committees who not only lobbied on behalf of villagers but also engaged in protest activity:

> In Shandong, the liberalization of nomination procedures in early 1999 led to the election of many leaders of collective protests. By October 1999, elected cadres had organized so many protests against township governments that the provincial organization department warned in an internal circular that elections had caused widespread chaos.[126]

In late 1999, four elected protest leaders in Shandong were reportedly arrested.[127] Case 5.10 from Hunan illustrates some of the dynamics involved.

Case 5.10 In the summer of 1995, two peasants, Li Mingfa and Li Guobao from Queshan county, Henan, led several hundred people to skip administrative levels by submitting petitions to the prefectural and provincial governments. Because of this incident, the village Party secretary and three cadres were dismissed, as were two leaders of the county Party committee. Three years later the two peasants, known as "burden reduction heroes," were elected chair and vice-chair of the VC. Once in office, the Lis saved the peasants money by economizing on expenses. They stopped holding banquets for higher-level visitors, stopped collecting a reception fee, and reduced village-level assessments and imposition of fines. Li Mingfa told his constituents: "I was popularly elected. As long as I keep in line with you and with Party Central, I am not afraid of anything.... Those further down, referring to basic-level government, are a bunch of fools so don't obey them. If problems arise I'll be responsible."

With regard to the T and V levies, the two Lis claimed that their town government had erred on the high side in setting them. They decided to collect only 30 yuan from each resident calculated on the basis of 600 yuan per capita income. In 1998, the VC collected 7,000 yuan but used it all up, failing to deliver the township's share. In 1999, Li Mingfa claimed that past accounts had to be cleared up first and that the previous VC chair's

---

[124] We are greatly indebted to Professor Li Lianjiang for sharing with us his important unpublished paper, "Elections and Popular Resistance in Rural China," Hong Kong, spring 2000.

[125] Stratfor Report (www.strafor.com [Nov. 2, 1999]).

[126] Ibid., based on interviews.

[127] *Washington Post* Foreign Service (Nov. 12, 1999).

expenses for injuries had to be paid for, before the agricultural tax and the T and V levies be turned over (the latter were administered by the township).

On July 5, the town deputy Party secretary, who was concurrently the secretary of the village Party branch, led twenty town finance and tax cadres to the village to mobilize Li to turn over the procurement quota and agricultural tax. He agreed to turn over two sacks of wheat in place of the agricultural tax. But when the town cadres started to take the wheat, they were obstructed by peasants and a fight broke out. The county-level Political and Legal Committee thereupon had the two Lis arrested for the crime of "conspiring to incite the masses to resist implementation of state laws and administrative regulations."

Some of the people thought this was unfair in that the county authorities were retaliating for Li Mingfa's past activities of leading peasants to petition the higher levels and to oppose random fee collection. On the other hand, "some basic-level cadres" felt that if Li hadn't been arrested there would never be peace in the county. And indeed, just at that time, the neighboring county of Suiping also arrested a "reduce burden hero" who was a VC chair and who had refused to hand over the T and V levy and the agricultural tax, while leading peasants to surround and attack county legal personnel. Li's temporary replacement as VC chair observed that this episode showed that the peasants' legal outlook had not kept pace with the rise in their democratic consciousness. It is not clear from the account what ultimately happened to the two Lis.[128]

A trend – however small – emerged toward the end of the 1990s as elected village leaders, some of whom had already led protests before they held office, began leading collective actions once in office. In doing so they risked arrest, but then the regime was depriving itself of leaders of proven effectiveness in reducing the endemic cadre-peasant conflicts. The dilemma was compounded because top leaders approved village elections on the grounds that they would promote stability. If elected leaders acted on a wide scale as protest leaders, this rationale would be severely undermined.

The Role of Unelected Cadres. Accounts published in the Hong Kong press in the mid-1990s claim that "in almost all the serious incidents in Shanxi, Henan, and Hunan, the 'ringleaders' were local cadres." In some villages and townships,

---

[128] Paraphrased from Li Junde, "*'Jianfu yingxiong' za chengle fanzui xianyiren*" (How did "burden-reduction heroes" become criminal suspects), *Banyyuetan* (*neibuban*) (No. 2, 2000: 13–14).

virtually the entire cadre force was guilty of inciting to riot.[129] In the Jiangxi disturbances in 1997, township and village Party and government cadres were said to have "participated and encouraged peasants to protest."[130] The April 1998 State Council document quoted earlier in the section on repression repeatedly mentioned cadre and Party member participants, as did the investigation report of the Central Committee's Organization Department. One of the Hunan peasant hero leaders was a Party member who said that he didn't represent any faction or clan and only wanted to help peasants to understand central policy.

The image of cadres as protest leaders, however, is counterintuitive, given the powerful evidence of conflict between local officials and the masses. The bulk of our evidence emphasizes the severe tensions between peasants and cadres as the major line of cleavage. In the cases examined in this study, even village cadres, not to speak of township-level officials, almost invariably enforced the collection of levies. Career considerations, especially on the part of township cadres, stood in the way of support for or leadership of protest movements. This was less true of village cadres but in their cases, Party discipline could be invoked, since village branch secretaries were subordinate to the township Party committees. Village committees were bound to obey the law and follow the "guidance" of the township governments.

Cadre morale suffered not primarily from pressure from peasants but more so from lack of support from above when higher authorities, especially the Center, repudiated their actions. In the Renshou case many cadres said angrily: "The central authorities have betrayed us." During the riots, many cadres were beaten by peasants but couldn't voice their grievances. Reportedly, a third of Fujia district's village cadres "refused to work."[131] In Sheyang county, Jiangsu, villagers reportedly took advantage of central rules to frame and attack basic-level cadres under the pretext of reducing burdens. Some individuals who had been punished in the past for refusal to pay fees filed appeals with law enforcement organs, demanding "reversal of verdicts" on them.[132] Some villagers took advantage of the weakened power of cadres by refusing to pay taxes altogether on the ground that they were helping to reduce burdens.[133] Demoralized cadres complained:

Right now, it is getting harder and harder to do work among the masses. In the past, money was invariably collected through administrative means

---

[129] Guan Jie (1996).

[130] Li Zijing (1997).

[131] Sheng Jung (1993).

[132] *Zhongguo Xinxibao* (July 21, 1993, *JPRS*, No. 74, Oct. 1993: 35).

[133] For a later example, see *Neibu Canyue* (No. 28, July 21, 1999) on Changpu county, Fujian.

to be "turned over to the higher authorities." Now, deducting anything from the amount peasants receive by selling their agricultural and sideline products is not allowed. Nor is it permitted to go to the masses and collect money by force. Many village and team cadres feel helpless, when they encounter difficulties in carrying out their work.[134]

Concern about the damage that was being done to the regime's political base by pitting farmers against officials was voiced in the fall of 1993 by two State Council officials, Yuan Mu and Yang Yongzhe:

The purpose of sternly punishing these people [basic-level cadres who abused people] is to protect the majority of grass-roots-level cadres and give full play to their enthusiasm. In rural work, under no circumstances should we set grass-roots-level cadres against the vast numbers of peasants. Whether the rural areas are stable or not depends to a great extent on the stability and quality of the ranks of cadres at the basic level. If the rural areas are not stable, there will be no foundation for political power. Rural work can in no way be separated from the grass-roots-level cadres, who cannot be replaced by cadres of the central, provincial, or county levels.[135]

Having said this, it is important to note that throughout the era of Communist rule, there always had been village cadres who identified not only with their superiors but also with their clients with whom they had personal and family ties.[136] Some data suggest that those closest to the peasants at the very lowest level of the hierarchy, the former production teams, now called "groups," were more likely to sympathize with and side with the peasants. In a case in Hubei in which a peasant was harassed to the point of suicide, the group chief, who was a member of the collection team, told *Xinhua* reporters that he "was very ashamed to have been an accessory to this crime. These days, when the masses see me approach, they say 'the devils are coming [that is, the wartime invading Japanese], hurry home and dig tunnels.'"[137] Many village cadres felt trapped by their situation.

We are all peasants, our families contract for land, we understand the peasants, but who understands us? . . . We get blamed by both sides. The higher levels demand money from us . . . each year we have to ask several times, causing the elders and our relatives to feel offended.[138]

---

[134] Ibid.

[135] Yuan Mu and Yang Yongzhe (1993: 39), *FBIS*, No. 199.

[136] See Bernstein (1970: 239–67), Shue (1988), and Oi (1989).

[137] See Case 5.4, above, and *Xinhua Neican Xuanbian* (No. 2, 1996: 16–18).

[138] *NMRB* (Sept. 26, 1988).

These complaints smack of demoralization, self-pity, and discontent. Some village cadres caught in the middle of competing pressures from above and below resigned their offices, but some responded by encouraging or even leading protests, thus to a certain extent qualifying our argument that the major line of cleavage was between ordinary peasants and office-holders.

At the township and higher levels, younger, better educated, and more open-minded township or county officials were also more likely to sympathize with the peasants' plight.[139] Chapter 3 related the case of a Hubei township Party secretary, Li Changping, college-educated but of peasant origin, who protested against the crushing tax, fee, and procurement burdens borne by peasants in his township. Rather than lead a popular movement, however, he protested by sending a detailed report to the State Council in which he pleaded for help from the Center, which, indeed, his township eventually received. His courageous exposé angered other local officials and he eventually was pressured into resigning his post and leaving the area.[140] But township officials were under intense pressure to extract funds both for career reasons and because townships depended on such funds. It is not plausible that they would risk their careers by leading peasant protests. A Chinese scholar pointed out, however, that if planned severe cutbacks in the township bureaucracies actually took place, then laid-off and disgruntled cadres might end up supporting peasant protests.

Staying Power, Networks, and Coordination. The significance of collective protest grows in proportion to its horizontal spread beyond a village or a township. Most of the anti–tax-and-fee protests were confined to one village. Only a subset, but clearly a growing one, involved one or more townships. According to a central document quoted in *Cheng Ming*, in 1993 out of a total of 6,230 cases of turmoil, 820 affected more than one township or 13 percent. In 78 cases several townships or possibly counties were involved.[141] In the disorders in Shanxi, Henan, and Hunan in the fall of 1995 rural underground organizations were said to have fomented unrest by coordinating protest activity between several villages.[142] Deliberate coordination played a role in the disorders in Renshou, Qidong, and Ningxiang, in which several townships took

---

[139] When the journalist Chen Daolong interviewed cadres, one, an older ex-Party secretary who had been dismissed because of a suicide, blamed peasant recalcitrance on anarchists and the descendants of rich peasants and landlords, in sharp contrast to other officials who recognized the difficult situation they were in. See Chen Daolong (1994: 16–22).

[140] See Li Changping (2002).

[141] Lu Nong (1994: 28).

[142] Guan Jie (1996: 18–19) and Li Zijing (1997: 19–21).

part. In Renshou, some villagers sought to enlist the cooperation of peasants in neighboring Pengshan county. Significant coordination enabled close to five thousand peasants from five townships and villages, in Pengzi county, Jiangxi, in 1997, to engage in a protest that reportedly led to violence and deaths.[143] Just how deliberate coordination among protestors was, in more than one village or even township, is often quite unclear. In many cases, it may well have been news of a protest spreading to nearby villages and townships that created a contagion effect. This was more likely if peasants heard that the grievances of villages in which collective protests occurred were subsequently remedied without the imposition of punishment.

But what is most noteworthy about a subset of cases of collective protest that have occurred in recent years is their staying power, made possible by sustained networks of contact among activists and leaders, such cases being characterized by continuity in leadership. But collective actions were only intermittent, as indeed one would expect in communities bound by the agricultural work cycle. This was so in Ningxiang, Hunan and in the clash with police in Yuntang, Jiangxi, in April 2001, where a village had sustained a tax boycott for three years, fending off at least one previous police invasion.[144] Increased staying power seems to be an important new feature of protest in the late 1990s. Rapid improvements in communication facilitated the building of larger networks. As rural discontent became chronic because authorities could not find a solution to the burden problem, broader circles could well become involved. As one Chinese scholar noted, school graduates were a potential group from which networks could be built. Lower-middle school graduates had classmates in the township; higher-middle school graduates had classmates in the district or county. Businessmen whose relatives were suffering from burdens also might use their contacts to stir up trouble. Horizontal networks of activists thus had the potential of organizing collective actions among several townships or, even, countywide protest.

Some protests erupted in neighboring counties at more or less the same time, which could be suggestive of coordination. In Sichuan, from April to June 1993, peasant protests took place in ten counties. A set of three and a set of two were in close proximity to one another. The remaining five were farther away from each other.[145] In Shanxi, all five of the counties where riots erupted in October 1995 were located in the southwest of the province. Three of the

---

[143] Yue Shan (1997: 21).

[144] *NYT* (April 20, 2001) and *Baltimore Sun* (April 18, 2001).

[145] Zong Lanhai (1993: 14–15). The three counties were Santai, Pengxi, and Yanting; the set of two was comprised of Bazhong and Nanjiang.

counties were close together and the other two, fairly distant from the three, were close to one another. In Henan, also in October 1995, protests erupted in Nanyang, Tanghe, and Xinye counties, all in Nanyang prefecture and all connected by road. In Hubei, in May and June 1997, four counties in Jingzhou prefecture, all geographically quite close to one another, mounted significant protests. The Hubei counties in which major protests occurred two months later, in July and August, are in prefectures distant from Jingzhou prefecture but close to one another. Four counties – Baokang, Fang Xian, Zhushan, and Zhuxi – are located along a major highway and are roughly fifty kilometers apart. On the other hand, five protest movements in Jiangxi which took place in May and June 1997 were located in three different prefectures, as were protests in Anhui.[146] In July and August, when large-scale protests occurred in fifteen counties in Jiangxi, four of them had already experienced protests in May and June. It is not clear, however, whether the same townships were involved. On a provincial scale, waves of protests erupted in neighboring provinces at the same time: in the fall of 1995, in Shanxi and Henan and in May and June 1997, in Hubei, Hunan, Anhui, and Jiangxi.

Without explicit evidence of cross-county organization and coordination, these cases may not indicate a large-scale threat to the regime. In most cases it appears that peasant protests were short-lived and localized and most often the villagers were unable to sustain organized activity for long periods. The new development is that prolonged organized resistance has become increasingly possible.

POTENTIAL ALLIES

If sustained antitax movements were to develop, the question of joint action with protestors who had other grievances needs to be considered. In the countryside, financial burdens were not the only source of individual or collective protest. Rural Chinese had multiple grievances against the authorities, which might have but evidently did not coalesce. For instance, in Suining county, Jiangsu, the "masses" carried out 381 acts of "revenge" against village and group cadres in 1987 and the first five months of 1988. There were 122 resulting from enforcement of birth control; 115 from enforcement of grain purchases and the extraction of taxes; 51 from disputes over house building; and 45 over rules requiring cremation of the dead rather than traditional burial (the purpose being to save precious arable land). But aggrieved peasants in this county either did not join

---

[146] Guan Jie (1996: 18–19), and Li Zijing (1997: 19–21).

together in a common cause or were unable to do so.[147] The one exception where joint action occurred was over a grievance most closely related to taxes and fees, grain procurement. Procurement abuses were often indistinguishable from tax and fee abuses, since they also entailed extraction or withholding of resources from farmers, as when cadres issued IOUs rather than cash to farmers or deducted taxes and fees from procurement payments. When the price scissors widened, farmers evaded selling to the state, leading cadres to use force in collecting grain. This happened in numerous places in 1988 and again in the mid-1990s.[148] In 1992 and 1993, tax-and-fee protests seem to have merged with protests against IOUs and this strengthened their impact.

Three other important grievances against state authorities elicited rural collective protests: first, the requisitioning of land for industrial or other developmental projects, especially in rapidly developing provinces such as Guangdong and in the rural suburbs of cities such as Zhengzhou. Availability of land was crucial to a locality's ability to attract investors. When land was leased to entrepreneurs, local officials were sometimes able to pocket huge sums without paying adequate compensation to the peasants whose land they requisitioned, or they failed to allocate industrial jobs to them, prompting peasants to seek redress, including resort to collective action.[149]

Second, unrestrained rural industrialization led to severe contamination of the rivers and the water supply, poisoning fields and causing illness. In the absence of adequate enforcement of environmental statutes, collective or state-owned enterprises often failed to pay compensation to those suffering damage or to eliminate the source of pollution, provoking confrontations, including riots. One of the first of many such conflicts occurred in the Beijing suburbs in 1988.[150] River pollution affected downstream farming villagers but did not apparently lead to joint protest with those aggrieved by taxes and fees.

Third, abuses in the administration of the birth control program – imposition of heavy fines, favoritism in the allocation of birth quotas, arbitrary enforcement of rules that stipulated when and under what circumstances couples could have

---

[147] *NMRB* (Sept. 26, 1988).

[148] See *NMRB* (March 31, 1989), for an extensive report on procurement abuses in northern Hunan, including an example of collective passive resistance.

[149] See especially Zweig (2000: 120–42) for analysis and a prolonged case of conflict in suburban Nanjing. See also Wu Jieh-min (1998). And see the cases reported in *SCJP* (Sept. 18, 1997 and March 27, 1998) and *Ming Pao* (Dec. 23, 1998, *SWB-FE*/3419/11, Dec. 29, 1998).

[150] See AFP (July 1, 1998) and *Xinhua* (June 30, 1988, both in *FBIS*, No. 127: 17–18). For other cases, see *Lien Ho Pao* (Sept. 22, 1995, *FBIS*, No. 193: 40–1), and *Xinhua Ribao* (March 20, 1998, in *SWB-FE*/3194, G/4–8).

a second child, coercive abortions, and sterilization – were sources of protest, potentially in all villages. In 1997 in Gaozhou city, Guangdong, fines of several thousand yuan provoked collective protests that spread to thirty towns.[151] All these grievances could in principle merge into a broad-gauged movement of resistance against state agents or perhaps the regime itself, but this has not happened, at least thus far.

Religious Sects and Movements. Because the Party-state arrogated to itself the right to eliminate "feudal superstitions," that is, peasant folk religion, there was an inherent conflict between peasants and the state.[152] During the reform era, as long as religious practices were confined to the family, the regime was fairly tolerant. But larger assemblies were not tolerated, resulting in occasional clashes. In 1982, in Yingde county, Guangdong, a large-scale Daoist sacrificial festival was organized. Five to ten thousand people attended; order was maintained by a volunteer security force. "When commune leaders tried to put a stop to this event, hundreds of peasants stoned them" and public security had to be called in.[153] When authorities callously disregarded peasant beliefs, collective responses could also occur. In 1997, a huge demonstration took place outside Nanhai city, Guangdong, against the removal of thousands of graves at a site intended for a tourist facility. The disturbance spread to numerous towns.[154]

What was highly disturbing to the regime was the revival of heterodox religious sects, cults, and movements, which had played an important role in the rebellions that punctuated Chinese history, erupting in times of social and economic hardship and dynastic decline. The enormously destructive Taiping Rebellion in the middle of the nineteenth century is an example. The appeal of heterodox sects usually lay in their millenarian predictions of an impending "great event" in which the dynasty would be overthrown and replaced by a truly just one. In the PRC, where the Party zealously guarded its monopoly over organization, such movements had a unique capacity to recruit, organize, and maintain followers in diverse localities. One such movement, the supreme spirit sect (*Zhushen Jiao*), operated in Hunan in the mid-1990s. It originated in Anhui in the late 1980s. In 1993, Liu Jiaguo, who had joined the Anhui sect in 1989, was sent to Hunan to recruit sect members. His activities were not suppressed until 1998. The Supreme Spirit sect "continually expanded its forces into other provinces and cities" and grew to have as many as eight thousand followers in

---

[151] *Ming Pao* (Sept. 7, 1997, *SWB-FE*/3021, G/4–5).
[152] For a trenchant analysis, see Cohen (1991: 113–34).
[153] *NFRB* (Jan. 26, 1983), cited in Perry (1985: 433).
[154] *Ming Pao* (Oct. 21 and 23, 1997, *SWB-FE*/3057, G/3–4).

ten provinces. It had "a marked political tinge." It called for the overthrow of the kingdom of man and its replacement by the kingdom of God and predicted great calamities. It had a cohesive eight-level hierarchical, territorial organization, based, ironically enough, on Leninist principles of democratic centralism. It trained "backbone elements" and dispatched them on conversion missions to remote mountain areas but also to suburbs. Contributions from followers were used to buy "mobile phones, pagers, and motorcycles." Between 1993 and 1997, the sect "held more than ten large illegal assemblies," five of which drew delegates from all over the country. In April 1996, it held its "first national congress" in Hengshan, Hunan, and claimed that this signified "the emergence of a political power and a state." After his arrest, Liu Jiaoguo, like other leaders of such sects, was tried and executed.[155]

Estimates of the number and size of such movements vary greatly. According to one report, six major sects and roughly one hundred minor sects flourished in the 1980s and 1990s. Each of the six reportedly had between one hundred thousand and six hundred thousand members. The Supreme Spirit sect, whose membership was put at eight to ten thousand by mainland sources, was estimated in Hong Kong to have one hundred thousand members.[156] Because of their longevity and geographical range, such sects had the potential of pulling together peasants with diverse grievances. In the European context, Tarrow, writing of heretical sects, suggests that "it was only when religious fervor joined with tax revolts, dynastic ambitions or interstate conflict, that rebels against [established] religion gained access to the tools of the modern social movement."[157] Thus far, this evidently has not happened in China.

The possibility that religious movements might bring together members of diverse social groups has been of great concern to Chinese leaders, since it is one of their control strategies to block social groups from forming alliances with one another. This is one factor in the harsh crackdown on the Falun Gong movement from 1999 on. Founded in 1992, this sect, whose name literally means "Dharma Wheel Practice," preached a doctrine of salvation and acquisition of supernatural powers by means of mental and physical exercises grounded in Buddhist and Daoist beliefs. The movement's estimated size ranged from two to seventy million. According to the charges leveled against it, it was well organized, borrowing techniques from the Party's Leninist structure and making

---

[155] *Xinhua* (Oct. 14, 1999, *SWB-FE* 3666, G/7–8); and *Xinhua* (Oct. 15, 1999, *SWB-FE*/3670, G/9–11). For a Henan case which involved recruitment of soldiers, see *Liaowang* (No. 7, 1994, *JPRS-94-25*, April 19, 1994: 59).

[156] Report by Hong Kong Information Centre of Human Rights and Democracy in China (Nov. 2, 1999, *SWB-FE*/3683, G/8–9).

[157] Tarrow (1994: 38).

use of modern communications technology. The Falun Dafa Research Society of Falun Gong had a top-down, "tight organizational system made up of 39 general instruction stations, 1,900 instruction centers, and 28,000 exercising sites in localities throughout the nation."[158] Falun Gong was able to stage an entirely peaceful sit-in of ten thousand people around the top leaders' Beijing compound, Zhongnanhai, in April 1999, totally surprising the authorities. Moreover, once the crackdown began, Falun Gong exhibited extraordinary staying power. It was able to stage further demonstrations characterized by passive resistance and to send petitions signed by thousands of followers to the leaders to explain the harmless nature of its activities. A deep sense of unjust persecution arose among its members.[159] In the face of repression, Falun Gong leaders appointed "second and third echelons" of leaders to replace those arrested, thus acquiring the capacity for "long-term confrontation against our Party and government."[160] Its practices resemble those of other popular exercise (*qigong*) groups and hence are hard to detect. It was elusive and hard to pin down, its social networks well coordinated. It had strong support from Falun Gong practitioners abroad, who organized a number of web sites.[161]

From the vantage point of social movement theory, a major attribute of Falun Gong was that it transcended some of the vertical barriers that divide Chinese from one another, both territorial and urban-rural. Its members came from a variety of social groups, from retired cadres, housewives, unemployed workers, students, peasants, and alarmingly, from among Party members and high government officials, including the military and the Ministry of Public Security.[162] Undoubtedly, Falun Gong had a following of unknown size in the countryside.[163] In August 1999, one of the authors of this study was refused access to a Hunan county in part because of the campaign then in progress against Falun Gong. Its promise of salvation and miracle cures was no doubt attractive to the aggrieved and deprived in rural society. But Falun Gong did not take up concrete economic or social causes, perhaps in part because it sought to protect itself from even harsher repression by claiming to be apolitical. The persecution to which it has been subject could, however, drive it into the explicitly political arena and hence to take up broader causes.

Unofficial or semi-official Christian movements also offered an organized challenge. Unregistered Christian "house churches" proliferated in the rural

---

[158] *RMRB* (Nov. 1, 1999).
[159] *SCJP* (Oct. 25, 1999).
[160] Ibid.
[161] See Madsen (2000: 243–7).
[162] *Xinhua* (Oct. 25, 1999, *SWB FE*/3678, G/9–11).
[163] Interview with Falun Gong adherent in the United States, October 2000.

areas of several provinces, especially Henan, in the 1980s and 1990s. An "extensive underground network of Protestants proselytizes aggressively in the countryside, claiming hundreds of thousands of adherents every year."[164] Catholics who recognized the authority of Rome also maintained underground networks. Some of these activities crossed over into the realm of social and economic grievances. For instance, Protestant and Catholic churches have legal claims to land confiscated after 1949 which have led to conflict with land developers. "Such cases are already on the boil in Shanxi and Liaoning provinces, where parishioners have been beaten up by hired thugs for protesting against land-grabs." In addition, in the early 1990s, some Christians aided the organizers of an illegal trade union by providing "a ready supply of scriptural references and spiritual authority," suggestive of linkages between different groups of dissidents, a development about which the regime is particularly anxious.[165]

The rapid rise in the number of unregistered Christian churches, especially in the rural areas, was seen by some as having potential for supporting political change. A 1992 campaign against unregistered churches likened the Christian movements in China to the collapse of communism in Poland, in which the Catholic Church played a major role. Warnings were voiced that the "terrible changes" in Poland could also occur in China. "If China does not want such a scene to be repeated in its land, it must strangle the baby [of Christianity] while it is still in the manger."[166] Thus far, evidence of linkages to tax protests has not come to light.

Urban Allies. In contemporary China, the major and overwhelming reality has been the absence of linkages between urban and rural protest. There was growing unrest in the urban sector in the second half of the 1990s.[167] The major source was the regime's massive effort to downsize state industry, which led to large-scale unemployment and to the marginalization of a hitherto privileged and protected class, industrial workers, for whom downward mobility was a painful experience. Enforced early retirements and failure to pay pensions added to the grievances, especially at a time when the state's nascent social safety net still had enormous holes. Cities as well as smaller industrial towns experienced numerous demonstrations, strikes, confrontations, and riots more or less parallel to those occurring in the countryside at the same time.[168] In principle, this would seem to provide fertile soil for cooperation between urban and rural

---

164 *FEER* (June 6, 1996: 46–53).
165 *FEER* (May 5, 1994: 26).
166 *SCMP* (June 9, 1992, *FBIS*, No. 112: 16–17).
167 See Ching Kwan Lee (1999).
168 See, for instance, *FEER* (June 26, 1997:14–16) and *Financial Times* (April 3, 2000).

protesters. But as of the late 1990s there was no evidence that this was happening, even in the suburban areas, where peasants' anger over land seizures was often acute.

The underlying obstacle to urban-rural cooperation was the deep cleavage between the two sectors that developed during the Mao era and that continued to persist in the reform era. Most urban residents had enjoyed privileges since the mid-1950s – lifetime employment and welfare benefits – from which peasants were excluded. Stark status differences developed between urban and rural residents. From the mid-1950s on, peasant migration to the cities was largely forbidden. Peasants were essentially bound to the land, separated by strict enforcement of the rural and urban household registration system (*hukou*). Many peasants came to harbor deep resentment at their second-class status and toward the urban sector. These distinctions began to break down in the reform period as lifetime employment and guaranteed benefits for state workers were phased out. Restrictions on migration were greatly relaxed. Tens of millions of rural migrant workers flocked to the cities in search of employment. But the unequal status was maintained. Migrant workers were for the most part not allowed to establish urban residence. They were, in Dorothy Solinger's words, excluded from "urban citizenship."[169] Thus while urban-rural linkages were restored, there was no accompanying rise in urban-rural solidarity. Urbanites looked down on the migrants, blaming them for crime and disorder.

Moreover, the massive layoffs of industrial workers that began in the later 1990s had the potential of exacerbating worker-peasant tensions. A two-tier labor market had developed as peasants took jobs disdained by urbanites, but with unemployment and increased desperation among unemployed workers, competition between them and rural migrants began to develop. Some cities began to impose restrictions on migration, barred peasants from a number of occupations, and mobilized migrants to return to their native villages.[170] Were this to occur on a large scale, rural resentment toward the urban sector would no doubt increase, all the more because migrant remittances were essential supplements to many a rural family budget.

The literature on revolution emphasizes the forging of urban-rural linkages as a key to success. In the Chinese Communist revolution, urban intellectuals and students went to the countryside to mobilize peasants, providing leadership, organization, coordination, and a vision that linked parochial rural grievances to broader, national, and even international goals. Such links were absent in the 1990s. In the reform period those in the urban sector, mostly students and

[169] See Solinger (1999).
[170] See Solinger (1998).

intellectuals who were the mainstays of the urban Tiananmen protest movement in 1989, were not interested in rural grievances or in making contact with rural people. Urban protest was thus isolated from the countryside. The momentous Tiananmen democracy movement of 1989 was a classic illustration. Although there was some rural participation, urban protestors did not reach out to the peasants. Of course, there were constraints, such as fear of repression and the sheer lack of time for detailed planning in a rapidly evolving situation. But Elizabeth Perry's observation about Tiananmen is telling: "In failing to take seriously the peasantry's capacity for collective action, would-be democrats deny themselves a powerful and essential ally."[171] On the rural side, one peasant's contemptuous comment to a foreign anthropologist about the 1989 protests probably was typical of rural attitudes.

> What did they have to complain about? They are *jumin* (urbanites). They live in cities. They have jobs. They eat the state's grain. We can do without them but they cannot do without us. We peasants are the pillars of the state.[172]

Urban-rural income inequality, which increased significantly from the late 1980s on, has contributed to rural resentment against the urban sector.[173]

Many Chinese intellectuals had strongly elitist attitudes. They disdained peasants and their superstitions. They blamed Mao's despotism on the peasants' "feudal" backwardness, that is, the peasants' propensity to put all their trust in an emperor. Many urbanites, including officials, intellectuals, and students, were often not willing to accept backward, poorly educated, and "feudal" peasants as legitimate participants in the political process.[174] In the 1990s, these attitudes were reinforced by the attractiveness of neo-conservative thinking and the rejection of popular mobilization as too dangerous to China's development. In 1994, a book entitled *Viewing China through the Third Eye* predicted that lifting restrictions on peasant mobility would plunge the country into chaos.[175] Not all intellectuals shared these condescending and fearful attitudes; some strongly defended peasant interests (see, second section in Chapter 7), but by all accounts, negative attitudes were dominant. Formation of alliances between the countryside and the cities faced formidable obstacles.

---

[171] See Wright (1999) and Perry (1992: 153, 74–92).
[172] Quoted in Ruf (1998: 162).
[173] Riskin et al. (1999: 66–70).
[174] See Kelliher (1993: 379–96).
[175] Lo Yi Ning Ge Er (pseud.) (1994: 27 ff).

CONCLUSION

Large parts of rural China were in a volatile state in the 1990s. Peasants protested against a variety of perceived abuses by state authorities, of which excessive burdens were probably the most important. Collective actions, organized and unorganized, broke out with increasing frequency. Identifiable leaders emerged and in some villages and townships, resistance activities were maintained over several years. Improved communications and learning played a significant role. Peasants in widely separated areas seemed to share "repertoires of contention" of which social movements theorists speak. The organizational controls which the Party had built in the countryside after 1949 were in some disarray. Much illegal or disapproved activity in the villages was beyond the control of the local authorities and required the mobilization of forces from the townships to suppress.

This situation would seem propitious for the rise of large-scale peasant social movements. But several critical ingredients were missing: Leaders who might actively have overcome societal segmentation, dispersion, and cleavages to forge a significant social movement around a common set of grievances and goals were simply not in evidence. Neither were organizers who could transcend the predominantly localist character of collective protests. Vertical cleavages, it is important to emphasize, were due not only to "natural" social conditions, such as lineage segmentation and other forms of localism, but also to the long-standing separationist state policies. A major goal of regime strategy was to maintain social stability precisely by forestalling the formation of cross-group alliances. Given the ubiquity of grievances in town and country, this vigilance was justified.

There were trends that pointed toward greater coherence, coordination, and duration. If such trends gain in strength the Chinese leaders will face a much more difficult situation. Similarly, if the number of protests mushroom but still remain fairly localized, their sheer number could conceivably overwhelm the regime's capacity to repress and control. A true challenge to the regime's existence from below, however, can probably only arise if there is a political opening from above which would provide opportunities for cross-societal mobilization.

6

Containing Burdens: Change and Persistence

PEASANT protest and violence were a major reason why the Party-state sought to solve the burden problems. Ever since the mid-1980s, central leaders have taken measures to curb excessive taxes and fees. Nonetheless, despite years of effort, the state was unable to solve the problem as of the year 2002. This chapter examines three state strategies adopted by the government to address the problem. First, the war on burdens was waged by means of exhortation, promulgation of rules and regulations, and campaigns. These were efforts to pressure and constrain local officials to reduce burdens. This approach was important. It served to call widespread attention to the problem and to indicate to lower-level officials that the issue was a core concern of the central leaders and that therefore it had to become part of their agendas. And it served to inform the peasants that the Center was on their side.

A second strategy was to allow peasants themselves to seek redress using these tactics: by the "letters and visits" system, which enabled peasants to lodge complaints with the local and higher authorities in the hope of enlisting their aid in curbing burdens; by making the legal system more accessible to villagers in the hope that legal intervention, including lawsuits, would remedy particular grievances; and by promoting village democracy to enhance the accountability of cadres (see Chapter 7).

A third strategy consisted of attempts to address some of the institutional roots of the burden problem in the financial and bureaucratic systems. This included reform of township and village financial management, administrative streamlining, and most important, increasingly significant experiments of converting fees into regular taxes, which in 1999 became a national goal. The last showed the greatest promise of making a dent in the problem, but according to official estimates, would require three to five years of effort to register real results. None of these strategies, however, could attack the problem at its core.

To do so effectively would have required even more fundamental changes in central-local and state-society relations.

Even in the reform era, the Chinese government relied heavily on the old strategy of mobilization through exhortations and campaigns. This began in the mid-1980s, when the Central Committee and the State Council, separately or jointly, as well as central ministries, issued the first of a stream of "notices," "urgent," or "emergency notices," "circulars," "decisions," and regulations that specifically addressed the burden problem. In 1996, the *Legal Daily* listed twenty-four such central directives that appeared between 1985 and 1996.[1] All but one were issued in the 1990s, when Beijing sent out new edicts on burden reduction virtually every year. According to another count, between 1991 and 1999, seventy-six regulations and policy circulars were issued by the Central Committee or the State Council or both or by the central ministries.[2] As recently as July 2001, the State Council issued a decree warning against any attempt to raise unapproved local levies and fees.[3] To these must be added *People's Daily* editorials or articles by "commentators" that reflected the views of the policy-making establishment.

Broadly speaking, these documents contained similar themes. They acknowledged the failure of previous directives to reduce burdens or to prevent burdens from "bouncing back" (*fantan*) after they had been cut. They diagnosed the problem as very serious. They exhorted officials seriously to deal with the problem and to put generalist leaders, especially the territorial Party secretaries, in charge of the matter. They acknowledged that officials needed to raise their level of "ideological understanding" of the burdens problem, a stance that reflected a general tendency to attribute lack of compliance not to conflicts of interest but to lack of understanding of the real situation. According to this view, officials must realize that peasants were still poor and their capacity to "endure" was limited.

The main aim of these documents was to regulate burdens by defining and delimiting legitimate burdens from those the Center deemed excessive. In 1991 a regulation specified that peasants' T and V levies "must not exceed five percent of the preceding year's net per capita income," taking the township as the

---

[1] *FZRB* (May 21,1996).

[2] Zhonggong Zhongyang Zuzhibu Ketizu (2001: 84).

[3] See *http://www.sina.com.cn* (July 30, 2001).

unit.[4] Five years later, a central government decree demanded that incomes be averaged at the village level in recognition of the inequities that resulted from using so large a unit as a township. Although the document recognized that household incomes varied and that this should be taken into account, it did not actually require that each household's income should be the basis for determining the five percent, presumably because of the administrative difficulties involved.[5] Regulations also forbade using projected income increases as the basis for calculating these payments.

With regard to fees, fines, and assessments – the largest, most unpredictable, and most hated part of the burden system – regulations simply forbade imposing unauthorized fees and fines or forcing peasants to make contributions to projects. The most dramatic instance of this came in 1993, when the leaders were greatly alarmed by widespread peasant protests. The central authorities eliminated thirty-seven fees, demanded revision of seventeen, and an end to the compulsory imposition of fourteen types of assessments, as well as "piggy-backing" of fees on other payments (*dache*). Twenty-nine fees were allowed to continue, but forty-three target-setting activities that required imposition of burdens were canceled.[6] Regulations were promulgated restricting the scope of permitted fees.

Central decrees also outlawed a variety of practices used to extract more money. State agencies could no longer make a profit from fees charged for licenses, nor could they deduct levies from grain or cotton procurement payments due peasants, nor could expenses incurred by officials visiting villages be apportioned among households, nor could there be any "extravagant wining and dining and presenting of gifts." A wide variety of abusive practices were identified and prohibited, such as those described in Chapter 3. Thus, force, or "utilizing the instruments and methods of dictatorship to collect money and goods is strictly forbidden."[7]

Violators were to be subject to Party discipline and the law. In 1993, the Ministries of Supervision and Finance issued joint "Regulations on Punishment for Those Who Increase the Peasants' Burdens."[8] And in early 2000, "Interim Provisions" for punishment of officials who violated the burden regulations were issued.[9] These included criminal liability but earlier regulations had done this as well. As for career incentives, in 1996, Circular No.13 of the

---

[4] *ZRGYGB* (No.41, 1991; Jan. 1, 1992: 1430–5).

[5] *RMRB* (April 1, 1997).

[6] *ZRGYGB* (No. 18, Sept. 2, 1993: 850–6).

[7] *RMRB* (April, 1997).

[8] *Xinhua* (Oct. 24, 1993, *FBIS*, No. 209:31–3), and *Xinhua* (Oct. 9, 1993, *FBIS*, No. 203: 30).

[9] For a summary, see *Xinhua* (Feb. 17, 2000, *SWB FE*/3767, No. G/7).

CCP Central Committee called for tying officials' careers to burden reduction, which

> will be used as an important criterion in the appointment and evaluation of leaders at each level, especially at the county and township levels. . . . Core leaders of any locality or agency that increase burdens will be held strictly responsible. Any cadre who is subject to disciplinary action for increasing burdens will not be eligible for promotion or appointment to an important position for the period specified.[10]

As far as we can tell, however, severe punishment of offenders was rare. Some officials were expelled from the Party and dismissed from their posts, but there apparently were no jail sentences. Most offenders were disciplined, warned, demoted, or, probably most commonly, transferred to another post.

Central decrees, beginning in 1991, authorized peasants to "refuse" to pay illegal exactions. Indeed, the "Agriculture Law," adopted in July 1993, used the term "right to reject" illegal imposts in four different articles, but without specifying remedial mechanisms that peasants could use.[11] The purpose, scope, and limits of specific impositions were to be made known to the population by means of "energetic publicity" and transparency. Village assemblies, people's congresses of the townships, and the people's congress standing committees of the counties had to approve specific imposts.

Regulations specified complex examination and approval processes involving central ministries and commissions, some of which had themselves authorized burdens. In 1990, a Central Committee "Decision" on fees, fines, and apportionments required that imposition of fees be examined and approved by the Ministry of Finance and the State Administration of Commodity Prices, or their provincial counterparts. "Major projects" required approval by the State Council or the provincial government. Fund-raising and imposition of fees had to be strictly regulated.

> The scale of fund-raising should be incorporated into the local investment plan assigned by the State Planning Commission. . . . Revenues from fines should be submitted to the treasury and all forms of retention of a percentage of fines should be abolished. . . . Unauthorized use, misappropriation, or setting up of "private coffers" with collected fees or fines are strictly forbidden.[12]

---

[10] Quoted in Whiting (1998: 13) from *ZRGYGB* (No.12, 1997:563–8), and Whiting (2001: 286).

[11] *ZRGYGB* (No.12, 1993: 548).

[12] See decision by CCP Central Committee and the State Council, *Xinhua* (Oct. 15, 1990, *FBIS*, No. 202: 1–34).

A year later, the Ministry of Agriculture (MOA) was authorized to screen central-level departmental decrees. It discovered, as noted in Chapter 3, that forty-eight ministries and commissions had issued 148 rules for payments by the public, an admission that burdens were not imposed by errant local authorities alone.[13] In the fall of 1993, MOF was given "principal responsibility" to take charge of curbing "unwarranted fees," together with the State Planning Commission, the State Economic and Trade Commission, the MOA, and the Ministry of Supervision.[14]

The State Council set up a Leading Group on Burden Reduction in the early 1990s, and so did the provinces and counties throughout the country. By 1997, twenty-seven provinces had established them.[15] At all levels of the hierarchy, burden reduction offices (*jianfuban*) were set up but without giving these offices power independent of the local Party committees. Their mandate was to monitor the implementation of laws and regulations related to burdens, to approve local government decrees related to burdens, to assist in litigation cases of peasant burdens, and to train inspectors in burden monitoring.[16] Twenty-five provinces promulgated their own local regulations to reduce levies and fees on peasants. By 1997, 73 percent of the counties nationwide had established accounting systems for peasant payments and two-thirds of them conducted annual special audits on peasant payments.[17]

Government investigation and inspection were also used in burden reduction. In the autumn of 1992, the State Council Leading Group on Burden Reduction organized a large-scale investigation which sent teams to nineteen provinces, their members coming from the State Council's Bureau of Legislative Affairs, MOF, MOA, the Ministry of Supervision, and the State Planning Commission to obtain information directly from farmers and local officials.[18] A year later inspection teams from the same units were dispatched to fifty-four counties in eighteen provinces. In nine weeks, these inspection teams investigated 215 villages to check on the drastic burden reductions decreed that year.[19] A recent inspection was launched nationwide by the State Council in August 2001.[20]

[13] Ibid. and *ZRGYGB* (No. 41, Jan. 7, 1992).

[14] General Offices of CCP Central Committee and State Council, "Provisions on Controlling the Collection of Unwarranted Fees," *Xinhua* (Oct. 24, 1993, *FBIS*, No. 208: 31–3).

[15] These offices had a variety of names. See *Nongye Jingi* (No. 12, 1996: 18); *Zhongguo Gaigebao* (Sept. 17, 1998).

[16] Li Wenxue (1997).

[17] Ministry of Agriculture circular, February 1997.

[18] *NMRB* (Dec. 29, 1992).

[19] Jianchabu (1995).

[20] *Xinhua Online*, August 28, 2001 (*www.sina.com.cn/c/2001-08-28/341716.html*).

Central leaders personally intervened and frequently commented on the issue. Less than a year after his ascendance to the position of the Secretary General of the CCP, Jiang Zemin commented at a meeting on rural work: "These [burden] problems have caused serious discontent among peasants. We must try our best to solve them."[21] In December 1992, General Secretary Jiang Zemin and Premier Li Peng held meetings in six provinces and a general nationwide tele-conference on agriculture and burdens in particular, in which Jiang and Li made "specific demands" on local governments with regard to burden reduction. In 1993 central leaders intensively focused on both burdens and IOUs, and in later years, Premier Zhu Rongji and other central leaders voiced strong concern and a determination to reduce burdens.

Some provinces innovated on their own, devising peasant burden monitoring and regulation systems. Heilongjiang issued burden regulations as early as 1989. More than a thousand personnel slots were created in the agricultural economic administration at the county and township levels charged with power to audit rural taxation. In 1994, the province conducted intensive training sessions for 20,208 cadres from seventy-one counties as "peasant burden monitors."[22] In almost every year, the provincial government organized large-scale inspections. In 1990, it dispatched some four thousand cadres from counties and prefectures to townships and villages in an effort to "clean up collective finance, land, and taxation." This campaign disovered 153 million yuan worth of burdens that had been illicitly imposed. In 1991, 107 million yuan were found. Special inspection teams were also dispatched in 1992, 1993, and 1995.[23]

In Jiangsu province, where peasant income variations were more pronounced than elsewhere, provincial authorities targeted the unfairness of tax and levy rates. In 1998, the province decided to change the "average burden" to "fair burden." Jiangsu forged ahead of national regulations by attempting to base levy rates on the actual incomes of villager families, including both farm and off-farm incomes. This was done by first setting a total amount to be paid by the village and then by identifying high- and low-income families. Families with commercial and other business incomes paid at higher rates than farming families. The poorest families received exemptions. This progressive taxation scheme overcame at least some of the inequities in burden sharing, assuming proper implementation.[24] Moreover, by merging nonagricultural with agricultural incomes, this reform reduced the bias against farming, for in many places farming

---

[21] Li Wenxue (1997).

[22] Jiang Ming'an (1998).

[23] Jiang Ming'an (1998: 135).

[24] *Zhongguo Gaigebao* (June 1, 1998).

households bore relatively heavier burdens than nonfarming households. At the same time, these reports did not make clear how the dfficult problem of ascertaining actual household incomes was to be solved.

Several burden reduction efforts took the form of campaigns typical of Maoist mobilization practices. The most comprehensive national campaign was carried out in 1993, when central leaders greatly feared peasant unrest. In March, an "Emergency Circular" was issued followed by the summer directives mentioned earlier that ordered the wholesale slashing of burdens, all amidst a great deal of publicity. Intense pressure was generated on local officials as central and provincial inspection teams descended on the countryside. Local officials could not ignore or evade the pressures from above to reduce burdens, and in fact, unauthorized collections, especially those that exceeded the 5 percent T and V levies, did decline in 1993 in many places. In the autumn of that year, MOA claimed that peasants had saved 10 billion yuan, a substantial amount since one estimate of burdens resulting from fees, fines, and apportionments put them at 13.9 billion.[25] A circular issued by the central government in 1994, "Report of Inspections on Burden Reduction in 1993," also claimed significant successes.

The 1993 campaign was only partially successful, however.[26] In an interview in October 1993, then Minister of Agriculture Liu Jiang revealed that central government pressure was not effective everywhere. According to Liu, "some localities" did not implement the new rules properly, interpreted them in a "flexible manner," pretended to have eliminated burdens, or had simply ignored the central government order that fee collection be halted pending the completion of the screening process. "Comrades of some localities" had still not become aware of the seriousness of the problem. Liu acknowledged that localities were faced with insufficient budgets but exhorted them to give primacy to the general interest by reducing burdens.[27] The 1993 State Council inspection teams discovered that many local officials were reluctant to implement the directives on cuts, since "the current core task is economic development, not burden reduction."[28]

Most important, wily officials compensated for the loss of revenue from the reduced township and village levies by shifting extraction of these levies to miscellaneous fees, fines, and apportionments, the "three irregulars" (*sanluan*), which were more difficult to track and which became the major burden problem in the later 1990s. Rural officials displayed much ingenuity in maintaining excessive extractions even while pretending to comply with regime demands.

---

[25] Interview with Liu Jiang, Minister of Agriculture, *Xinhua* (Oct. 9, 1993, *FBIS*, No. 203: 29–31).
[26] Jianchabu (1995: 35).
[27] Liu Jiang, Interview (Oct. 9, 1993).
[28] Jianchabu (1995).

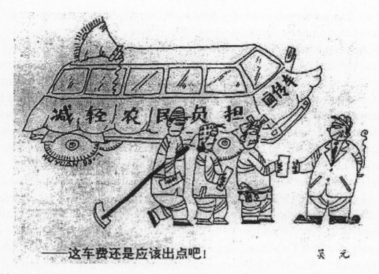

Figure 6.1 Three peasants have to pay a fee in order to enter a roving exhibit on reducing peasant burdens. The cadre says: "You still have to pay a fee." *Source: Fengci yu Youmo*, No. 16, August 20, 1993.

Thus, one village committee amalgamated all charges into a comprehensive set, labeled it the "agricultural tax," and assigned quotas of 80 yuan per *mu* and 40 yuan per household, thereby dramatically cutting the number of charges although the actual amount collected increased. Another reduced charges, but raised the fee for putting the indispensable seal on official documents to 50 yuan.[29] In Yunnan, in August 1994, no fewer than ten departments still collected illegal road-user fees.[30] In Hunan province, despite claims that peasant burdens were being kept below 5 percent in 1998, investigation found that actual burdens including fees ranged between 10 and 15 percent and in some areas even reached 20 percent.[31]

After a major campaign to reduce burdens, burdens would "bounce back," prompting the central authorities send to out new edicts and launch new drives, only to see the problem spring up once again. This happened after edicts were issued in 1990 and again after 1993. Formal compliance (*yangfeng yinwei*) was a widespread bureaucratic practice, but it is essential to keep in mind the under-lying structural problem. The inability of the regime to curb burdens more than temporarily was rooted in the reality that the remedial measures failed to specify

[29] *FBIS* (No. 116, June 18, 1993: 16).
[30] *Chuncheng Wanbao* (Aug. 15, 1994).
[31] *ZNJ* (No.9, 1998: 37–42).

how the financial needs of local governments were to be met once burdens had been reduced and how economic development goals were to be achieved.

When compliance was attained, therefore, a new problem arose: Who would pay for services and programs that were worthwhile, such as development and even those that would benefit the farmers? As shown in Chapters 3 and 4, taxes and fees opened up plenty of incentives and opportunities for predation, but they were also used for public purposes, at least some of which constituted essential services. The villagers, had they been asked, might well have approved of them, especially if the payment methods had been fairer and adjusted to the villagers' ability to pay.

In Sheyang county, Jiangsu, burdens were reduced in the spring of 1993, but the cost was immediately apparent. Water conservancy and basic agricultural construction projects, such as building culverts or pumping and draining stations, had been funded jointly by higher levels, the village committees, and households. "Now these funds are no longer available."[32] The projects, which had begun in April 1993, ground to a halt even though the late summer flooding season was about to start. In Sheyang, as elsewhere in rural China, crime and social disorder were disturbing people. "Rural public security teams" reportedly struggled effectively against crime and people did not want these teams to be disbanded. "However, the collection of money for rural public security has been canceled." With respect to education, Wei Houkai and Yang Dali found that the 1993 burden reduction campaign led to stoppages or cancellation of fundraising for school buildings and repairs, because there was a "huge decline in social donations for education in many regions."[33] Teachers were often not paid. In 1994, the situation in education was described as "catastrophic."[34] Villagers might well have agreed to make contributions to education that were within their means. Thus, a slash-and-burn approach was as irrational as an approach that required uniformity in the provision of services and public goods.

From the point of view of the performance incentives of local officials, burden cuts were a threat. As the chairwoman of a Sichuan township, who had lost a court case in which a group of peasants sued for refunds of illegal exactions, put it:

If we handle everything in accordance with the "Regulations on Burden Reduction," we will not be able to accomplish the tasks assigned by the

---

[32] *Zhongguo Xinxibao* (July 21, 1993, *JPRS*, No. 74, Oct. 7, 1993).

[33] Wei Houkai and Yang Dali (1998: 13–31). "Decentralization and Disparities in Local Education in China," *Social Sciences in China* (No. 3, autumn 1998, 13–31).

[34] Zhou Xiang (1994: 50–52). Minzhu yü Fazhi, April 7. This article discusses both urban and rural education.

higher authorities. All the quotas are set by relevant authorities. If we fail to [fulfill them] our salaries will be reduced and bonuses withheld.[35]

That burden reduction would have an adverse impact on the implementation of various government programs is highlighted by the fate of an important innovation designed to inform peasants as to just what their burdens were. A "peasant burden card" stipulated to each household its obligations with respect to funds, goods, and labor. Any additional charges not specified on the card could be refused. Introduced on the initiative of some provinces, the cards were to be issued to each farm household nationwide. In 1994, at least nine provinces, where peasant burdens were relatively heavy, implemented the burden card system.[36] In 1993, Hengyang city, Hunan province, printed two hundred seventy thousand copies of its "farmer burden card," but only a fourth of them were handed out. Distribution was stopped because officials realized that making good on the limits stipulated on the cards would throw towns and townships into deficit. In one township, eleven of eighteen nonstate payroll personnel were paid entirely from apportionments among farmers, the rest being paid only in part by the county and its departments. Cadres and staff who would have been fired included the telephone operator and those in charge of household registration and family planning. Because of this, Hengyang officials felt unable to inform farmers about the limitations of their legal obligations.[37]

Local officials, put in the contradictory position of having to cut burdens yet deliver on their assignments, and with the Center demanding that the rules and regulations be made widely known to villagers, sometimes took extraordinary measures to prevent peasants from learning about the rules and from acquiring "the imperial sword" with which to petition higher authorities for relief (*shangfang baojian*).[38] In Sichuan, Center regulations were treated in some localities as "internal documents" not to be transmitted to the peasants.[39] In some cases villagers broke through this barrier accidentally when, visiting village or township offices, they came across a booklet or circular on burdens.[40]

A widely publicized incident of blocking information occurred in July and August 2000, when the deputy editor of a rural journal published by the Jiangxi Provincial Party Committee, published a handbook on peasant burden reduction. This was a 147-page collection of rules and decrees from the central authorities,

[35] *RMRB* (Sept. 12, 1992).
[36] Ibid., 512.
[37] *RMRB* (May 18, 1993).
[38] *Jiage Lilun yu Shijian* (No. 7, July 1994: 41); and *RMRB* (Oct. 16, 1993).
[39] *SCRB* (Jan. 3, 1993).
[40] Authors' interviews, September 1998.

as issued in Jiangxi and Hunan, along with a section on "frequently asked questions" and a phone number where farmers could lodge complaints. On the cover was a picture of Premier Zhu Rongji. Twelve thousand copies were sold in two weeks. Some farmers traveled from distant places to buy the book. Just as the publisher was planning a second printing, the journal was notified by "departments concerned" to stop the sale and recall all the books that had been sold. Local cadres were mobilized to go from house to house to retrieve the book, giving refunds or even more money. Eleven thousand copies were recovered. One farmer was detained for fifteen days for selling the book. The editor of the booklet was relieved of his duties. The incident was reported by media outside of the province including Central Television and became something of a cause célèbre.[41]

How well were peasants acquainted with the rules? A State Council survey in 1992 based on a sample of 1,284 peasants and village cadres found that a majority of peasants lacked a thorough knowledge of the regulations on taxation and burden control. Thirty-four percent of respondents were unaware of them; 39 percent did not know about the 5 percent limit on exactions or the rules about compulsory labor, or about their right to refuse to pay excess burdens; 48 percent didn't know which "department above the township level had supervisory control" over the peasants' tax obligations; 44 percent did not know how to safeguard their legal rights; and 35 percent were unaware they had any legal recourse concerning fines levied on them. "A fairly large number" said that knowing about the rules and their legal rights "was useless" and even if one did know, "I am afraid to say anything."[42] In 1994 a survey found that 52.3 percent of peasants had not heard of the 5 percent ceiling on T and V levies.[43] More recently, in 1999, a survey conducted in nine provinces, mostly in agricultural rural China, showed that although 100 percent of a sample of rural youths knew about the NATO bombing of the Chinese Embassy in Belgrade and other national-level events, only 53 percent were aware of the fee-to-tax reform to reduce burdens and other matters affecting their livelihoods.[44]

The regime was undoubtedly serious about reducing peasant burdens, if only to avoid a further deterioration in state-peasant relations, but central circulars themselves reflected the unsolved dilemmas resulting from fiscal constraints

---

[41] *Nanfang Zhoumo* (Oct. 10, 2000, *www.nanfang* daily.com.cn). CCTV reported on this case on November 11, 2000 in its "Economy Half Hour" program. For other media reports on this case, see Hunan TV (*www.hunantv.com/block/talkeasy/htjs/htjs72*) and *Zhejiang Agriculture* (*www.agzj.com/ncxxb/201021*). See also *Wall Street Journal* (Nov. 20, 2000).

[42] *Xinhua Ribao* (Oct. 30, 1992, *JPRS*, No. 95, Dec. 22, 1992: 32).

[43] Jianchabu (1995).

[44] Cao Weiqiu, et al. (2000: 34–8).

and development goals. Even as section six of Document No.1 of 1984, a major central directive on rural reforms, demanded reduction of "unreasonable assessments and of the 'above-quota' burdens on the peasants," section five called for joint efforts by the state, the collectives, and individuals to raise funds for infrastructure projects.[45] In 1984, the State Council authorized the townships to levy a surcharge for education and to arouse "the enthusiasm of rural collective economic organizations and social forces for education." The 1985 central directive on burden reduction also called for encouragement of "voluntary" contributions from society. Later burden reduction decrees also upheld the principle of fund-raising as long as it was properly authorized.[46] The education taxes and other educational levies became, as shown in Chapter 3, the major burden in the 1990s. Fierce denunciation of unreasonable burdens thus went hand in hand with sanctions for societal fund-raising, a practice deeply rooted in a tradition of charitable giving for local needs, but one that was often involuntary.

"LETTERS AND VISITS" AND THE ROLE OF THE MEDIA

The second strategy the regime used to cope with the burden problem was to permit peasants to petition the authorities for redress of grievance. When peasants complained to higher authorities above the townships, there was the possibility that officials might respond and order adoption of remedial measures. From the point of view of the local cadres, higher-level intervention of this sort was unwelcome because it drew negative attention to their bailiwicks. The regime also encouraged press coverage. Investigations by journalists and press publicity of abuses served as a form of pressure on the local authorities singled out while sending a message to officials generally. From the regime's point of view, these two channels served as sources of information, which for obvious reasons local officials were not anxious to have disclosed, at the same time assuaging peasant anger by demonstrating to them that the regime cared about their plight. From the point of view of villagers seeking redress, outside ignorance of their situation was a serious obstacle. Given the likelihood that local power holders, especially at the township level, would not listen to their grievances or would block their transmissions to higher levels, villagers had to devise strategies to communicate with the outside world. One way was to make trouble: Often, illegal protests – sit-ins, demonstrations, blockades of railroads

---

[45] *RMRB* (June 12, 1984). We are indebted to Professor Tyrene White for bringing this point to our attention.

[46] See decision on burdens, *Xinhua* (Oct. 15, 1990, *FBIS*, No. 202: 31–4).

or roads – were motivated by the hope that higher-level officials would hear about them and come to their aid.[47] Another was to try to communicate by letter or in person or to hope for media coverage, particularly by newspapers such as the *Nongmin Ribao* (*Farmers' Daily, NMRB*).

The "letters and visits" (L&V) system was the major channel through which peasants could communicate their grievances to higher-level leaders, by writing letters, individually or in groups, or, particularly important, by individual or collective visits to higher authorities (*jiti shangfang*). Established in the 1950s and revived early on in the reform period, the L&V system was supported by numerous statements by top leaders and by the demand that those who staff these L&V offices deal seriously with complaints.[48] L&V offices were established by the Party and government from the Center on down to the counties to handle complaints from the masses.[49] The National People's Congress and its lower-level counterparts also maintained offices to receive visitors and process letters. The state-run media were part of this system, since they too received letters and visits from the public.

Ordinary people sent huge numbers of letters. As of 1988, the *NMRB*, according to its editor-in-chief, received about a thousand letters a day, most consisting of "complaints by farmers against ill treatment by local tyrants."[50] Ten years later, in 1998, the State Council and Central Committee Letters and Visits Office alone processed four hundred sixty thousand complaints, more than half from the countryside, a not atypical number judging by statistics for the mid-1990s.[51] Provincial offices also received numerous complaints. Hunan handled more than three hundred thousand in 1998, the largest number since the mid-1980s. In 1996, 488,177 peasants contacted the provincial authorities in Jiangsu.[52]

In 1995 and 1996, burdens were the largest source of complaints, accounting for more than 30 percent of rural complaints lodged at all levels from the county on up, and over a third of all collective visits. The second most important source, also related to burdens, concerned violations of law and discipline by basic-level cadres.[53] In Jiangsu, burdens also topped the list of grievances,

---

[47] Interview, Beijing University, September 1998.
[48] For the most recent of many such exhortations, see *Xinhua* (Feb. 14, 2000, *SWB-FE*/3766, G/3–4), reporting on Zhu Rongji's inspection of the Central Committee's complaints office.
[49] See Nathan (1985: 80–1).
[50] *Asiaweek* (April 1, 1988).
[51] *RMRB* (Feb. 9, 1999) and *Liaowang* (No. 11, March 11, 1996: 6–20).
[52] *Hunan Ribao* (Jan. 16, 1999, *SWB-FE* 3442, G/4), and *Jiangsu Nianjian-1997* (Jiangsu Yearbook-1997).
[53] Chen Weihua (1998).

most of them complaints coming from the poorer northern and central regions of the province which lacked nonagricultural income. In Sichuan, burdens constituted the second most important complaint and in Hebei, burdens ranked fourth.[54]

Letters served as a source of information on local conditions for central leaders. The Letters and Visits Office of the Central Committee/State Council (nominally separate but actually one unit) was supposed to sort through the letters according to subject, compile summaries, forward some "directly to leading comrades for comments," and direct others to the appropriate ministries and agencies. Information from citizens reportedly played a major role in the work of the central and local Discipline Inspection Departments, since 80 percent of the clues about cadre misconduct and financial irregularities came from letters of complaint sent by the public.[55]

Newspapers, which also received a huge number of letters from the public, published some of them, but in addition, the "mass work department" of each paper compiled the letters in internal journals intended only for the leadership. An issue of *Gansu Daily*'s "Extracts from Letters" contained a letter signed by an entire village complaining about the brutal and grossly excessive collection methods of town cadres.[56] Other provincial newspapers also published letters internally. The editorial department of *Xinhua Ribao* (Nanjing) published a monthly collection of letters that included graphic descriptions of abuses.[57] In Beijing, the *Farmers' Daily* distributed "Internal Reference: Extracts from Letters by the Masses," to eighteen central agencies beginning with the Standing Committee of the Politburo. One three-page issue contained a letter from a Hebei village, written in the name of eight hundred members of the village, detailing the abusive fourteen-year reign of their Party secretary, who was depicted as corrupt and brutal and who, among various other misdeeds, imposed excessive levies.[58] The openly circulated newspapers apparently did not publish letters written by large groups of people. The internal reports were accompanied by requests for leader comments and instructions.

The central authorities handled letters in several ways. One was to launch follow-up investigations to verify the charges. Reportedly, 60 to 70 percent of complaints about cadre misconduct were found to be "true or basically true."[59] In one case, Jiang Zemin ordered verification of a report that higher-level officials

---

[54] *Jiangsu Nianjian 1997*; *Sichuan Nianjian 1997*, and *Hebei Xinfang* (No. 3, 1998: 15).

[55] *Liaowang* (No. 11, 1996: 6–20).

[56] *Laixin Zhaibian, Gansu Ribao* (No. 603, Oct. 17, 1998).

[57] *Laixin Zhaibian, Xinhua Ribao* (No. 18, Aug. 25, 1998).

[58] *Neibu Cangao: Qunzhong laixin zhaibian* (No. 1, Jan. 8, 1999).

[59] *Liaowang* (No. 11, 1996).

visiting the rural areas had behaved dishonestly, ordering that if it was true, "we must circulate a notice through the whole Party."[60]

A letter writer might receive a direct response. One such letter about burdens was sent by an Anhui farmer directly to Jiang Zemin in December 1992, stating that "It would be a big problem if there were unrest among the eight hundred million peasants. The Party Center should try every possible means to lessen the burden of the peasants!" A week later, the L&V office replied: "Your letter has been forwarded to the relevant authorities. The State Council is about to take measures to redress this problem. Thank you for your enthusiasm in taking part in the administration and discussion of state affairs."[61]

A letter might simply be forwarded to the relevant local authorities with a request to handle the matter, possibly exposing the sender to retaliation. And many letters ended up in the files or in the wastebasket.[62] Central leaders repeatedly criticized neglect of the L&V work: "It is strictly forbidden to cover up, ignore, transfer through different levels, pass around, and leave such cases unsettled."[63] In 1999, a Party secretary of Xinxiang city, Henan, was dismissed in part for having ordered two hundred letters from citizens destroyed.[64]

Central units were sometimes mobilized to initiate remedial action immediately. In 1990, the central L&V Office received a series of letters complaining about the withholding by rural post offices of remittance payments to farm families sent by migrant relatives. Instead, they issued IOUs called "green slips," comparable to the "white slips" issued in lieu of cash for procurement sales. The L&V office collated these complaints and sent out a circular, whereupon the Ministry of Posts and several other units held a teleconference, demanding that all green slips be redeemed within seven days. This allegedly solved the problem.[65] *NMRB* claims to have been the first national paper to have exposed the IOU problem, publishing letters from Hubei that its journalists had investigated, causing local leaders to take remedial steps.[66]

A case of decisive responsiveness occurred in 2000, when Li Changping, the Hubei township Party secretary mentioned in Chapter 3, wrote the State Council about burdens and the desperate financial situation in the countryside. His letter was received, prompting an investigation by plainclothes officials

---

[60] Ibid.

[61] *Liaowang* (No. 11, 1996).

[62] Information from a Chinese student who worked in a Beijing City Letters and Visits office in the 1980s, New York, 1993.

[63] *Liaowang* (No. 11, 1996).

[64] *Xinhua,* cited in *SJRB* (Nov. 9, 1999).

[65] Ibid.

[66] Interview with *NMRB* editors, August 4, 1994.

who verified the truthfulness of Li's complaints. State Council leaders ordered Hubei authorities to deal with these very serious problems and in early June, the Hubei Party secretary and governor visited the township and drastic measures were taken to reduce burdens, eliminate equal assessments (for example, of the slaughter tax) and other abuses, and ordered payment of the official grain protection price. Further steps were taken to eliminate village indebtedness and to reduce the bureaucracy of the county by 850 personnel and to cut education costs by amalgamating schools and reducing staff. Whether this slash-and-burn campaign remained effective or whether burdens bounced back is not clear. Li Changping, whose exposé had made him many enemies, resigned his Party post in October and moved to Shenzhen.[67]

Collective Visits. Tens of thousands of citizens did not just write letters but visited L&V offices, often traveling all the way to Beijing in search of redress, showing up at various L&V reception offices. Some persisted for years in their efforts to get help.[68] Visits by groups were by definition more difficult to deal with. In 1988, villagers in Zhongxiang county, Hubei, wrote 402 letters lodging complaints about cadres, but also made 500 collective visits to county offices to appeal for help.[69] In a Henan city, 170 collective visits were made in the first nine months of 1993, the groups ranging in size from 7 members to 145, "with an average of 20 to 30, whereas larger delegations often had 60 to 70 members."[70] Wei county, Hebei, registered 4,559 cases of collective petitioning between 1993 and 1995, or 1,533 per year.[71] In 1997, Hebei province alone experienced 6,047 group visits, each averaging 22 members, 44 per county.[72] According to the Ministry of Agriculture, in 1996 eighteen provinces experienced ten or more cases of burden-related group visits in which petitioners skipped over administrative levels, the cases adding up to 1,260, or 70 per province. Eleven provinces had ten or fewer such cases.[73]

Collective visits, according to interviews conducted in 1998, became more frequent in the 1990s but there appeared to be enormous variation. In some cases, an apparent contagion effect led to a multiplicity of collective visits. In the early 1990s, Huixian city, Henan, attained national fame on this account, since recurring "fairly large-scale collective visits" were organized by villagers

---

[67] *Nanfang Zhoumo* (Aug. 25 and Oct. 14, 2000).
[68] See *NYT* (Dec. 7, 1998), for some pitiful stories.
[69] Wang Chongru (1990).
[70] Cited in O'Brien and Li (1995: 760).
[71] *Hebei Xinfang* (No. 3, 1998: 7).
[72] Ibid.
[73] Zhang Heping and Ren Yiqin (1999).

in more than one-third of the townships and towns. Convenient transportation facilitated the groups' travel, first to the city, then to the province, and finally to the State Council. This locality had a long history of "hard struggle" to build collective projects during the Mao period, which may have left a legacy of solidarity that facilitated collective mobilization in the 1990s.[74] Eighty percent of the collective visits were about excessive burdens and chaotic village finances.

A telling case of a visit to the *Farmers' Daily* Beijing office by a farmer who in effect represented a large number of people was published on the paper's front page in 1991. Wang Diancai, from Taian county, Liaoning, a long-time reader of *NMRB*, was inspired to visit by a December 1990 article that called for laws to reduce the very sorts of burdens that had bankrupted him. He sold his last oxen to pay for the trip. Wang did not simply come on his own behalf. Before his journey, he mobilized a large network of contacts and visited six hundred families in ten-odd townships, tape recording their stories and bringing six reels of audio tape with him to Beijing. He expressed the hope that *NMRB* would appeal to the State Council to bring relief to the hard-pressed villagers. Staff members of the paper accompanied an investigation group of the Ministry of Agriculture to Liaoning and found a distressing situation which confirmed the truthfulness of the reports.[75] Whether remedial steps were taken was not reported, however.

According to O'Brien and Li, most collective complaints "are formal, written complaints physically carried by a group of villagers to higher levels. . . . The complaint cannot be anonymous and must be signed or thumb printed." It usually consisted of a joint letter written, signed, and delivered by a group of villagers, which detailed the particular grievance and cited supporting evidence. Reference to specific policies, laws, and regulations was likely to make their case more persuasive.[76] Li and O'Brien rightly call this "policy-based resistance," since villagers sought redress on the basis of rights contained in particular center rules and policies.[77]

Collective visits were clearly a form of pressure on officialdom. From the official point of view, when a sizeable group of villagers appeared at a county Party and government compound, it disrupted normal routines, giving the local leaders a "big headache."[78] As noted in Chapter 5 when officials sought to placate a group of visitors with empty promises or resorted to bureaucratic trickery, angry and frustrated petitioners could and did resort to sit-ins, demonstrations, or

---

[74] Xu Yong (1998b).

[75] *NMRB* (April 18, 1991).

[76] O'Brien and Li (1995: 758).

[77] Li and O'Brien (1996: 40–7).

[78] Xu Yong (1998b).

riots. The largest of the collective visits in Wei county, Hebei, consisted of three hundred villagers who fruitlessly petitioned their township. There followed an outbreak of violence in which more than a thousand persons surrounded the township headquarters and beat the Party committee secretary.[79] Violence did not always result, but collective visits were viewed as harbingers of instability.[80]

It is remarkable that a state which attempts to suppress any unsanctioned organized activity and which is obsessed with stability, did not prohibit collective petitioning outright. "Regulations on Handling Complaints" promulgated in 1995 limited and regulated but did not outlaw group visits. These rules stipulated that aggrieved groups should use the telephone and letters to transmit their complaints. If visits were necessary, no more than five representatives should be sent. Complaints should be made to the next higher administrative unit or to the one above that. If petitioners didn't abide by this rule and contacted a higher administrative level, the higher level should not accept the complaint, unless "it regards it as necessary to deal with it directly." The Regulations called on the authorities to handle promptly charges regarding violations of law and "infringement of the villagers' legal rights and interests," and "resolutely" to deal with cases that "might have strong social repercussions," that is, cause riots. Other provisions warned petitioners not to "nag, insult, beat, or threaten" the staff of the reception offices and not to cause disturbances.[81] These rules suggest that the regime viewed visits as important outlets for the voicing of grievances and as a form of pressure on local officials even as it was uneasy about the larger group visits, which demonstrated the villagers' capacity to engage in collective action.

Although complaints were supposed to be directed to the township authorities, villagers preferred to "skip administrative levels" (*yueji*) in the hope of securing a more sympathetic hearing higher up, since the complaints were mostly directed against township and town officials. In Hebi city, Henan, 60 percent of two hundred groups of rural complainants bypassed at least one level on their way to the municipal government.[82] A high rate of groups skipping levels drew unwelcome attention to the village, township, or county from which they came. Among the stratagems used by collective groups to increase the likelihood of obtaining a hearing locally was to threaten to appeal further up the hierarchy or to send a group when important official meetings were in progress, thereby

---

[79] Zhu Shouyin (1998: 45).

[80] Xu Yong (1998b).

[81] "Regulations on Handling Complaints," *Xinhua* (Oct. 30, 1995, *FBIS*, No. 216: 13–16). The Chinese version is in *ZRGYGB* (No. 185, 1995). We are indebted to Laura Luehrmann, Ohio State University, for a copy of these documents.

[82] O'Brien and Li (1995: 778).

embarrassing the local leaders.[83] This not only might lead to higher-level demands for corrective action but also possibly to negative performance evaluations of the local officials, who had failed to handle their relations with the masses properly.[84] Conversely, absence of collective visits was a sign of good performance. A Shanxi journal boasted that in 1997 the province had the nation's fewest number of collective visits. Even big cases in Shanxi generally didn't end up in Beijing but were settled locally. Ordinary ones were handled at county level or below.[85]

Collective visits sometimes did have results. Before 1995, some villages in Taihe county, Anhui, bore burdens that took 30 percent of net incomes, resulting in constant collective visits. One peasant went to the State Council three times. This reportedly prompted the county authorities to take corrective action. Burdens were lowered to the 5 percent level and stability was restored.[86] Comprehensive data showing what proportion of such visits actually yield improvements have not been released.

Local officials clearly had an incentive to prevent, halt, or abort collective visits, either by taking action to defuse the grievance in question or by forcibly preventing petitioners from going further up the hierarchy. Village and township cadres had the biggest motivation to block or punish complaints and petitions. Engaging in collective protest boosted villagers' courage and determination to press claims, since there was safety in numbers. It was more difficult to retaliate against groups than individuals. Still, news of beatings and killings of complainants have come to light.[87] One instance of local officials seeking to crush collective petitioners took place in Yilong county, Sichuan. In late 1999, four veteran petitioners were formally charged with having organized an illegal organization, a "County-wide Command Center" for the exchange of information among peasants, which they set up because local officials had fended off their requests to see official burden reduction directives. Attempts to arrest the four met with strong peasant resistance. Ultimately, the four were able to secure assistance from provincial, city, and county units, which organized a team to investigate and indeed found serious abuses. Some cadres were dismissed and money illegally extracted was refunded.[88]

---

[83] Ibid., 778–9.
[84] Zhu Shouyin (1998).
[85] *Shanxi Nongjing* (No. 2, 1999: 40).
[86] *Banyuetan—Neibuban* (No. 4, 1999: 22–3).
[87] In 1993, 1994, and 1998 cases of farmers beaten to death for complaining were reported. See *Zhongguo Qingnianbao* (April 22, 1993; *FBIS*, No. 18: 8–10); *FZRB* (April 10, 1996); and Zhu Huaxin (1998: 365).
[88] Jiang Zuoping and Yang Sanyun (2000: 15–16).

Role of the Media. Many newspapers and popular journals, including the *People's Daily*, wrote extensively about burdens, IOUs, and other abuses, also publicizing relevant laws, regulations, and policy statements. As can be seen from the source citations throughout this study, the various Chinese media used this permissiveness to run exposés, sometimes written by aggressive investigative journalists. The regime explicitly told the media to play a stronger "supervisory role" in the campaign to lighten burdens.[89]

One newspaper, the *Farmers' Daily*, published under the auspices of the Ministry of Agriculture, emerged as a self-proclaimed champion of peasant interests. In an interview with *Asiaweek* in 1988, the editor-in-chief, Zhang Guangyou, noted that peasants had "few platforms to air their views on policies affecting their lives," hence, *NMRB* should play this role.[90] As an editorial entitled, "Reporting on the voice of the peasants is an obligation we should fulfill to the utmost" put it:

> To be concerned about the suffering of the peasants, to give voice to them, to speak for them, to protect their legitimate interests are not only our very important tasks but our greatest obligation. It must be acknowledged that we have not done enough in this regard and that we must exert ourselves to improve our efforts. . . . We hope that we will be supported by the leaders at various levels.[91]

Sympathetic local officials praised the paper as a courageous defender of the peasants. The deputy head of the CPPCC of Feng county, Jiangsu, characterized the paper as "spiritual food for cadres and peasants:"

> Now, at long last, peasants have a newspaper of their own. If we didn't have a newspaper that dared to tell the truth about the peasants, others would misunderstand us even more. . . . In this way, *Nongmin Ribao* will serve to raise the peasants' social position in carrying out a dialogue among various circles of society.[92]

Similarly, the head of the rural work department of a Jiangxi county Party committee called *NMRB* "our newspaper." He pointed out that during the current period of agricultural difficulties, a paper was needed that voiced our "calls" (*huhan*) and that reported objectively on the situation without evading and

---

[89] See, e.g., the Central Committee "Decision" in *RMRB* (April 1, 1997).
[90] *Asiaweek* (April 1, 1988).
[91] *NMRB*, Editorial Department (Nov. 17, 1988).
[92] *NMRB* (Sept. 8, 1988).

dodging the issues. *NMRB* helped fill this need. Several other local officials expressed similarly enthusiastic views about the role of *NMRB* as a substitute for a farmers' organization.[93] Significantly, even though after the Tiananmen incident *NMRB* was criticized for one-sidedly emphasizing peasant grievances, the paper kept on reporting them.[94]

With a circulation of eight hundred thousand, *NMRB* was able to reach most villages. Some ordinary peasants subscribed and many wrote letters to the editors. As noted earlier, forcing villagers to subscribe to publications was one of the burden grievances. But in this case, subscriptions served to provide farmers with information local officials wanted to deny them. In one village, cadres cancelled subscriptions to the *NMRB*, allegedly because of the costs, but a complaining farmer's letter noted pointedly that these same "frugal" cadres freely spent 200 to 300 yuan entertaining visiting officials. This case prompted *NMRB* to insist on the peasants' "autonomous power" to decide on subscriptions, not failing to observe that they should choose the *Farmers' Daily*, since only it served as a bridge to, and "mouthpiece" for, nine hundred million peasants.[95]

In the reform period, television became the most important mass medium in the countryside. As of 1997, two-thirds of rural households owned black and white TVs and a fourth owned color TVs.[96] Peasants avidly watched programs that exposed official misconduct, such as the highly popular "Focus of Coverage" (*Jiaodian fangtan jiemu*), whose daily fifteen-minute broadcasts were directly supported by the Premier, Zhu Rongji.[97] Some villagers, unable to secure redress locally, wrote to the program asking it to send an investigative team. In one of the Jiangxi cases, a peasant ruined by his township secretary's ruthless exactions phoned "Focus of Coverage" in the hope of getting his case publicized.[98] Local officials sometimes took out their anger on offending journalists who exposed their illegal activities. Punishments included dismissal of locally based journalists from their jobs and sometimes violence.[99]

The difficulties of getting effective help from higher levels is illustrated by Case 6.1, reported in 1996 by the journal *Minzhu yu Fazhi* (*Democracy and*

---

[93] Ibid.

[94] See *NMRB* (Sept. 11, 12, 1989).

[95] See *NMRB* (Sept. 14, 1993, Sept. 28, 1993).

[96] *ZTN* (1998: 355).

[97] See *Boston Sunday Globe* (Feb. 21, 1999).

[98] *Ping Kuo Jih Pao* (Nov. 25, 1996, *SWB-FE*/2783, G/4–5). Whether this plea was successful is not known; also *SCJP* (Nov. 26, 1996).

[99] See *www.stratfor.com*, Global Intelligence Update (March 1, 2000), citing a report from *Shanghai Star* (Feb. 29, 2000).

Rule of Law), of an eight-year struggle by a Hunan village against excessive burdens.[100] The account is remarkable for several reasons:

1. The involvement of one of the small democratic parties, which are part of the CCP-led united front and have normally been quiescent.
2. The absence of institutionalized means of securing redress since neither local courts, village committees, nor local people's congresses played a role.
3. The complete dependence of villagers on provincial-level intervention.
4. Villagers' capacity for sustained collective action.
5. The extraordinary tenacity of the township leaders' resistance and county-level foot dragging.

Case 6.1. Sometime in 1988, the newspaper of the Hunan branch of the China Association for the Promotion of Democracy (*Zhongguo Minzhu Cujin Hui*, CAPD) ran an article about a poor village in Qingting township, Hengyang county. This was the result of a letter or visit from the village and subsequent investigation by reporters and "responsible comrades" from the CAPD's Provincial Committee. The article recounted the dismal burden situation in Qingheng and the peasants' acute suffering. Accompanying the story was a note from the Hengyang county government accepting the newspaper's criticism and promising to take remedial steps. Why the village made contact with the Association was not explained.

Some time later the villagers told the CAPD Committee that township cadres had thwarted implementation of the county's burden reduction measures and were retaliating against those who had exposed the situation. "Some cadres" also were scheming to lodge a complaint or bring suit against the newspaper. In 1992, when the Center vigorously demanded burden reduction, "some local power holders" played the "same old tricks," evading implementation.

Two years later, in September 1994, the villagers wrote a new, lengthy letter to the provincial CAPD Committee, detailing the severity of the "three irregulars" and the abusive behavior of township cadres who searched homes and beat people, asking that the Committee forward their letter to provincial leaders.

In mid-November 1994, the CAPD Committee organized a group including members of the national and provincial CPPCC [a united front organization], the provincial People's Congress, and journalists, to go to Qingheng village unofficially and incognito (*weifu sifang*). Villagers reported that after 1993 the burdens had rebounded and they told the familiar story of harsh and endlessly increasing exactions. They were most upset

---

[100] Li Shengping (1996).

by the "vile" high pressure work style of some township cadres, who, *inter alia*, extorted a fine for having a bad attitude. The Qingting township CCP secretary, Hu Weiping, was both abusive and corrupt. The harsh extractions prompted twenty families to move elsewhere; others thought of abandoning farming. Nearly one-third of the women reportedly sold blood simply to survive. Following this investigation, the provincial CAPD Committee reported to the national chairman of the CAPD who gave instructions to the Hunan branch to pursue the matter.[101]

On February 20, 1995, the CAPD Committee head spoke at a meeting of the provincial Communist Party committee about Qingheng village and offered remedial suggestions. His speech elicited stormy applause. Provincial CCP secretary Wang Maolin praised the report and activated the relevant provincial Party and government departments to investigate further, incognito, and to make Qingheng village a model for the entire province, since its situation was representative of the province.

Thus mobilized, on February 23, 1995, provincial officials went to Hengyang city and Qingheng village in the company of city burden-reduction officials, spending the afternoon and evening meeting with peasants. Only three days later, Wang addressed a provincial anticorruption conference, described the Qingheng situation and ordered severe penalties for the offending cadres. He also told the returning investigators to inform the CAPD Committee and solicit their opinions. Much publicity resulted. The national press carried articles praising Secretary Wang's personal initiative and the role of the CAPD.

In the meantime, Hengyang city Party and government launched their own campaign, publicizing Qingheng's plight. The Hengyang county Party secretary went to Qingheng and canceled eleven fees. Hu Weiping, the township Party secretary was dismissed and subjected to disciplinary sanctions. The issue seemed settled.

It was not. Qingheng villagers kept visiting and writing to the CAPD, complaining that once more, township cadres continued to flout higher-level instructions, pressing peasants to pay some of the canceled fees and levying still new ones, while pressuring and intimidating villagers. Some CCP cadres dismissed the united front organizations such as the CAPD as lacking political authority and power. "You must not obey them. We are the government and [the Communist] Party. They are not. You must obey us!" Hu Weiping, despite his dismissal, boasted that his turn to run things would come again. Villagers were very worried about retaliation.

---

[101] *NMRB* (March 8, 1997).

The CAPD leaders proposed to settle the matter once and for all, based on CCP Secretary Wang's instructions. They organized still another investigation team to visit Qingheng, again incognito. Once more the team gathered data. The team reported its findings to a county meeting attended by the key leaders, who didn't dispute the findings but emphasized the problems and difficulties in carrying out higher-level instructions: "The crux of the matter is that a small number of lower-level cadres harbors conflicting ideas and feign compliance." The county leaders promised to eliminate this "intestinal obstruction."

The CAPD group also transmitted its finding to the provincial Party and government, which pressured the Hengyang county leaders to take further action. The county Party committee thereupon once again sent a team to Qingheng to reduce burdens and also to promote the collective economy in order to create a foundation for prosperity, thereby solving the burden problem. These steps prompted some of those who had left the village to return.

Remarkably, the story still did not end here. Ex-Party secretary Hu Weiping, who had been dismissed but not otherwise disciplined, continued to retain influence. Peasants still worried about retaliation. Thirty villagers wrote a joint letter that specified twelve grievances and asked the higher levels to correct them. After still further investigation, the CAPD Committee wrote another report in late December 1995. CCP secretary Mao sent it to the Hengyang city Party secretary with instructions to act firmly and make the county leaders understand the importance of the issue.

In January 1996, the Hengyang city Party secretary, accompanied by legal personnel, started intensive work on burdens, meeting with peasants and listening to reports. Hu Weiping and other township cadres were expelled from the CCP and subjected to disciplinary and "economic" punishment. A campaign to rectify the township cadre work style was to be launched. Burden management was to be made a public matter within the county and there was to be democratic supervision. The county also sent "reduce-burdens and attain-prosperity work teams" to Qingting township and seven other villages where peasants also had protested vehemently. At the annual meetings of the National People's Congress and the CPPCC held in March 1997, burden reduction in Qingting was hailed as a great success and as exemplifying the supervisory role of the small democratic parties. And so, amidst celebrations, the story ended, at least for the time being.[102]

[102] Ibid.

ENABLING VILLAGERS TO SEEK LEGAL REDRESS

China's leaders wished for the courts to play a significant role in the resolution of rural grievances. In April 1993, the Supreme People's Court issued a circular calling on courts to play their part in curbing excessive burdens. Courts were to call to account officials who retaliate "against those who inform against, expose, or file charges against" illegal impositions.[103] Also in 1993, *People's Daily* ran an article on burden reduction on its front page, headlined "Give peasants the imperial sword of the rule of law."[104] Three years later, in 1996, the vice president of the Supreme People's Court, Luo Haocai, again called for the courts to get involved with burden management, noting that "the majority of peasant burden cases brought to court are reasonable and correct."[105] In late 1998, Politburo member Luo Gan told a national court conference that "cases in rural areas embody contradictions that could easily explode, so just decisions are especially important."[106]

These exhortations responded to the reality that peasants seeking judicial redress faced major obstacles. A legal infrastructure, albeit thin, was established. By 1988, for instance, 17,411 branch county court branches had been set up in townships. Legal services, though far from adequate, became increasingly available. Laws, including the Administrative Litigation Law adopted in 1990 (henceforth ALL), were passed authorizing citizens to sue officials. And substantial efforts were devoted to educating ordinary rural people about their legal rights, including the specific procedures that had to be followed to bring suit.[107] Greater awareness of rules and regulations, the distribution of "burden cards," and the posting of permissible fees also enabled many peasants to determine whether or not their rights had been violated. There is a good deal of evidence that many peasants became much more conscious of their rights.

Courts were reluctant, however, to take burden cases:[108] "Farmers have always found it very difficult to take the local authorities to court because their applications to file writs are routinely turned down and they are still not guaranteed fair hearings." This was due to the close ties between the courts and the local power structure. Local governments sought to influence court decisions, thereby "depriving peasants of their rights to seek justice." The president of

---

[103] *Xinhua* (April 9, 1993, *FBIS*, No.46, 47).

[104] *RMRB* (Oct. 16, 1993).

[105] Luo Haocai (1996).

[106] *Xinhua* (Nov. 28, 1998, *SWB-FE*/3397, G/2).

[107] See Pitman Potter (1991: 96). On its implementation, see Minxin Pei (1997). For a booklet on law designed for rural consumption, see Huang Mengdi and Li Ning (1990). For a handbook on how to bring a lawsuit, see Beidou Falü Shiwusuo Yanjiu Shi (1995).

[108] *ZXS* (Oct. 28, 1996, *FBIS*, No. 209).

the Supreme People's Court charged that some townships treated court staff as their own employees, thereby preventing independent and fair trials. He called for improving the image of the courts and raising the people's confidence in law. If the county courts failed to take cases, the intervention of higher courts was needed.[109] In one case, a court responded positively to a village committee petition for "an order of payment" against a peasant who had no cash because of harvest failure and who owed 298.5 yuan in taxes. The judge ordered the defendant to pay the amount within fifteen days and charged 50 yuan for the petition fee. "The public, filled with indignation . . . organized themselves [sic] spontaneously and appealed to the intermediate people's court and relevant departments to demand that justice be upheld."[110]

Despite these obstacles, villagers did sue. An impressive but highly variable number of lawsuits was filed against rural local governments in the 1990s, of which an unspecified proportion concerned burdens. In Sichuan: 3,717 cases were filed in 1991 and 1992, but the number dropped to 614 in the years 1993 to 1995. In Hebei there were 2,600 cases between 1993 and late 1997, but in Shandong, as many as 2,600 burden cases were brought in the first half of 1995 alone.[111] It is not clear whether these cases were brought under the Administrative Litigation Law. Nationwide, ALL cases actually tried increased from 12,040 in 1990 to 79,527 in 1996. The two most litigious provinces, Henan and Hunan, were predominantly rural. They accounted for 28 percent of the 35,083 suits accepted by the courts in 1994. Half the suits involved public security, land use, forestry, urban zoning, and real estate. Unfortunately, burdens did not appear as a separate item in the national breakdown of the cases but were apparently subsumed under the category "other," which amounted to 40.7 percent of the 51,370 cases brought in 1995. A subset of the "other" cases was about taxes. A sample of 236 cases tried in the early 1990s showed that 6 percent involved taxes; 17 percent were brought by peasants and 3 percent by collective groups. It seems fair to conclude that burden suits made up only a small fraction of the ALL cases.[112]

Nationally, according to an assessment made by Minxin Pei, the proportion of cases in which the courts revoked an administrative act ranged between 17 percent in 1990 and 15 percent in 1995, reaching 19 to 21 percent of cases in the intervening years. The proportion of cases in which administrative acts were upheld, however, declined steadily from 35 percent in 1990 to 17 percent

---

[109] *Xinhua* (Nov. 29, 1998, *SWB-FE*/3397, G/2).

[110] Chen Wenmin (1993).

[111] *SCRB* (Dec. 15, 1992, reported in *SJRB*, Dec. 16, 1992), all other data in *RMRB* (Oct. 27 1997).

[112] Minxin Pei (1997: 832–62).

in 1995. In addition, the proportion of suits withdrawn by the plaintiffs rose from 36 percent in 1990 to 51 percent in 1995. This apparently was largely due to out-of-court settlements, in which the government agency rescinded its actions, satisfying the plaintiffs. Settling out of court made sense given the difficulty of enforcing judgments. "These results show that the very act of filing a lawsuit can generate substantial benefits for the plaintiffs even without going to trial."[113] The Administrative Litigation Law appears to have been playing "a limited role in curbing and rectifying unjust treatment by government officials." In one poll, 74 percent of government officials surveyed said that they had become more cautious in their work because of the law. Moreover, ALL has also played a significant role in raising popular awareness of legal rights.[114]

To make the county court system play a more significant role required serious commitment on the part of judges and the local political apparatus and extensive work among peasants. Thus far such a commitment has not been in evidence on a large scale. There were some cases of success. In 1995, Neixiang county, Henan, made burden reduction via the courts a priority. The court's administrative department sought to educate peasants about the rules, their rights, and how to defend them by compiling a booklet for each household. An educational campaign was also launched among peasants and county cadres. All these initiatives had the support of both the county Party secretary and the magistrate. These measures bore fruit: In 1995, the court handled 869 burden cases, 689 of which the administrative agencies lost. For instance, villagers in Chimei town, having studied the materials, "dared" to bring suit against the town government complaining about an increase in the special products tax. As the suit was being heard, the town government itself revoked the increase, whereupon the peasants withdrew their suit. All told, this judicial campaign led to countywide burden reduction of several million yuan. Moreover, these successes prompted villagers who had planned several collective visits to higher levels not to make them.[115] This successful case was the product of empowerment of peasants on the initiative of and with the strong support of county-level authorities.

What is particularly noteworthy was villagers getting together to file collective lawsuits. This practice resembles class action suits, which the Civil Procedure Law permits, but such suits did not set binding precedents for similar cases elsewhere.[116] Much publicity was devoted in 1992 to Lezhi county, Sichuan, where groups of peasants from three different townships sued their respective

---

[113] Ibid., 843.
[114] Ibid., 859–62.
[115] Song Lixiao (1996). The author was chief justice of the county court.
[116] *Harvard Law Review* (1998: 1523–41). We are indebted to Kevin O'Brien for this reference.

governments for refunds for excess burdens and won. Lezhi county officials reportedly studied these cases and drew lessons from them. Successful burden suits were also brought in four other counties in Sichuan.[117] It may not have been accidental that these suits succeeded at a time when peasant anger was reaching a high point. This suggests that publicity about successful suits may well have been designed to demonstrate that villagers did have institutionalized alternatives to riots.

In one district court in Hubei, ten of fourteen collective cases were brought by peasants in 1996–7. These cases concerned burdens but also other issues such as land use and environmental damage suffered by villages.[118] In June 1996, 357 peasant families sued their township government for collecting taxes and levies in excess of the amount to which it had committed itself in writing in the preceding year. The county court ruled in the peasants' favor and ordered the excess collection to be returned to the peasants.[119] In June 1998, a group of 109 peasant families sued the county government of Congyang, Anhui, for misallocation of land. The court ruled in their favor and ordered the government to pay the litigation costs.[120] Whether these judgments were enforced is not clear. Case 6.2 illustrates the enormous obstacles that can arise when peasants bring suit.

Case 6.2. The largest known case of collective litigation took place in Zizhou county, Shaanxi, part of the Yan'an revolutionary base area. Remarkably, two-thirds of all inhabitants of Peijiawan township, 12,688 out of 18,841, signed an administrative complaint against the township government. The cause was the extraordinary violence and brutality that accompanied the government's campaign to collect arbitrarily increased taxes and fees in 1996, after a year of unprecedented natural disasters which inflicted large-scale losses on peasants. The funds demanded amounted to a quarter of the preceding year's income, far exceeding the legal limit. Teams of township cadres invaded the villages, using "high pressure tactics" to enforce payment, including severe beatings – numerous peasants suffered injuries – illegal detentions, and seizure of household belongings.

Shock and anger prompted villagers in the forty-five administrative villages to "link up" (*chuanlian*, a term used during the Cultural Revolution) and organize a lawsuit. From among the villagers, they chose sixty-eight

---

[117] *RMRB* (Sept. 12, 1992, *FBIS*, No. 185: 47). This report stated the amount to be returned was 50,000. *SCRB* (Nov. 24, 1992), put the amount at some 20,000. See also Pan Wei (1996: 109).
[118] *Faxue Pinglun* (No. 1, 1998: 109–12).
[119] *Hubei Nianjian* (1997: 119).
[120] *Zhongguo Gaigebao* (Jan. 5, 1999).

representatives of whom a subgroup of thirteen took charge. It is note-worthy that in addition to ordinary peasants, the representatives included retired county, township, and village cadres, several VC chairmen and a county people's congress representative. Many were Party members. This, then, was a case in which peasants were supported and probably led by the local elite.

Lawyers from the Yulin prefectural economic law office heard about the suit and volunteered to take the case pro bono. The case aroused the attention of the press and TV media, including the exposure show "Focal Point of Coverage" and of the top leaders of Shaanxi. Ma Wenlin, a teacher in Yan'an who came from one of the villages involved, and who was famous for having long sought justice for ordinary people, worked closely with the protestors, informing them of the burden-reduction rules in Party documents.

On April 30, 1997, the case was brought to the administrative division of Yulin Intermediate Court. The court dragged its feet, hearing the case only at the end of August and handing down a decision on March 23, 1998, two years after the brutal campaign. The court found that the township government had illegally collected 89,000 yuan in fees and assessments, which it ordered returned. But the court ruled that it lacked jurisdiction to decide on punishment for injuries inflicted on villagers and on compensation.

The villagers appealed to the Shaanxi Supreme Court on the grounds that the Yulin court had only counted a small portion of the excess taxes and fees forcibly collected by the township. The total claim was for 521,000 yuan. The appellants also demanded 80,000 yuan in compensation for losses suffered. The Supreme Court heard the case on August 11, 1998, taking extensive additional testimony. The court then ruled that more investigation was needed and recessed.

In April 1999, Ma Wenlin organized a delegation from eight townships to appeal to the State Council to reduce burdens and punish those officials who had inflicted injuries on peasants. Instead of gaining a hearing, Ma was arrested by Beijing police, severely beaten, and returned to Shaanxi. Peasants were pressured into testifying that he had organized a hostage-taking incident. Ma was sentenced to five years in a reform-through-labor camp "for disrupting social order" and several peasant leaders were also jailed.

In December 1999, the Shaanxi Lawyers Association and the Shaanxi Legal Institute organized a forum on the case and wrote a petition asking for justice for the peasants. One of them was the chair of the Law Committee of the Shaanxi People's Congress, who wrote a letter to the secretary of the Shaanxi Party Committee, Li Jianguo, urging him to have the case handled justly, and charging gross violations of the law.[121] In the absence of redress there were fears of violence. Reportedly ten thousand peasants put their thumbprint on an "Appeal to get rid of evil creatures and rescue Ma Wenlin from prison." Premier Zhu was said to have learned about this but did not intervene, to the chagrin of the protestors.

During these years, the township did not take any steps to rectify its abusive tax and fee policies. It failed to issue the burden card which all households were supposed to have. To be sure, the township head and the Party secretary of Peijiawan were both dismissed, but the secretary reportedly was transferred to manage the Zizhou county TV station – he was said to have suppressed all TV news about burdens – while the ex-township head was appointed deputy Party secretary of another township and promoted in rank. No one was prosecuted for illegal imprisonment and the injuries inflicted on peasants.[122]

In August 2000, peasants of Zizhou mobilized once more. Thirty thousand one hundred sixty-six peasants from eight townships signed a "joint letter to the Shaanxi Provincial Higher People's Court to request the reversal of the court decision on Ma Wenlin."[123] By any account, the feat of organizing the signature drive stood as a benchmark in peasant protest.

In 1998, an Anhui county official suggested the establishment of tax burden courts because it is "extremely necessary to involve the law in solving this problem." If this were not done, he emphasized, village collective appeals to higher authorities would persist. Burden courts would strictly supervise the legality of township and village levies. They would accept suits by peasants and use their judgments for propaganda purposes. This would restrain the townships from abusive behavior (for example, the confiscation of peasant property to enforce payment), thereby preventing the eruption of "vicious cases." And, since some peasants did evade payment of legal taxes, these courts could also be used for enforcement.[124] Apparently this proposal did not get anywhere in Anhui. But in Heilongjiang special "peasant burden case courts" were in fact set up. Township courts also organized circuit tours in villages to make

---

[121] *SCJP* (Jan. 19, 2000).
[122] For this case, see Wang Hai'an (1998). Additional sources include Becker (2000: 4–9) and *SCJP* (Jan. 19, 2000). The accounts by Wang and Becker, who interviewed peasants in Yulin, differ in important details but not on the key points.
[123] Centre for Human Rights and Democracy, Hong Kong, August 11, 2000 (*SWB-FE*/3918, G/8).
[124] Li Zhuanshui (1998: 56).

access to courts easier. Heilongjiang handled over two thousand cases related to the burden issue in 1996. A commentary on these cases noted their political sensitivity and the fact that courts handling these cases faced pressure from the local Party committees and governments.[125]

Other legal innovations by local governments included drawing up written "peasant burden contracts" between governments and peasants and notarized by legal authorities. This method was first implemented in Weifang city, Shandong province, and subsequently extended to the province as a whole. These contractual documents specified the amounts and the time payment of taxes, levies, and approved contributions. Both sides were to act in accordance with their rights and duties. If disputes occurred, courts could be petitioned. This way, peasants were supposed to be protected from arbitrary actions by government officials and governments could collect legitimate taxes and levies without undue resistance.[126] Burden complaints continued to emanate from Shandong, however, so the impact of this innovation was probably limited. Another measure originated in Shandong in 1998, the opening of a legal services hot line for villagers to provide advice and information about hiring lawyers. By early 2000, almost all the counties in the country were linked in this way. According to the Ministry of Justice, 1.35 million peasants availed themselves of this new resource, whereas another four hundred thousand visited law offices.[127] Innovations of this sort indicate that some local governments were using their imaginations to come up with new ways of regularizing burdens. A skeptical interpretation might attribute their inventiveness to pressure to be seen as doing something to alleviate the problem.

An overall assessment of the contribution that the legal system made to burden reduction is necessarily somewhat bleak. By the end of the century, judicial redress was becoming increasingly available to China's peasantry, but still only to a fairly small minority. Even if those who sued won, enforcing a judgment was quite another matter. Nationally, as of mid-1999, eight hundred fifty thousand court rulings involving 259 billion yuan had not been executed because "illegal official orders and violent activities interfering in the enforcement of court rulings" were said to be common across the country.[128] As the journal *Zhongguo Gaigebao* (*China Reform*) lamented in early 2000, "the law can hardly govern the officials."[129]

[125] *Heilongjiang Nianjian* (1997) and Jiang Ming'an (1998: 138–9).

[126] Bi Jingquan, Xiong Zhongcai, and Wang Caiming (1996).

[127] *Zhongguo Gaigebao* (Jan. 11, 2000, *SWB-FE* 3761,G/5–7).

[128] *CD* (Aug. 14, 1999). As of 1997, the courts had accepted nearly 3.3 million civil cases. See *ZTN* (1998: 791).

[129] *Zhongguo Gaigebao* (Jan. 11, 2000, *SWB-FE* 3761,G/5–7).

TOWARD EFFECTIVE INSTITUTIONAL CHANGE

Burden reduction did bring institutional changes that were aimed at rooting out structural causes of heavy taxation on peasants. Structural changes got underway in the 1990s, with the introduction of village elections and of financial transparency at the village level (see Chapter 7). This section examines three structural changes that, as of 2000, either had already gotten underway or were getting off the ground: financial management reform, administrative streamlining in the townships, and, most important, a reform that aimed at a wholesale overhaul of the tax-and-fee system in rural China.

Township Finance and Administrative Streamlining. The section on "muddled finances" in Chapter 4 dealt with the irregularities and malpractices associated with off-budget funds. To redirect more of these funds into the regular revenue stream, in 1996 the State Council promulgated new "Regulations on Extrabudgetary Funds" which stipulated that all surtaxes collected by local governments as extrabudgetary funds be integrated into the regular budgets. Self-raised funds were redefined EBFs but were to be subject to budgetary control.[130] This was an effort to regularize and make accountable the disposal of the T and V levies and of other revenues at both the township and village levels. The finance departments were now given control over these funds, whereas in the past in a third of the townships other agencies had controlled them.[131]

In many provinces, the township finance department was charged with managing not only the township part of the T and V levy but the village part as well. The rationale was that with funds managed at the township level, villages which usually lacked trained bookkeepers and standard accounting procedures would have their collective funds administered more efficiently and honestly. In Hebei province, for example, half the villages adopted this system.[132] Many localities also established a peasant burden budget system, which required that the amount of collective funds be budgeted in advance and known to households. At year's end, a financial statement was to specify the disposal of the collective funds. Budgets were to be proposed by village committees, approved by the village assembly, and checked by the township finance department. Similarly, townships were also to draw up a revenue budget which would be examined by the county government or its city equivalent.[133] This too was intended to insure greater accountability and predictability.

---

[130] See Ye Baozhu (1997: 54).
[131] Su Ming (1998: 58–62) and *Zhongguo Caizheng Nianjian* (1997: 124).
[132] Zhao Shifeng, Gao Lifeng, and Xu Shaoyi (1998).
[133] *Nongye Jingji* (No. 1, 1997: 32; and No. 3, 1997: 43).

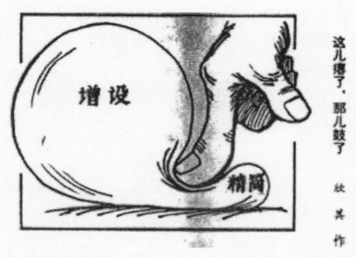

Figure 6.2 The caption reads: "If you press here, it pops up there," meaning that reducing the size of the bureaucracy in one area merely leads to an increase in another. *Source: Liaowang*, No. 37, September 14, 1992.

Chapter 4 shows that the bloated bureaucracies with their insatiable appetite for money were a major cause of increased burdens. Prior to 1998, drives to cut their size had failed. In that year, Premier Zhu Rongji unveiled a major plan for cutting the size of the entire bureaucracy by 50 percent or so. This project began at the central level. It drastically reduced the number of central agencies, and claimed a personnel reduction of 50 percent. This reform was intended to be extended downward, beginning with the thirty-one provincial-level units following suit, and was ultimately to reach the townships.[134] The goal of subprovincial administrative downsizing was to reduce 20 percent of existing staff. The results of this new round of downsizing, which was set in motion in February 2001, remain unclear.[135] See Figure 6.2.

However, even before the nationwide campaign, some localities had already taken significant initiatives to reduce the size of the township bureaucracies. The 116 townships and towns of Jiaoshi city, Henan, reduced their 696 administrative units to 507, cutting personnel by 21 percent, and their 1,100 non-profit units down to 837, cutting personnel by half. At the same time, however, there was additional hiring of personnel in education. Costs were reduced by 12.3 million yuan, significantly lightening burdens.[136] Hebei's 3,202 townships

---

[134] *Xinhua* (Jan. 29, 2000, *SWB-FE* 3752, G/11–12).

[135] *Xinhua* (Feb. 2, 2001, *http:/dailynews.sina.com.cn*).

[136] *Zhongguo Gaigebao* (May 25, 1999).

and towns were staffed by an average of fifty to one hundred "eaters of imperial grain" as of 1995, even as the population averaged twenty thousand per
township. In 1996 the province merged the 3,202 units into 1,970, permitting
cuts in personnel of 37,000. Wages and administrative costs for each person
were about 5,000 yuan per year; 180 million yuan was thus saved and burdens
reduced. These officials were apparently paid entirely out of peasant funds. Reportedly, those laid off successfully turned to economic pursuits, presumably in
the private sector.[137] By the late 1990s, amalgamation of townships and towns
became a national policy. By the summer of 2000, provinces such as Jiangsu,
Shandong, and Zhejiang were said to have cut their township personnel by about
30 percent.[138]

Some localities also took initiatives to reduce the number of village officials.
Jiangsu province, where villages often had to feed a dozen cadres and in some
places twenty or thirty, reportedly cut the number of village cadres by one
hundred thousand after 1996, saving a total of 500 million yuan a year or 10 yuan
per farmer.[139] In Shandong province, Liaocheng city decided to reduce the
number of village officials by having Party branch secretaries who were elected
to the post of village committee chair serve concurrently in both positions. In
addition, members of Party branches also became village committee members.
This led to the elimination of 26,000 village officials and relieved peasants from
paying the extra 20 million yuan in taxes that would otherwise have been needed
to support those additional officials.[140]

Fees into Taxes. This idea of amalgamating all exactions into formal taxes,
thereby largely eliminating the multitude of unauthorized fees, was the most
significant prospective structural reform, one that promised to have the greatest
impact on peasant burdens. Its proponents hailed it as the "third revolution"
since 1949, the previous ones having been land reform and decollectivization.
Like many other reforms, it began with local initiatives. The first experiments
were launched in 1993 in three counties in each of Guizhou, Hunan, Hebei,
and Anhui provinces. By 1998, seventy counties in these provinces as well
as counties in Henan and Shanxi had conducted similar experiments. Central authorities took more direct charge from that year on. This new approach
indicates recognition that simply demanding burden reduction using old mobilization approaches or even providing legal redress was not enough. Instead, the

---

[137] Yu Shaoliang and Pu Liye (1997: 32).
[138] *Banyuetan* (No. 1, Jan. 2001).
[139] *Zhongguo Gaigebao* (Nov. 25, 1999) and *Xinhua* (Oct. 30, 1998, *SWB-FE*/3372, G/7).
[140] *NMRB* (Dec. 11, 1999). See Chapter 7 for comment on the implications of this measure for
village democracy.

underlying structural problems had to be addressed, that is, the revenue system as a whole. If the main problem of peasant burdens was uncontrollable and irregular fees imposed by government agencies, converting all nontax levies into taxes would permit elimination of irregularities if not all of the arbitrariness of the old system. The hope was also that by converting levies into taxes, the central government would find it easier to control off-budget revenues, thereby increasing regular tax revenues, which in turn might enable it further to subsidize local governments. This was a crucial issue, since the main problem with the fee-for-tax reform proposals was that they were not revenue-neutral but aimed at reducing peasants' burdens. This would jeopardize the operations of the township and village governments. As Table 4.3 indicates, many were already heavily in debt by the late 1990s. Moreover, since much of the administrative apparatus, beginning with the ministries, charged fees, abolishing them would harm their interests as well.

Several experimental approaches to reforming the existing rural taxation system emerged.[141] One combined levies and taxes (*feishui heyi*). The T and V levies were combined with agricultural taxes into one payment in kind. Peasants wouldn't have to pay any other levies, but it wasn't clear what the status of the numerous fees outside the T and V levies was. The new tax would be higher than the old agricultural taxes set in 1958, rising to 8 to 10 percent of normal yields over a three-year time span. The revenue would be divided between the counties, the townships, and the villages. This model targeted the uncertainties and unpredictability associated with the township and village levies in that their incorporation into the regular tax would eliminate the discretion of township and village officials. From the point of view of the peasants, the major stumbling block for widespread implementation was lack of trust. Peasants were hardly likely to welcome a major legal tax increase accompanied by promises to abolish all other levies. This required a degree of credibility and trust that simply was not there, given the history of the burden issue.

Another approach was called the "public grain system" (*gongliangzhi*) as in the precollectivization period of the early 1950s, when peasants only paid the agricultural tax in kind. Its most radical feature was that it abolished the state grain procurement system, which, as shown in Chapter 3, had imposed heavy "hidden burdens" on farmers. The goal was to eliminate all irregular exactions beyond taxes paid in kind – the so-called "public grain" – to the state. The strong opposition to this approach came from those who argued that the compulsory grain procurement was necessary for a state responsible for the food supply of

---

[141] See Su Ming (1998: 58–62) and Zhu Shouyin (1998: 143–53).

so huge a population. It would be premature for China to fully liberalize the grain market and only collect the tax grain.

A third approach consisted of consolidating all informal levies into new, money-based formal taxes. In some places, this took the form of a "rural public project tax," collected by the township to provide local revenue under the control of the financial department. Unlike other approaches, the levy-to-tax conversion did not change the existing agricultural tax regime.

Various approaches were tested in different localities, and in general, results appeared positive. Peasant burdens were reduced and the number of cases of peasant petitions and complaints declined.[142] The Hunan provincial government ordered at least one township in every county to start an experimental system of levy-to-tax conversion beginning in 1997. Township officials were more enthusiastic about the new system than village officials who believed that the total amount of tax would not be reduced. Peasants predictably were also skeptical. They too doubted that the village portion of the local tax – 50 percent – would really be remitted to villages under the new taxation system.[143]

A national conference on agriculture organized by the CCP Central Committee in 1998 praised the fee-into-tax reform experiments but considered them to be inadequate, apparently because the models did not consider all the complexities of the proposed reform, meaning how townships and villages were to be adequately funded. The conference decided that a nationwide reform in the levy regime required further experimentation before being adopted nationwide.[144]

At the March 1999 NPC meeting, Finance Minister Xiang Huaicheng announced that the fee-to-tax reform – an issue that affected all sectors of society, not just the countryside – would take three to five years to accomplish. Xiang pledged a "breakthrough" in 1999 with respect to fees levied on transportation and vehicles and the formulation of plans for fee-to-tax reform in the countryside.[145] A year later, the Central Committee and State Council issued a circular on the selection of the entire province of Anhui as a site for experimenting with a standardized rural tax and fee system. In April, Politburo member Wen Jiabao addressed a "mobilization conference" in Anhui. He hailed this reform as equal in importance to the land reform and decollectivization. "It is a radical measure for genuinely reducing peasants' burdens. . . . it is also an important move for improving relations between cadres and masses and maintaining stability in the rural areas." Wen laid down several principles to be

---

[142] Zhu Shouyin (1998).
[143] *ZNJ* (No. 9, 1998: 37–41).
[144] *Neibu Canyue* (No. 17, May 6, 1998).
[145] *Xinhua* (March 6, 1999, *FBIS*, No. 305).

followed: Lightening burdens was most important, but he warned that attaining this goal had to be aligned with township governments needs for adequate funds. In addition, the fee-and-tax reform had to be tied to organizational reform and structural reform of rural education as well as to the downsizing of local governments. Equally important, Wen demanded that unrealistic target setting activities be stopped, a demand that, if implemented, would have reduced the pressures on local officials to achieve results even at the cost of burdening peasants. This was top-level recognition that a fundamental change would have to be made in the incentive structure of local officials. Even after tax-and-fee reform, Wen observed, tight management of burdens would be needed. He also indicated that the third of the three models was to be the primary focus, that is, fees would be replaced by the agricultural tax and its "supplementary tax." The goal was the establishment of a standardized system with a stable level of taxation, thereby insuring predictability. Wen characterized this reform as arduous and complex, given the multiple factors that had to be taken into account. He again stressed that the central authorities "take it very seriously."[146]

As applied in Anhui, the new system had dramatic results in reducing peasant financial burdens, to the delight of many taxpayers. In 2000, the average burden in Anhui province decreased by 25.6 percent from the 1997 level.[147] In the summer of 2000, a progress report on the implementation of the new system from Huiyuan county, Anhui, claimed that now that only "the regular taxes and surtaxes" were being collected instead of the myriad of ad hoc levies, peasants were happy. Before 1999 the county was one of those with the most complaints and petitions. In one village, more than two hundred of the eighteen hundred villagers lodged complaints every year. Now, it turned into a "peaceful village."[148]

However, the Anhui experiments had an enormous downside: Township and village finances, already in trouble, were plunged into an even more difficult situation. According to a ten-village study, the new system resulted in an average 62 percent decrease in village public revenue.[149] Ending fees and the education surcharge sharply reduced available funds for education on which village schools had long depended. Education was the first to suffer when local governments faced the new hard budget constraints. One reason was that the bloated township bureaucracy had not as yet been touched. On average, townships in

---

[146] *Xinhua* (April 14, 2000, *FBIS*, No. 414).

[147] Lu Zexiu (2001: 36–41).

[148] CCTV (Aug. 5, 2000, *SWB-FE*/3914, G/2–3).

[149] Zhu Baoping (2001: 12–16).

Anhui financed 310 staff in the year 2000.[150] As long as the local government payroll remained large, the fee-to-tax reform would be undercut.

But even cutting the rural bureaucracy would still leave a substantial gap in the resources available locally once the fee-into-tax system was in place. At the March 2001 NPC meeting there was for the first time public, highest-level acknowledgment that a large infusion of funds from the outside was essential if the fee-into-tax reform was to work. Premier Zhu Rongji informed a news conference that the central government planned to transfer 20 to 30 billion yuan to local governments to offset their expected budgetary shortfalls. Zhu explained that 120 billion yuan or more was being extracted from the villages each year: 30 billion in taxes, 60 billion in T and V levies, and the rest in unauthorized fees. The T and V levies and the irregular exactions would be cut. The gap this would create would be partially filled by an increase in the agricultural taxes from 5 to 8.4 percent or 30 to 50 billion yuan in the aggregate, as well as by a 20 to 30 billion infusion from Beijing targeted at provinces in difficulty. The tax increase and the central subsidy would still mean reduced funding for townships and villages. Zhu indicated that since most fees were devoted to education, a fundamental educational reform would also be necessary.[151]

The nationwide fee-to-tax reform was postponed in the summer of 2001 on the grounds that further local experimentation was needed. But a major reason was financial stringency. As Premier Zhu noted, the central capacity to provide funds "has be further examined."[152] As will be recalled, financial decentralization had sharply cut the proportion of the total revenue flow to the Center in the 1980s and early 1990s, greatly inhibiting its capacity to redistribute resources. In 1994 a major tax reform was enacted designed to increase the share of taxes taken by the Center, which could only be done by increasing the tax load borne by the richer provinces. In the intense bargaining that preceded the legislation, the richer, eastern provinces were pitted against those of the interior. The former saw the tax-sharing reform as "robbing the rich to help the poor" (*jiefu jipin*). The governor of Anhui fully supported the reform since it would replace a very "unfair" system of fiscal contract.[153] In this contest, the richer provinces won. They succeeded in securing a package of refunds to the provinces from the Center's enriched coffers that favored them. As Pak K. Lee put it, "The central pledge that tax refunds would be pegged to local growth in the [new] consumption and value added taxes has worked in favour of the more urbanized,

---

[150] *Liaowang* (No. 50, Dec. 11, 2000: 12–19).

[151] *RMRB-0* (March 16, 2001).

[152] *RMRB-O* (July 23, 2001).

[153] Jae Ho Chung (1995: 3, 13–14).

industrialized coastal regions." Central transfers of revenue disproportionately benefited the coastal provinces and some of the very poorest, minority provinces, notably Tibet. "The recipients of the lowest subsidies were the provinces of Anhui and Henan in central China and Sichuan in the southwest." Most of the other provinces in agricultural China also received below-average subsidies.[154] Thus the central government's capacity to assist these provinces continued to be limited.

The fee-and-tax reform was also challenged by "patterns of vested interests" of government departments that had become entrenched with the deconcentration of state power. The abolition of most fees affected the funding of numerous specialized governmental agencies from Beijing down to the townships. Interest conflicts were discussed with great frankness in the media in 1999 and early 2000. The proposed abolition of all EBFs and of all levies and fees "that had the character of taxes" into actual taxes and allowing only a few user and regulatory fees to remain in standardized form meant that revenue would accrue to the tax and finance departments as part of the regular budget. The reform would meet even greater obstruction than the 1994 tax reform, because the latter only affected vertical relations between the Center and provinces whereas the new one affected horizontal relations between administrative departments as well. Everyone agreed that the fee-into-tax measure was necessary but "how to avoid increasing the burden on peasants, how to ensure the return of all the increased revenue to the peasants, how to prevent the recurrence of wanton collection of fees, and how to determine tax sharing by the central and local authorities" were all knotty issues.[155]

CONCLUSION

Despite prodigious efforts spanning almost two decades, the Chinese regime was not able to make a significant dent in the burden problem. There were temporary successes as in 1993 but peasant tax burdens remained a persistent problem for the regime. It was not an isolated phenomenon. As with other economic issues, the difficulties were rooted in the practices, values, and norms of Chinese institutions. The Chinese government attempted to contain and/or eliminate the problem by what it knew best: ad hoc campaign-style mobilizations with exhortations from the highest level. One can safely say that these failed. The solutions had to be institutional ones, in large part codeterminous with the transformation of China's bureaucratic, legal, and financial systems.

---

[154] Pak K. Lee (2000: 1017–19). See especially Table 3.
[155] *ZXS* (June 21, 1999, *FBIS*, No. 711).

The long, arduous trajectory of burden reduction was both similar to and unique from other reform processes in China. The regime did attempt institutional solutions, engaging in trial-and-error experiments based on local initiatives. But burden reduction was unique because it involved a large yet underrepresented group that held the key to stability in China. Nowhere else in China was the strategic interplay among the central state, local state, and peasants so clearly manifested.

The most promising of the institutional reforms, turning fees into taxes, was suspended in the summer of 2001 because it could not be undertaken without first or simultaneously solving the problems of redistribution and the funding of institutions. Times have changed since the Yongzheng emperor's effort in the eighteenth century to turn fees into taxes failed, but thus far the new effort to do so has also encountered major obstacles. In the short term, the success of this reform seemed to hinge on three main issues: How successful would the downsizing of the townships be? How committed was the central government to the prioritizing of burden reduction by finding and committing adequate resources? Could the Center gain the redistributive capacity required by such a large undertaking, given the interests of wealthier provinces?

At the same time, a more optimistic prognosis is also warranted. First, the burden problem was a learning experience for the Chinese leaders. They gradually moved toward a more systemic understanding of what the underlying issues were and how greatly burdens impacted on social stability. Their enhanced understanding has already had a significant impact on the policies they have adopted. Second, the long history of the burdens has left its imprint on the peasants, who asserted themselves more and more as their rights consciousnes increased, and as many more peasants used available channels to secure those rights. This suggests that a sense of empowerment has become more entrenched among them. And third, the burden problem was a learning experience for local officials. Whatever their recalcitrance, obstructionism, and resistance, "lightening the peasants' burdens" unquestionably became part of their official lives and could not be ignored.

7

Burden Reduction: Village Democratization and Farmer National Interest Representation

THE financial and administrative reforms analyzed in the preceding chapter did not make much of a dent in the burden problem. They therefore did not end the crisis in state-peasant relations caused to a significant extent by the imposition of unreasonable financial levies. Attempting to control local officials only from above was simply inadequate. Pressure on cadres had to be exerted from below as well, that is, by the peasantry. Otherwise, as officials of the Ministry of Civil Affairs argued in seeking to convince central leaders of the necessity for village elections, it would not be possible to contain the explosive potential of peasant anger.[1] Villagers needed legitimate institutionalized means through which to advance their claims and seek redress lest they be compelled to take to the street.

The regime recognized this. As shown in Chapter 6, it allowed the system of individual and collective petitioning to function and it fostered the establishment of legal institutions in the countryside. In addition, it promoted democratization, including elections of village leaders, village self-rule, and "open and transparent" conduct of village affairs (*cunwu gongkai*). The latter applied especially to finances, in which villagers had a keen and vital interest. Empowering villagers to defend themselves against illegal exactions and the abuses associated with them entailed alterations in the triangular relationship between the central state, the local state, and the peasants, essentially to the disadvantage of the local authorities. As did other empowerment measures such as letters and visits, media exposure, and litigation, village self-governance entailed the implicit or explicit authorization for peasants to act collectively.

The first part of this chapter asks whether village democracy and self-government curbed tax-and-fee abuses. A conclusive answer cannot be given, if only because of wide local variation in practices and the continuing evolution of

---

[1] See Tianjian Shi (1999a) on how the Ministry of Civil Affairs promoted elections.

village democratization. It is difficult to generalize about the impact of village elections on the relationships between peasants, elected village committees, the Party branches, and the townships, all of which are important actors in local governance. Nonetheless, when fair and open elections were held, there was a real possibility of significant change in the village structure of power to the advantage of the peasants, especially with respect to the fairness and modes of collection of burdens, and to some degree with respect to reduction of burdens. There may even be an impact on those imposed by the townships, since elected village leaders were more likely to defend the interests of their constituents against the township.[2]

But even if these empowerment measures had been highly effective, they could not by themselves cure the entire excessive burden problem. As this study has emphasized throughout, local officials, whether at the level of the villages or the townships, were not the only culprits. Burdens originated from the administrative system as a whole. Burdens were embedded in and the consequence of policies of taxation, finance, resource allocation, and development strategies which were decided by the Center. If rural interests, and especially those of agriculture, acquired an effective voice at the Center, there would be a greater chance that decision makers would take those interests into account, thereby affecting burdens in a more comprehensive way. Part two of the chapter deals with this issue. Complaints about inadequate representation of peasants at the Center were raised with considerable intensity in the late 1980s and in the 1990s, when villagers harbored increasingly intense grievances about burdens, procurement prices, and inflation. Demands were voiced not only for substantive policy changes but also for greater inclusion of peasant interests in policy making. Proposed remedies included strengthening their role in the NPC and establishment of a national farmers' association. Some changes were made but the idea of an organized interest group did not find favor. Nonetheless, discussion of the issues indicated awareness among segments of the elite that rural problems, including the burdens, required larger political reforms if China's peasants were to be enabled to defend their legitimate interests.

THE IMPACT OF VILLAGE DEMOCRATIZATION ON BURDENS

Elections. Why did China's conservative leaders who were determined to maintain the Party's monopoly of power permit and even promote free village elections? They did so not because they became converted to democratic values

---

[2] Lianjiang Li (2000).

but because village democratization held out the promise of fostering rural stability by improving the conduct of village cadres. Village elections, in other words, were designed to strengthen the Chinese state not to weaken it.[3] In interviews, Chinese scholars cited the Renshou county riots as demonstrating that it wasn't democracy that led to instability; it was lack of democracy that led to disturbances. Villagers in neighboring Pengshan refused to join their Renshou compatriots because their elected village representative assemblies had settled the funding issue to the satisfaction of the inhabitants.[4] Without elections, according to an MCA official, disturbances (*naoshi*) would keep on erupting. Village democracy, by involving peasants in the decision-making process, would improve compliance with taxation, assuming of course that the taxes were fair.

Policymakers were naturally ambivalent about the scope of permissible village autonomy. The creation of effective, institutionalized checks on village officials raised the specter of elected village leaders beholden to their constituents and openly challenging higher authority on their behalf. As described in the leadership section of Chapter 5 on protest, cases were reported of elected village cadres organizing and leading collective antitax or corruption protests. These amounted to instances in which elections seemed to promote instability. Even if most elected leaders did not take that route, there was still the possibility that they would lobby energetically with township officials on behalf of villager interests. They might not, in other words, confine their activities to intravillage matters, but seek to represent their villages in making claims for redress. Village officials were supposed to carry out a wide range of higher-level policies, from implementing family planning to grain procurement. What if they refused to do so or demanded modifications? Policymakers seem to have agreed that the balance of power had to be tilted somewhat in favor of villagers. At the same time, they were concerned about whether the "wrong" candidates might get elected and what they might do once in office. What was wanted was the election of leaders who would stand up for the "legitimate rights and interests" of peasants but who at the same time would willingly implement those higher-level demands which the regime considered to be legitimate, even if they ran counter to perceived villager interests, such as family planning. The regime wanted the election of energetic and able young leaders who could promote economic development, lead the peasants to prosperity, and maintain stability. What it did not want was the election of lineage leaders, political dissidents,

---

[3] This point is made with great clarity in an unpublished paper by Xi Chen (1999).

[4] Zhu Huaxin (1998: 365). According to the author, the Pengshan county Party secretary was transferred to Renshou to introduce democratic management.

local tyrants, or leaders of collective protests. If an election failed to produce the right outcomes, intervention from above was clearly not ruled out.[5]

The linkage between democracy and taxation was well understood in rural China. One need only recall the Shandong farmer quoted in the Introduction of this book who tied his demand for democracy to financial accountability.[6] Tianjian Shi, who conducted a national survey in 1993–4, found that, "When authorities ask for money from peasants, the latter will ask for the right to participate in the decision-making process."[7] It is this relationship between taxes and democracy that suggests that the strongest demand for democracy should come from those villagers who had the greatest interest in changing the abusive and unpredictable tax-and-fee system. Shi and other scholars found that the connection between taxes and interest in elections was strongest in the middle-income areas of agricultural China, where the lack of revenue from TVEs put the burden of funding local governments mainly on the peasants. In the poorest parts of China, acute poverty translated into political passivity, whereas in the richest, coastal areas, TVE profits largely relieved ordinary farmers from having to shoulder heavy burdens. This pattern would indicate that rural China is an exception to the widely accepted generalization that demands for democracy increase monotonically with growth in income. There is evidence, however, that in developed, richer areas, demand for broader participation, including elections, was also strong, but for other reasons. There was resentment at the tight control often exercised by one or a few local bosses over economic resources, exemplified by the corrupt sales of arable land to industrial users without adequate compensation for farmers.[8]

For our purposes the question is whether and to what extent village democracy succeeded in reducing peasant grievances about taxes and fees. Assessing this issue first requires some remarks about village elections themselves. Villagers elected the chairman of the village committee (VC) and committee members for

---

[5] Interviews with MCA officials, New York, March 1999. See also Alpermann (2001) on the ability of township Party leaders to remove elected village cadres in villages in southern Hebei.

[6] *NMRB* (Jan. 20, 1988).

[7] Tianjian Shi (1999b). Shi's article is based on a sample survey which he conducted in 1993 in cooperation with Chinese People's University.

[8] See Guo Zhenglin (1999) and Wang Rentian, ed. (1999: 333, 335) for arguments that the corruption of village leaders gave a big impetus to elections in industrialized villages. For a different view, see Tianjian Shi (1999b: 13). Shi argues that local bosses in TVE-rich areas bought off ordinary farmers. Jean Oi emphasizes the benefits of authoritarian rule in industrialized villages. See Oi (1999: 112 ff.). In analyzing the incentives of villagers and village leaders to take part in elections, Oi and Scott Rozelle (2000: especially 527–37) note that in industrialized villages, incomes are much more closely tied to outside resources than to village land, hence reducing interest in village elections.

three-year terms. A village assembly of adults, the village congress, or, in the case of large villages, a villager representative assembly (VRA), was charged with discussing and approving major decisions, including financial ones.[9] Direct elections began in the late 1980s on an experimental basis and gradually spread across China. As of 1998 "more than 60 percent" of China's villages had "initially established village self-government centering on democratic elections, democratic management, and supervision."[10] There was, however, wide variation. Guangdong, which had had a system of administrative districts under the townships, did not hold elections until 1998.[11] Sichuan reported in May 1999 that two-thirds of its 33,139 villages had held competitive elections, apparently for the first time, whereas more advanced areas had already held three or more rounds.[12] A nationwide survey conducted by Li Lianjiang in early 1999 – he employed Chinese students to poll a random sample in their home villages, located in eighty-three counties and twenty-five provinces – found that 798 of 1,140 respondents (57 percent) reported that elections had been held in their villages and 342 (43 percent) reported that no elections had been held.[13] Nationwide data on the proportion of elections held in accordance with rules that provided, inter alia, for freedom of nomination and secret ballots have not thus far become available.[14] Surveys show a mixed picture. Tianjian Shi's 1993–4 nationwide survey found that about half the respondents (51.6 percent) had voted in elections in which there was more than one candidate.[15] Five years later, Li's 1999 survey found that only 39.6 percent of the 789 respondents in villages with elections reported multiple candidacies, and a mere 18 percent reported that elections had been "very democratic or relatively democratic." Additional sources also indicate that somewhere between a fifth and a half of the elections conformed to the rules.[16]

[9] In November 1987 a trial law on the organization of village committees was passed and eleven years later, the final draft. For the first, see *ZRGYGB* (No. 27, Dec. 15, 1987); for the second, see *FZRB* (Nov. 5, 1998). See also a Central Circular, "Open and democratic management of village affairs" (April 18, 1998, *Xinhua*, June 10, 1998, *SWB-FE* 3252, G/5–8, June 13, 1998). There is extensive literature on village elections, much of which focuses on the electoral process. For analyses of policies toward elections and the way in which they have been implemented, see the special issue of *China Quarterly* (No. 162, June 2000), "Elections and Democracy in Greater China."

[10] *Xinhua* (June 18, 1998, *SWB-FE*/3258, G/6), reporting on a State Council directive calling for universal application of the new system.

[11] Guo Zhenglin (1999).

[12] *Xinhua* (May 24, 1999), in FBIS (No. 526).

[13] Lianjiang Li (2000).

[14] Carter Center Report on Chinese Elections (2000: 26). A project of the Carter Center is to set up a nationwide election monitoring operation.

[15] Tianjian Shi (1999b).

[16] O'Brien and Lianjiang Li (2000: 485–6).

Over the years, Chinese media have carried numerous reports of coerced elections, fraud, manipulation, and other abuses especially by the townships. Township officials have been a major obstacle to the holding of free and fair elections. They have a vital interest in the outcome, since instructions and assignments must be implemented through the village leaders. Without their cooperation, the unpopular "five hard policies" – tax collection, grain procurement, allocation of land for household building, cremation of the dead, and birth control – could not easily be implemented. From the township perspective, obedient village cadres were a necessity and many township officials did their best to maintain control over the elections. As late as the mid-1990s, as many as 60 percent of China's villages were classified by Xu Yong, a prominent researcher on village democracy, as "administered villages" (*xingzhenghua cun*).

Although the VCs in these villages were elected, the electoral process was strongly influenced by the township government and the basic-level Party organization. The mass basis was weak and the level of democratization low even to the point of administrative manipulation.[17]

In "administered villages," the township-village cadre relations were those of obedience and subordination. The VCs executed township orders even when they were unreasonable. The masses "were in a politically passive position."

As the quote suggests, township manipulation of the electoral process, often in conjunction with village Party branches, which under the principle of democratic centralism were directly subordinate to the township Party committees and not to the voters, was a strategy widely employed by township officials.[18] "In quite a few localities" the village Party branch nominated candidates and then asked the township to investigate and approve the candidates. Often enough, township Party and government officials themselves selected the nominees to ensure that dependable candidates were chosen.[19] Frequent press accounts of the imposition on villagers of candidates or the removal or harassment of popular candidates who were unacceptable to the authorities attested to the widespread nature of the problem. [20] In some places, dissemination of information about elections was blocked. In one case, a villager "accidentally" found a booklet

---

[17] Xu Yong (1997: 144–5).
[18] Interviews with academics in Wuhan and academics and officials in Beijing, September 1998.
[19] See, for instance, He Xuefeng (1998) for a telling analysis of how this manipulative process operated in two Hubei villages. The Hebei villages investigated by Bjoern Alpermann revealed a similar pattern of township control. See Alpermann (2001).
[20] For a telling case in which a township in Hunan used Public Security to impose its preferences, see *Nanfang Zhoumo* (Oct. 16, 1998, *SWB-FE*3367 G/7–8). See also *SJRB* (May 7, 1997).

in a town office that contained the village organization law. He "stole" it and informed fellow villagers who appealed to the county for redress.[21]

In order to enhance villager autonomy, Lishu county, Jilin, a national demonstration site of the Ministry of Civil Affairs, introduced a practice known as *haixuan* – "sea" or mass elections – in the mid-1990s. A county election rule stipulated that both township and village Party branches had to step aside and allow peasants to nominate candidates without interference. A competitive election was based on a primary, which weeded out those candidates who received the lowest number of votes. According to a Chinese scholar's field research in Lishu, this method was able to break the dominance of the existing power holders by opening up electoral opportunities to newcomers. In one township, half the village chairpersons were newly elected and Party secretaries actually lost elections. In this way the longstanding ties between township and village cadres were severed. In the past, when the township and Party branch controlled the nominations they would simply oust the winner if their candidate lost. But now this was no longer possible.[22]

The "sea election" model was widely emulated but by no means everywhere. The final law on village organization, adopted in November 1998, stipulated that villagers "directly" nominate candidates for election without mentioning the role of organized groups, the Party, or governments, thereby giving legal imprimatur to this practice.[23] Nonetheless, reports of manipulation of the elections by the township leaders and the Party branch continued to appear.[24] In early 2000 the head of the MCA's office of rural governance observed that there were no well-defined channels or institutional mechanisms to challenge violations of the law on village organization. Aggrieved villagers had no choice but to petition the authorities.[25] Still, local authorities came under increasing pressure from above to allow peasants a free choice.

Candidates usually did not make specific promises during the election campaign. Ministry of Civil Affairs officials frowned on active campaigning or canvassing for votes, worrying that this would give rise to illegal networks and allow wealthier candidates to gain advantages.[26] Cultural constraints also

---

[21] Zhu Huaxin (1998: 353–4).

[22] Ibid., 355–6 and interviews with academics and officials, Beijing (Sept. 1998).

[23] *FZRB* (November 5, 1998).

[24] See *NMRB* (March 16, 1999), for an NPC Henan deputy's complaints about violation of election rules and formalistic democratization.

[25] Carter Center Report (2000). See also Zhang Shuhuai (1998). This skepticism is shared by other researchers as well. See, for instance, Chen Youfu (1994: 52–5).

[26] Ibid., 20. The Carter Canter delegation recommended adoption of methods that would allow villagers to learn about the plans of the candidates.

inhibited self-promotion. Li Lianjiang found that only 8.7 percent of the 798 respondents from villages with elections reported that candidates delivered campaign speeches. The issue of burdens, therefore, was not central to the electoral process. But some candidates, when introducing themselves to their electors, did promise that no new fees would be imposed and especially that they would manage village affairs frugally and honestly. Usually they explained or were asked by villagers to explain their plans for developing the village economy.

Although burdens were not discussed much in public before ballots were cast, elections did have the effect of raising popular expectations that those elected would defend village interests vis-à-vis the townships. Li Lianjiang's survey found that two-thirds of respondents "said they would base their voting on whether they thought the candidates would dare to speak up on behalf of villagers."[27] Most strikingly, Li found a strong positive correlation between the extent to which the elections were free and democratic and the likelihood that ordinary villagers would contact their elected leaders and urge them to defend their interests.

Village Self-Rule and Burdens. The 1998 law on village self-government required that the VCs submit to their VRAs (or village congresses) the major issues over which the villages had jurisdiction, for discussion and ratification. The scope of what village authorities could do was quite narrow. VCs and VRAs did not gain the right to determine or even to co-determine (with the township government) the amount of the township and village levies. Village governments were limited to deciding the method of collection of both levies, thereby implicitly empowering the VCs and VRAs to adjust burdens according to income. VCs and VRAs were, however, allowed to determine how the village fund would be used. This included deciding on the number of village cadres who qualified for remuneration for lost productive working time and the criteria to be used for setting the amount, as well as the use of income from collectively owned village properties. Village authorities could also decide on fundraising for village public works such as village-run schools and road building. And they acquired the right to have a voice on the collection of fees for water and electric power (high prices for electricity became a serious issue in many villages in the 1990s).[28] These were significant, if limited, responsibilities. Cadre pay, fundraising, and fees were core concerns of budget-conscious peasants.

In addition, the law demanded that village affairs be public and transparent, meaning peasants had to be kept informed about village finances, VC incomes

---

[27] Lianjiang Li (2000).
[28] *FZRB* (Nov. 5, 1998).

and expenditures, the accounts of village collective enterprises, the award of economic contracts, allocation of land for household building, and the setting of birth quotas. The goal was to overcome the chronic suspicions of villagers of cadre malfeasance, a major source of grievance and confrontation. The collection and disposal of village public funds had long been controlled solely by village cadres in collaboration with the bookkeepers. Ordinary villagers had little knowledge as to how village funds were spent. During the Mao era, political campaigns such as the "Four Cleans" of 1964, targeted petty corruption and as corruption rose in the reform period, many peasants came to harbor nostalgic memories of those campaigns.[29] Even if corruption was not at issue, accurate bookkeeping had long been problematic in many villages. Well-trained bookkeepers were few and there was a general lack of standardized accounting procedures.

The introduction of transparent governance began experimentally in Gaochen county, Hebei, in 1989, and spread in the early 1990s. In Liaoning province, village finance became a target of rural reforms from 1991 on. By 1998, of the 15,738 villages in this province, 14,430 had installed new "democratic" financial procedures.[30] Local initiatives included opening the books to villagers by publicly posting monthly financial statements, setting up an elected "democratic financial monitoring group" (*minzhu licai jiandu xiaozu*) composed of villagers, and biannual auditing of village finance.[31] Village bookkeepers were also required to attend monthly "conference accounting" meetings at the township agricultural economy office, at which township accountants examined the requests for reimbursements from village collective fund accounts.[32] The 1998 law on village governance also allowed peasants to appeal to the township or the county governments to enforce the transparency provisions.[33]

An experiment was launched in Huixian city in Henan, in 1991, where, in one-third of the townships, peasants had participated in large-scale collective actions, including many collective visits and petitions in search of curbs on the financial abuses of village cadres.[34] One of the townships, Nancun, adopted a "transparent village governance system" for its twenty-five villages in 1991. This was deemed a success as measured by the criterion of drops in the number of collective petitions. Over a five-year period, no collective petitions were submitted in Nancun. In 1994, the Nancun model was applied to all of Huixian's

---

[29] O'Brien and Lianjiang Li (1999).
[30] *Nongye Jingji* (No. 7, 1998: 36–7).
[31] *Nongye Jingji* (No. 9, 1997: 30–1).
[32] *Nongye Jingji* (No. 12, 1996: 18).
[33] Bai Gang (1998b: 88–104).
[34] Unless otherwise noted, the material in this case comes mainly from Xu Yong (1998b).

villages and proved successful by cutting collective visits and petitions in half by 1997. In 1997 the Henan provincial government decided to implement the reform in all villages. Sichuan and Hebei provinces had done so in 1996. In Sichuan, 80 percent of all villages implemented the transparent financial system; as of 1998, 30 percent were reported to have done so successfully.[35] In Bazhong prefecture, the new system reportedly lowered the proportion of villagers who distrusted their cadres from 78 to 12 percent.[36]

As a villager in Liaoning put it, "Elected cadres have a harder time pocketing our money or wining and dining at our expense now that all the figures are put up on the village notice boards."[37] Hebei's Party committee replaced 12,600 village Party secretaries for resisting the implementation of the new system. Again, the early results of Hebei's efforts were positive: Peasant collective petitions and visits complaining about local officials decreased by 12.5 percent and those about burdens by 5 percent in 1997, but the decline in petitions was modest in comparison to the results achieved by other jurisdictions.[38]

For cadres, the prospect of financial openness gave rise to what was tellingly labeled the "three fears": fear of loss of special privileges; fear of investigation; and fear that the masses would understand what was really going on.[39] Accordingly, these leaders were strongly motivated to find ways to get around the new requirements. As a researcher on village democracy noted, openness was very hard to enforce. Even when accounts were made public, not all transactions were necessarily reported. Fines, for instance, were not listed in the accounts. Village cadre incomes were often high but the sources were murky because of cash transactions, which made proving corruption difficult, especially in the face of cadre mutual protection networks.[40] The problem of cadre friends and relatives who were in charge of finances and engaged in favoritism or corrupt dealings was not easily overcome.[41] The law did set forth a procedure for ousting incumbents. At least one-fifth of voters had to sign a petition asking for the dismissal. This had to be followed by a meeting of the village assembly, which could approve the petition, but only if over half the villagers with the right to vote agreed. Some elected village chiefs were in fact ousted for corruption in accordance with this provision.[42]

---

[35] Li Renshi and Chen Daichang (1998).
[36] Ibid., 11.
[37] Quoted in Jakobson (2001).
[38] *Liaowang* (No. 9, 1998: 20–1).
[39] Bai Gang (1999: 2–7).
[40] Interviews with scholars, Wuhan (Sept. 1998).
[41] See a case from Shandong, in Wang Rentian, ed. (1999: 329).
[42] *Xinhua* (June 11, 1999, *SWB-FE*/3560, G/8).

In 1999, the MCA made a nationwide assessment of the performance of village committees. Its investigation yielded the finding that although village elections had generally been held, only two-thirds of villages had actually put in place the required "democratic management and transparency." The MCA had received a "series of complaints" that "some village governments" issued fraudulent reports to deceive their publics and continue their corrupt practices. Progress in establishing accountability thus was slow and monitoring difficult. "Political instructors" were needed to go to the villages to teach proper procedures.[43]

In the final analysis, a straightforward answer to the question of whether democratic reforms at the village level reduced burdens cannot be given. Case 7.1, a comparative case study, sheds some light on this question. It shows that democratic management and especially openness of village financial affairs did lead to improvements in the methods of collection and did reduce grievances associated with burdens. But the size of the burden load was not affected by democratization. Moreover, the case introduces a major intervening variable, that burden reduction significantly hinged on the presence or absence of village resources from TVE revenues, a point emphasized throughout this study.

Case 7.1: Village Democracy and Burdens

In his book on village self-government, Xu Yong compared two villages, Baihe in Hunan, with freely elected leaders, and Baishi in Sichuan, where the township manipulated the vote and controlled the village cadres. This included their remuneration, which was paid by the peasants but set by the township depending on cadre performance. Baihe was well-off; Bashi was very poor. In both, burdens constituted major grievances. They had risen sharply in 1996, when the investigation took place. In Baishi, where average incomes were only 400 yuan per capita, a family of five saw its burdens leap forward from 485.10 yuan in 1995 to 695.93 yuan in 1996. In Baihe, because nearby villages had been severely damaged by floods and this village was supposed to help them, burdens rose from 133 yuan per capita to 250 yuan per capita.

In Baihe, village leaders defended peasant interests against the township. In this village, three elections had been held by 1996 and a strong village representative system was in place. Because of the elections cadres felt a sense of responsibility toward villagers. They "actively reported to the town government on villager difficulties and demands." In this cotton growing village, income from cotton sales was the main source of

---

[43] *Xinhua* (July 11, 1999, *SWB-FE*/3585, G4) and *SCMP* (July 13, 1999).

tax-and-fee payments. Farmers wanted to delay selling the cotton (and hence delay paying taxes) because at harvest time the purchasing units offered lower prices than they might in the winter. The cadres informed the town government about this demand. The village deputy Party secretary in charge of agriculture attended a special meeting in the town and again demanded that the town leaders solve the problem with cotton sales. Xu Yong did not, however, report the result of these initiatives.

Democracy made a big difference in the methods used to collect burdens. Village cadres employed the "mass line," successfully avoiding the use of "crude and simple" work methods. Party members and cadres set examples by paying early and each guaranteed payments from three to five households. Although peasants were discontented with the big increase in levies in 1996, there was "no fierce resistance."

A big problem in handling burdens in Baihe was intravillage inequality. One-fourth of the households averaged more than 2,000 yuan per capita per year, but one-fourth earned under a thousand and some less than 300 yuan per capita. Equal assessment on all households thus created severe hardship for the poor. Richer households, however, were opposed to differentiating by income because this would have penalized them and their views prevailed. Assessments continued to be based on family size and amount of land contracted. But it nonetheless proved possible to grant some exemptions and postponements for old people and households in deep distress, because the village had set up several TVEs and their profits were tapped for this purpose. Democratization was credited with fostering the development of nonagricultural sources of incomes in Baihe because it created a spirit of cooperation between peasants and cadres.

Collective resources thus made the difference. One villager who was in great difficulty due to illness said that he chose not to protest by blocking cars, because cadres cared about his situation, reduced his payments, and helped him in other ways. He realized that if he blocked cars, the village cadres would lose face and the reputation of the village would be damaged.

In contrast, in Baishi village in Sichuan, village cadres were not responsive to villager interests. They very rarely reported peasant grievances to the township. One of the biggest complaints concerned a hog raising fee imposed by the township designed to compel peasants to raise pigs. The fee had to be paid in January and would only be returned if in fact the households did rear pigs that year. Villagers strongly felt that pig raising was their business and besides, they lacked grain with which to feed them. Village leaders failed to defend peasant interests by demanding that the fee be canceled. In the end, a villager managed to contact higher levels which eventually ordered the township to cancel the fee. The village cadres had simply obeyed township orders, just as they did with regard to burden collection. There was mutual distrust between cadres and peasants. A potentially beneficial road project to which peasants were in principle willing to contribute could not get off the ground because villagers suspected that cadres would waste their contributions.

In Baishi, collection of levies required a bitter struggle. Cadres harshly coerced a group of recalcitrant villagers (*dingzi hu* or "nail households"), some of whom were simply too poor to pay. With township assistance, furniture and tools were confiscated in order to speed up payment. Most of the other households tried to delay making payments until the pressure became too intense. But the villagers were not united: Many worried that if the "nail households" succeeded in their resistance, their quotas would be shifted to them.

In both villages, the issue of redistribution of burdens in favor of the poor and elderly arose. In both, this prospect was opposed by the richer households. But Baishi was entirely dependent on agriculture and hence was unable to adopt the solution available to Baihe of tapping collective resources.[44]

Baihe thus exemplified the developmental approach to solving the burden problem advocated by the regime. One of the major goals of village democracy was to spur self-reliant local development by motivating popular participation in collective undertakings. But this required that untapped resources be available for exploitation. In Baishi, opportunities for the generation of collective incomes were not only stifled by cadre-peasant tension and pervasive distrust, but by the village's remote location and poor soil. Its county was included in the national antipoverty program, but apparently funds to start businesses had not trickled down to Baishi.

Villages, Townships, and Party Branches. Most burdens were imposed by the townships, often acting as the agents of their superiors. Hence, a crucial question was the extent to which the elected VCs were able to stand up to township officials. On the legislative level, how to define the relationship between the VCs and the townships had in fact been the source of spirited debates during the adoption of both the trial law in 1986–7 and the final law in 1998 by the NPC Standing Committee. One side demanded that village autonomy be tightly circumscribed. The village committees, though not a formal level of

[44] Xu Yong (1997: 275–88).

government – they had the status of a mass organization – should be made explicitly subordinate to the township, the lowest level of the government hierarchy. The relationship should be one of "leadership" (*lingdao*) rather than "guidance" (*zhidao*) to insure the fulfillment of state tasks. The opposing side argued in favor of maximizing autonomy by confining the township's role to "guidance" of the VCs, meaning that it could not issue binding orders. As a Chinese scholar put it, the VCs were not simply to be the "agent" of the townships (*daili ren*); they were also to act as managers or bosses (*dangjia ren*) of village affairs.[45] Even the more permissive side agreed that the VCs would still be obligated to abide by laws and regulations and to carry out state assignments.[46]

Both the 1987 and the 1998 versions of the law opted for the looser "guidance" formulation. Townships were to "guide, support, and help" but not to interfere in the work of the VCs on issues which fell within their legal jurisdiction. The VCs were to "support" and "help" the townships, but also to report villager opinions, demands, and suggestions to them. Another provision called on VCs to protect the "legitimate rights and interests of villagers." This presumably could apply to illegal tax-and-fee demands from higher up. The stipulation that the collection of the township fee be discussed by the village assembly could conceivably enable the VRAs to question items on the township burden list that were not in conformity with the regulations, thereby turning the legal refusal to pay unauthorized levies into a collective rather than an individual (or household) matter.[47] This would substantiate the hope voiced by some Chinese academics and officials that village democracy would in fact entail a change in the power relations between the village and the township.[48]

But the new law did not include a crucial provision found in the 1993 Law on Agriculture and in many Central Committee–State Council documents on burden reduction, that villagers had the "right to refuse" to pay illegal levies. This omission and other restrictions apparently prompted a member of the Standing Committee of the NPC, Pu Zhaoshu, to observe during the debate on the final law that it didn't really protect peasants' economic interests. The law did not provide for mechanisms to enable peasants to resist withholding of procurement

---

[45] Xu Yong (1997: 291).

[46] For reportage on the debate in 1987, see *RMRB-O* editorial (March 17, 1987), and *RMRB* (April 5 and April 10, 1987). On the debate in 1998, see *CD* (Aug. 28, 1998), and *Xinhua* (Oct. 29, 1998, *SWB-FE*/3373, G/9–10).

[47] That "contradictions" could arise between VCs and townships over the township and village tax, and the funding of road and school construction and other public interest projects was acknowledged in an unpublished paper by a Henan civil affairs official (Aug. 28, 1998).

[48] Interview, Beijing (Sept. 1998).

payments or demands for fees. "If the organic law of the villagers' committee, a fundamental law affecting the nine hundred million peasants, cannot resolve this issue, the peasants' democratic rights will end up being empty words," he argued.[49] Three other Standing Committee members supported this minority view.

Adoption of the "guidance" relationship continued to be challenged even after the passage of the final law. In the summer of 1999, for instance, an article by members of the Policy Research Office of the Shanxi Party Committee argued strenuously in an internal publication in favor of formal restoration of "leadership" relations and for township "administrative supervision" of villages. The Research Office claimed that an investigation had shown that 22 percent of directly elected village cadres openly declared that they would no longer obey the township Party committee secretaries and government chiefs. "Abolition of the leadership relationship will shake the mass basis and organizational guarantee of rural political power and will weaken the worker-peasant alliance, which is the foundation of the people's democratic dictatorship." That village leaders would pursue local interests rather those of the Party was seen as a particularly serious problem in poorer areas, where lineage and blood relations exerted powerful influence. Without higher-level intervention, "small groupism," "local protectionism," and "fortified village politics" (*tuweizi zhengzhi*) would, in their view, flourish.[50]

These Party officials did indeed zero in on the core problem raised by free and fair village elections – their potential for conflict with the townships. As emphasized earlier, the more VC cadres owed their elections to their constituents rather than to appointment by higher authority or the Party secretary, the greater their incentive to be responsive to their electorate. According to a village chief in Yunnan, "As an appointed official he carried out township orders without thinking about their effect on villagers. Now, he worries about his constituents and vows that they will not regret giving him their support."[51] Whether this commitment prompted him to stand up to the leaders of the township was not clear, but free elections had the potential of tilting the balance of competing pressures on elected cadres toward the peasants, if they felt empowered to respond to their demands and reject unlawful demands of township officials. Village leaders might bargain with the officials, using the threat of peasant protest as chips.

One way for townships to maintain control was through the village Party branches, a point vigorously stressed by the cadres of the Shanxi Party Research

---

[49] *Xinhua* (November 2, 1998, *SWB-FE*3373, G/9–10).
[50] Li Chun and Guo Lingji (1999).
[51] Epstein Gadsden and Thurston (n.d.: 15).

Office quoted above, who argued that the Party units should maintain "leadership" relations with the VCs.[52] Party branches were directly subordinate to the township Party committees and Party discipline could be invoked to secure compliance if the VCs turned out to be recalcitrant. The final Village Committee Law stipulated that the CCP play the "core leadership role" in the village. Its task was "to support and ensure villager self-rule, thereby enabling villagers to exercise their democratic rights directly." So ambiguous a delimitation of the respective spheres of competence could lead to two kinds of outcomes. First, the Party branches remained in control and decided on important policy issues while the VCs implemented them. Second, the VCs gained in power and the role of the Party branches was confined mainly to political education and the recruitment and training of new members. This could happen because the prestige and authority of a popularly elected VC chairman were likely to exceed those of the appointed Party secretary. Some secretaries perceived the consequences of the elections as reducing them to impotence, especially when they had hitherto been the unchallenged bosses of the village, but now had to turn over to the VC the administrative seal and control of finances, including those of collective enterprises. Some elected VC chairs vigorously defended their prerogatives against those of the Party branch on the grounds that the law was on their side. In other cases, Party secretaries hung onto the levers of power.[53]

An important trend relevant to burdens was to merge the posts of Party secretary and VC chair. This resolved the jurisdictional conflict but left open how to resolve the dilemma of conflicting pressures from townships and peasants. Merging posts was popular among peasants because it saved them money, since they would only have to pay for one chief, not two. In Shanghai 36 percent of village secretaries served concurrently as VC chairs. In Hubei, Zhejiang, and Jiangsu, the percentages were lower (11, 8, and 7), but in Guangdong as of 1999, the average was 56 percent, and in some jurisdictions, Nanhai city and Xinhui city, the proportions were as high as 60 and 80 percent.[54] In 1999, Liaocheng city, Shandong, innovated by making concurrent officeholding more or less compulsory, in that it required Party secretaries to run for election. As a result, 4,933 branch secretaries were elected VC chairs, or 77.1 percent of the total. Six hundred thirteen Party secretaries were "readjusted," thereby raising the concurrence rate all the way to 86.7 percent. In one town, seven out of thirty-eight Party secretaries lost the VC elections, whereupon the winning

---

[52] Li Chun and Guo Lingji (1999).

[53] For such cases, see Guo Zhenglin (2000) and *NMRB* (Dec. 11, 1999). For an overview of relations between the Party branch and the VC, see Xu Yong (1998a: 89–92).

[54] Guo Zhenglin (2000: 19).

VC chairpersons took over their Party posts. Moreover, 16,089 members of the village committees served concurrently in Party branches, permitting a reduction of the village cadre force by 26,000, thereby saving the peasants a total of 20 million yuan. Cadre-mass relations reportedly improved significantly whereas the position of the CCP as the "core" basic level organization was consolidated.[55] Making the Party secretary at least in part accountable to the electorate changed the incentive structure of the secretaries in the direction of paying attention to the demands of constituents rather than only to their Party superiors. In the discussions that preceded adoption of this measure, township secretaries voiced their concerns precisely on this point, that exposure to electoral pressures would make it more difficult for them to secure the compliance of village Party secretaries.[56] This realignment of the pressures under which Party secretaries labored held out the promise that village leaders might present a united front vis-à-vis the townships in defending villagers' interests, including those that affected burdens. Bjoern Alpermann's findings from field research in southern Hebei, however, did not sustain these hopes. Instead, village leaders operated jointly as the "*lingdao banzi*," the leadership groups, and they were primarily responsive to the townships.[57] Mergers eliminated dual rule but another outcome could be restoration of rule by one boss (*yibashou*).

Expanding Democracy to the Townships? There is widespread agreement among researchers and officials strongly supportive of democratizing the countryside that major progress in holding the authorities accountable will only come when direct elections are extended to the townships themselves, where real power lies, at least with respect to village finance. Even if village elections turn out to have a strong impact on burdens, it is direct elections of township leaders that would make a real difference in securing official responsiveness to villager interests and curbing official arbitrariness, and hence burdens. Direct township elections would be a major step forward in boosting the capacity of villagers to pressure officialdom. Villagers could elect township heads who promised not to launch compulsory drives to raise funds or not to impose fees or arbitrary fines. A popularly elected township head might well take energetic

---

[55] *NMRB* (Dec. 11, 1999).

[56] *NMRB* (Dec. 11, 1999). Other experiments elsewhere sought to enhance the popularity of the Party secretaries by modifying the rule that they be elected only by Party members. In some villages in Hequ county, Shanxi, a kind of popular straw vote tested the candidate's acceptability to the masses and only afterward did the branch members vote. This change, which undermined basic Leninist principles, was supported by higher-level Party committees but not generally adopted. See Lianjiang Li (1999).

[57] Alpermann (2001).

action to reduce overstaffing, a major source of excessive burdens. And, just as the direct election of village leaders might motivate them to resist unreasonable impositions by the townships, so direct township elections might similarly motivate the leaders to stand up to higher-level illegal demands in the name of their constituents.

Direct election of the township head and the extension of the financial openness policy to the township and even higher levels have been discussed internally by researchers and by Ministry of Civil Affairs officials from the mid-1990s on.[58] But it took a local initiative in Buyun township, Suining city, Sichuan, sanctioned and supported by reform-minded district officials, for a direct election of the head of a township actually to take place.[59] Direct election of the township head by sixteen thousand residents was much more complex than a village election, requiring fairly complex organization. An election steering committee set the rules. The nominations were made by an appointed group of one hundred fifty individuals who selected three candidates out of fifteen who had nominated themselves or were nominated by the Party or by mass organizations. The fifteen were able to campaign, engage in debate, and answer questions, as were the three finalists. The winner, by a narrow margin, turned out to be the nominee of the Buyun Party Committee, Tan Xiaoqiu, who was already the deputy township head. Apparently the people thought he was capable and could get things done. The open debates were "characterized by angry complaints" about "the exorbitant hog tax," excessive fees, an increased education tax, and cadre corruption. Burdens were thus an important facet of the electoral campaign. One of its by-products was that district officials finally became aware just how deeply farmers resented the hog tax and how suspicious some voters were that the township was "cheating ordinary people by imposing taxes."[60]

Did the elections make a difference in reducing burdens? A year later, a visiting reporter learned that although Tan had fulfilled some of his campaign promises, this did not include his pledges to lower taxes, which were, in fact, slated to increase significantly in 2000. Tan fulfilled his promise to build a road but imposed a 10 yuan fee on each resident to help pay for it. Grumbling continued.[61]

The Buyun election provoked a great deal of debate. Doubts were raised about its constitutionality since only the township People's Congress was supposed to choose the township head. The regime at first took a wait-and-see attitude, neither repudiating nor approving the election. Further experiments

---

[58] Bai Gang (1998a), Zhu Huaxin (1998: 367), and interviews, Beijing (Sept. 1998).
[59] This paragraph is based on Yawei Liu (1999).
[60] Yawei Liu (1999).
[61] *Los Angeles Times* (Feb. 27, 2000).

were conducted in a Shanxi township and in a village in Shenzhen. China's leaders are likely to proceed very cautiously on this issue, given that direct township elections have the potential of increasing peasant power far more than village elections.[62] Much will depend on how the village elections work out. If a major trend emerges of elected village leaders vigorously defending the interests of their constituents to the point of organizing mass protests, the top leaders are likely to conclude that direct township elections would jeopardize social stability even more. They might, in fact, not only decide to squash further electoral experiments with township elections, but also cut back on the relative electoral freedom in the villages. Reemphasis on Leninist Party principles, especially the requirement that subordinate Party bodies unconditionally obey their superiors would be one possibility. And indeed a major theme in nationwide political discourse around the turn of the century was to emphasize the continued primacy of Party leadership.[63]

The following tentative conclusions seem appropriate:

1. When elections were genuinely open, cadre-peasant relations improved and tax collection was characterized by greater fairness and less abuse. This was even more likely if village leaders planned to run for reelection.
2. With regard to actual reductions in burdens, decreases could occur when elections were accompanied by genuine financial transparency enforced by the VRA, which would curb cadre corruption, for example, embezzlement or misuse of funds, or the conspicuous consumption of "wining and dining." In addition, some burden reduction could come from cutting village cadre compensation and from limiting their number.
3. However, if the Party branch secretary retained full power as the village boss, positive change was likely to be minimal.
4. Burdens could be reduced if elected village leaders bargained with or pressured township officials.

STRENGTHENING FARMER INTEREST REPRESENTATION AT THE CENTER

As this study has emphasized, central leaders were strongly concerned with peasant and agricultural problems and sought to solve them. Yet, with respect to burdens, fifteen years of centrally decreed remedial measures were, as of 2001, not effective. One of the contributing factors in this record of ineffectuality was the weak political strength of the agricultural sector in policy-making.

---

[62] Interview, Beijing (Sept. 1998). See also Zhu Huaxin (1998: 367) for a strong expression of hope that elections be expanded. Some reformers see village elections as the proverbial foot in the door leading eventually to national elections.

[63] Exemplified, for instance, by Jiang Zemin's "three represents" campaign.

Burdens were to some degree the product of a set of political institutions that systematically favored the urban-industrial sector and discriminated against agriculture and the peasants. As Susan Shirk points out:

> CCP leaders set up China's national economic bureaucracy in 1953 to reflect their developmental priorities, industry over agriculture and heavy industry over light industry. . . . Chinese leaders established an administrative structure that would give heavy industry the strongest voice.[64]

In the era of the planned economy industrial interests dominated in the coordinating agencies such as the State Planning Commission, in large part because of the overwhelming presence of the many industrial ministries, especially those for heavy industry and for defense. Officials in the heavy industrial sector had greater prestige and status and were able to recruit the most talented cadres. The industrial bureaucracies overshadowed the economic agencies concerned with agriculture which had "little political clout" and were considered "political lightweights." Agriculture produced little budgetary revenue, in contrast to the industrial sector, whose profits or taxes provided the bulk of central revenue. "The privileged bureaucratic position of heavy industry and the weak position of agriculture were reflected in the allocation of resources." With respect to state investment, the proportion allocated to agriculture during the reform period dropped even below the levels of the Mao era. "In a system that gave agriculture only a feeble bureaucratic voice China's eight hundred million rural dwellers remained a disenfranchised majority."[65]

In this respect China resembled other Third World states which, as Robert Bates writes, were dominated by

> a development coalition of industrialists, urban wage earners, bureaucrats, and intellectuals . . . who see the future prosperity of their nations tied to their ability to secure rapid industrialization and who are committed to elicit, if necessary, the transfer of resources from agriculture with which to secure this transformation. In many countries, these interests dominate policy making."[66]

According to Bates and William Roerson, agricultural interests have difficulty in forming alliances with other interests, because "agricultural producers constitute relatively unattractive partners, for should they be granted a price rise,

---

[64] Shirk (1993: 107–8).

[65] Shirk (1993: 108–10, 133). According to interviews with several retired high officials in Beijing in August 1994, "many government departments" were simply not interested in agriculture.

[66] Bates (1987: 179).

this would be very costly to all other members of the coalition."[67] Agricultural interests tended to make redistributive demands which urban and industrial interests naturally opposed. These structural obstacles to the establishment of a strong peasant voice in policy-making applied well to the Chinese case.

The discriminatory status of the agricultural sector did not go unchallenged during the reform period. Some in elite circles spoke out on behalf of agriculture and advocated a variety of remedial measures designed to help that sector, such as increasing state investment in agriculture, reducing or eliminating the scissors gap between industrial and procurement prices, allocating more resources to rural education, and more broadly, ending the exploitation of the agricultural sector.[68] Among the advocates were deputies to the National People's Congress who came from agricultural provinces, sometimes as successful model peasants or local entrepreneurs, sometimes as deputies who held major posts in the rural Party-government hierarchy and who had an interest in securing more resources for their areas of responsibility. Advocates also came from the media, from some ministries, such as Agriculture and Civil Affairs, and from members of the academic and research community both within the State Council and the Central Committee, universities and the social science academies, as well as provincial Party research offices.[69] What is of interest is that some of these elite advocates not only demanded remedial policies, but also argued that the influence of the farm sector on policy-making needed to be strengthened and even to be given institutional expression. Some of the recommendations and demands made by elite advocates were in fact adopted but this did not fundamentally alter the second-class status of the agricultural sector. Five such demands were particularly noteworthy. One, the demand for a national farmers' association, is treated in some detail in this chapter.

First, advocates demanded that the status of peasants be raised. They criticized the widely noted unwillingness of urban people, especially intellectuals, to accept peasants as legitimate participants in politics.[70] This stemmed from deep rooted assumptions, that only the educated were entitled to rule, that peasants were backward, feudal, reactionary, and superstitious, and that they put their trust in good officials and benevolent emperors. Many intellectuals saw in peasants a tragic drag on democratization, dooming the country to authoritarian rule until agriculture had been modernized and peasants enlightened. As the

[67] Bates and Roerson (1989: 523).
[68] Editorial Department, *NJW* (No. 10, 1991) and Wang Yuexin (1995).
[69] For an analysis of elite advocacy, see Bernstein (1999: 197–219).
[70] See Kelliher (1993), Cohen (1993: 151–70), and Goldman (1994: 177).

astrophysicist and democracy advocate Fang Lizhi put it in 1986 at a meeting with students:

> Question: Not long ago Deng Xiaoping said that China would have to wait twenty or thirty years before being able to hold competitive elections. Can you imagine that China will have full-scale democracy? (laughter)
>
> Answer: The right answer is this: You can go to the villages and see the peasants' uneducated and traditional consciousness. You would have a hard time stirring up a democratic consciousness among them. They just want upright officials. If no one looks after them, they become uncomfortable. This is the AQ mentality that Lu Xun talked about.[71]

Similarly, an NPC official was heard to say in 1999 that "Teaching democracy to peasants is like playing the piano to cows."[72]

Advocates chastised the unwillingness of the urban sector to take peasant opinions seriously. "They (urbanites) must not neglect them simply because peasants are poorly organized and their voice is weak. They must hold more dialogues with them."[73] The difficulty of rural NPC deputies in asserting themselves was an example of these exclusionist attitudes. In the past peasant deputies had often been models who were chosen for the NPC for essentially symbolic reasons and who didn't speak up in the NPC's group meetings. But this changed, in part due to the enlivening of the NPC as a genuine forum for debate.[74] By 1988, peasant deputies spoke with an "unexpectedly loud voice." They articulated their resentment of the low esteem in which they were held by their colleagues from urban and intellectual backgrounds. "Some people" insisted that peasant deputies were not qualified to be participants in political debate (*zhengyi*) because their educational levels were lower than those of urban deputies. Rural deputies strongly objected to this, insisting that competence to participate was not simply a function of education but of social practice.[75] A woman deputy from a Liaoning county, the director of a textile factory, acknowledged that peasant deputies did have difficulties participating: "I am afraid we won't be able to convey the peasants' views." She nonetheless expressed determination to speak on peasant problems, saying, "we peasants can draw up accounts. We may not have much other knowledge, but this we can do."[76] In other words, she put forth the classic argument for democracy for

---

[71] Xu Xing, ed. (1987: 134). We are indebted to Harold Tanner for this source.
[72] Jakobson (2001).
[73] *RMRB* Commentator (March 6, 1989).
[74] For two studies on the changing role of the NPC, see O'Brien (1990) and Tanner (1999).
[75] *NMRB* (April 12, 1988 and March 26, 1988), and *Xinhua* (March 25, 1989, *FBIS*, No. 58: 20–1).
[76] *NMRB* (March 28, 1988).

all, that even the uneducated know "where the shoe pinches" and hence have a right to be heard.[77]

Second, advocates from within the NPC complained about the underrepresentation of peasants in that body. This had been deliberate policy since the early 1950s, since it "gives expression to the leading role of the working class in our country and the need to realize the four modernizations."[78] According to the 1979 Election Law, a deputy from the rural sector represented eight times the number of people as one from the urban sector. In the seventh NPC, elected in 1988, 315 or 10.6 percent of the 2,970 deputies were counted as peasants. In contrast, workers made up 12.4 percent and intellectuals 23.5 percent.[79] As of 1993, one rural deputy represented 825,000 people, an urban one 106,300.[80] At the 1990 NPC session, several deputies called for an "appropriate increase" in the number of rural deputies to both the NPC and the CPPCC, "to provide more chances for rural citizens, who make up the bulk of the Chinese population, to participate in and discuss government and political affairs." They complained that peasant membership on the crucially important Standing Committee of the NPC had shrunk from twelve to two in the 1980s.[81] In 1995 the Election Law was changed so that one rural deputy represented "only" four times as many people as did an urban one and this was hailed as a step toward equalizing representation. Unfortunately, separate breakdowns of the number of peasants and workers were no longer provided, and it is difficult to tell how close the additional deputies were to agriculture as opposed to, say, rural industry.

Third, a persistent chorus of voices in the NPC from the later 1980s on charged that the top leaders, including Premiers Zhao Ziyang and Li Peng, were not paying enough attention to agriculture.[82] Deputies complained that leaders often paid only lip service to the importance of agriculture, practicing "slogan" or "conference" agriculture (*kouhao* and *huiyi nongye*),[83] and criticized the tendency to pay attention to agriculture only during times of natural disaster when the supply of grain to the cities was in danger. As a woman leader of a Zhejiang village put it at an NPC meeting:

> China is an agricultural country. The government should pay more attention to the opinion of us peasants when formulating policies in the future. When

---

[77] Lindsay (1943: 269–72).

[78] Quoted in Burns (1988: 30).

[79] *Beijing Review* (April 2–8, 1990: 20).

[80] Zhe Sun (1999: ch 6, 46).

[81] *ZTS* (April 13, 1990, *FBIS*, No. 71: 28). One of the deputies who made this proposal was a nationally prominent model village Party secretary from Henan, Shi Laihe.

[82] O'Brien (1990: 118–20).

[83] See, e.g., *NMRB* (March 3, 1998).

eight hundred million peasants are satisfied with the government . . . there will be no task that cannot be accomplished properly.[84]

These complaints were tied implicitly or sometimes explicitly to demands for strengthening the position of agricultural interests in the central executive apparatus. In 1990, an NPC deputy from Jiangxi, Wang Shufeng, asked that a "strong and powerful department in charge of rural work should be formed by the CPC Central Committee to guide and coordinate agricultural development."[85] In 1992, a *Farmers' Daily* editorial proposed establishment of a "powerful supervisory mechanism" to control IOUs and burdens.[86] The rise of the socialist market economy did not mean that agriculture could be left to itself. Governments in advanced capitalist countries played a powerful role in supporting a flourishing agricultural sector. "We must consider setting up a comprehensive agricultural department with the power to balance all interests" which would be able to effectively take charge of all aspects of agriculture and by implication defend the interests of that sector in policy-making.[87]

Fourth, from the late 1980s on, NPC deputies vigorously advocated passage of laws to institutionalize protection of agriculture and the peasants. Demands were voiced for a general law on agriculture, plus a law on state investment that would legally stipulate agricultural investment by the state, a law on burdens, and one on land. These demands were part of the regime's determination to rule the country by law. The intent was clearly to bind the government to a series of laws that would insure credible commitments by the government to the agricultural sector, thereby protecting it from frequent adverse shifts in policy. After several years of NPC agitation, a law on agriculture was enacted in 1993, which, as noted earlier, gave peasants the "right to refuse" to pay illegal taxes and fees. This law also stipulated that state investment in agriculture should increase at a rate faster than the increase in overall state revenues. In 1997, NPC and CPPCC investigations claimed that the state had "basically" complied.[88] In 1999, deputies made a motion for a law to protect peasants' rights and interests (*quanyi*) on the grounds that there had been no progress on burdens, which, if anything, had gotten more severe, despite numerous Party-state decrees.[89]

---

[84] *Xinhua*, Beijing (Nov. 2, 1988, *JPRS*-CAR-88-81: 43–4).

[85] *Xinhua* (March 26, 1990, *FBIS*, No. 60: 9). In the wake of the Tiananmen crackdown the Rural Policy Research Office in the Party Secretariat and its State Council counterpart, the Rural Development Research Center, were closed. See *Washington Post* (Oct. 27, 1989).

[86] *NMRB* editorial (Dec. 16, 1992).

[87] Zhang Qingzhong (1993a: 38).

[88] *NMRB* (March 14, 1997).

[89] *NMRB* (March 9, 1999).

In 1998, an NPC Committee on Agriculture was finally established, evidently in response to many years of entreaties by deputies. Until then, the Finance and Economics Committee handled agricultural legislation but only as part of a much broader agenda. A separate committee raised the status and visibility of the agricultural sector. A year after its establishment, the committee reported on its activities, which included processing deputies' motions; drafting legislation, including that on the final law on village organization; receiving reports on various aspects of the rural sector, including burdens; and investigating the implementation of laws. Its projects for 1999 included drafting a law on the household responsibility system and the aforementioned law on protecting peasant rights.[90]

One possible indicator of the increasing clout of agricultural interests in the NPC was the repeated rejection of an amendment to China's Highway Law. In November 1998 the State Council proposed to end the collection of all highway fees, licit or illicit, and instead to substitute a tax on fuel and motor vehicle sales. Since road fees had long been a severe burden on peasants – in 1996, 249 tolls yielded 116 billion yuan in revenue – this amendment seemingly would have helped them. But closer examination indicated that farmers, who were no longer allowed to drive farm machinery on major highways, would be burdened by the increased fuel costs. The Standing Committee of the NPC rejected the amendment. Half a year later, the State Council submitted a revised amendment that called for reimbursement of farmers for the increased fuel tax. Members of the Standing Committee questioned whether such a scheme would work, wondering whether the money would actually reach the farmers or be diverted; others worried that the new tax would give rise to gasoline smuggling. Again, the amendment failed to be adopted, falling one vote short of the required majority of the 154 members.[91] Finally, in October 1999, the Standing Committee did approve the amendment.[92] The Ministry of Finance promised that 5 billion yuan would be distributed to farmers via local governments to offset the increased cost of fuel. Yet, two years later, the fuel tax had not yet been imposed, indicative of continued opposition. The delay could also have been caused by increased oil prices which would make the tax even less palatable.

Whether this chain of events was in fact an indicator of the clout of farming interests is by no means clear. As Christine Wong suggests, the peasant issue may have been only the public argument against the amendment. The real issue

---

[90] *NMRB* (March 13, 1999). A law on household contracting was designed to reassure peasants about its permanence, which had long been a source of concern. See Bernstein (1992: 146–66).
[91] Cui Bo (1999: 10–11).
[92] *www.finance.sina.com.cn* (Nov. 1, 1999).

was that under the amendment, control over revenues from the fuel and car sales taxes would accrue to the Center, not to the localities that had benefited greatly from the fee system.[93] Farm interests evidently played a role but they may have been invoked by local interests simply to strengthen their case.

A NATIONAL FARMERS' ASSOCIATION?

The fifth of the demands and proposals for improving peasants' capacity to participate in state affairs took pride of place. The proposal to establish a national farmers' association sought sharply to raise the capacity of farming interests to find a voice in Beijing. Proposals for FAs kept being made during the reform era. The first was made in 1980 and into the late 1990s they continued to be a topic of internal discussion among scholars and officials. The idea was reportedly discussed within the State Council. In evaluating the proposals, it is important to bear in mind that none of those that surfaced was a detailed blueprint. They did not answer such questions as how China's vast and increasingly differentiated and diverse farm population could be represented by one national organization. In other large and diversified countries, several farmer organizations represented competing agricultural interests. And, most important, the proposals did not directly address the crucial question of just how far such a group would be able to go in pressing its claims in China's authoritarian system.

A major and recurring theme in the litany of advocates' complaints about exclusion was that China's eight hundred million peasants had no organization of their own. In striking and painful contrast, workers had a trade union, women the women's federation, and young people the Communist Youth League. Even private entrepreneurs and consumers had their own organizations. Only peasants were not allowed to have one, demonstrating their inferior and unequal status. Gaining equal status with other groups was an important motive for demands for a national farmers' association.

What would an FA accomplish for the peasants? First, it would raise their status and give them a strong voice in national affairs. Peasants constituted "a gigantic interest group," yet they lacked the capacity to protect their social and economic interests.[94] The high status of a nationwide organization, capped by a central-level headquarters, would provide farmers with greater access to the Party and government and would enable them to carry on "an equal dialogue" with the authorities. Representing the peasants, it would transmit

---

[93] Personal communication with Professor Wong.
[94] *FZRB* (June 21, 1996).

their opinions and demands to the leaders, thereby providing a basis for the country's leaders to respond to farmers' pleas. As two scholars pointed out in 1987, "peasants must be allowed to have a real organization of their own, which can exercise popular supervision and guarantee their participation and discussion in politics."[95] "Merely by relying on some government supplement and relief, peasants could not basically change their situation of having their interests seriously encroached upon," observed another. An FA would represent peasant interests and would allow them to "participate in the formulation of state policy (*zhiding*)."[96]

Second, according to Gu Wenshao of the Rural Work Department of the Hebei Party Committee, a major task of an FA network would be to check administrative acts that violated peasant interests. Since various administrative units failed to obey Central directives, they could severely harm peasant interests. An FA organized at all levels of the hierarchy would "struggle" against departments and individuals that "dug pits" for the peasants. State industrial and administrative organs "block peasants, injure them, and eat them up" (*ka nong, shang nong, chi nong*). A unified organization would be able to protect villagers' legal interests, such as the right to refuse to pay illegal burdens imposed by some organization or other, he wrote.[97]

Third, also according to Gu, the establishment of an organization that represented peasant interests was a necessary component of socialist democratic political development. Without an FA, peasants were put into an unfavorable, passive position when interest conflicts arose between them, departments, and urban social groups. An FA would contribute to the adjudication (*xietiao*) of conflicting social interests.[98] As things stood, peasants could not enter into an equal dialogue with other societal circles and engage in equal exchange with the cities.[99]

Advocates usually couched their arguments in terms of the benefits for the regime of establishing an FA. It would strengthen the ties between villagers and the Party, promote peasant ideological education, and foster the growth of the "two civilizations." An FA would mobilize peasants to fulfill "to the utmost" their various legal duties and obligations to the state and to the collectives. A farmers' association would contribute to the growth of legality and of

---

[95] Liu Huazhen and Xu Wenan (1987: 61) and Liu Huazhen (1989). For similar formulations, see Chen Youfu (1994).

[96] Zhang Qi (1989: 49–51).

[97] Gu Wenshao (1993).

[98] Ibid.

[99] *NMRB* (March 30, 1993), article by Wang Yushao, the deputy head of the State Council Development Research Center.

legal norms. Its local branches would help farmers at the various stages of the production cycle, organize peasants to enter markets, and disseminate market information and technical knowledge. Most important, it would promote social stability.

FAs should be organized at all levels of the hierarchy, not simply at the grass roots level, where they had existed in revolutionary times, in the 1960s as associations of poor and lower-middle peasants, and in the reform period as functional groups devoted to the advancement of specialized agricultural undertakings (beekeeping, duck raising, technology promotion, and so forth).[100] A national association, in contrast, would be led and coordinated by its central bureau. It would have its own charter and membership and representative meetings. Its status would be that of a mass organization.[101] One idea was that an FA should not be run by officials (*guanban nongxie*), although from the county on up, state cadres would be needed to staff it and state financial help would be necessary. Another one was that an FA should not "eat imperial grain" but be independent financially.[102] The FA would differ from existing collective or cooperative organizations, which in reality were administrative organs of the government and could not genuinely protect peasant interests. Specialized trade associations could also not serve as substitutes to an FA.[103]

Several proponents looked to foreign models for a Chinese FA, noting that developed countries had agricultural interest groups, including the United States, France, Romania, and Hungary. A CASS researcher, for instance, wrote that:

Japan's agricultural association is an oriental style peasants' cooperative organization. We must borrow from the experiences of other countries in setting up a nationwide peasant organization that will enable the peasants to maintain a direct dialogue with the government and protect agriculture.[104]

He added that Japan's farmers had a national organization, with a branch for every thousand individuals. It had three hundred thousand employees, was an internally democratic organization, and one that acted in a representative capacity vis-à-vis government. It was able to secure government attention to and subsidies for agriculture, thereby making a contribution to stability. However,

---

[100] Such functionally specific service-oriented local associations had Jiang Zemin's imprimatur. See *NMRB* (March 17, 1998).

[101] Chen Youfu (1994).

[102] Li Xiuyi (1992b).

[103] Gu Wenshao (1993).

[104] Zhang Qingzhong (1993b: 12); see also "Riben nongxie jiankuang" (1993: 27–8).

the author did not mention the great electoral power of Japanese rural districts and the difference that this made in enhancing agricultural influence.[105]

Advocates for an FA came from a wide range of organizations, including the NPC, the CPPCC, the Policy Research Office of the Central Committee Secretariat, State Council and CASS research institutes, the Hebei Provincial Rural Work Department, and the Shanxi Provincial Agricultural Office. Within the NPC, deputy Wang Deli, together with thirty-one colleagues – both rural cadres and peasants – submitted a motion during the 1989 session demanding the establishment of a farmers' association from "top to bottom." The *NMRB* reported this demand, which was echoed at the concurrently held CPPCC congress. After all, "workers have a trade union, why shouldn't eight hundred million peasants establish their own organization?" "The peasant masses" want one, they claimed. When meeting with reporters, "many" farmer deputies asked that *Nongmin Ribao* issue an appeal (*huyu*) on behalf of this cause. In the same issue in which the *NMRB* reported on NPC deputies, it also printed a letter from a Hubei rural deputy, who had in "recent years" received letters from "friends of peasants" nationwide which "urgently demanded" both national and local FAs. Because farmers had in recent years been cheated and harmed, their interests could not realistically be safeguarded. A farmers' association would be able "to consult and coordinate" (*cuoshang xietiao*) with the government and the departments concerned on the issues. A local organization would also help in combating feudal evils and raising peasants' cultural level, thereby serving regime purposes.[106]

In 1990, after the crushing of the Tiananmen Protest Movement, when political reforms were hardly in favor, these same demands were nonetheless voiced, even more intensely, by NPC deputies. Among those who spoke on behalf of FAs was Shi Laihe, a long-standing nationally prominent model village Party secretary from Xinxiang county, Henan, a member of the NPC Standing Committee, who had been received by Mao Zedong nine times as well as by Zhou Enlai and Deng Xiaoping.[107] During the NPC session, *Farmers' Daily* prominently reported that "departments concerned" in the State Council were examining the proposals for an FA made a year earlier at the NPC.[108]

Nothing came of this examination, but proposals continued to surface as the 1990s progressed. For example, in 1992, Luo Hanxian, vice chairman of the

[105] Ibid. Gu Wenshao (1993) and Chen Youfu (1994).
[106] *NMRB* (March 28, 1989).
[107] *NMRB* (April 4, 1990); see also *ZTS* (April 3, 1990, *FBIS*, No. 71: 28). Shi Laihe also spoke out on behalf of increasing the number of peasant deputies.
[108] *NMRB* (April 4, 1990).

Democratic League and a member of the Standing Committee of the CPPCC, proposed establishing a farmers' association, which would join the CPPCC and guarantee the "legal rights and interests" of three-fourths of the country's population.[109] The issue was discussed by Wang Yushao, the deputy head of the State Council Development Research Center at a meeting of the Agriculture-Forestry Small Group of the CPPCC in March 1993.[110] Proposals for a farmers' association were reportedly seriously examined at interministerial meetings after 1990. In the later 1990s FAs continued to be a subject of discussion among researchers in academia and government. The idea was cautiously raised in a text on the process of government.[111] It surfaced again in 1999 during Premier Zhu's visit to the United States. Zhu invited the president of the American Farm Bureau Federation to visit China and explain how his group worked. He reiterated the old point that workers had a trade union but farmers had no equivalent, adding that the question was being studied, and that it was an important issue for China's agricultural development.[112]

In 2001, Dang Guoying, a CASS researcher, wrote that unorganized peasants were a greater danger to stability than organized ones. They might fall prey to leaders of religious sects or to political extremists. Since the countryside was something of a pressure cooker, some way of relieving political pressure would have to be found. Among various solutions, Dang suggested that peasants needed organizations, which, in his view, would incline rural people toward reformism rather than radicalism. They would enable holding dialogues with the government and mediate "sudden incidents" (see Chapter 5). Dang suggested encouragement of localized and specialized economic organizations, which would form the basis for the future establishment of a national peasant association.[113]

Appraisal of the Proposals. As of 2001, these proposals were not implemented but they were also not rejected. The regime was not as yet willing to allow peasants even a transmission-belt mass organization, such as the trade union or the women's federation largely continued to be, not to speak of a formally

---

[109] *SJRB* (March 20, 1992). Other proposals were published in *NMRB* (March 10 and 30, 1993) and Zhou Yichun and Ai Fuzhen (1994).

[110] *NMRB* (March 30, 1993).

[111] Interview with government official, August 1994, Beijing, and with Wuhan agricultural economists, September 1998. See Zhu Guanglei (1997: 118–19) for a brief discussion of the issue, in which the author cites proponents of an FA but then suggests that it would be more efficacious to continue to promote local-level cooperative organizations, of which there were 1.46 million as of 1993.

[112] *www.chinesenewsnet.com* (March 7, 2001).

[113] See *FEER* (Aug. 2, 2001, 24–5), Dang Guoying (2001) and Dang Guoying (1999: 7).

established independent interest group. It seems clear that proponents saw in a farmers' association an organization able to defend farmer interests and not simply to transmit policy downward. The first proposal, made in 1980 by Liao Gailong, a member of the Party Secretariat's Policy Research Center, was the bluntest of all in calling for "independent organizations" to enable farmers to defend their interests, to democratize grass roots political life, and to check bureaucratic power.

> By establishing such organizations, we can [correct the problems] that the prices of our agricultural products have been too low for a long time, that the price scissors have not been narrowed but have sometimes even widened, that the interests of the peasants are not safeguarded, and that the cost of planting rice cannot be recouped.[114]

Liao voiced confidence that farmers' associations would "carry out their work independently and responsibly under the leadership of the Party's line, principles, and policies." He did not, however, explain how interest conflicts would be resolved. Liao's proposal was made during the year of the spectacular rise of Poland's Solidarity trade union, which shocked the Chinese regime and no doubt contributed to the demise of Liao's proposal. Yet, as noted, even after the Tiananmen incident, the regime tolerated discussion of an FA and of its role. One researcher, writing in 1992, sought to distinguish between the creation of "pressure groups" (*yali zuzhi*) and organizations that would exert some influence (*yixie yingxiang*) on government. The former could "naturally" not be allowed, but, he added, to establish an organization that had no influence at all would rob it of its purpose.[115]

Perhaps one reason why the proposals were not decisively rejected is that China's leaders might have been interested in establishing some form of authoritarian corporatism. Following Philippe Schmitter's famous definition, authoritarian corporatism – translated by some Chinese scholars as *quanwei hezuo zhuyi* – is that case where the government confers a legal monopoly of representation on an association, giving it a voice within its functional sphere and enabling it to bargain on behalf of the specific interests of its members. The leaders of the association are approved, if not selected, by the regime. Regime policies favorable to the members of the group are then exchanged in return for its political quiescence, which is ensured by its leadership.[116] From

---

[114] Liao Kai-lung (1981) and Falkenheim (1982: 261).
[115] Li Xiuyi (1992b: 17). A shortened version was reprinted in *Hebei Nongcun Gongzuo* (Oct. 1992: 7). We are indebted to Kevin O'Brien for a copy of the latter.
[116] Quoted in Chalmers (1991: 61).

this perspective, an officially sponsored farmers' association would be able to bargain with policy makers over investment, taxes, prices, subsidies, and legal reform designed to increase the efficiency and honesty of local officials, all of which would help satisfy farmers. In return, the association would undertake to influence farmers not to make trouble and to adhere to regime goals on a variety of issues, ranging from paying taxes to birth control. These were among the advantages of an FA to which proponents pointed. In other words, the association would contribute to one of the most cherished goals of the Chinese Party-state, maintenance of social stability.

In the mid-1990s, the possibility that China might be headed in a corporatist direction briefly attracted the attention of western scholars.[117] In the absence of liberalization, which would include recognition of independent interest groups, China's corporatism would be authoritarian, in distinction to the societal corporatism of democracies.[118] Jonathan Unger and Anita Chan found that even while carrying out government policies, the All-China Federation of Trade Unions had been playing something of a corporatist role by becoming more assertive in its defense of workers' interests than would be expected of a Leninist transmission-belt mass organization.[119] A concrete example of the participation of the trade unions in governmental bargaining was reported in early 1988, when the deputy director of the State Administration on Commodity Prices wrote about a meeting at which prices were being set:

> At every meeting, departments in charge of production will demand price increases for their products. In a meeting attended by a dozen departments, the Commodity Price Administration will have only "one ally," that is, the National Federation of Trade Unions, which represents the workers and staff and is strongly opposed to price increases.[120]

If leaders of a farmers' association had been present, the Commodity Price Administration would have had a second ally, at least with regard to input prices, though not with regard to the prices of agricultural products. But in fact, little concrete evidence of corporatist-type behavior has come to light with regard to workers or other groups.

---

[117] See Unger and Chan (1995).

[118] Liberal corporatism can be found in some Western European democracies, where the peak associations of labor unions and business groups bargain over wages and prices together with the government, which confers official recognition on the former as the authoritative representatives of the participating social groups. See, for instance, Keeler (1981: 185–208).

[119] Unger and Chan (1995: 41).

[120] *Xinhua* (Jan. 12, 1988, *FBIS*, No.13: 25).

Even an authoritarian corporate arrangement for farmers would enable agricultural interests to gain a stronger voice in central decision making, hence altering the balance of power in policy-making between urban-industrial and agricultural interests, in which the latter were at an enormous disadvantage, as farmer advocates kept emphasizing. An FA that truly represented farmers and the countryside would make demands for redistributive policies that would favor agriculture. The very prospect that strong pressure might be exerted is undoubtedly the fundamental reason why the creation of an FA was not allowed. As a senior researcher of the State Council Development Research Center put it in an interview in September 1998, the state simply could not afford to subsidize agriculture. As a developing country, China had to give priority to industry. The only way out for agriculture was to achieve a decisive reduction in the proportion of the population engaged in agriculture, from the then 70 percent to below 50 percent. With increased urbanization and a shift to industrial-urban occupations, those who remained in agriculture would be able to increase their incomes as urban demand for agricultural products rose and rural-urban disparities declined. A national farmers' interest group could only be allowed when the agricultural population had become a relatively small minority and its demands could no longer threaten the country's developmental goals.[121] The consequence of the regime's determination to insulate policy-making from the intensive pressures that formally organized interest groups could bring to bear was exemplified by the bargaining among ministries over the terms of China's accession to WTO. The agreement reached in 1999 will demand painful sacrifices from agriculture, especially those sectors not able to compete against foreign imports.[122] These probable hardships will come on top of the hardships described in this volume. Had an effective farmers' organization participated in the decision making process, a different outcome could have resulted.

China's leaders, deeply worried about domestic upheaval, are likely to continue to be suspicious of any organizational development that could turn into a challenge to their power and priorities. And, looking at the outside world, they might have noticed that legal interest organizations do not necessarily prevent social instability, for example, in the form of "direct action." They need only have examined the French case, where farmers quite frequently demonstrated and blocked highways. Recurrently in the 1990s, radical farm organizations mobilized hundreds of thousands of farmers to march through Paris. That huge

[121] Interview, Beijing, September 1998.
[122] *Neibu Canyue* (No. 28, July 2, 1999), *SCMP* (May 26, 1999), *Hsin Pao* (May 28, 1999), in *FBIS* (May 28, 1999), and *China Business Review* (Jan.–Feb. 2000: 40–1).

numbers of farmers might go to the cities not simply to work but to agitate has been something of a nightmare for Chinese leaders.

Fear of the peasant majority is a major factor that will delay China's transition to democracy. The same scholar who gave the developmental reason for denying farmers effective interest representation also thought that greater political participation of the peasant population could not be allowed until the peasants had become a minority of the population. Otherwise, the voting strength of the rural sector would enable it to dominate the urban sector. From the regime's vantage point, democratization, which would undoubtedly give rise very rapidly to peasant political organizations, will not be on the agenda as long as peasants are in a majority.

This argument is sustained by the Indian case. Ashutosh Varshney has shown that peasants, who constitute 70 percent of the population, made impressive political gains by using the vote and gained substantial financial benefits. But Varshney also notes that the rural majority was not able to gain control of the central government because of intrarural crosscutting cleavages (for example, caste), and also because the powerful Ministry of Finance restricted the concessions that could be made to agriculture.[123] In western democracies and Japan, powerful agricultural interest groups combined with representation have succeeded in gaining extensive subsidies. But there are also cases, such as that of democratizing Taiwan, where agricultural interests have lost out on the issue of international agricultural agreements. Another case is that of Russia in the 1990s, where rural interests were not able to make much of an impact in the political arena, also in part because of intrarural divisions.[124] In China, industrial villages are sharply differentiated from the agricultural villages and in a democracy, such cleavages would undoubtedly make themselves felt.

CONCLUSION

Open and fair elections have been held in only a minority of villages. In that subset of villages, democratization seemed likely to result in fairer and less abusive management of burdens in the villages and in actual reduction of burdens if there was genuine financial accountability and if the popular demands reduced the cadre force and its costly maintenance. But only if democratization were to extend upward to the townships, and perhaps to even higher levels, can significant burden reductions be brought about.

---

[123] Varshney (1995: 181–8).

[124] See Chien-pin Li (1998: 558–602) and Wegren (2001). The special issue of the *Journal of Development Studies*, "Beyond Urban Bias," contains several articles that shed light on the reduction or elimination of "urban bias" in various Third World states. See Varshney (1993).

At the national level, some steps were taken to give agricultural interests greater representation, mainly in the NPC, but China's leaders have shied away from permitting the establishment at the national level of agricultural interest groups. Doing so would be a structural change that could genuinely empower China's farmers to pressure policymakers and thus modify the urban-rural balance of power. In sum, China's rural people continue to be essentially disenfranchised. As China's senior agricultural official, Du Runsheng, put it, the "first step" in solving the problems of the countryside is to "treat the peasants as citizens and to give them their basic rights."[125]

---

[125] This he did in a foreword to the book cited earlier by the former Hubei township Party secretary who had lodged serious complaints with the State Council. See Li Changping (2002: 1–3).

8

Conclusions

NEARLY a century ago, Schumpeter wrote in his treatise on the relationship between the state and taxation: "Taxes not only helped to create the
state. They helped to form it. The tax system was the organ the development
of which entailed the other organs.... The tax brings money and calculating
spirit into corners in which they do not dwell as yet, and thus becomes a for-
mative factor in the very organism which has developed it."[1] The study of
peasant burdens and rural taxation in China offers a glimpse into the direction
in which Chinese reforms have been evolving. This conclusion recapitulates
major empirical findings and discusses their theoretical import.

The Three Rural Chinas. Our first major finding is that to understand the complexities of the countryside, it is essential to differentiate between "industrializing rural China," middle-income "agricultural China," and low-income
western China. China's unitary state designed policies at the Center for the entire
country. Although lip service was paid to the principle of implementing policies
according to local circumstances (*yin di zhi yi*), in fact performance demands
on localities seem to have been quite uniform. (There were some exceptions,
such as Tibet.) With regard to the rural sector, this greatly contributed to increased regional differentiation with respect to development. Policies of fiscal
decentralization allowed localities to retain more revenues and thereby stimulate development. This worked well in some parts of the country but not so
well in others. Hence, our distinction between "industrializing rural China" and
"agricultural China," the former mainly located in the eastern provinces and
around major cities in the other parts of the country, and characterized by the
spectacular, even miraculous growth of township and village industries in the
1980s and into the mid-1990s. This success naturally aroused the attention of

---

[1] Schumpeter (1991: 108).

241

scholars who sought to explain the mushrooming of TVEs and to understand their evolution over time. They addressed important puzzles, such as how rapid growth was possible in the absence of well-defined property rights.[2] But these successes were confined to only a part of rural China.

Rural industry grew much more slowly if at all in "agricultural China," the great agricultural regions of central China, not to speak of the poor western and southwestern provinces, which we call "subsistence rural China." In these areas conditions for TVE development were less propitious. They lacked market access, availability of investment funds, especially from overseas, and favorable natural endowments. Hence, promotion of rural industrialization and other developmental projects was much more difficult. Scholars have rightly devoted much attention to "industrializing rural China," but the problems of the less favored regions have not been highlighted in the literature. Our study of the peasant tax burden issue, which focuses primarily, but not exclusively, on agricultural China, endeavors to contribute to our understanding of these relatively neglected areas.

Historical Continuity. China's long history of the difficult relations between the central and local governments under a nominally unitary structure has shaped patterns of rural taxation. It is in this sense that we see striking similarities between the late imperial, the Republican, and post-Mao peasant burden problems. Nor is conflict over tax policy and tax collection unique to China. Post-Mao China can be fruitfully compared with state building in western Europe in the eighteenth century, where central control over revenue was a core issue. The success or failure of tax policy and revenue collection by a regime was generally affected by the ability of the Center to control the local revenue collection. In China, in the Qing, the county magistrate, though centrally appointed, had to pay his staff out of his own resources, just as in the PRC, numerous local bureaucrats had to be paid out of informal resources gathered locally. Thus local officials were not only agents of the central state but they also had their own interests which they to varying degrees succeeded in pursuing. As Hopcroft notes, this situation also obtained in some European states, including England, motivating officials to be "more concerned with maintaining their local standing than carrying out the often unpopular will of the central government."[3]

Although peasant tax protest was by no means confined to agricultural China – in industrializing China, for instance, villagers protested inadequately

---

[2] See, for example, Montinola, Qian, and Weingast (1995), Oi (1999), Whiting (2001), Zweig (1997).

[3] See, inter alia, Hopcroft (1999).

compensated land confiscations – impressionistically, the highest incidence of protest activity was to be found in provinces such as Hunan, Jiangxi, Anhui, and northern Jiangsu. In these provinces, it is worth noting, numerous peasant riots took place in imperial China, suggesting that repertoires of protest had roots in premodern practices. The discovery of striking continuity in the regional distribution of tax revolts is significant in that some of the same provinces had also been the ones where major rebellions and revolutions got their start. We do not claim that the small-scale tax riots of the 1990s will inevitably evolve into major regime-threatening directions. In the 1990s, all were essentially localized outbreaks. For its part, the regime strove to maintain barriers making the expansion of local protests to coordinated cross-group mobilization very difficult. Peasants might hope for a Chen Sheng or Wu Guang (leaders of rebellions in early China), but thus far, at best, only a few local counterparts have emerged. Protest has not been "nationalized."

Sources of Heavy Tax Burden. The sources of the tax-and-fee problem are rooted in the political and administrative system as a whole, especially in central-local relations. They are not simply the product of abusive and predatory officials in the localities. A major source of the heavy burdens is that China's leaders devised a set of policies to speed up rural development and modernization but without adjusting those policies to the conditions of central and western China. Demands for progress were made on all of rural China without sufficient consideration of how it was to be paid for. In industrializing rural China, expanding resources from TVE revenues allowed for the provision of public goods, including the building of infrastructure, schools, and other facilities without burdening rural households with onerous taxes and fees. Agricultural China did not have this option. Fiscal decentralization, which enabled the regions with favorable conditions to develop rapidly by retaining revenue, had the further effect of reducing revenue flows to the Center, thereby curtailing its redistributive capacities and thus its ability to offset the lack or inadequacy of the local tax base in agricultural China. Not willing to allow for lower developmental capacities, the central government essentially compelled less favored regions to practice self-reliance by mobilizing local initiatives and local resources. Beijing, in other words, wanted to have its cake and eat it too. It wanted maximization of local development but at the same time it assigned top priority to the maintenance of political and social stability in the countryside. For the central government, the perfect outcome of combining maximizing local development efforts with bearable tax burdens and social stability remained elusive.

Local officials acted as agents of development within the hierarchical institutional constraints in which they operated. Both their organizational and individual incentives motivated them to press on with faster local development. In our depiction of arbitrary tax imposition and collection, local government and officials often appear as the culprits. But as we have shown in our analysis, they were not simply "bad" or corrupt. They did what rational actors would normally do in such an institutional environment, namely to satisfy their superiors. Attainment of development targets was a major career incentive for local officials on matters that could be monitored relatively easily, a main factor contributing to overexaction in agricultural China. Organizationally, *unfunded mandates* from the central authorities compelled local agents to maneuver within the muddled boundaries of off-budget financing. To comply with higher-level demands, they had to pressure, cajole, and coerce the peasants. Despite the heavy taxation, there were no public finance process and control per se in rural China. Peasants, the taxpayers, had no say in how much local governments should tax and how the money should be spent. Officials at the township level and above were not accountable to taxpayers.

In the view of the officials, peasants were tax-evading shirkers who were unwilling to support the creation of new public goods intended to benefit them. Predation and development coexisted side by side. Predation was accentuated by the lack of accountability, with ample opportunity for corruption, malfeasance, and misuse of funds. Lying to superiors about local circumstances, for example, peasant incomes, was commonplace. In the end, a significant proportion of the public goods that were supposed to benefit peasants never materialized. Moreover, as peasant incomes stagnated or even fell, more people used connections to get jobs in the local bureaucracies, thereby exacerbating the growth of the costly and parasitic township staff, which in turn required extraction of even more funds. Even as the central authorities sought periodically to reduce the size of various bureaucracies, staff kept growing, paid out of off-budget funds.

Deconcentration of Power. The burden problem was further accentuated by the horizontal deconcentration of power that characterized the post-Mao politico-administrative system, a phenomenon often ignored in the literature. Deconcentration entailed an increase in the number of agents – both agencies and persons – who exercised state authority at each level of the administrative hierarchy. They acquired the de facto power to accumulate their own extrabudgetary funds and to charge fees for various services. The multiplicity of agents inevitably caused great difficulties for the principals in monitoring the behavior of the agents. Agents routinely withheld information from their principals as they accumulated "small treasuries." Thus, as seen in Chapters 3 and 4, it required major investigations to uncover the dozens and dozens of fees imposed by central ministries and commissions. Opportunities for shirking and abuse of authority naturally increased.

In a nondemocratic system, oversight of agents has to be done exclusively by administrative means – by higher authorities in the case of decentralization and horizontal authorities in the case of deconcentration. The peasants, the clients of the agents, had little or no effective capacity to influence the behavior of officials. Establishment of performance criteria (*zhengji*) was an effort to monitor what agents did. But the principals were unable to detect hidden information about what kinds of fees were being imposed or adequately to monitor the actual behavior of the agents. Deconcentration created multiple principals and agents with conflicting interests. Uncoordinated competition among agents generally does not generate welfare, as Przeworski notes.[4] His finding that in other transitional countries the division between "spending ministries," supposed to promote substantive goals, and the finance ministry, supposed to control spending, failed to produce the desired results is readily applicable to the situation of "unfunded mandates" in China.

Equally important, deconcentration further increased the costs of government at all levels, since it created opportunities for bureaucratic sprawl, which, in the countryside, contributed directly to the heavy tax burden on the peasantry. In a broader context, this can be seen as reflecting the changing role of the state in the emerging market economy. The state delegated more regulatory power to, and expanded the service responsibilities of, various agencies even as it withdrew from its old productive and redistributive roles. Although such redefinitions of the state's role were necessary to adapt the state to the market economy, the change had many unintended consequences, a prominent one being rent seeking by government agencies.

What then can be said about state capacity? The central authorities were not able to craft a differentiated developmental program suitable for all parts of the country. Center relations with local officials were problematic, since local officials complied with only one of two demands made from above. Local officials complied with the policies of the Center that called for rapid development. But they didn't comply with the central authorities' demands, made again and again, to reduce burdens and to stop mistreating peasants. Of course, the two demands were contradictory. From the vantage point of local officials, promoting development projects at the expense of the peasants was rational and took priority since their careers were tied to performance.

[4] See Przeworski (1997: 422).

Peasants as Active Players. Thus far, we have treated the burden issue as a two-player game between the central and local governments. But peasants were an important set of third players. Peasants resisted compliance, necessitating reliance on force. In the eyes of the peasants, tax-and-fee collecting officials were arbitrary, predatory, and brutal. This to a significant extent explains the sharp deterioration in cadre-peasant relations in the 1990s to the point where some observers spoke of enmity. Peasant violent and nonviolent collective actions, especially against township officials, increased in the 1990s. There were indicators in the late 1990s and into the twenty-first century that the scope of protests was rising and that leaders and coordination were playing greater roles. But as of 2001, rural tax protests had not turned into broad-based social movements as generally understood, especially because of the absence of protest linkages between the countryside and the cities.

Just how extreme were the economic hardships to which peasants were exposed as a result of the burdens and low procurement prices? The question arises in relation to China's past. In contrast to pre-Communist China, we have not come across reports of food riots or of looting of foodstuffs.[5] This suggests that physical survival was not in the main at issue and that subsistence was more or less guaranteed. The reason lay in the entitlements of the household responsibility system under which land was collectively owned and could not be sold. China's residual socialist system continued to treat land as a collective rather than a private good. Each household was entitled to a plot of land, leased on the basis of contracts with the village committees. Use rights to land were indeed the major form of social security for China's peasants and prevented the rise of an immense landless proletariat. The right to a plot of land, however minuscule, meant that sheer survival was possible. This is not to say that extreme hardship did not exist and that people were not driven to desperation. Witness suicides and the sale of blood in such provinces as Henan. But there was something of a floor for China's peasants.

Opportunities to earn income by engaging in commerce and working in towns and cities were another factor that mitigated the hardships. With the relaxation of the household registration system, millions of peasants from agricultural China took advantage of the booming economy in the eastern provinces. Remittances from the cities played a significant role as an economic buffer. This source of security seems to have led to some land lying fallow because there was no profit to be made from farming, an exit from agriculture disturbing to a regime determined to maintain a stable food supply. Urban job opportunities were increasingly constrained in the late 1990s, however, because of the growth

---

[5] Cf. Lucien Bianco (2001: ch. 8).

of urban unemployment, a consequence of the restructuring of state-owned enterprises. If this constraint becomes more severe and results in the return of numerous peasants to their home villages, tensions in agricultural China will intensify further.

Many peasants learned that the higher the administrative level of authority, the greater the sympathy for their plight. Central authorities were on their side with regard to excessive burdens. New evidence strengthens the finding that peasants tended to trust the Center while distrusting the basic-level authorities.[6] The central authorities, as emphasized in this study, harshly criticized local officials for abusing their power and attempted to regulate burdens. For their part, hoping to secure redress, peasants increasingly made use of the letters and visits systems, individually or collectively, some going up all the way to Beijing. Some sought national media assistance in publicizing their plight. One result of this was conflict between peasants and local authorities over access to information about the national rules and regulations. The central government, the principal, attempted to disseminate information about tax rates and regulations to give peasants "the imperial sword" against local agents. Local governments tried to hide such information from peasants to minimize possible resistance to taxation. Note the famous case of the burden handbook in Jiangxi province.

The Center's siding with the peasants was an important fact. Something of a Center-peasant alliance emerged in which both targeted abusive local authorities and the Center sought to lighten the peasants' burdens. For peasants, the Center presented itself as a "clean and upright king" opposed to the corrupt "lords." Their protests and revolts were not directed at the regime but only at local officialdom. This is a very important limitation to rural protest, and will remain so, assuming that it is possible to extrapolate from the present to the future.

At the same time, the central authorities had to maintain a delicate balance between supporting peasants and inciting them to rebel. As shown by the Renshou riots of 1993, central documents unwittingly served to legitimate collective protest and rioting against local authorities. This unanticipated consequence of siding with the peasants had the potential of disrupting the regime's local organizational base of political power, posing a difficult dilemma for a regime obsessed with the maintenance of stability. As rural disturbances increased, the regime sought to balance increased repression with the expansion

---

[6] A recent survey found that the majority of villagers surveyed in two provinces had greater trust in higher levels of government than in the lower ones, particularly those of the townships and villages. Nearly half the respondents reported a high level of trust in the central government, but less than 15 percent thought the same of village Party branches and township Party committees. Only 1 percent did not trust the central government at all. See Li Lianjiang (2001).

of peaceful avenues for redress of grievances such as the courts and the letters and visits systems, as well as village democratization.

Toward Effective Solutions. The future will undoubtedly see continued regime efforts to press forward with various kinds of incremental reforms. Although these reforms have not thus far made much of a dent in the burden problem, they should not be dismissed out of hand. Some are promising and may in due course show real results. There is a sense of urgency that something has to be done about burdens, propelled by rising rural unrest. It is not inconceivable that as village democracy becomes more entrenched, townships will feel increasing pressure to reduce both abuses and arbitrary fee collection. The legal system will no doubt make further inroads into the rural areas. Bureaucratic rationalization and streamlining could in due course cut the township bureaucracies, making possible significant burden reduction. Research by Dali Yang on the rationalization of government suggests substantial progress in the streamlining of the bureaucracy in the later 1990s, in making bureaucrats more accountable, and in raising the ethical standards of officialdom.[7] The changes analyzed by Yang have not trickled down to the grass roots in the countryside, but they may eventually have a significant impact there.

Having said this, it seems clear to us that deeper institutional changes, both formal and informal, are needed, changes that would alter the rules of the game that govern the behavior of the main set of actors – peasants, local officials, central authorities. As comparative institutional analysis suggests, institutional change involves arriving at a new equilibrium of the endogenous rules of the game.[8] The focus of such institution-altering reforms has to be on the redefinition of central-local relations. As some Chinese scholars argue, the main formal institutional reform has to come from "*lishun zhongyang yu difang guanxi*" – rationalization of central-local relations. Take the issue of subsidizing agricultural China. Simply pointing to an irrational public finance system misses the important role played by the constitutional relationship between the central and local governments.[9] Political reforms are needed. The suspension of nationwide implementation of the promising fees-into-taxes program in the summer of 2001 was to a significant degree motivated by central budgetary difficulties, as pointed out by Premier Zhu Rongji.[10] Yet, the 1994 tax reform was supposed to have increased the flow of resources to the Center. Although this flow did

---

[7] Professor Yang is completing a major study of governmental reform.

[8] See Aoki (2001).

[9] For this type of argument, see Christine Wong (1997) and Wang Shaoguang and Wang Youqiang (2001).

[10] *RMRB-O* (July 23, 2001).

increase, it turned out that the tax reform, intent notwithstanding, benefited the richer provinces much more than those in agricultural China. The bargaining clout of the richer provinces was clearly much stronger than that of their poorer relatives to the West.[11]

The experience of the 1994 tax reform suggests that solutions to the problem of redistribution do not simply lie in strengthening the bargaining position of all provinces vis-à-vis the Center and each other. The real problem is how to strengthen the power of the agricultural provinces that lost out.[12] How is this to be achieved? One answer is to modify or even abolish China's unitary constitutional system. Some scholars have argued that China already has "federalism, Chinese style."[13] But this arrangement has serious drawbacks. Fiscal decentralization was undertaken within the old framework of the centralized state, leading to an odd coupling of fiscal federalism and politico-administrative centralism, which as we have seen, resulted in the "unfunded mandates" problem. A more explicit rearrangement of political and administrative power sharing between national and local governments is needed, not just new versions of tax sharing. Such an institutional arrangement would address core questions: What public goods are to be provided by national and local governments? Who will pay for them? Provinces would have to be empowered to set their own developmental goals in the light of their own circumstances. They would have to have discretion to set their own tax rates. And they would have to have the power to refuse to fulfill unfunded mandates. Thus, there would be a constitutional or at least a statutory and legally enforceable division of responsibilities. It is conceivable that such reforms could be undertaken by an authoritarian regime. China's top leaders seem to have recognized the deep institutional or structural roots of the burden problem, but whether they would be willing to take such drastic steps remains to be seen.

Changes along these lines would also require changes in deeply entrenched informal institutions of norms and modes of operation. There has been recognition of the need for change in this realm in top-level criticism of such practices as target setting (*dabiao*). But whether anything will actually be done is not clear. Target setting is one of a set of assumptions that originated in the Mao era and that persist in the mind-set and incentives of officials. Another is the belief that as long as the goals are lofty and oriented to the collective, the means don't really matter and that "faster is always better." Still another of socialism's

---

[11] See Pak K. Lee (2000: 1018–19).

[12] In contrast to most of agricultural China, the very poor West, including Tibet and other provinces, benefited from central redistribution and now, from the Western Development Program.

[13] See Montinola, Qian, and Weingast (1995).

legacies is that both citizens and officials hold the belief that many goods and services are public and that the government is responsible for providing them, which has led to adoption of unrealistic programs. Changing these rules of the game is not easy. In times of transition, conflicting rules of the game may coexist and be hard to reconcile.

Another solution, advocated by China's "neo-authoritarian" state-strengthening school of scholars, is a more complete recentralization of control, especially financial control, to give the Center power insulated by the bargaining clout of various interests to allocate resources and thereby take major redistributive and equalizing measures. Whether this is politically feasible given the realities of dispersed economic power in China is a question. Recentralization would also perpetuate and even strengthen the Center's power to set policies for all of China's diversified regions. It would require a truly sophisticated central policy-making process that could meaningfully adjust for diversity. Problems of continued uniform prescriptions of policy directives could well become even more serious. Most important, as Huang Yasheng has suggested, recentralization of economic control would make China's political system even more authoritarian, given that the Center already has control over the appointment of the major provincial officials.[14]

Grass Roots Democratization and Taxation. Underlying the issue of peasant burdens is the relation between state and society and hence the issue of democracy. Giving the central government greater power as suggested by some does not by itself insure that misuse of power will not recur. Giving provinces greater power over finances and policies raises the possibility that provinces might abuse their powers vis-à-vis the peasants. There is no logical reason why, in an authoritarian regime, provinces should be any more sensitive to the interests of ordinary people than the Center. Financial and politico-administrative decentralization that would really benefit the local population would seem to require making all levels of local government more accountable.

Thus, the foundation of China's arbitrary tax collection system in the rural areas, namely the authoritarian nature of China's regime, shows no signs of disappearing, so there will always be opportunities for renewed abuses. Even if the peasant tax problem is eventually resolved, the possibility exists of the regime arbitrarily imposing new exactions or programs on citizens without securing their consent. There is, however, a price tag. Even though authoritarian regimes are able to decide the tax rates and extract revenues, collecting taxes tends to be more costly than in democratic regimes. Under an authoritarian regime,

---

[14] Huang Yasheng (1996: 327–9).

taxpayers tend not to comply voluntarily, requiring governments to maintain larger numbers of tax collectors and monitoring devices.[15] Our study of Chinese rural taxation confirms this point.

We have been skeptical about the effectiveness of village-level democracy in significantly enabling peasants to hold officials accountable. Democratization is a moving target, as so much else in China and its potential has not been exhausted. The main reason for the small impact so far is that the power of village committees over taxes and fund-raising is very limited. The township officials and their superiors are the main extractors of funds and they have not been touched by democratization, except in a few experimental townships.

More research on the relationship between democratization and taxes is needed. One of the weaknesses of the growing body of studies on grass roots democratization in rural China is its primary focus on electoral processes and institutions and the lack of adequate attention to the role of taxation. The relationship between taxes and democracy is an age-old one, as the slogan "no taxation without representation" suggests. It is therefore appropriate to speculate further on the relationship between the two in rural China. Although the evidence is not conclusive, one can hypothesize that the major mass impetus for democracy in China comes from those areas in rural China where the tax burdens are most severe. When governments take money from people arbitrarily and without accountability, the "shoe pinching" argument for democracy put forth long ago by A. D. Lindsay is likely to be most compelling.[16] The distinction between the three rural Chinas comes into play here. In the richer parts, ordinary people don't feel the weight of tax-and-fee burdens so strongly. In the poorer, western parts there is less to extract to begin with and the consciousness of being a taxpayer may be less strong than where the direct tax burden is high, visible, and arbitrary.[17] So it is in middle-income agricultural China, where the burdens are most keenly felt, that the impetus for democratization is likely to be the strongest, beginning with a growing rights consciousness.[18]

Will such rising consciousness lead to fundamental changes? Over seventy years ago, Thomas Millard made this sobering observation about the relationship between taxation and revolutionary change in China: "It has been said that

---

[15] See Levi (1988) and Chebub (1998).

[16] Lindsay (1943: 269–72).

[17] In China, due to the elimination of the personal income tax during the Maoist period, there was a lack of *"nashuiren yishi"* or "consciousness of a taxpayer." The term did not even exist in the political vocabulary. Now such consciousness has begun to form in a limited way as the term is being increasingly used.

[18] As noted in Chapter 7, we do not claim that rural people in industrializing China don't also want democracy, but the reasons are likely to be different, having less to do with taxes than with corruption and the economic power exercised by village Party secretaries.

revolutions start with the tax collector. Taxation may bring about the completion of the revolution in China. Taxes may be the straw which finally breaks down the patience of the Chinese under present misrule. . . . Therefore it is conceivable that China's ancient evil, official 'squeeze,' as applied through the tax collector, eventually will arouse among the people the spirit and the will to accomplish national reconstruction."[19] No doubt China's leaders are well aware of this point.

It is widely assumed in the literature that the impulse for democratization originates in cities, where levels of education are higher, where democratic discourse is likely to flourish – "*Stadt Luft macht frei*" in the city, where one can breathe freely and where the middle class provides the mass base for political change. If our hypothesis is accurate, China would seem to be an anomaly. As some enthusiastic officials of the Ministry of Civil Affairs have put it, in China the revolutionary pattern is replicating itself. Just as the Communist revolution took hold first in the countryside and only in its last stage liberated the cities, so democracy will first grow in the villages and ultimately surround and bring democracy to the cities. This is not the place to analyze the potential for democratization in the cities but simply to note that the Marxist contempt for the "idiocy of rural life" does not tell the whole story. The full potential of rural pressures for democratization has not been exhausted.

Future Prospects. As of late 2001, the prospects for agricultural China are at best uncertain, at worst bleak. The fee-into-tax reform is progressing slowly and it is by no means clear whether it can succeed in solving the burden problem. China became a member of the World Trade Organization which, according to estimates, will likely drive millions of peasants off the land as foreign competition makes itself felt. Yet, rising unemployment in the cities and the consequent shrinking of opportunities for peasants are making the "exit" option for peasants less plausible. Unless these opportunities are replaced by others, for example, new-job-creating industrialization in small towns in the interior, the pressure on China's farming population is likely to increase. Whether the resulting increase in discontent will swell to the point of posing a genuine threat to the regime or whether it will become a source of more substantial democratization are questions for the future.

[19] *NYT* (April 4, 1926).

Bibliography

Alitto, Guy S. 1979. *The Last Confucian: Liang Shu-ming and the Chinese Dilemma of Modernity.* Berkeley: University of California Press.

Alpermann, Bjoern. 2001. "The Post-Election Administration of Chinese Villages." *China Journal*, No. 46 (July: 45–67).

Amsden, Alice. 1989. *Asia's Next Giant: South Korea and Late Industrialization.* New York: Oxford University Press.

Aoki, Masahiko. 2001. *Toward a Comparative Institutional Analysis.* Cambridge, MA: MIT Press.

At China's Table. 1997. Washington DC: The International Bank for Reconstruction and Development/World Bank.

Bai, Gang. 1999. "Woguo cunmin zizhi buru guifanhua fazhan jieduan" (China's village self-rule has entered the stage of regularization). *Neibu Canyue*, No. 13: 7–9.

Bai, Gang. 1998a. "Woguo jiceng minzhu zhengzhi jianshe de zhanlüe yu celüe" (Strategy and tactics of building basic-level democracy in China). *Neibu Canyue*, No. 24: 7–10.

Bai, Gang. 1998b. "Zhongguo cunmin zizhi fazhi jianshe pingyi" (Villager self-governance and rule of law in China). *Zhongguo Shehui Kexue,* No. 3: 88–104.

Bates, Robert. 1987. "Agrarian Politics," in Myron Weiner and Samuel Huntington, eds., *Understanding Political Development.* Boston: Little Brown, 160–95.

Bates, Robert and William P. Roerson. 1989. "Agriculture in Development: A Coalitional Analysis." *Public Choice*, 35: 513–27.

Becker, Jasper. 2000. "Might Is Right." *China Forum* (Spring): 4–9.

Beidou Falü Shiwusuo Yanjiu Shi, eds. 1995. *Da guansi 400 wen* (400 questions about lawsuits). Beijing: Xueyuan chubanshe.

Bernhardt, Kathryn. 1992. *Rents, Taxes, and Peasant Resistance.* Stanford: Stanford University Press.

Bernstein, Thomas P. 1999. "Farmer Discontent and Regime Responses," in Merle Goldman and Roderick MacFarquhar, eds., *The Paradox of China's Post-Mao Reforms.* Cambridge, MA: Harvard University Press, 197–219.

Bernstein, Thomas P. 1992. "Ideology and Rural Reform: The Paradox of Contingent Stability," in Arthur Rosenbaum, ed., *State and Society: The Consequences of Reform.* Boulder, CO: Westview, 143–66.

Bibliography

Bernstein, Thomas P. 1984. "Stalinism, Famine, and Chinese Peasants: Grain Procurements during the Great Leap Forward." *Theory and Society* 13, No. 3: 339–77.

Bernstein, Thomas P. 1970. "Keeping the Revolution Going: Problems of Village Leadership After Land Reform," in J. W. Lewis, ed., *Party Leadership and Revolutionary Power.* New York: Cambridge University Press, 239–67.

Bi, Jingquan, Xiong, Zhongcai, and Wang, Caiming. 1996. "Shandong, Henan nongmin fudan wenti diaoyan baogao" (Investigation report on peasant burden problem in Shandong and Henan). *Zhongguo Wujia* (China Price), No. 10: 16–21.

Bianco, Lucien. 2001. *Peasants without the Party: Grassroots Movements in Twentieth Century China.* Armonk, NY: M. E. Sharpe.

Bianco, Lucien. 1995. "Peasant Responses to CCP Mobilization Policies, 1937–1945," in Tony Saich and Hans van de Ven, eds., *New Perspectives on the Chinese Communist Revolution.* Armonk, NY: M. E. Sharpe, 175–87.

Bianco, Lucien. 1978. "Peasant Movements," in J. K. Fairbank and A. Feuerwerker, eds., *The Cambridge History of China–Republican China, 1912–1949,* Vol. 13. New York: Cambridge University Press, 280–301.

Blecher, Marc and Vivienne Shue. 1996. *Tethered Deer: Government and Economy in a Chinese County.* Stanford: Stanford University Press.

Brockett, Charles D. 1991. "The Structure of Political Opportunities and Peasant Mobilization in Central America." *Comparative Politics* 23, No. 3: 253–74.

Burns, John P. 1988. *Political Participation in Rural China.* Berkeley: University of California Press.

Cai, Yongshun. 2000. "Between Supervisors and Peasants: Local Cadres and Statistical Reporting in Rural China." *China Quarterly,* No. 163 (Sept.): 783–805.

Caizheng nianjian (Finance yearbook). 1935. Shanghai: Shangwu yinshuguan.

Caizhengbu (Ministry of Finance): *Zhongguo nongmin fudan shi* (A history of peasant burden in China). Vol. 1 (1991), Vol. 2 (1994), and Vol. 4 (1994). Beijing: Zhongguo caizheng jingji chubanshe.

Cao, Weiqiu, et al. 2000. *Qianfada diqu qingnian nongmin suzhi de diaocha* (A survey on the quality of young farmers in less developed areas). *Qingnian Yanjiu* (Youth Study), No. 2, 34–8.

Carter Center Report on Chinese Elections. 2000. *Observations of Chinese Village Elections in Hebei Province, January 4–13, 2000.* Atlanta, GA.

Chalmers, Douglas. 1991. "Corporatism and Comparative Politics," in Howard J. Wiarda, ed., *New Directions in Comparative Politics.* Boulder, CO: Westview Press.

Chebub, José Antonio. 1998. "Political Regimes and the Extractive Capacity of Governments: Taxation in Democracies and Dictatorships," *World Politics* 50, No.3 (April): 349–76.

Chen, Dajie and Wu, Zunpei. 1994. *Nongcun Caizheng* (Rural public finance). Beijing: Nongcun chubanshe.

Chen, Daolong. 1994. "*Xiangcun zai huhan*" (Cries from the countryside). *Yuhua,* special reportage issue: 2–22.

Chen, Junqi, 1987. *Yan'an shiqi caikuai gongzuo de huigu* (Recollections of the financial and accounting work in Yan'an). Beijing: Zhongguo caizheng jingji chubanshe.

Chen, Weihua. 1998. "Cong xinfang gongzuo jiaodu dui dangqian jianqing nongmin fudan wenti de zai sikao" (Reexamination of the question of lightening the peasants' burden from the vantage point of letters and visits). *Renmin Xinfang,* No. 9: 28–31.

Chen, Wenmin. 1993. "Peasant burdens are an invisible knapsack." *Xin Shiji,* No. 50: 17, *FBIS,* No. 116.

Chen, Xi. 1999. "The Role of the State in the Development of Village Self-Government in China," unpublished paper, Columbia University. May.

Chen, Xiwen. 1998. *Zhongguo Shichang Jingjibao,* May 28, in *SWB-FE,* 3263, S 1–7.

Chen, Yimin. 1983. "Nongmin fudan ji dai jianqing" (It is urgently necessary to reduce peasant burdens). *Nongcun Gongzuo Tongxun,* No. 8: 19–20.

Chen, Yizi. 1989. *Zhongguo: Shinian gaige yu bajiu minyun* (China: Ten years of reform and the '89 popular movement). Taibei: Lienjing Chubanshe.

Chen, Youfu. 1994. "Nongmin fudan wenti de shenceng toushi" (Deep perspective on the peasant burden question). *Gaige yu Lilun,* No. 1: 52–5.

Chen, Yun. 1982. "Tiaozheng guomin jingji, jianchi an bili fazhan" (Adjust the national economy; adhere to proportionate development, March 21,1979), in Zhonggong Zhongyang Wenxian Yanjiu Shi Bian, *Sanzhong Quanhui yilai,* Vol. 1 Beijing: Renmin Chubanshe: 74–9.

Chen, Yung-fa.1995. "The Blooming Poppy under the Red Sun: The Yan'an Way and the Opium Trade," in Tony Saich and Hans van de Van, eds., *New Perspectives on the Chinese Communist Revolution.* Armonk, NY: M. E. Sharpe, 263–98.

Chou, Wen-tao. 1993. "A look at the agricultural crisis through 'popular rebellion' caused by officials' tyranny." *Hsin Pao* (April 20, *FBIS* 81: 10–12).

Chung, Jae Ho. 1995. "Central-Provincial Relations," in Lo Chi Kin, Suzanne Pepper, and Tsui Kai Yuen, eds., *China Review 1995.* Hong Kong: Chinese University Press.

"Class Action Litigation in China." 1998. *Harvard Law Review* 111, No. 6: 1523–41.

Clubb, O. E. 1964. *Twentieth Century China.* New York: Columbia University Press.

Cochrane, Willard. 1979. *The Development of American Agriculture: A Historical Analysis.* Minneapolis: University of Minnesota Press.

Cohen, Myron L. 1993. "Cultural and Political Inventions in Modern China: The Case of the Chinese Peasants." *Daedalus* (Spring): 151–70.

Cohen, Myron L. 1991. "Being Chinese: The Peripheralization of Traditional Identity." *Daedalus* (Spring): 113–34.

Cui, Bo.1999. "Yi piao zhi cha: Yuanhe wei huo tonggu." (One vote short: Why it didn't pass). *Minzhu yu Fazhi,* No. 12: 10–11.

Dang, Guoying. 2001. "Qingnian nongmin shi dangjin Zhongguo" (Young peasants are the China of today). *Zhongguo Guoqing Guoli,* No. 5.

Dang, Guoying. 1999. "Zhongguo xuyao chongjian nonghui" (China must reestablish a peasant association). *Zhongguo Guoqing Guoli,* No. 7.

Davis, Deborah and Ezra Vogel, eds. 1990. *Chinese Society on the Eve of Tiananmen.* Cambridge, MA: Harvard University Press.

"Decisions of the Central Committee of the CPC on some questions concerning the acceleration of agricultural development" (draft: Jan. 11, 1979). *Issues and Studies* (July 1979): 104–5.

Deng, Sanlong. 1998. "Jiceng wenti de baogao" (Reports from the grass roots). *Zhongguo Gaigebao* (June 17).

Dong, Yongyu and Shi, Binghai, eds. 1998. *Zhengzhi Zhongguo: Mianxiang xin tizhi xuanze de shidai* (Political China: Facing the era of choosing a new structure). Beijing: Jinri Zhongguo Chubanshe.

Du, Ying. 1992. "Recommendations for focus in rural reform," *Zhongguo Nongcun Jingji*, October, in JPRS No. 8, 1993: 37.

Duan, Chinglin. 1998. "Woguo nongye shuishou jiqi tidai jizhi de ruohua yu gaige wenti yanjiu" (A study on China's agricultural tax system and its replacement). *ZNJ*, No. 2: 49–56.

"Dui 'nongmin caichan quanli yu shenfen ziyou shuangchong jiefang' de zhiyi yu zhuisu" (Searching for the 'double liberation of the peasants' property rights and personal freedom'). *NJW,* No. 3 (1989): 49–51.

Eastman, Lloyd E. 1984. *Seeds of Destruction: Nationalist China in War and Revolution, 1937–1949.* Stanford: Stanford University Press.

Eastman, Lloyd E. 1974. *The Abortive Revolution: China under Nationalist Rule, 1927–1937.* Cambridge, MA: Harvard University Press.

Editorial Department. 1991. *NJW*, No. 10 (Oct. 23, 1991): 32–6, *JPRS*-CAR-92-009, February 16: 43.

"Elections and Democracy in Greater China," special issue. 2000. *China Quarterly*, No. 162 (June).

Epstein, Amy. 1996. "Village Elections in China: Experimenting with Democracy," in U.S. Congress, Joint Economic Committee, *China's Economic Future: Challenges to US Policy.* Washington, DC: U.S. Government Printing Office.

Evans, Peter. 1995. *Embedded Autonomy: States and Industrial Transformation.* Princeton, NJ: Princeton University Press.

Evans, Peter, Dietrich Rueschemeyer, and Theda Skocpol. 1985. *Bringing the State Back In.* New York: Cambridge University Press.

Falkenheim, Victor. 1982. "Political Reform in China." *Current History* (September).

Fan, Gang. 1998. "Market-Oriented Economic Reform and the Growth of Off-Budget Local Public Finance," in Donald J. S. Brean, ed., *Taxation in Modern China.* New York: Routledge, 209–28.

Fang, Xiancang. 1998. "Nongmin fudan jianer buqing de zengjie hezai" (What's behind the persistence of the peasant burden?), *Nongye Jingji*, No. 7.

Fewsmith, Joseph. 1994. *Dilemmas of Reform in China: Economic Debate and Political Conflict.* Armonk, NY: M. E. Sharpe.

Gadsden, Amy Epstein and Anne F. Thurston. n.d. *Village Elections in China: Progress, Problems and Prospects.* Washington DC: International Relations Institute.

Gamble, Sidney. 2000. "The People's Middle Kingdom: Tax Evasion in China." *Foreign Affairs*, November–December, 16–20.

Gansu Sheng Tongji Ju and Nongyeweiyuanhui. 1997. *Gansu Nongcun Tongji Nianjian-1997.* Beijing: Zhongguo Tongji Chubanshe.

Gao, Shangquan and Chi, Fulin, eds. 1997. *The Reform and Development of China's Rural Economy.* Beijing: Foreign Language Press.

Gao, Xiaosheng. 1979. "Li Shunda Zaowu" (Li Shunda builds a house). *Yuhua*, No. 7.

General Offices of the Central Committee and State Council. 1998. "Transparent and democratic management of village affairs." *Xinhua* (June 10), *SWB-FE*3252, G/5–8, June 13.

Gilley, Bruce. 2001. "A Plot for the Farmers." *FEER,* August 2: 24–5.

Goldman, Merle. 1994. *Sowing the Seeds of Democracy in China: Political Reform in the Deng Xiaoping Era.* Cambridge, MA: Harvard University Press.

Goldman, Merle and Roderick MacFarquhar, eds. 1999. *The Paradox of China's Post-Mao Reforms.* Cambridge, MA: Harvard University Press.

Gu, Kang, et al. 1999. "Liudong guiwei – 'feigaishui' de jiben silu" (Basic thoughts on the integration and distribution of funds by means of substituting taxes for fees). *Neibu Canyue*, No. 22: 2–7.

Gu, Wenshao. 1993. "Jianli nongmin zuzhi, baohu nongmin liyi" (Establish a peasant organization to protect peasants interests). *Neibu Wengao*, No. 1: 24–6.

Gu, Yanwu. 1879. *Tianxia Junguo Libingshu* (A treatise on the strength and weaknesses of nations). Sichuan: Tonghua Books.

Guan, Jie. 1996. "Peasant Riots in Shanxi, Henan, and Hunan." *Dongxiang*, No. 124 (1995): 18–19, trans. in *China Perspective*, No. 3 (Jan./Feb.): 6–9.

Guo, Zhenglin. 2000. "The Village Party Branch after Elections: Confusion, Struggles, and Configurations of Power," unpublished paper, Lund Center for Chinese Studies, Sweden, May.

Guo, Zhenglin. 1999. "Shishi cunmin zizhi: Guangdong nongcun guanli tizhi de zhuan-xing" (Implementing villager autonomy: the transformation of the administrative system in Guangdong), unpublished paper, Zhongshan Daxue, July.

Guojia Shuiwu Zongju Nongshuiju Ketizu. 2000. "Nongmin fudan yu nongye shuizhi gaige wenti" (Peasant burdens and the issue of reform of the agricultural tax system). *Shuiwu Yanjiu*, No. 4: 22–32.

Guojia Tongjiju (State Statistical Bureau), ed. 1993, 1998, 1999. *Zhongguo Tongji Zhaiyao.* Beijing: Zhongguo Tongji Chubanshe.

Han, Hongjie. 1997. "Nongmin fudan yu xiangzhen fuzhai" (Peasant burdens and township debts). *Nongcun Jingji* (Rural Economy), No. 6.

He, Huiyuan. 1934. "Lun tianfu fujia" (On land tax and surtaxes). *Duli Pingjia* (Independent Review), No. 89: 6.

He, Xuefeng. 1998. "Cunweihui xuanju weihe chuxian daotui?" (Why do village elections give rise to retrogression?). *Zhongguo Nongcun Guancha*, No. 4: 49–53.

Heilongjiang Nianjian (Heilongjiang Yearbook).1997. Har'erbin: Heilongjiang Nianjianshe.

Henan civil affairs official. 1998. "Xuchang shi shishi cunmin zizhi shi nian de huigu he sikao" (Recalling and reflecting on ten years of Xuchang city villager autonomy), August 28.

Hopcroft, Rosemary. 1999. "Maintaining the Balance of Power: Taxation and Democracy in England and France, 1340–1688." *Sociological Perspectives* 42, No. 1: 69–95.

Hu, Angang. 2002. "Jiaru WTO hou yingshi 8 yi nongmin shouyi zui da hua, fengxian zui xiaohua" (After entry into WTO the 800 million peasants should benefit the most and incur the least risk), unpublished paper.

Hu, Jiayong. 1998. "Woguo zhengfu guimo weishenme chixu pengzhang?" (Why does the Chinese government size keeps growing?). *Gaige* (Reform), No. 3: 87–92.

Hua, Sheng. 1993. "*Wuguan butan daozhi wushang bujian*" (The corruption of officials has led to the illicit behaviors of businessmen). *Tansuo* (Probe), (April): 84–7.

Huang, Jizeng. 1990. *"Hebei nongcun jinzhang dangqun ganqun guanxi zhuangkuang ji dai jiejue"* (The tensions between the masses and Party and non-Party cadres must be speedily resolved). *Neican Xuanbian,* No. 123: 3.

Huang, Mab and James D. Seymour. 1980. "Introduction" in Seymour, ed., *The Fifth Modernization: China's Human Rights Movement, 1978–1979.*

Huang, Mengdi and Li, Ning, eds. 1990. *Nongcun falü duben* (Rural legal reader). Jinan: Shandong Kexue Jishu Chubanshe.

Huang, Philip. 1990. *The Peasant Family and Rural Development in the Yangze Delta, 1350–1988.* Stanford: Stanford University Press.

Huang, Yanxin. 1994. *"Nongmin fudan guozhong de zhiduxing genyuan yu duice"* (The systemic sources and remedy for heavy peasant burdens). *Zhongguo Nongcun Jingji,* No. 5.

Huang, Yasheng, 1996. *Inflation and Investment Controls in China: The Political Economy of Central-local Relations during the Reform Era.* New York: Cambridge University Press.

Hubei Nianjian (Hubei Yearbook). 1997. Wuhan: Hubei Nianjianshe.

Hunter, Guy. 1969. *Modernizing Peasant Societies.* New York: Oxford University Press.

Information Centre of Human Rights and Democracy, Hong Kong, November 2, 1999. *SWB-FE*/3683, G/8–9, November 4, 1999.

Jakobson, Linda. 2001. "Pursuing More Effective Governance: Village Elections and Their Implications in China," paper presented at ISA Convention, Hong Kong, July 27.

Jia, Kang, Bai, Jingming, and Ma Shaoling. 1999. "Fenliu guiwei – Fei gai shui de jiben silu" (The basic road of transforming fees into taxes is to end dispersion). *Neibu Canyue,* No. 22 (June 9): 2–7

Jianchabu. 1995. *Xingzheng Jiancha Wenjian Xuanbian 1992–94* (Documents on administrative supervision 1992–4). Beijing: Zhongguo jiancha chubanshe.

Jiang, Ming'an. 1998. *Zhongguo xingzheng fazhi fazhan jincheng diaocha baogao* (A study of the development of the administrative legal system in China). Beijing: Fazhi chubanshe.

Jiang, Xiaowei. 1997. "Woguo caizheng kunnan de yuanyin yu duice" (Causes and solutions to the financial difficulties). *Zhongguo Jingji Wenti,* No. 1: 59–64.

Jiang, Zuoping and Yang Sunyun. 2000. "Chuanhuan siwei 'lingxiu' xingcheng yichang fengbo" (Summoning four 'heroes' to court creates a storm). *Banyuetan-neibuban,* No. 2: 15–16.

Jiangsu Nianjian (Jiangsu yearbook). 1997. Nanjing: nianjianshe.

Jiangsu Sheng Tongji Ju, ed. 1997. *Jiangsu Nongcun Jingji Ziliao* (Materials on Jiangsu's rural economy). Ninjing: Jiangsu Sheng Tonji Ju.

"Jianqing nongmin fudan, zuo hao xinfang gongzuo – Sichuan shengwei shuji Xie Shijie zai sheng jianqing nongmin fudan zuotanhui de jianghua." 1998. (Lower peasant burdens and do well the letters and visits work – speech by Sichuan provincial Party secretary Xie Sihjie at a provincial conference on reducing burdens). *Renmin Xinfang,* No. 2: 14–15.

Johnson, Chalmers. 1987. "Political institutions and economic performance: the government- business relationship in Japan, South Korea, and Taiwan," in Frederick C. Deyo, ed., *The Political Economy of the New Asian Industrialism.* Ithaca, NY: Cornell University Press, 136–64.

Johnston, Bruce and Peter Kilby. 1975. *Agricultural and Structural Transformation.* New York: Oxford University Press.

Jowitt, Kenneth. 1992. *New World Disorder: The Leninist Extinction.* Berkeley: University of California Press.

Jowitt, Kenneth. 1970. "Time and Development under Communism," in Dwight Waldo, ed., *Temporal Dimensions of Development Administration.* Durham, NC: Duke University Press, 233–63

Kamenitsa, Lynn. 1998. "The Process of Political Marginalization: East German Social Movements after the Wall." *Comparative Politics* 30, No. 3: 313–33.

Kau, Michael Y. M. and John K. Leung, eds. 1986. *The Writings of Mao Zedong, 1949–1976,* Vol. I. Armonk, NY: M. E. Sharpe.

Keeler, John. 1981. "Corporatism and official union hegemony: The case of French agricultural syndicalism," in Suzanne Berger, ed., *Organizing Interests in Western Europe: Pluralism, Corporatism, and the Transformation of Politics.* New York: Cambridge University Press.

Kelliher, Daniel. 1993. "Keeping Democracy Safe from the Masses: Intellectuals and Elitism in the Chinese Protest Movement." *Comparative Politics* 25, No. 4: 379–96.

Ketizu. 1998a. "Xiangzhen tongchou zijin zhidu gaige yanjiu" (A study of reforming township unified funds). *Caizheng Yanjiu,* No. 10: 21–30.

Ketizu. 1998b. "Xianji caizheng weiji ji qi duice" (County fiscal crisis and its solution). *Caizheng Yanjiu,* No. 5: 55–9.

Ketizu. 1997. "Jiaqiang xiangzhen yusuanwai zijin guanli yanjiu" (How to improve the management of extrabudgetary funds of townships). *Caizheng Yanjiu,* No. 7: 40–5.

Khan, Azizur Rahman and Carl Riskin. 1998. "Income and Inequality in China, Composition, Distribution and Growth of Household Income, 1988 to 1995." *China Quarterly,* No. 154: 221–53.

Kuhn, Philip. 1980. *Rebellion and Its Enemies in Late Imperial China: Militarization and Social Structure, 1796–1864.* Cambridge MA: Harvard University Press.

Lardy, Nicholas. 1983. *Agriculture in China's Modern Economic Development.* New York: Cambridge University Press.

Lee, Ching Kwan. 1999. "The politics of working class transition in China," paper prepared for Conference on Wealth and Labour in China: Cross-cutting Approaches to Present Development, Paris, December 6–7.

Lee, Pak K. 2000. "Into the Trap of Strengthening State Capacity: China's Tax Assignment Reform." *China Quarterly,* No. 164: 1007–24.

Lee, Sing and Arthur Kleinman. 2000. "Suicide as resistance in Chinese society," in Elizabeth Perry and Mark Selden, eds., *Chinese Society: Change, Conflict, and Resistance.* New York: Routledge, 221–40.

Levi, Margaret. 1988. *Of Rule and Revenue.* Berkeley: University of California Press.

Levine, Steven I. 1987. *Anvil of Victory.* New York: Columbia University Press.

Li, Changping. 2002. *Wo xiang zongli shuo shihua* (I spoke the truth to the premier). Beijing: Guangming Ribao Chubanshe.

Li, Cheng. 2001. *China's Leaders: The New Generation.* Boulder, CO: Rowman and Littlefield.

Li, Cheng. 1997. *Rediscovering China: Dynamics and Dilemmas of Reform.* New York: Rowman and Littlefield.

Li, Chien-pin. 1998. "Domestic Bargaining in Taiwan's International Agricultural Negotiations." *Asian Survey* 38, No. 6 (June): 585–602.

Li, Chun and Guo Lingji. 1999. "Shixing cunmin zizhi xu chuli hao sanzhong guanxi" (Three important relations have to be resolved in implementing villager autonomy). *Neibu Canyue*, No. 30 (Aug. 4): 209.

Li, Jingtian. 1991. "Miqie nongcun ganqun guanxi" (Close relations between rural cadres and masses). *Zhongguo Minzheng*, No. 6: 11–12.

Li, Kang, ed. 1992. *Zhongguo nongcun jiceng shequ zuzhi jianshe xin tansuo* (A new study of grass roots community organizations in rural China). Beijing: Zhongguo kexue jishu chubanshe.

Li, Kang. 1990. "Jiceng zhengquan yu jiceng shequ" (Grass roots government and community). *Shehui Gongzuo Yanjiu* (Social Work Study), No. 3.

Li, Lianjiang. 2001."Peasant Views of the Chinese Party-State," unpublished paper.

Li, Lianjiang, 2000. "Elections and Popular Resistance in Rural China," unpublished paper, Hong Kong.

Li, Lianjiang. 1999. "The Two-Ballot System in Shanxi Province: Subjecting Village Party Secretaries to a Popular Vote." *China Journal*, No. 42: 103–18.

Li, Lianjiang and Kevin O'Brien. 1999. "The Struggle for Village Elections," in Merle Goldman and Roderick MacFarquhar, eds., *The Paradox of China's Post-Mao Reforms.* Cambridge, MA: Harvard University Press, 129–44.

Li, Lianjiang and Kevin O'Brien. 1996. "Villagers and Popular Resistance." *Modern China* 22, No. 1: 28–61.

Li, Qin. 1992. "Dui woguo nongmin fudan zhuangkuang de fenxi" (Analysis of the condition of peasant burdens). *Zhongguo Nongcun Jingji*, No. 8: 47–51.

Li, Renshi and Chen, Daichang. 1998. "Sichuan nongcun shixing cunwu caiwu gongkai de diaocha" (A report on the transparent village finance and governance in Sichuan). *Lilun Yu Gaige* (Theory and Reform), No. 4: 9–12.

Li, Shengping. 1996. "Jianfu' jiandu zai Qingheng cun gaojie" (Burden reduction supervision is victorious in Qingheng village). *Minzhu yu Fazhi,* No. 11: 18–20.

Li, Wenxue. 1997. "Guanyu nongmin fudan wenti de yanjiu baogao" (A research report on the peasant burden problem). *Jingji Yanjiu Cankao*, No. 21: 2–36.

Li, Xiande. 2000. "Rethinking the peasant burden: Evidence from a Chinese village," paper prepared for the Sixth Conference on Agricultural and Rural Development in China, Leiden, January 5–7.

Li, Xiuyi. 1992a. "'Nongmin Xiehui' fanying le shenhua nongcun gaige de yaoqiu" (A 'Farmers' Association reflects the demands of the deepening of rural reform). *Hebei Nongcun Gongzuo* (October): n. p.

Li, Xiuyi. 1992b. "Guanyu shiban 'Nongmin Xiehui' de ruogan wenti" (Several questions pertaining to the experimental establishment of "farmers' associations"). *ZNJ*, No. 6: 15–18.

Li, Xueju, Wang, Zhenyao, and Tang, Jinsu, eds. 1994. *Zhongguo xiangzhen zhengquan de xianzhuang yu gaige* (Current state of township government and its reform). Beijing: Zhongguo shehui kexue chubanshe.

Li, Zhuanshui. 1998. "Guanyu jianqing nongmin fudan de liangdian lifa jianyi" (Two suggestions for two types of legislation for lightening the burdens of the peasants). *Xingzheng yu Fa*, No. 1: 56.

Li, Zijing. 1998. "Duifu jihui shiwei de xin zhengling" (New government decree on dealing with demonstrations). *Cheng Ming* (May): 17–18.

Li, Zijing. 1997. "Si sheng wushiwan nongmin kangzheng" (Half a million peasants resist in four provinces), *Cheng Ming* (April): 19–21.

Lian, Jimin. 1999. "Qiangkou buneng zhi xiang qunzhong" (The gun can't be pointed at the masses). *Minzhu yu fazhi*, February 21: 10–12, in *SWB-FE*/3520, G/7–8.

Liao, Kai-lung. 1981. "Historical Experiences and our Road to Development." *Issues and Studies*, No. 12: 91–2.

Lieberthal, Kenneth. 1995. *Governing China: From Revolution through Reform*. New York: W. W. Norton.

Lindsay, A. D. 1943. *The Modern Democratic State*. New York: Oxford University Press.

Lipton, Michael. 1977. *Why People Stay Poor*. London: Temple Smith.

Liu, Binyan. 1989. *Tell the World: What Happened in China and Why*. New York: Pantheon.

Liu, Guoguang, et al. 1998. *Zhongguo kuashiji sanda gaige* (Three major Chinese reforms that straddle the millennium), Vol. 3. Beijing: Zhongyang dangxiao chubanshe.

Liu, Huazhen. 1989. "Qie ji bu yao weibei nongmin de yiyuan" (Always remember not to violate peasant wishes). *Nongcun Jingji Wenti*, No. 6: 9–15, 21.

Liu, Huazhen and Xu, Wenan. 1987. "Jianyi chengli geji nongmin xiehui" (Suggestion for the establishment of a peasant association at the various levels). *Nongye Jingji Wenti*, No. 11: 61.

Liu, Jinghuai. 1992. "Jingbinjianzheng shizaibixing" (It is essential to cut the bureaucratic staff). *Liaowang*, No. 36 (Sept. 7): 18–19.

Liu, Yawei. 1999. "The Buyun Election and its Meaning," Appendix to Carter Center Report on Chinese Elections, "Observations on the Township People's Congress Elections, January 5–15 and Cooperative Activities with the Ministry of Civil Affairs, August 1, 1998–January 15, 1999. Atlanta, GA.

Lo, Yi Ning Ge Erh (pseud.). 1994. *Disan zhi yanjing kan zhongguo* (Seeing China through the third eye), Wang Shan, trans., Taiyuan: Shanxi Chubanshe.

Lu, Mai. 1999. "Developing the rural markets is a long-term strategy." *RMRB*, (Sept. 20), *SWB-FE*/3687, G/4–5.

Lu, Nong. 1994. "Nongcun bu wending qingkuang ehua" (The worsening of the unstable rural situation). *Cheng Ming*, No. 8: 28–9.

Lü, Xiaobo. 2000a. *Cadres and Corruption: The Organizational Involution of the Chinese Communist Party*. Stanford: Stanford University Press.

Lü, Xiaobo. 2000b. "Booty Socialism, Bureau-preneurs, and the State in Transition: Organizational Corruption in China." *Comparative Politics* 32, No. 3: 273–94.

Lü, Xiaobo. 1999. "From Rank-Seeking to Rent-Seeking: Changing Administrative Ethos and Corruption in Reform China." *Crime, Law and Social Change*, 32: 347–70.

Lü, Xiaobo. 1997a. "Minor Public Economy: Revolutionary Origins of the Danwei," in Xiaobo Lü and Elizabeth Perry, eds., *Danwei: The Changing Chinese Workplace in Historical and Comparative Perspective*.

Lü, Xiaobo. 1997b. "The Politics of Peasant Burden in Reform China." *Journal of Peasant Studies* 25, No. 1: 113–38.

Lu, Yu-sha. 1993. "Wan Li Delivers Speech, Expressing Worry about Peasant Rebellion." *Tangtai,* No. 25: 13–14, *FBIS* No. 72: 43.

Lu, Zexiu. 2001. "Cunyiji de jichu diwei yu zuoyong jidai jiaqiang" (The state and role of the village must be enhanced), *Nongcun Jingji Wenti*, No. 2: 36–41.

Luo, Fasheng and Sun, Zuohai, eds. 1993. *Zhonghua renmin gongheguo nongye fa shiyi* (Explication of the PRC Law on Agriculture). Beijing: Zhongguo Zhengfa daxue chubanshe.

Luo, Haocai. 1996. "Wei jianqing nongmin fudan tigong falü baozhang" (Provide legal guarantees for burden reduction). *Minzhu yu Fazhi*, No. 24.

MacFarquhar, Roderick, Timothy Cheek, and Eugene Wu, eds. 1989. *The Secret Speeches of Chairman Mao: From the Hundred Flowers to the Great Leap Forward.* Cambridge, MA: Harvard University Press.

Madsen, Richard. 2000. "Understanding Falun Gong." *Current History* 99, No. 638 (Sept.): 243–7.

Manion, Melanie. 1996. "Policy Instruments and Political Context: Transforming a Culture of Corruption in Hong Kong," paper delivered at the Forty-eighth Annual Meeting of the Association for Asian Studies, Honolulu, April 11–14.

Mao, Zedong. 1992. "On the Ten Major Relationships," in Michael Y. M. Kau and John K. Leung, eds. *The Writings of Mao Zedong, 1949–1976*, Vol. 2. Armonk, NY: M. E. Sharpe: 43–66.

Mao, Zedong. 1986. "Speech on the Victory in Resist U.S. Aggression and Aid Korea Movement," September 12, 1953, in *The Writings of Mao Zedong, 1949–1976*, Vol. 1. Armonk, NY: M. E. Sharpe, 386–92.

Mao, Zedong. 1976–7. "Speeches at the Chengchow Conference (February and March 1959)." *Chinese Law and Government* 9, No. 4.

Mao, Zedong. 1949. *Jingji yu caizheng wenti* (On economic and financial problems). Hong Kong: Xinminzhu chubanshe.

Mellor, John W. 1966. *The Economics of Agricultural Development*. Ithaca, NY: Cornell University Press.

Migdal, Joel. 1988. *Strong Societies and Weak States: State-Society Relations and State Capabilities in the Third World.* Princeton, NJ: Princeton University Press.

Montinola, Gabriela, Yingyi Qian, and Barry Weingast. 1995. "Federalism, Chinese Style: The Political Basis for Economic Success in China." *World Politics* 48 (1): 50–81.

Moore, Mick. 1998. "Death without Taxes: Democracy, State Capacity, and Aid Dependence in the Fourth World," in Gordon White and Mark Robinson, eds., *The Democratic Developmental State*. London: Oxford University Press.

Nathan, Andrew J. 1985. *Chinese Democracy*. New York: Alfred Knopf.

Nongmin Ribao. eds. 1998. *Jianqing nongmin de fudan shouce* (Handbook on peasant burden reduction). Beijing: Zhongguo Nongye Chubanshe.

Nongyebu. 1993. "Cong nongye dasheng kan nongcun zhengce de zhiding he zhixing" (Agricultural policy making and implementation as seen in the cases of large provinces). *Zhongguo Nongcun Jingji*, No. 9: 8–17.

O'Brien, Kevin. 1996. "Rightful Resistance." *World Politics* 49, No. 1: 31–55.

O'Brien, Kevin. 1990. *Reform without Liberalization: China's National People's Congress and the Politics of Institutional Change*. New York: Cambridge University Press.

O'Brien, Kevin and Lianjiang Li. 2000. "Accommodating 'Democracy' in a One-Party State: Introducing Village Elections in China." *China Quarterly*, No. 162: 465–89.

O'Brien, Kevin and Lianjiang Li. 1999. "Campaign Nostalgia in the Chinese Countryside." *Asian Survey* 39, No. 3 (May/June): 375–93.

O'Brien, Kevin and Lianjiang Li. 1995. "The Politics of Lodging Complaints in Rural China." *China Quarterly*, No. 143: 756–83.

Oi, Jean C. 1999. *Rural China Takes Off: The Institutional Foundations of Economic Reform.* Berkeley: University of California Press.

Oi, Jean C. 1990. "The Fate of the Collective after the Commune," in Deborah Davis and Ezra Vogel, eds., *Chinese Society on the Eve of Tiananmen.* Cambridge, MA: Harvard University Press.

Oi, Jean C. 1989. *State and Peasant in Contemporary China: The Political Economy of Village Government.* Berkeley: University of California Press.

Oi, Jean C. and Scott, Rozelle. 2000. "Elections and Power: The Locus of Decision-making in Chinese Villages." *China Quarterly,* No. 162: 756–83.

Oksenberg, Michel. 1982. "Economic Policymaking in China: Summer 1981." *China Quarterly*, No. 90 (June): 165–94.

Pan, Wei. 1996. "Politics of Marketization in Rural China," unpublished Ph. D. dissertation, University of California, Berkeley.

Pei, Minxin. 1997. "Citizens vs. Mandarins: Administrative Litigation in China." *China Quarterly*, No. 152 (Dec.): 832–62.

Perry, Elizabeth. 1992. "Casting a Chinese 'Democracy' Movement: The Role of Students, Workers, and Entrepreneurs," in Jeffrey Wasserstrom and Elizabeth Perry, eds., *Popular Protest and Political Culture in China.* Boulder, CO: Westview Press.

Perry, Elizabeth. 1985. "Rural Violence in Socialist China." *China Quarterly*, No. 103 (Sept.): 414–40.

Perry, Elizabeth. 1980. *Rebels and Revolutionaries in North China, 1845–1945.* Stanford: Stanford University Press.

Perry, Elizabeth. 1985. "Rural Collective Violence: The Fruits of Recent Reforms," in Elizabeth Perry and Christine Wong, eds., *The Political Economy of Reform in Post-Mao China.* Cambridge, MA: Harvard University Press.

Potter, David C. 1986. *India's Political Administrators, 1919–1983.* Oxford: Clarendon Press.

Potter, Pitman. 1991. "The Administrative Litigation Law of the PRC." *Chinese Law and Government* 24, No. 3.

Przeworski, Adam. 1997. "The State in a Market Economy," in Nelson, Tilly, and Walker, eds. *Transforming the Post-Communist Political Economy.* National Academy Press.

Qu, Liangsheng. 1997. "Xiangzhen zichou zijin guanli gaige chuyi" (A preliminary discussion on the reform of township self-raised funds). *Zhongguo Nongcun Jingji,* No. 3.

Remick, Elizabeth. 1999. "Big Plans, Empty Pockets: Local Exactions in Republican and Post-Mao China." *Twentieth-Century China* 25, No. 1: 43–70.

Renwubu. 1988. "Qing tingting nongmin de 'laosaohua'" (Please listen to the complaints of peasants), *NMRB,* January 20.

"Riben nongxie jiankuan." 1993. (Simple introduction to the Japanese Farmers' Association. No author. *Neibu Wengao,* No. 1: 27–8.

Riskin, Carl et al., eds. 1999. *China Human Development Report 1999: Transition and the State.* Beijing: China Financial and Economic Publishing House.

Rosen, Stanley. 1990. "The Chinese Communist Party and Chinese Society: Popular Attitudes Toward Party Membership and the Party's Image." *The Australian Journal of Chinese Studies*, No. 24 (July): 76–8.

Ruf, Gregory A. 1998. *Cadres and Kin: Making a Socialist Village in West China, 1921–1991*. Stanford: Stanford University Press.

Rural Development Research Institute and Office for Rural Social Economic Statistics, SSB. 1997. "Increasing peasants' incomes is top priority in rural economic development." *Zhongguo Nongcun Jingji* (April 20, *SWB-FE*/3020, Sept. 10, 1997, S/1–4).

Schumpeter, Joseph. 1991. "The Crisis of the Tax State" (1918). In R. Swedberg, ed., *Joseph A. Schumpeter: The Economics and Sociology of Capitalism*. Princeton, NJ: Princeton University Press, 99–140.

Scott, James C. 1990. *Domination and the Arts of Resistance*. New Haven, CT: Yale University Press.

Selden, Mark. 1971. *The Yenan Way in Revolutionary China*. Cambridge, MA: Harvard University Press.

Seymour, James, ed. 1980. *The Fifth Modernization: China's Human Rights Movement, 1978–1979*. Stanfordville, NY: Human Rights Publishing Group.

Sha, Qiu and Jiang, Nan. 1993. "Jiangsu nongcun shehui yanglao baoxian jishi" (Record of rural social insurance for the aged in Jiangsu). *Zhongguo Qingnian*, No. 3: 24–7.

Shanghai Lingdian Shichang Diaocha Youxian Gongsi. 1998. "Miaodian: huanjie pinkun guocheng" (Miaodian: the process of reducing poverty). *Zhongguo Qingnian Yanjiu*, No. 1: 24–8.

Shangyebu Shangye Jingji Yanjiusuo. 1984. *Geming genjudi shangye huiyilu* (Recollections of commerce in the revolutionary bases). Beijing: Zhongguo shangye chubanshe.

Shanin, Teodor. 1971. "Peasantry as a Political Factor," in Shanin, ed. *Peasants and Peasant Societies: Selected Readings*. Baltimore: Penguin Books, 238–63.

Sheng, Jung. 1993. "Great Impact of Agricultural Issue – Tracking Incident of Peasant Riots in Sichuan's Renshou County." *Hsin Pao*, Hong Kong (June 10), *FBIS*, No. 111: 10–15.

Shi, Tianjian. 1999a. "Village Elections in China: Institutionalist Tactics for Democracy." *World Politics* 51, No. 3: 385–412.

Shi, Tianjian. 1999b. "Economic Development and Village Elections in Rural China" *Journal of Contemporary China* 8, No. 2: 425–42.

Shirk, Susan L. 1993. *The Political Logic of Economic Reform in China*. Berkeley: University of California Press.

"Shixing cunmin zizhi xu chuli hao sanzhong guanxi" (In order to implement villager autonomy it is necessary to deal well with the three relations). 1999. *Neibu Canyue*, No. 30: 2–9.

Shu, Hua. 1987. "Liangshi dinggou hetong falü yiju de zhiyi yu duice" (Querying the legal basis of grain contracts and providing countermeasures). *Nongcun Jingji Wenti*, No. 11: 44–7.

Shu, Szu. 1993. "CPC works out anti-riot contingency plan." *Cheng Ming* (April): 34–5, in *FBIS*, No. 63: 28–30.

Shue, Vivienne. 1995. "State sprawl: The regulatory state and social life in a small Chinese city," in Deborah Davis et. al., eds. *Urban Spaces in Contemporary China*. New York: Cambridge University Press.

Shue, Vivienne. 1988. *The Reach of the State*. Stanford: Stanford University Press.

Sichuan Nianjian (Yearbook of Sichuan). 1997. Chengdu: Sichuan nianjianshe.

Sicular, Terry. 1988a. "Agricultural Planning and Pricing in the Post-Mao Period." *China Quarterly*, No. 116 (Dec.): 671–705.

Sicular, Terry. 1988b. "Grain Pricing: A Key Link in Chinese Economic Policy." *Modern China* 14, No. 4.

Solinger, Dorothy. 1999. *Contesting Citizenship in Urban China: Peasant Migrants, the State, and the Logic of the Market*. Berkeley: University of California Press.

Solinger, Dorothy. 1998. "The Impact of Openness on Integration and Control in China: Migrants, Layoffs, Market Formation and the Antinomies of Market Reform in Guangzhou, Shenyang, and Wuhan," unpublished paper, December. University of California, Irvine.

Solinger, Dorothy. 1991. *From Lathes to Looms: China's Industrial Policy in Comparative Perspective, 1979–1982*. Stanford: Stanford University Press.

Song, Lixiao. 1996. "Jianqing nongmin fudan, yunyong falü shouduan" (Use the legal method to reduce peasant burdens*). Liaowang,* No. 47: 22–3.

State Council. 1990. "Notice on Practical Measures to Reduce Peasant Burdens" (Document No. 12). *Xinhua* (Oct. 15), *FBIS*, No. 202: 31–5.

Steinmo, Sven. 1993.*Taxation and Democracy: Swedish, British, and American Approaches to Financing the Modern State*. New Haven, CT: Yale University Press.

Su, Ming. 1998. "Chonggou wo guo nongcun tongchou zijin zhidu de zongti silu" (General thoughts on restructuring our village comprehensive fund system). *Jingji Gaige yu Fazhan*, No. 8: 58–62.

Sun, Jun and Li, Yuchen. 1998. "Nongcun jiti jingji zuzhi caiwu wenti yuanyin ji duice" (Problems and solutions of rural financial management). *Nongye Jingji*, No. 8: 38.

Sun, Meijun. 1998. "Nongmin fudan de xianzhuang ji qi guozhong de genyuan" (Peasant burdens and the causes of their excessive heaviness). *Zhongguo Nongcun Jingji*, No. 4: 7–12.

Sun, Xiaocun. 1934. "Kejuan zashui baogao" (A report on informal taxes and levies). *Nongcun Fuxing Weiyuanhui Huibao* (Bulletin of the Rural Revitalization Commission), No. 12 (May).

Sun, Zhe. 1999. "The Remaking of the National People's Congress in China, 1979–99," unpublished Ph. D. dissertation, Columbia University.

Sun, Zifeng. 2001. "Xiangcun zhaiwu heshi le? Yi dui Anhui sheng xiangcun zhaiwu de fenxi" (When did townships and villages become indebted? An analysis from Anhui). *Diaoyan Shijie*, No. 3.

Tang, Ping. 1992. "Increasing Burdens of Peasants Examined," in *Zhonguo Tongji Xinxi Bao* (Sept. 10), JPRS-92-86: 32–4.

Tang, Yinsu. 1991. "Jianjue, renzhen de zhengdun ruanruo huansan de cunji zuzhi" (Resolutely and earnestly rectify village organizations that are weak and lax). *Zhongguo Minzheng*, No. 9: 18–19.

Tanner, Murray Scot. 1999. *The Politics of Lawmaking in China: Institutions, Processes, and Democratic Prospects*. New York: Oxford University Press.

Tanner, Murray Scot, et al. 2000. "Central-Local Relations and State Legal-Coercive Power: Decentralized Policing, Social Control, and Rule by Law in China," paper presented to Midwest Conference on Asian Affairs, Indiana University.

Tarrow, Sidney. 1994. *Power in Movement: Social Movements, Collective Action and Politics.* New York: Cambridge University Press.

Thornton, Patricia. 1999. "Beneath the Banyan Tree: Popular Views of Taxation and the State during the Republican and Reform Eras." *Twentieth-Century China* 25, No. 1: 1–42.

Tian, Zelin and Zou, Haisen. 1989. "Gaishan nongcun ganqun guanxi yao zuli gaige zonghe chili" (Improving cadre-mass relations must be based on comprehensive reform of governance). *Nongcun Jingji Wenti,* No. 5: 44–7.

Tilly, Charles. 1978. *From Mobilization to Revolution.* New York: Random House.

Unger, Jonathan and Anita Chan. 1995. "China, Corporatism, and the East Asian Model." *Australian Journal of Chinese Affairs,* No. 33: 29–54.

Varshney, Ashutosh. 1995. *Democracy, Development, and the Countryside: Rural-Urban Struggles in India.* New York: Cambridge University Press.

Varshney, Ashutosh, ed. 1993. "Beyond Urban Bias." Special issue, *Journal of Development Studies* 29, No. 4 (July).

Walder, Andrew. 1998. *Zouping in Transition: The Process of Reform in Rural North China.* Cambridge, MA: Harvard University Press.

Wang, Chongru. 1990. "Weixian de liehen: Nongcun dangqun guanxi shuli" (The danger of a rift: Estranged relations between the Party and masses). *Shehui,* No. 2: 9–11.

Wang, Dagao. 1991. "Gaige zhong de nongmin xinli daoxiang" (The psychological guidance of farmers during the reforms). *Zhongguo Jingji Tizhi Gaige,* No. 4: 40–2.

Wang, Haian. 1998. "Shangfang nongmin: Weihe shang fating" (Why do peasants appealing to higher levels go to court?). *Zhengfu fazhi,* No. 11: 15–17.

Wang, Qixiang. 1997. "Guanyu yusuanwai zijin de xingzhi cunzai de wenti ji duice" (Nature and solutions to the problem of extrabudgetary funds). *Jingji Pinglun* (Economic Forum), No. 7: 61–7.

Wang, Rentian, ed. 1999. *Xiangcun Zhengzhi: Zhongguo Cunmin Zizhi de diaocha yu sikao* (Rural politics: Investigation and reflections on China's village autonomy). Nanchang: Jiangxi renmin daxue.

Wang, Shaoguang. 1995. "The Rise of the Regions: Fiscal Reform and the Decline of Central State Capacity in China," in Andrew Walder, ed., *The Waning of the Communist State.* Stanford: Stanford University Press, 87–113.

Wang, Shaoguang and Hu, Angang. 1999. *The Political Economy of Uneven Development: The Case of China.* Armonk NY: M. E. Sharpe.

Wang, Shaohuang and Wang, Youqiang. 2001. "Gongmin quan, suodeshui yü yusuanjiandu: jiantan nongcun feigaishui de silu" (Citizenship, income tax, and budgetary oversight: Some ideas about fee-into-tax reform in rural China). *Zhanlue yu Guanli* (Strategy and Management), No. 3.

Wang, Xijia. 1991. "The Reasons for Strained Relationships between Rural Cadres and the Masses." *Shehui,* No. ll, *JPRS-* 92-016, March 20, 1992: 11–13.

Wang, Yanbin. 1995. "Nongmin fudan: Anxia hulu qilai piao" (Peasant burdens: Solving one problem only to have another crop up). *Minzhu yu Fazhi,* No. 13: 11–13.

Wang, Yanbin. 1993. "Nongmin fudan toushi" (Examining peasant burdens), *Banyuetan,* No. 10: 16.

Wang, Yaoxin and Lu, Xianzhen. 1997. "Nongmin fudan wenti jian zhe" (Simple analysis of the peasant burden problem), *Tongji Yanjiu.* No. 6: 7–12.

Wang, Yeh-chien. 1971. "The Fiscal Importance of the Land Tax During the Ch'ing Period. " *Journal of Asian Studies* 30, No. 4: 829–42.

Wang, Yuexin. 1995. "Dui nongmin fudan wenti de sikao" (Examining the peasant burden problem). *Zhongguo Nongcun Jingji*, No. 1: 33–6.

Wang, Yushao. 1997. "Yingdang zhengshi 'nongmin fudan kongzhi guiding' suo cunzai de biduan" (Attention should be paid to malpractices that arise from the directives on peasant burden control). *Liaowang*, No. 7: 30.

Wank, David L. 1999. *Commodifying Communism: Business, Trust, and Politics in Xiamen.* New York: Cambridge University Press.

Wasserstrom, Jeffrey and Elizabeth Perry, eds. 1992. *Popular Protest and Political Culture in China.* Boulder, CO: Westview Press.

Wedeman, Andrew. 1997a. "Looters, Rent-Scrapers and Dividend-Collectors: Corruption and Growth in Zaire, South Korea and the Philippines." *Journal of Developing Areas,* 31 (Summer): 457–78.

Wedeman, Andrew. 1997b. "Stealing from the Farmers: Institutional Corruption and the 1992 IOU Crisis." *China Quarterly*, No. 152: 805–31.

Wegren, Stephen K. 2002. "Democratization and Urban Bias in Post-Communist Russia." *Comparative Politic* 34, No. 4: 457–75.

Wei, Hongyun. 1990. *Jin-Cha-Ji kangri genjudi caizheng jingji shigao* (A short history of economy and finance in the Jin-Cha-Ji base area). Beijing: Dangan chubanche.

Wei, Houkai and Yang, Dali. 1998. "Decentralization and Disparities in Local Education in China." *Social Sciences in China*, No. 3: 13–31.

West, Loraine A. 1997. "Provision of Public Services in Rural PRC," in Christine P. W. Wong, ed., *Financing Local Government in the People's Republic of China.* Hong Kong and New York: Oxford University Press, 213–82.

White, Tyrene. 1990. "Post-revolutionary Mobilization in China: The One-Child Policy Reconsidered." *World Politics* 43 (October): 53–77.

Whiting, Susan. 2001. *Power and Wealth in Rural China: The Political Economy of Institutional Change.* New York: Cambridge University Press.

Whiting, Susan. 1998. "The Cadre Evaluation System at the Grassroots: The Paradox of Party Rule," unpublished paper presented at University of California, San Diego.

Wong, Christine P. W. 1997. "Rural Public Finance," in Christine P. W. Wong, ed., *Financing Local Government in the People's Republic of China.* Hong Kong and New York: Oxford University Press, 167–212.

Wong, R. Bin. 1997. *China Transformed: Historical Change and the Limits of European Experience.* Ithaca, NY: Cornell University Press.

Wright, Teresa. 1999. "State Repression and Student Protest in Contemporary China." *China Quarterly*, No. 157: 142–72.

Wu, Jieh-min. 1998. "Local Property Rights Regimes in Socialist Reforms: A Case Study of China's Informal Industrialization." Ph. D. dissertation, Columbia University.

Xiang, Guang and Zhang, Yang. 1988. *Kangri zhanzheng shiqi Shaan-Gan-Ning bianqu caizheng jingji shigao* (A short history of the economy and finance in Shaan-Gan-Ning border region during the Anti-Japanese War). Xi'an: Xibei daxue chubanshe.

Xiang, Guang and Zhang Yang. 1989. *Jiefang zhanzheng shiqi Shan Gan Ning bianqu caizheng jingjishi ziliao xuanbian* (Selected materials on the history of finance and economy in Shan Gan Ning border region during the liberation war), Xi'an: Sanqi Chubanshe.

Xu, Baojian. 1993. "He yi jian er bu qing" (Why the reduction cannot alleviate the burden), *JJRB*, Feb. 26. *JPRS*-CAR-93-027, 29 April: 41.

Xu, Gongmei. 1993. "Zoufang Songshuyu" (Visiting Songshuyu). *Tansuo* (April).

Xu, Hongbing. 1992. "Danwei sishe 'xiaojinku' xingwei dingxing chutan" (A preliminary study of illicit *danwei* small coffers). *Zhengzhi yü Falü*, No. 1: 32–3.

Xu, Kunrong. 1990. "Jingji zhengce de zhongyaoxing cong jiao xiaoyi kan tiaozheng nongcun" (The importance of economic policy seen from the comparative effectiveness of agricultural readjustment). *Jingji Guanli,* No. 11: 52–5.

Xu, Xing, ed. 1987. *Fang Lizhi–Zhongguo de Sahelofu* (Fang Lizhi, China's Sakharov). Hong Kong: Tianyuan Shuwu.

Xu, Yong. 1998a. "Lun cunmin zizhi beijing xia dang zuzhi yu zizhi zuzhi de xietiao" (On coordinating Party and self-governing organizations against the background of villager autonomy). *Xuexi yu Tansuo,* No. 1: 89–92.

Xu, Yong. 1998b. "Minzhuhua jincheng zhong de lujing xuanze" (Choice of paths in democratization). *Shehui Kexue,* No. 10: 26–30.

Xu, Yong. 1997. *Zhongguo Nongcun Cunmin Zizhi* (Rural self-governance in China). Wuhan: Huazhong Shifan Daxue Chubanshe.

Yan, Zhongping. 1989. *Zhongguo jindai jingji shi* (Modern Chinese economic history). Vol. 2. Beijing: Renmin chubanshe.

Yang, Dali. 1996. *Calamity and Reform in China*. Stanford: Stanford University Press.

Yang, Hao. 1999. "Nongmin de huhan" (Peasants' cries). *Dang Dai*, No. 6: 63–90.

Yang, Lianbai and Li, Xuezeng. 1980. "The Relations between Agriculture, Light Industry, and Heavy Industry in China." *Social Sciences in China*, No. 2:182–214.

Yang, Po. 1992. "Zhonggong yanfang minjian zuzhi" (The CCP strictly guards against popular organizations). *Cheng Ming,* No. 6: 26–7.

Ye, Baozhu. 1997. "Guanyu wanshan xiangzhen caizheng yunxing jizhi de sikao" (Some reflections on perfecting the operation of township financial systems). *Nongcun Jingji Wenti*, No. 8: 53–5.

Ye, Xingqing. 1997. "Lun nongcun gonggong chanpin tizhi de gaige" (The reform of the public goods provision regime in the countryside). *Jingji Yanjiu*, No. 6: 57–62.

Yu, Shaoliang and Pu, Liye. 1997. "Jingbing jianzheng: jianqing nongmin fudan de xianshi chulu" (Reducing the size of the bureaucracy is a real way to reduce peasant burdens). *Liaowang*, No. 12: 32.

Yu, Tianxing and Wang, Shisheng. 1999. "Zhengfu xingzheng guanli feiyong gaige de guoji bijiao" (An international comparison of the reforms in government administrative spending). *Neibu Canyue*, No. 15: 14–18.

Yuan, Mu and Yang, Yongzhe. 1993. "Several Questions on the Current Rural Situation and in Rural Work." *RMRB* (Sept. 17), *FBIS*, No. 199: 39.

Yue, Shan. 2000. "Shehui zhuangkuang ehua de jingren shuzi" (Worsening of the social situation is indicated by alarming numbers). *Cheng Ming*, No. 2: 23–4.

Yue, Shan. 1997. "Gan E wushiwan nongmin baodong" (Half a million peasants rebel in Jiangxi and Hubei). *Cheng Ming*, No. 9: 21–3.

Zelin, Madeleine. 1984. *The Magistrate's Tael: Rationalizing Fiscal Reform in Eighteenth Century Ch'ing China*. Berkeley: University of California Press.

Zhai, Liansheng. 1997. "Xiangzhen Zichou Zijin guanli gaige chuyi" (Opinions on the administration of township self-raised funds), *ZNJ*, No. 3: 26–9.

Zhang, Heping and Ren, Yiqin. 1999. "Baohu nongmin hefa liyi – qieshi jianqing nong-min fudan" (Protect the peasants legitimate rights and interests – earnestly reduce their burdens). *Shanxi Nongjing,* No. 2: 40–6.

Zhang, Jun and Jiang, Wei. 1998. "Gaige hou Zhongguo nongcun gonggong chanpin de gongji" (Public goods provision in China's countryside after the reforms). *Shehui Kexue Zhanxian* (Social Science Front), No. 1: 36–44.

Zhang, Qi. 1989. "Dui 'nongmin caichan quanli yu shenfen ziyou shuangzhong jiefang' de zhiyi yu zhuisu" (Searching for the "double liberation of the peas-ants' property rights and personal freedom"). *Nongcun Jingji Wenti*, No. 3: 49–51.

Zhang, Qingzhong. 1993a. "Accelerate Commodity Circulation System Reform; Foster Rural Markets." *Zhongguo Nongcun Jingji*, No. 2 (Feb. 20), *JPRS*, No. 25 (April 20): 12.

Zhang, Qinghong, ed. 1993b. "Peasant Income, Structural Adjustment, Market Devel-opment: China's Key Rural Reform in 1990s." *Zhongguo Nongcun Jingji*, No. 11, JPRS No. 12 (1993): 38.

Zhang, Shuhuai. 1998. "Zhiyue cunmin zizhi de yuanyin ji duice tanxi" (Analysis of the source of restrictions on village autonomy and of policy). *Zhongguo Nongcun Guancha*, No. 4: 60–2.

Zhao, Shifeng, Gao, Lifeng, and Xu, Shaoyi. 1998. "Guanyu Hebeisheng nongcun caiwu guanli zhuangkuang de diaocha" (Investigation on rural financial management in Hebei province). *Zhongguo Nongcun Jingji,* No. 5: 47–50.

Zhao, Xin. 1992. "Memorandum on Bringing 'Three Irregulars' under Control." *Minzhu yu Fazhi*, No. 9 (1991): 4–8, in *JPRS*-92-002 (Jan. 22): 78.

Zhao, Yining and Ye, Shudong. 1997. "Zhongguo Jigou gaige de xin qili" (A new turning point in China's bureaucratic structure). *Liaowang*, No. 39: 12–13.

Zheng, Xuwei. 1997. "Dangqian woguo caizheng kunjing de chengyin ji duice" (Current financial difficulties and solutions). *Jingji Tizhi Gaige* (Economic system reform), No. 4: 88–91.

Zheng, Ying. 1988. "Dalu minzhong saodong ciqibiluo" (People on the mainland stage more and more disturbances). *Chiushi Nientai*, No. 222: 38–40.

Zhongguo caizheng nianjian. 1997. (Finance Yearbook of China). Beijing: Zhongguo caizheng zazhishe.

Zhongguo Nongcun Tongji Nianjian (Rural Statistical Yearbook of China). Various years. Beijing: Zhongguo Tongji Chubanshe.

Zhongguo Shehui Kexueyuan Nongcun Fazhan Yanjiusuo (Institute of Rural Develop-ment, CASS). 1999. *Zhongguo nongcun jingji xingshi fenxi yu yuce 1998–1999* (Anal-yses and predictions of the situation in the Chinese countryside, 1998–9). Beijing: Shehui kexue wenxian chubanshe.

Zhongguo Laodong Tongji Nianjian (Chinese labor statistical yearbook). Various years. Beijing: Zhongguo Tongji Chubanshe.

Zhongguo Tongji Nianjian (China Statistical Yearbook). Various years. Beijing: Zhongguo Tongji Chubanshe.

Zhongguo Zhonggong Zuzhibu Ketizu. 2001. *Zhongguo Diaocha Baogao, 2000–2001: Xin Xingshi Xia Renmin Neibu Maodun Yanjiu* (China Investigation Report, 2000–2001: Study of contradictions among the people in the new situation). Zhongyang Bianshi Chubanshe.

Zhonghua Renmin Gongheguo Guowuyuan Gongbao. 1993a. "Zhonggong Zhongyang Bangongting, Guowuyuan Bangongting guanyu qieshi jianqing nongmin fudan de jinji tongzhi" (Emergency notice by the General Offices of Party Central and the State Council concerning earnestly reducing peasant burdens). No. 7 (May 27): 286–8.

Zhonghua Renmin Gongheguo Guowuyuan Gongbao. 1993b. "Zhonggong Zhongyang Bangongting, Guowuyuan Bangongting guanyu sheji fongmin fudan xiangmu shenhe chuli yijian de tongzhi"(Notice of opinion concerning the management of the examination of peasant burdens by Party Central and the State Council General Offices). No. 18 (Sept. 2): 850–7.

Zhonghua Renmin Gongheguo Guowuyuan Gongbao. 1992. "Nongmin chengdan feiyong he laoli guanli tiaoli" (Administrative regulations on fees and labor services borne by the peasants). No. 41 (Jan. 7): 1430–5.

Zhonghua Renmin Gongheguo Guowuyuan Gongbao. 1985. "Zhonggong Zhongyang, Guowuyuan guanyu jinzhi xiang nongmin luan paikuan, luan shoufei de tongzhi" (Note by the CC and State Council on prohibiting random assessments and fee collection from the peasants). No. 31 (Nov. 20): 1043–6.

Zhou, Xiang. 1994. "Increasing numbers of teachers, owed back wages, leave their profession." *Minzhu yu Fazhi*, April 7, *JPRS*, No. 36, June 10: 50–2.

Zhou, Yichun and Ai, Fuzhen. 1994. "Xin shiqi woguo 'nongxie' de jianli keburonghuan" (Establishment of a farmers' association for the contemporary era brooks no delay). *Changbai Xuetan*, No. 4: 52–4.

Zhu, Baoping. 2001. "Nongcun feishui gaige shidian de jinzhan, nandian ji sigao" (Progress, difficulties, and reflections on the rural fee-into-tax experiment). *Zhongguo Nongcun Jingji*, No. 2: 12–16.

Zhu, Guanglei. 1997. *Dangdai Zhongguo Zhengfu Guocheng* (The process of government in contemporary China). Tianjin: Tianjin Renmin Chubanshe.

Zhu, Huaxin. 1998. "Caogen minzhu" (Grassroots democracy), in Dong Yongyu and Shi Binghai, eds. *Zhengzhi Zhongguo: Mianxiang xin tizhi xuanze de shidai* (Political China: Facing the era of choosing a new structure). Beijing: Jinki Zhongguo chubanshe.

Zhu, Shouming. 1958. *Guangxuchao donghualu* (Historical records of the Guangxu emperor). Beijing: Zhonghua shuju.

Zhu, Shouyin. 1998. "Nongye shuifei zhidu gaige shiyan yanjiu baogao" (Report on experimental research on reforming the agricultural tax-and-fee system). *Guanli Shijie*, No. 2: 143–53.

Zong, Lanhai. 1993. "Dang kan 'zuowen' yuejin kouhao" (The leap slogan of a Party 'leftist document'). *Cheng Ming* (July): 14–15.

Zonghe Jihuasi, Nongyebu. 1990. "Guanyu nongmin fudan de diaocha" (Survey on farmers' burdens). *Nongcun Jingji Wenti*, No. 2: 57–60.

Zongzhengzhibu. 1989. *Zhongguo renmin jiefangjun qunzhong gongzuoshi* (The history of mass work in the PLA). Beijing: Jiefangjun chubanshe.

Zweig, David. 2000. "The 'Externalities of Development': Can New Political Institutions Manage Rural Conflicts?" in Elizabeth Perry and Mark Selden, eds., *Chinese Society: Change, Conflict, and Resistance.* New York: Routledge, 120–42.

Zweig, David. 1997. *Freeing China's Farmers.* Armonk, NY: M. E. Sharpe.

Index

271